CUSTOM AND CHERISHING:

The Arts in Elementary Schools

Studies of U. S. elementary schools
portraying the ordinary problems
of teachers teaching
music, drama, dance and the visual arts
in 1987-1990

Robert Stake
Liora Bresler
Linda Mabry

National Arts Education Research Center
University of Illinois

with assistance from
Nancy Ellis
University of New Hampshire

Council for Research in Music Education
School of Music
University of Illinois at Urbana-Champaign
1114 West Nevada Street
Urbana, IL 61801

1991

Layout and Production Editor: Martha L. Alwes

Table of Contents

Preface i
Foreword ii

Part One: Introduction

Chapter 1. Arts Education Case Studies 3
   Organizing the Case Studies
      Our Schools
      The Research Issues
      The Researchers
      The Research Rationale
   What Do We Expect a School to Be?
   Expectations for School Arts

Part Two: Case Studies

Chapter 2 19
   Anacortes Middle School, Anacortes, Washington
   Robert Stake

Chapter 3 55
   Washington and Prairie Schools, Danville, Illinois
   Liora Bresler

Chapter 4 95
   Armstrong Elementary School, Chicago, Illinois
   Liora Bresler

Chapter 5 137
   Alexandre Dumas Elementary School, Chicago, Illinois
   Linda Mabry

Chapter 6 177
   Colonial School District, Plymouth Meeting, Pennsylvania
   Linda Mabry

Chapter 7 217
   Oakwood School, Townsend, New Hampshire
   Nancy Ellis

Chapter 8 235
    Luther Burbank Elementary School, Las Lomas, California
    Robert Stake

Chapter 9 263
    Webster County School District, San Sebastian, Texas
    Linda Mabry

Part Three: Traditional and Emerging Issues

Chapter 10. The Content of Arts Education 301
    Differentiation and Standardization of Aims
    Integration with Other Subject Matters
    Discipline-Based Arts Education
    Band and Vocal Music Customs
    Personal Cherishing

Chapter 11. The Pedagogy of Arts Education 309
    Differences in Teaching the Arts
    Differences of Learnings Depending on the Context of the Art
    Teachers' Beliefs about Art
    The Context of Schooling

Chapter 12. Leadership in Arts Education 321
    The Arts and Educational Leadership
    What Constitutes Leadership?
    Persuasive Advocacy: An Arts Need
    Creative Habits of Mind: A Leadership Need

Part Four: The Several Arts

Chapter 13. The Several Arts 337
    Music Education
    Dance Education
    Theatre
    Visual Arts Education
    Final Summary

Finale

Appendix: References and Related Works 351

Preface

This publication is a product of the program of research carried on at the University of Illinois Site of the National Arts Education Research Center. The Center, funded by the National Endowment for the Arts and the U. S. Department of Education, opened in October 1987 and closed on December 30, 1990.

We are pleased to present *Custom and Cherishing* to the arts education community. We value it for its dramatic portrayal of reality in elementary school arts education.

Charles Leonhard
Director of Research

Jack McKenzie
Director for Management

CUSTOM AND CHERISHING:
The Arts in Elementary Schools

Foreword

These case studies present dramatic portrayals of principals, arts educators and classroom teachers exerting their leadership and imagination to enhance the quality of arts education in their own schools. Among the many lessons to be learned from reading the case studies is that in the final analysis the quality of arts education depends on the sustained efforts of teachers, whatever their specialization, who are passionate in their belief in the value of the arts and imaginative in devising means to reveal to their students the splendor of the arts.

The many currently active visionaries in arts education who proclaim that the arts should be elevated to full standing in the school curriculum appear to be having little or no effect on the content or implementation of arts education programs in the schools under consideration in the case studies. The message of the visionaries is either not reaching school administrators, classroom teachers and practicing arts educators or it appears to be unconvincing or irrelevant to them.

Arts education in America is unlikely to improve markedly without the efforts of a new corps of leaders consisting of arts specialists and classroom teachers who have the intellectual and artistic qualifications and the sense of mission necessary to bring about a reconciliation between the theoretical position of the visionaries and the limited prevailing conception of the role of arts education held by school administrators, parents and the public at large. Arts education theorists are prone to becoming so involved in thinking, talking and writing about what arts education could be or should be that they give scant attention to the reality of arts education in American public schools. Professor Stake and his associates have rendered the field of arts education a significant service by focusing attention on the reality of arts education as it exists in nine public elementary schools located in diverse communities in diverse parts of the country and characterized by diverse student populations and diverse levels of support for arts education.

The preparation of this corps of leaders for arts education represents a major challenge to persons charged with responsibility for the preservice and inservice education of classroom teachers, arts specialists and school administrators.

Charles Leonhard
Director of Research
National Arts Education Research Center
University of Illinois at Urbana-Champaign

PART ONE: INTRODUCTION

Chapter 1:
Arts Education Case Studies

American schools have an arts program. With emphasis on singing and making posters, with opportunities to participate in dramatic sketches, with after-hours activities in instrumental music and crafts, the American elementary school student is afforded opportunity to develop artistic skills. Learning objectives often have been stated in writing, responsibilities programmed. Yet the specialist in arts education, community advocates of the arts, and many parents are disheartened. In the 1980s they helped draw rhetorical attention to the arts but practices in the schools appear largely unchanged. Within the American school system, the priority given arts education is low. According to the National Endowment for the Arts (1988), "Basic arts education does not exist in the United States today."

So it seems we Americans have a program and not much education. There is little need for research to establish the low priority and fragmentation of arts education in the schools. What is needed is greater understanding of the obstacles to improvement and real insight into the opportunities for arts education. Communities surrounding the school abound with music, dance, theatre, and the visual arts. Much of it is trivial, some is trash, but, even among the popular expressions, there are vast opportunities for awareness, analysis, and discriminating appreciation. It is easy to be disheartened by the school effort, to conclude that money is scarce, that competition with the rest of the curriculum is discouragingly difficult. Both are true but there is more to be said. We as a people, we as a profession, without major reallocation of resources, without hundreds of newly trained arts teachers, could do better. We have not sufficiently studied the ways to challenge old convictions. We ourselves have failed to inspire arts education in the schools.

These case studies are committed to that purpose. These are studies of ordinary offerings of the American elementary school, noting exposure and engagement of students in school, community, and home activity. The studies are part of the 1987-1990 program of research undertaken by the National Arts Education Research Center at the University of Illinois under funds granted by the National Endowment for the Arts. (See Leonhard, 1991).

Our sites were not selected to be technically representative of the nation's schools but instances of schools from which we could learn. Unlike the cases studied by the Rand Corporation (McLaughlin & Thomas, 1984) for the J. Paul Getty Trust, these sites were not selected from nominations for exemplary commitment or instruction. We did not intend these to be award-winning schools. Our sites were selected to touch a variety of demographics but primarily because it was judged by the research team that each would be a place where the vitality of school arts might be studied.[1] The hospitality of school district and teachers, the availability of local associates who might help, and the complexity of the arts offerings of schools and community were given careful attention in selecting the sites.

Issues for organizing our observations at the sites were partly those queries and concerns raised in professional and popular literature but also those puzzlements discovered at the sites. It was important for us to establish what is happening, both within arts courses and activities but also in the many contexts: curricular, administrative, fiscal, political, historical and social. The questions we raised were not so much "What are the children learning?" but "What are the schools providing as opportunities for learning?" Figure 1 is a stylized representation of the issues used for initial planning at each school site.

But each site was unique. Our interest was not in comparing them in terms of various criteria but in giving each school a chance to tell its story of arts education. Our curiosity as researchers focused on the uniqueness of each site, the special ways that a few teachers or advocates at that site dealt with the opportunities and barriers to arts education. Many of the issues of arts education are well known and we could have organized this report around them. We believe it serves the purpose better, however, for the reader to examine each site in itself, coming to understand the local dynamics, not so much as a generic concept but as a personalistic and situational instance, similar to but unlike the others and perhaps useful in understanding the reader's own arts education context. We have offered interpretations and generalizations but have tried to leave it up to the reader to add this vicarious experience, these special cases, to what the reader already knows. We feel that refinement of the reader's existing conceptualizations will be the payoff of these studies.

We presume our readers to be people concerned about education, particularly people responsible for arts education in American schools at the end of the ninth decade of this century. We do not expect to have any readers without already strong persuasions about what is happening in the schools and why. We hope to provide our readers with a carefully selected, recognizably portrayed description of events pertinent to certain issues, descriptions dependent on our interpretations of what was happening in classrooms and boardrooms at the end of the 1980s.

Organizing the Case Studies

Immediately we faced the question, "Will this research be embarrassing?" We wanted to look at ordinary teaching of the arts in elementary schools around the country and we knew that teaching of visual arts and music is often not done well, sometimes not done at all. Many of the advocacies of the American Art Education Association and the Music Educators National Conference are unheeded. Drama and dance teaching are rare. The JDR III Fund slogan (1975), "all the arts for all the children," is seldom voiced by educators. What more of the problem do we need to know? Can we learn how to educate by studying malpractice? In many

---

[1] Our visits to sites needed to be inexpensive. The budget for the research was small, about $30,000 per year, about $6,000 per site. Field researchers, even in modest appraisals, often estimate per-site costs of $10,000 as minimal.

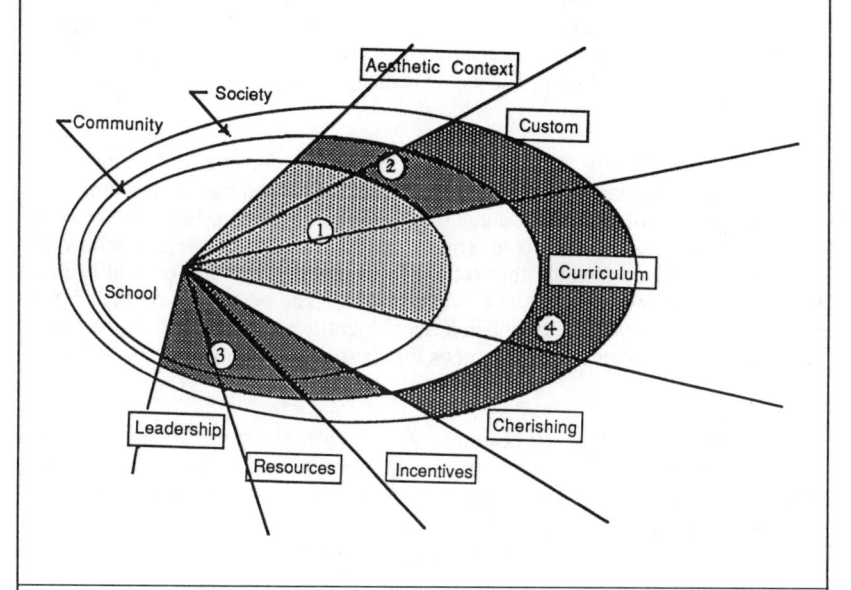

1. **THE SCHOOL; ITS CUSTOMS; ITS CURRICULUM; ITS AESTHETIC CONTEXT:** What constitutes the formal arts education offerings of school districts for the arts-talented and for the ordinary youngster? What is the balance between fine and popular arts? What is the interest in and strength of efforts to teach the "disciplined-based" arts to all youngsters? Is there aesthetic vitality?

2. **THE COMMUNITY; ITS CUSTOMS; ITS AESTHETIC CONTEXT:** In the community, when are the arts important? What are the out-of-school arts opportunities for ordinary youngsters? How and how much do the schools take responsibility for using out-of-school opportunities for educating their students? What is the interaction between fine and popular arts? How does the community constrain arts experience?

3. **SCHOOL AND COMMUNITY; THEIR RESOURCES AND INCENTIVES; THEIR LEADERSHIP:** What are the existing and what are the potential resources of school and community for arts education? What kinds of people are the leaders? How are arts education leaders unique? What are the incentives for teachers to teach the arts? What are the incentives for students?

4. **THE SOCIETY; ITS CUSTOMS; ITS CHERISHING; ITS CURRICULUM:** To what extent are youngsters drawn by teachers and the society into a personal beholding of artistic works, or even of the elegance of certain non-arts works, personal experience or momentary high? How does "enlightened cherishing" occur? What are the messages (including casual and indirect messages) to youngsters from the culture concerning knowledge about and participation in the arts? How is the societal arts agenda manifest in the experience of youngsters?

Figure 1. Schematic of Foreshadowing Questions for These Case Studies

ways, arts education in America is embarrassing—how could our study of the ordinary school not further the embarrassment?

But our years of curriculum evaluation studies led the four of us to realize that advocacy for high quality education is driven more by ideological yearning than by realistic assessment of schools and classrooms. We know that educational critiques focus on the best and worst of teaching and often fail to portray ingenious and tenacious efforts of ordinary teachers. Ordinary classrooms are understudied, often misunderstood.

We have been strong in the belief that effective reform is seldom born of goal-setting and standards-raising but rather of intensive analysis of problems and careful delineation of areas susceptible to improvement (Fullan, 1982, and Odden & Marsh, 1987). As consultants to schools, we do not, for example, know how to get people to behave rationally, thus rational remediation plans may be of little use. Ideology sometimes gets in the way. Voltaire said, "The best is the enemy of the good." We wanted to look at schools in order to identify what needs protection from change as well as to identify opportunities for assisting evolutionary change (Stake, 1986).

Some readers *may* find our accounts of arts teaching embarrassing. In those situations in which the teachers or others might be embarrassed or jeopardized by what we saw or wrote, we anonymized the accounts. Our purpose is not to belittle or to arouse the indignations which fuel reform. Our purpose is to improve our collective understanding of what is happening in American elementary schools.

Our Schools

Our National Center assignment called for case study of elementary schools. We limited our sample to public schools grades K-8 and gave most of our attention to grades 3-6. We looked first at a middle school, then at seven primary-elementary schools.

A collection of eight case studies, even with long-term fieldwork by expert observers, cannot—in a social science sense—be representative of a large population of cases. The teachers, classrooms and schools portrayed in our case studies were not randomly chosen. Even if they had been, it would be too small a sample to represent properly the American school system. Our aim was not representation, nor explanation, it was understanding of particular situations. (von Wright, 1971).

We chose to increase our understanding of a few schools, attempting to balance east, west, north, and south; urban, suburban, and rural; schools with and without arts specialist teachers; socioeconomic status and ethnic mix; and communities with higher and lower art-orientation. We deliberately sought to avoid school systems with high reputation for arts education and those where innovative new arts education projects were underway, thinking those were already being studied.[2] We hoped

---

[2] A number of school systems with good reputations were described in Getty Center (1985). A Rockefeller Brothers Foundation study was examining a number of innovative schools.

to choose schools moving with the current, not ahead or behind, not spurting nor moribund. We chose schools where we found persons, inside or outside, offering help with access to classrooms and with interpretations of our observations.

To facilitate early field operations, we chose Danville, Illinois, a small blue-collar city with economic woes, not distant from the University of Illinois In Danville, we studied the largest and most comprehensive of the elementary schools, partly to observe the role taken by an up-and-coming new principal.

We chose a Texas coastal town, here called San Sebastian, because of acquaintances there who already knew a lot about the arts scene in both community and schools. We looked particularly there for an ethnic mix not only of Caucasians, Hispanics and Afro-Americans but also newly settling Vietnamese and Taiwanese.

We chose two urban schools in Chicago, one in a most economically impoverished neighborhood, an all-Afro-American elementary school. On our exploratory visit, we were attracted to the new principal's intent to revitalize the school through an arts orientation. Our other Chicago public school was in a stately old building in a handsome neighborhood where neighbors sent their children instead to private school. Our school was attended by students bussed from afar. The contrast between teacher culture and student culture intrigued us.

We chose a middle school in Anacortes, Washington because the arts advocate there was known across that state to be a tireless and effective creator of learning opportunities. Then we worried that the community might be too much an arts colony, then realized that many communities across the country are home to small or large cadres of professional as well as casual artists.

We chose a New Hampshire elementary school because colleague Nancy Ellis was supervising teacher trainees there and had opportunity to observe classrooms regularly. Also the community was similar to many lying just outside the fringe of metropolitan areas, diminishing as centers of agricultural production, growing as centers for those who want a quiet, yet not too isolated, place to live.

We more or less blindly selected among the Philadelphia suburbs, wanting within the Atlantic megalopolis a site where the best of resources would be available but not wanting to know in advance whether and how those resources were being used for arts education.

For our eighth selection we went to California, the largest state school system, the one with perhaps the most diverse populations and probably the most sophisticated school reform efforts. Though Californians are among the most mobile of Americans, we chose a community where many parents themselves had once attended the school system. And we sought a classroom where a teacher minimally teaching the arts would be happy to show-and-tell what he cared about as a teacher and as a person.

A ninth visitation site at rural Brookwood, Alabama, was abandoned even before started. We ran out of time. We settled for those eight sites—yet in a way we had 50 additional sites. As part of our National Center work, for over a year we sought observations and opinions of arts education correspondents in each of the

50 states, comments on topics of concern to us and of concern to them. We wanted the views as background, to help us orient to what was going on around the country. We will quote these Fifty States correspondents a few times in this report.

As indicated, our sample was not designed to capture a certain kind of arts program or situation. We looked for diverse sites, found some agreeable hosts, identified some foreshadowing questions, and walked in with the idea that these places had stories to tell, stories we needed to see, hear and tell ourselves (Denny, 1978).

We cannot make a strong argument that these eight schools represent the nation's elementary schools. There are aspects about them that are typical, others unique. To some extent, our experience with schools in general and with arts programs, extended by the assurances and cautions of our colleagues, invited us to work toward certain generalizations—but these should be treated both by us and by our readers with caution. We have tried in a deliberate way to provide our readers with sufficient contextual and operational detail so that, coupled with their own experience and understanding, they can strengthen or modify their own generalizations about arts education (Stake & Trumbull, 1982).

We wish researchers had better ways to draw generalizations than they do.[3] At a glance, education appears more-or-less the same simple story everywhere; but under sustained examination of individual cases, its complexities and uniquenesses are obvious. We in the social sciences have our *uncertainty principle*: you cannot simultaneously know both the complexity and typicality of a phenomenon. Statistical surveys (where the same questions are asked of large numbers of respondents) give important but often superficial information about teaching and learning; case studies give in-depth information about individual cases. At increasing levels of complexity it is increasingly difficult to know how typical the case is. When samples are carefully drawn, the probability of a universal relationship among variables can be estimated but the probabilities do not hold for an individual case. Much of what happens in a classroom is situational. In a survey questionnaire, the complexity of the classroom situation can be alluded to but not captured. And without the survey, we cannot establish the typicality of the situation.

Such social science uncertainties do not disturb most readers. Encountering our descriptions and dialogue, they mix and match, chortle or grouse, and often think some more. Our purpose here is to present a few well-chosen vignettes with interpretations, not to identify the national conditions but to aid thinking about what is and ought to be happening in our classrooms.

The Research Issues

Many things happen in the classroom—only some did we want to study. We identified a small list of issues at the outset but remained alert to other issues that might emerge as even more important.

---

[3]From research methods courses and books, the generalization seeker is seldom adequately told of the role of common sense, intuition, and presumption. The problems are discussed in Greene and David (1984).

Some research is driven by theory: social theory, education theory, arts theory.[4] As researchers we are not oblivious to theory but, here, our studies were driven by what we found in the schools, by events, by problems. We oriented our observations to certain key issues, especially teacher issues (Elbaz, 1983). They were not derived from formal theory, nor aimed to create theory, yet constituted an evolving grounded theory, a conceptual structure for organizing and coordinating our work (Glaser & Strauss, 1967).

We used the diagram in Figure 1 as a background map and, for initial observations, divided the questions into the four categories represented by the shaded areas. As we became familiar with our sites, our issues became fewer, our foci narrowed. Increasingly we pursued the following issues:

1. In our elementary classrooms, formally and informally, is there attention to aesthetics (Smith, 1971), to beauty, to intellectual understanding of the arts which individuals and societies cherish?

2. With limited time for arts instruction, are teachers encouraged to meet arts education needs by integrating arts activities into the teaching of other subject matter? When instruction is integrated in this way, are important knowledge and skill in the arts or any other legitimate arts education goals actually pursued?

3. When significant artists and exemplary artworks are studied, are classroom teachers and the authorities to whom teachers appeal expanding arts education beyond classical European culture toward popular and multicultural arts?

4. Schoolwide emphasis on explicit goals, prespecified instructional materials and procedures, performance evaluation, and various schematic views of teaching pressure teachers to feel they must be authoritative about what they teach in the classroom. Does such responsibility diminish classroom attention given to arts events and experiences occurring outside the classroom?

5. In these elementary schools do we find advocates for a more discipline-based arts education or for any other high quality arts curriculum to replace the present custom?[5]

6. What forms of arts education leadership are to be found and how do they match the needs for leadership?

Each of the four of us continued to modify the conceptual structure for our case studies not only according to what was going on at schools visited but also as to what

---

[4]Our view was a bit like that of Degas. According to Paul Valéry (1960), "Degas, with little tenderness for anything, was not apt to be indulgent of criticism, or of theories. He was always ready to assert — and later in life he would harp on it — that there is no arguing among the Muses. They work all day, very much on their own. In the evening, work finished, they get together and dance; they do not talk."

[5]We felt it of primary importance to understand what constitutes a curriculum, not so much by district specification but experientially for the teacher and the individual child. See Stanley Madeja (1977).

he or she felt could be learned by pursuing it. Each of course in part followed personal interest and previous experience.

The Researchers

The team of researchers worked under the auspices of the National Arts Education Research Center at the University of Illinois, first directed by Ted Zernich and later by Charles Leonhard and Jack McKenzie. The Center existed between 1987 and 1990 as a creation of the National Endowment for the Arts.

Bob Stake directed the study. A curriculum evaluation specialist, he was the director of CIRCE, the University of Illinois Center for Instructional Research and Curriculum Evaluation. From a background in psychometrics and study in many of the traditional subject matters, but neither trained nor experienced in the arts, Stake had become involved with program evaluation problems raised by CEMREL, SWERL, the JDR III Fund, the Cleveland Area Arts Council, and the J. Paul Getty Trust. He authored *Evaluating the Arts in Education, A Responsive Approach* and related papers (see bibliography). Though professing to be a measurements specialist, he frequently opposed the ways achievement tests and other indicator variables were being used to measure or evaluate education. He was recognized as an advocate of qualitative research methods, especially the case study.

Liora Bresler, a performing pianist and musicologist, became involved in art education in her work as musical director at the Tel Aviv Museum. Her principal conversion occurred at Stanford University working with Elliot Eisner and the Getty case study project. Captivated by the case study approach, she found her musical training useful in attending to rhythms, form and orchestration. At the University of Illinois, Liora was an assistant professor in CIRCE and the Department of Curriculum and Instruction, writing about music more than playing it. Her special interests were in aesthetic education, qualitative methodology, teacher training and computer mediated communication.

Linda Mabry was a research and teaching assistant at CIRCE. A doctoral student and Bagley Scholar, she studied aesthetics with Ralph Smith at the University of Illinois before engaging in qualitative research and evaluation. While at CIRCE she conducted several case studies and program evaluations, mostly involving arts education. Previously, she taught in public and private elementary schools and directed religious education programs. Her background included familiarity with the visual arts, music, theater, dance and literature.

Nancy Ellis was an assistant professor of education at the University of New Hampshire, Durham, with interests in arts education and professional development of educators. In 1987, after studying with Elliot Eisner and specializing in design and evaluation of educational programs, she received her doctorate in education from Stanford University. From 1970 until 1983 she had been a visual arts consultant and classroom teacher in the Burlington, Vermont, public schools. In 1984, she served as site evaluator for the National Endowment for the Arts in six states.

Among the people who helped us conceptualize these case studies were Harry Broudy, Richard Colwell, Dale Costello, Howard Gardner, Madeleine Grumet,

Jerry Hausman, and Ralph Smith. At each site we found people such as Phyllis Ennes, Pat Iannelli, Carolyn Lutgen and Mary Kay Mabry who drew us toward a better understanding of what we were seeking. Assisting us with early arrangements was Jonathan Block; in review of manuscripts were Berit Askling, Darla Cohen, Terry Denny, Janet Hatano, Charles Leonhard, Giordana Rabitti, Debbie Rugg, and Patricia Tracy; and with final organization of the book, Leigh Little.

The Research Rationale

Intending to portray how, as observers, we interacted with the happenings of the classroom, we might call this research *constructivist* case study. We think of our case study findings not so much as discoveries but as experiences (Stake, 1985) which, in part, we ourselves have constructed. We have sought not to minimize but to preserve interactions between researcher and phenomena. We acknowledge interpretation in each datum. Even though the researcher strives to document what every observer might see, each observation is expected to hold meanings that others would not see. Still, key observations are to be triangulated (Denzin, 1970), each narrative is to be trustworthy (Guba & Lincoln, 1989). Dialogue and contextual detail are chosen not only to portray the event but to develop issue-based assertions. Assertions are formed uniquely by each researcher, disciplined but drawing on personal experience and study (Erickson, 1986).

We call the research *naturalistic*. We want to see ordinary happenings in ordinary settings. We use instruments including questionnaires as little as possible, for they direct activity toward our issues, away from *every-day* pursuits. We cannot be on hand to see much of what we want to know about, thus through interviews and review of documents we indirectly look at happenings. We believe the happenings are best understood with a careful attention to their contexts and, partly for that reason, also think of our studies as *holistic*.

We call the research *service-oriented*. We not only hope it will be useful to people puzzled by arts teaching, engaged in improving programs, or setting arts education policy. We try to check out potential for use as we go along. We hope the report will be useful to quite different types of people but generally our concern is more for those close at hand, those who have most to gain and lose from a particular arts education program.

We call it *empathic* research. It attends to the intentions of the people studied, their value commitments, their frames of reference. We start with our own notions of what is important but increasingly try to highlight issues of importance to the teachers, parents, and others closely associated with the case. We try to report things in ways that provide vicarious experience.

This type of research has been supported and refined by the methodological writings of those cited so far and other researchers such as Herbert Glaser, Egon Guba, David Hamilton, Helen Simons, Lou Smith, and Anselm Strauss. Valuable precedents were set for us in the case studies of Howard Becker, Eleanor Farrar, Ernest House, Alan Peshkin, Harry Wolcott and Barry MacDonald and his East Anglia colleagues, Clem Adelman, David Jenkins, Saville Kushner, and Rob Walker. Examples are identified in our bibliography.

Here we have tried to emphasize the uniqueness of the situation as much as the general. Every site has its own story to tell and none is adequately representative of others. Still in each, most readers see parallels reflecting and informing about their own arts classrooms. A special aspect of the particularization in this report is our rather personalistic presentation. Many educational researchers consider staff and student personalities façades which must be penetrated. We consider personalities to be determining factors, thus a central part of the stories. For all the effort to cast education into a technical and standardized operation, it remains greatly a product of spontaneity and intuition on both sides of the desk. The particulars of arts education cannot be understood, we believe, without the personalistic dimensions.

Among the several drawbacks[6] of naturalistic case study are its personal intrusiveness and risk of exposé. Usually we are guests of the people we are studying, in some ways intruding into a space that—regardless of funding and crowding—is by custom a private space. We come *intending* to make it public. Along the way, we ask our hosts to read drafts of descriptions not only to correct our errors but to help us recognize their vulnerability. Teachers and especially educators who have a public rostrum, we prefer to identify by name, date and place, to facilitate reader understanding. But often, even when they do not ask for it, we find it best to anonymize. Thus, several of the case studies here carry pseudonyms and a few events have been distorted to diminish recognition. Still, within their own communities, individuals may be recognizable in our anonymized accounts. We believe this risk worth taking: problems, shortcomings, and personal dismay are essential to understanding but we are pained to think that we sometimes may leave a site having made it more difficult for the educators to carry out their responsibilities.

What Do We Expect a School to Be?

The frame around understanding is expectation. Nothing is meaningful without previous encounter. An encounter raises expectation for subsequent encounter. We approach new experience with expectation. We understand the new within frameworks of past experience. The next school we encounter will surely be something like the schools we already know. Even when forewarned that this one will be different, the expectation of difference is meaningful in terms of variation previously experienced. "You will find this school in touch with the arts community." "This school is striving to deal with the technological uncertainty of the future." "This school is backing away ever so slightly from 'the basics' toward exploratory studies." "This school is less oriented to music than most." Advance notice is meaningful only in terms of what we already know.

Our expectation of schools, like all perceptions, tends toward the concrete. We see first the shape of buildings and the scurry of people, only later the philosophies

---

[6]We do not want to deny that case study research has, in addition to the propensity for intrusion, several important defects. It is costly, wordy, subjective, biased toward attention to social interaction, seldom sufficiently cautious in interpretation, and its regimen of inquiry (or lack of it) is difficult to establish. Yet to probe some complex phenomena, it can be the best way to go.

of faculty and the impressions left on students. We expect the building, the faculty, and the philosophies to be a reflection of the community. Rich communities have 'country club' schools; ghetto communities have 'trashed' schools. Reality sometimes contradicts our expectation but the stereotypes run deep.

We expect a school to prepare the community's youngsters for college, for work, for young adulthood. We expect a curriculum heavy on the core subjects, language skills, science, and math, with options in vocational subjects such as office practice, food preparation, and agriculture, and the extracurricular activities such as athletics, band, and computer games. And we expect attention to the humanities, particularly the arts, available at least to the more talented and interested.

For a century, we have expected American schools to raise the level of education of each successive generation, to provide teachers more knowledgeable than parents, and to make youngsters even better educated than their teachers. Hopes remain but expectations are changing. In America today, schools are not thought to satisfy needs for technological competence, literacy, and readiness for an as-yet-unimaginable twenty-first century.

In all the 50 states, campaigns are underway to improve the schools, to raise the standards of education.[7] Expectation for the success of the reforms does not run high. People are used to educators and politicians promising more than they can deliver. For the country as a whole, further disappointments are on the way. But satisfaction with local schools remains surprisingly high. Expectation is that good teachers will continue to teach, that youngsters will learn. Prevailing still is the expectation of a healthy compromise between commercial-industrial needs and the competencies of graduates.

Americans have maintained considerable expectation that the sophistications of adults can be produced on a foundation of elemental skills, that all children need to master certain basics in order to advance to higher mental proficiencies. "One must walk before one runs." So in the 1970s and 80s the aim of school curricula has been to teach the competencies well, to postpone the interpretive studies. In his book *Should We Educate?* philosopher Carl Bereiter assessed school ability to teach basic skills and interpretive learnings, found the former attainable, the latter largely beyond our reach. The schools have not abandoned the teaching of reading comprehension, critical thinking, writing composition and music appreciation but those aims regularly are postponed at least until assessments of student accomplishment show the basic skills—arithmetic computation, reading as decoding and vocabulary—to be attained.

The states have responded to public disappointment by declaring increasingly that education is not only a local responsibility but state responsibility as well. Formal expression of standards has become more frequent and more explicit,

---

[7] Defining curriculum components is a common aim in planning reform. A strong argument for better definition of arts education has been made by Michael Day (1984) and Bennett Reimer (1989). Clearly, better definitions can aid communication. But the record does not show that specification regularly leads to improvement. Often it leads to simplistics, sometimes to dissention among reformers. In these case studies, we sought instances where poor definition of art education seemed to be an obstacle to good instruction—and found none.

implying that standards are being raised. Goal statements are worded to encompass almost all possible good learnings. But those statements serve mainly to raise expectation that traditional scholastic subjects will be addressed with more vigor than the vocational, the humanities, and the extracurricular. As exemplified in Figure 2, the arts are included in many state goal statements but the regulations developed to enforce state responsibility leave definition of arts education open, with computer keyboarding and photo processing as legitimate as chorus.

Contemporary recommendations of the National Endowment for the Arts (1988) include arts education for all the children: "Arts education should provide all students with a sense of the arts in civilization, of creativity in the artistic process, of the vocabularies of artistic communication, and of the critical elements necessary

---

Message from the Superintendent of Public Instruction

Inherent in our role as educators is the obligation to provide the best, most comprehensive education possible for all young people in our state. Included in this mandate is the necessity to include the arts—dance, drama, music, and the visual arts—in the core curriculum. The Basic Education Act of 1977 states that the goal . . .

shall be to provide students with the opportunity to achieve those skills which are generally recognized as requisite to learning. Those skills shall include the ability:

1. To distinguish, interpret, and make use of words, numbers, and other symbols, including sound, colors, shapes, and textures:

2. To organize words and other symbols into acceptable verbal and nonverbal forms of expression, and numbers into their appropriate functions;

3. To perform intellectual functions such as problem solving, decision making, goal setting, selecting, planning, predicting, experimenting, ordering, and evaluating;

4. To use various muscles necessary for coordinating physical and mental functions.

Properly taught, the arts embody and develop all of these skills.

In order to increase the quality of learning for Washington students the State Board of Education requested my agency to prepare curriculum guidelines in all content areas. These guidelines reflect the desire to achieve excellence at all levels and in all areas, as well as assist students in developing competencies for college, work, and life.

Figure 2. Opening to the Introduction to Visual & Performing Arts Curriculum Guidelines for Washington Schools, Frank B. Brouillet, State Superintendent of Public Instruction, 1987.

to making informed choices about the products of the arts." But as visitors to the schools, our expectation is less idealistic and more immediate. Our expectation of schools, across the country and already in Anacortes, Danville, and elsewhere, is less that they will educate, more that they will offer courses—pretty much the courses offered early in the century. We encounter little talk about what it means to be an educated adult but lots of talk about the illiterate. To hear some discussions, it seems the most important thing a school should do is to avoid illiteracy.

Expectations for School Arts

We expect the schools to have an arts program. In many places, what they have is a program in name only. An elementary school is likely to have a specialist teacher in music. According to Thomas Hatfield of the National Art Education Association, only four states have a specially trained art teacher in every school. In most places, the classroom teacher will provide a few minutes of art activity a week. Attention to drama will be confined to a performance of some kind a few times a year. These will be productions, something to be put on exhibit. The experience of participation will be esteemed. For the more talented youngster, knowledge of the arts is not expected to exceed that of an embryonic performer; for the others, almost no knowledge of the arts is expected.

Middle schools, junior high, and senior high schools are expected to provide regular instruction as optional enrollment for students in visual arts, crafts, choir, and band. Again the orientation is largely to performance, the junior class play, synchronous movement at "halftime," making of announcements and gifts for one's parents. The arts are participatory arts, production arts (Efland, 1976).

A typical school district hires only enough teachers specially-trained in elementary music to assure a weekly lesson for each child, only enough secondary teachers to provide courses for students electing band or chorus. A typical school district hires teachers specially-trained in the visual arts to provide an occasional elective for that minority of high schoolers not committed to academics, athletics, or other avocations. Faculty help is needed to assure direction of class plays and holiday programs and supervision of visits to museums and concerts, but these usually are handled by volunteer teachers and outsiders. Most school districts see little obligation to employ elementary teachers with more than incidental preparation in arts education. Our fundamental expectation of teacher preparation falls short of art education qualification.

We expect a school to help youngsters approach opportunities for further education by providing credentials of coursework, good performances on tests, and a disposition to undertake the burdensome assignments of professional training. We expect a school to acquaint youngsters with the arts, partly because it might be some part of their career activity, largely because it might become avocationally enriching, but mostly because it helps round out the school experience. We expect a school to be serious about its arts education, even about activities mainly purported to reduce the strain and tedium of other schoolwork.

Across the years, within and outside the schools, there have been urgings that art education be something more. John Dewey spoke of *art as experience*, Harry Broudy of *enlightened cherishing*, Elliot Eisner of *conceptual imagery*, Edmund Feldman of *humanistic* art education, the study of man through art. There are teachers in almost every school who reverberate to these purposes. But the ordinary expectation of school arts is for occasional, direction-following, momentarily-captivating activity that culminates in audience-pleasing productions.

It is with such expectation that we visit Anacortes, Washington. We go to a middle school there, then to grade schools in our other seven sites.

PART TWO:
Eight Case Studies

Chapter 2:
Anacortes Middle School
Anacortes, Washington

■ *Robert Stake*

Although I did not intend my case study of arts education in the middle school at Anacortes, Washington, to focus on purposes, that is the issue which repeatedly drew my attention. I anticipated finding instruction highly purposive—but would the teachers' purposes fit the rationales offered by national spokespersons?

During our 1985 study of art education in Decatur, Illinois we discerned that, in word and deed, advocates of graphic arts education collectively identify seven purposes. Art education exists "to develop a youngster's (1) cultural knowledge base, (2) imaging and other critical-thinking skills, (3) artistic expressiveness, (4) self-understanding, (5) membership in and support for the world of art, (6) opportunities for enjoyment and change of pace, and (7) appreciation and cherishing of the arts. Benefits to teachers, school, community and society were alluded to as well. I wanted to analyze the teaching at Anacortes in terms of these purposes.

The Research Plan

I chose the site from several recommended by Gina May, state supervisor of visual and performing arts, and Mike Croman of the Washington State Arts Commission. I had asked what programs among those having more or less ordinary funding would be good places to learn about ordinary teaching and learning but also would have people sensitive to arts education issues. I also chose the site because Dick Smock, a long time program evaluation colleague was available there for assistance in observation and interviewing. (I had told him I would ask him to help but then did not.) I was not acquainted with the community or anyone at the schools. I spent 12 days on site in 1988.

As a researcher, my background includes case study research in arts education and gifted student education as well as curriculum evaluation and testing broadly. Here in Anacortes I used naturalistic research methods outlined in my own writing and that of Fred Erickson (1986), Egon Guba (1978), Robert Bogdan and Sari Bicklin (1982); not the more structural case study approaches of Matt Miles and Michael Huberman (1984) and David Labaree (1988). I did not seek to identify the typicality of matters. Instead, I wanted to provide something of vicarious experience for the reader, especially in dealing with what I saw to be the uniqueness of the site, offering opportunities for naturalistic generalization, yet still providing much in the way of my own critical analysis.

The next section provides observations more or less in the order encountered to get immediately into both classroom and administrative situations. To squeeze the report together most interview quotations have been considerably cut and smoothed over, using a subsequent check with the interviewee to locate inaccuracy and insensitivity. The final section deals with the issues, first those such as standardization of the curriculum, interaction with community affairs, reliance on artists-in-residence, and rationale for arts education, ending on the two I felt most worthy of pondering as a result of this encounter: leadership and utilization of informal educational opportunities.

The Site

The Anacortes School District has four elementary schools, a high school and a middle school, the latter for the 325 students in grades 7 and 8. The middle school is housed under the same roof as the district administrative offices (called the management support center) and is but a short walk to the high school. Both stand on high ground overlooking the Anacortes community and looking northeastward into Puget Sound.

The school day is broken into seven periods of 48 minutes each. An eighth grader's schedule might look like this:

1	Math	Mr. Jones
2	PE/Health	Ms. Needler
3	Science	Mr. Rogers
4	Intermediate Band	Mr. Love
L U N C H		
5	Eighth grade block (Reading and Language Arts)	Mr. Moore
6		"
7	U. S. History	Mr. Slotemaker

Every middle school student is expected to be enrolled in an arts course every semester. The unified arts course includes: home economics, shop, visual art, and crafts. For music courses, i.e., band and chorus, the students take a quick bus ride to the high school. Presently a student can take formal coursework in visual art, music, drama, literature, and crafts, but not in dance or art history. A vigorous artist-in-residence program and organized trips to arts exhibits and performances extend the regular curriculum.

The students who come from the elementary schools in the community have been exposed to weekly music classes taught by a music education specialist. Activities in the other arts have been organized by the classroom teacher. Each teacher has considerable autonomy as to what to teach and what purposes to pursue. Over a period of several years, with support from the Washington State Arts Commission and coordination by Kathy Hastings (earlier an artist-in-residence, later a consultant), district administrators have redirected a number of staff development sessions toward development of an elementary school arts curriculum guide, *The Fourth R*. The Superintendent is proud of the work; he publicizes it and speaks of selling the guide to other districts.

Anacortes Middle School

Observations

Phyllis Ennes' Speech and Drama Class

The speech and drama class meets in a special room just off the library. Five tables provide workspace for the 25 seventh graders identified by teachers as not needing concentration on reading and for whom enrollment was requested by parents. The room has a tiny stage, a felt-pen board, a wall of letter fonts, a wall of windows opening on Fidalgo Bay. Behind the stage, space has been commandeered for costumes and props. A Young Authors group uses the room for case-binding their creative writing collections.

Ms. Ennes opens this morning's class with commentary on the flurries of student-made marking-pen snowflakes on the butcher-paper "graffiti sheets" covering each table, observing that graffiti can be ugly and can be beautiful. Skye, a blonde boy with a big smile, reads the morning announcements, including the fact that on the previous evening Matt—who is present—won the middle-high spelling bee. Applause. Ms. Ennes asks Matt the word on which he won. "Binomial." She asks two other competitors present the words that put them out. She encourages expression; these answers are cryptic. Commenting on the accomplishment of all three she adds 190 honor points to the whole class tally for this semester. Ms. Ennes notes that at yesterday's teacher meeting two words came to her attention. As a "gift" to the class she offers the two: "mutuality" and "civility." They work a few minutes to define them. Then she adds, "I learned something scary yesterday about mutuality and civility. When you lose either one, you cannot get it back." Then another "gift:" a numerical puzzle. After each student is led through a string of convoluted arithmetic operations, a surprising sum is reached, the home address house number of the person sitting next to him. After expressing a certain amazement, Ms. Ennes asks Quang to determine how it worked and to report to the class on Monday. Ten minutes later Quang indicates he has the answer. Ms. Ennes asks him to explain it. He moves to the podium and board and, using graphics and algebra, in clear voice and with pedagogic flair, explains it.

Within that 10 minutes occurred a matter of letters for Donna Rawhauser, retiring children's room librarian at the city library. The students had composed letters; now Ms. Ennes wants the letters prepared suitably for a gift collection. She indicates they need to be on nice paper, in ink or typewritten, well spaced, well spelled, possibly with borders. "It must look beautiful." She wants today to see a draft, with the final copy due Monday.

And finally to the primary class activity, the reading of Moliere's *Tartuffe,* a play they will see (as will the Eighth Grade Drama Club) at the Seattle Repertory Theatre next month. Ms. Ennes indicates that she failed to receive the brief "summaries of action" she had assigned. But it's a misunderstanding and clearing it up takes a while, partly because she keeps asking students to explain their understanding. Intended or not, another declamatory exercise.

She asks about the following passage in the Moliere plot:

> Dorine: It's your turn now, Sir, not to be listened to;
> You'd not trust us, and now she won't trust you.

"Who was Dorine speaking to?" "Who else gives him advice?" She asks the class to name the elements of theatre, and gets: plot, theme, dialogue, character, spectacle, music, et cetera—some right, some wrong. The study of *Tartuffe* is aided by a study guide distributed by the Repertory Theatre. On the examination Ennes has prepared are such questions as: "Tartuffe grew out of the traditions of French farce and Italian *commedia dell 'arte*. Discuss the similarities and differences in these dramatic forms and *Tartuffe*."

Phyllis Ennes and Two Eighth-Grade Students

As the session draws to a close she indicates she wants each of them, over the weekend while watching television, to select a scene and contemplate how they would make a "storyboard" of that scene, including all the elements. She says that later there will be a major assignment along these lines and she wants them to help her figure out what will work. The students are withdrawn, perhaps reeling a bit under the succession of assignments. Finally Ann asks for clarification. The answer: "Think about it."

Throughout the 50+ minutes Mrs. Ennes conveys high expectation of work, of punctuality, of attention, of care about presentation, and of individual interpretation. She expects the children to analyze, interpret, understand, as well as to know the right answers. She knows, and expects them to know, to acquire knowledge. Her standards are high. She doesn't smile much. She shows respect for individual youngsters and insists on respect from them. Her orientation to aesthetics is transparent. It appears she raises student expectation of what they can do partly by not acknowledging they can do less.

Why *Tartuffe*? "I chose it from perhaps eight plays to be performed in Seattle theatres. *Tartuffe* was the best. I was pleased the Rep was using the Richard Wilbur translation. Of course *Tartuffe* isn't the only play we have read this year:

Antigone and *Androcles and the Lion*. We usually read Shakespeare. I am looking over next year's possibilities. It's not wholly an aesthetic decision, it never is. But if I don't like what is playing, we won't see any of them!"

Charlie Kiel, Middle School Principal

Charlie Kiel has been the principal here for 11 years. I learned quickly that he has studied the curriculum carefully. While chatting over coffee in the kitchen by the Board Room, midmorning, I asked: "What is your view of arts education?"

Kiel: I am a Cultural Education Program Committee member. I believe in counterpoint between basic skills and the arts. We need variety, change in activity, creativity, higher order thinking skills, imagination, unique personal expression. Sometimes the school district waffles but we try to provide a variety in arts education.

Stake: What is the middle school arts program?

Kiel: We have one period out of seven for the arts. Students take music or unified arts, a full year course with one quarter for each: crafts, fine arts, shop and living skills. Band and chorus meet at the high school the first period, intermediate band fourth period. And we have 25 kids in speech-and-drama the second period. Another part of the program is the Young Authors project. It brings quite a bit of recognition to the middle school.

Stake: What issues do you face?

Kiel: Several. Whether or not the arts should be elective or required; right now, it's every kid, every year. Also, how best to use the Artists-in-Residence. One key problem is staff development. Another is making the building more appealing, more attuned to our fine graphics and stained glass. Also, we may need to add dance to physical education and more literary arts to language arts.

Stake: Are teachers rewarded for bringing the arts into general instruction? Does the administration applaud identification of elegance in math and science?

Kiel: Not systematically. But more than in most districts, we *do* the arts.

Stake: What is your opinion of the Artists-in-Residence program?

Kiel: It's a good opportunity to integrate the arts with other subject matters. It's inexpensive and labor intensive. A dollar goes a long way. We were particularly fortunate in having Kathy Hastings as one of our visiting artists. She did lots of staff development and helped us develop our guide, *The Fourth R*.

Stake: How do you decide which artists to invite for a residency?

Kiel: It isn't by administrative decree. The decisions are made by teachers. Teachers request the funding, identify needs of other teachers, review the list of available artists, and decide what to do. I should add that both Phyllis Nelson and I are on the committee that does those things but it really is an activity run by teachers.

The draft for next year's proposal was written by Phyllis Ennes. She will take several teachers, probably to Seattle, to interview prospective artists. They take the advice and requests of many teachers with them. It seems requests for music regularly end up in the minority—but it's an important minority, so for next year two weeks have been set aside for a musician. We have been thinking particularly of music related to social studies, the centennial songbook, and instrument making.

Stake: And it fits into the regular curriculum?

Kiel: Next year, as part of a five-year improvement plan, we will be reviewing the entire curriculum.

Stake: Who will be advocating more attention to the arts?

Kiel: Well, certainly Phyllis Ennes and Ann Moore. You've met Phyllis. Born and raised in Anacortes, she's our librarian, heads our cultural education program committee, teaches speech and drama, and does all sorts of things. Ann Moore teaches eighth-grade literary arts. They both are advocates of all the arts for all the children.

Stake: Is the middle school itself undergoing change?

Kiel: For two years enrollments have been declining. But next year we will get enough kids to need another teacher. Probably a math teacher. The district is not likely to be hiring more arts teachers. The academic diploma is reducing the high school arts and music program. It greatly limits arts electives.

Stake: Aren't the new state requirements for the arts helping?

Kiel: No. We already meet them.

Stake: What areas would Superintendent Lowell like to see enhanced?

Kiel: Computers. Programs for at-risk students.

Stake: At the expense of the arts?

Kiel: At the peripheries. A visit by a group of 20 seniors to Ashland, Oregon's Shakespeare Festival was in jeopardy of being cut, but reinstated. Two or three years ago the district's Suzuki violin program was on the way out. Parents raised $3000, got it back.

Stake: The arts have taken deeper cuts than other areas?

Kiel: It is hard to say. The swimming program, individual sports have been cut. For each cut a special interest group raises a fuss. But the situation really isn't as bleak as I paint it. We are running in the black.

Duane Lowell, Superintendent

In the superintendent's office, early the first morning on site, I said, "In the few hours I have been here I have been impressed by the district's assets."

Lowell: You must be thinking about Phyllis Ennes and what she does. I agree. She is a most unusual person. As an arts educator she has tremendous standards. She keeps everyone honest, including me. Our district arts program is recognized statewide, largely because of her leadership. Thanks to her we are able to bring in an array of artists and art forms.

Stake: What can you tell me about the Artists-in-Residence program?

Lowell: It is run by teacher committees. It's their baby. We keep hands off. But of course I keep an eye on what's going on. I'm impressed by the linkage between the art activity and the skills programs.

Stake: Isn't there an over-reliance on these itinerant artists to do a job that should be done by specially-trained teachers?

Lowell: We were badly hit by the budget crunch. We had to abandon having art specialists for the elementary grades. So we expect the classroom teacher to teach art, an assignment the teachers continue to resist. We still have an elementary music teacher, Pat Rein, but he is spread awfully thin. For 7-8 years we have relied a lot on visiting artists. One was Kathy Hastings, a muralist and maker of stained glass windows. (You can see her work in our halls and stairway.) For several years Kathy was in effect our arts consultant. She did staff development K-6 and helped our teachers develop a curriculum materials package.

Stake: Were you pleased with the results?

Lowell: I was very pleased with the whole project. We called it *The Fourth R*. You'll want to have a good look. Phyllis Nelson has a copy of the document. Kathy helped us overcome a lot of negative feeling. And there were rough spots along the way. Talented people can get upset. Rigid guidelines can be troublesome. Now we have an exemplary program, K-8. The teachers have a fun program, with good educational structures.

Stake: What else about the arts program are you proud of?

Lowell: Certainly the Suzuki program. This one is worked out with individual parents. We have a strong instructor, Mary Carrol, who really knows what she is doing.

Stake: Only a few children will study violin. What is the district's position on the theme of "all the arts for all the children?"

Lowell: In grades K-6 we have basic learning objectives for all the students. In grades K-12 we are in compliance with the basic education requirements of the state. Phyllis Nelson can inform you more of that. The state has an arts requirement but it can be satisfied by a single course-enrollment and it really doesn't have to be visual or performing arts. We are technically in compliance. But we want to do much better than that. I believe that there are lots of ways of looking at things. The arts provide one important way. We want all our children to be acquainted with that way.

Stake: Is your community willing to support arts teaching for all the children every year?

Lowell: No, but they have supported our current program. If you come to the Board Meeting on the 29th you will probably hear about the community's priorities.

Stake: What will the Board be considering?

Lowell: A number of things are on the agenda. Officially the one curriculum item is the selection of social studies texts. We review our text materials every 5-6 years or so. No-one on the Board takes a particular interest in arts education. A recent advocate is now gone.

Stake: All in all, how are things going?

Lowell: Well, we have an up-to-date curriculum. Our teachers are strong and there is limited staff turnover. On the whole we have good community support. We follow the "effective schools model." We are working on leadership. We keep busy maintaining community support to keep the schools running.

Diana Lim, Dancer, Artist-in-Residence

Diana Lim completed her work at the middle school several weeks ago. Today we are in Gail Joyce's second grade room at Island View School. Lim will work with this group for 45 minutes each day for two weeks. After asking their names: "How many kinds of dance do you know?" "Ballet!" "Square Dance!" "Boogie!" and others. "Good. We aren't going to do any of those! You are going to make up your own dances. But first we need to warm up our bodies. Let's move quickly to the gym."

Down a short hallway, we enter the gym, single file, no talking. Lim marks the middle of the gym with a make-believe wall through which we pass by opening and closing a make-believe door. They'll work every day in the far half of the room. They start with a circle that fills the half. First, it's "Flex and extend, flex and extend...," then it's "swimming," then there's "happy cat, mad cat" and finally back to "Flex and straight, let ten toes take the weight."—five minutes of warm-up. At the sound of the tambourine, each kid is to twist the body to shape a letter and hold it.

What is happening here? The kids are all caught up in it. Ms. Joyce is smiling, yawning, not "doing it" today but tomorrow she'll be dressed more casually and doing it too. Lim and the music are upbeat, demanding. Neither teacher nor children seem bent on "learning" something. For them it is not the time to memorize. It's participation time. A little competition. A little showing-off. Not much self-consciousness. While twirling on the floor, one kid is kicked (lightly) in the head, cries, is ignored, gets over it. The circle is awhirr with action. And before you know it, it's over—for today. I guess what we have done is identify a repertoire of poses and moves. Do you suppose that we might string them together later and that would be the dance we make up?

With an M.S. in Dance, Diana Lim works with the Co-Motion Dance Company of Seattle. Here in Anacortes she says, "During this residency the students will be observing *themselves* dance as well as me. Dance is an underexposed art. Many people say they don't understand it. This residency provides the students with basic tools for viewing and participating in dance. These tools will be presented as the dance elements: energy, time and space. Finally, we culminate with a show, something to be seen."

Forming letters during Diana Lim's residency

"We also work with content, with stories as a take-off point. Mood is a part of any dance. In class, I present shapes, mirroring and other techniques for movement improvisations. However, just because an improvisation or exercise emphasizes a movement element it doesn't mean we're ignoring the meanings inherent in the movement.

"The primary teachers have been very helpful showing me how to relate dance with stages of development their children are in. Likewise, we dancers share how dance can be used with their classroom work to present concepts they are working on: spelling, arithmetic, reading readiness. An excellent book is *Teaching the Three R's Through Movement Experience* by Anne Green Gilbert."

The links between the three R's and creating "our own dance" seem to me as tenuous as linking letter-shaped body-twists and pre-reading. But, it *is* a language art, a body language, a social communication, a medium of expression, a construction of word, sentence, and paragraph. Not all of this gets said, and indeed, only when skeptical questions are raised do advocates seek out usefulness in some academic tally. Behavior control may be a stronger appeal for many teachers than intellectual or creative expression. Even this seemingly skeptical teacher applauds the discipline of rhythm, a conformance to theme, the capture of individuality by creative togetherness. The lasting impression is that dance is not a bad thing to be doing in school, at least for a while. It's participatory. And possibly as Superintendent Lowell says, "it's one way of seeing things."

Laurie Julius and the High School Choir

This is the second year Julius has been teaching in Anacortes. When she arrived just 14 girls and a pair of boys were signed up for choir. Now the number has reached 40, but the gender disparity continues. Julius is not sure why. Twenty years ago choir was equally popular among boys and girls. With the choral group the "winningest team" in the high school, she is surprised about the continuing low popularity. Less than 20% of the students apparently take any high school music. Still she has enough to make presentations at Kiwanis Club and at the nursing homes.

School music has not been built up in the earlier grades. There is one music specialist for the elementary grades; he gets around to each class about once a week. Middle school students have an option to take chorus. Not many do.

Ostensibly Julius is free to teach any music she wants. Her repertoire does not test the limits. Seeking simplicity and arrangements for higher voices, she relies heavily on classical religious selections. I had just listened to them working through a handsome "Praise Be to God" with an SSAB arrangement. Modern music selections that fit her requirements are "generally over our heads."

Julius completed her teacher training at Western Washington University in 1985. In class, her style is brisk, businesslike. She treats the youngsters with respect but pushes them hard toward the performance she wants. But she avows only a secondary interest in performance. She strives to teach music so that students will enjoy music, if not now, eventually. It should be something they will "use later, one way or another." The question, "For what they would use it?" drew no delineating answer.

When asked what knowledge she hopes to share with students, Julius speaks of understanding such things as tempo markings. Reading music is a skill she wants all students to have by middle school. She makes no mention of the value of music history or criticism skills. She likes to keep the students aware of special music events in the community. She encourages them to bring their own tapes for listening in the music room. She goes along with the many whose first choice is rock, but insists upon setting decibel limits.

Her choral groups give four concerts a year. She plans to tour every other year. The tour this spring will take them to Seattle, with stops at high schools along the way. A schedule is easy to arrange because other schools regularly want a performance in the fine auditorium in Anacortes. She makes all the arrangements, including finding money to cover the costs. A supportive principal says, "Fine, you pay for it." What is the tour's educational purpose? The experience—partly the experience of dealing with problems.

When asked how she is different from the last music teacher Julius says she selects less difficult scores and she distances herself more from the students. "Trying to be counselor as well as teacher can be asking for trouble."

Phyllis Nelson, District Curriculum Coordinator

After examining the competing social sciences instructional materials laid out for selection committee review, I asked Phyllis Nelson: "By what pathway did you come to your present position?"

Nelson: I didn't aim for it. I guess I just moved from responsibility to responsibility, keeping alternatives open. I taught in junior high, then in kindergarten, then in a private school for emotionally disturbed boys. I taught junior high math and reading for six years. I was a high school teacher for eight years. I have been a school psychologist. I was vice principal of the high school for two years. This is my fifth year in the district curriculum office. In each of these responsibilities I was expected to come up with my own ideas.

Stake: What has been the theme of your ideas?

Nelson: A people theme. Of course I have had to deal with curriculum scope and sequence, with an emphasis on coordination of individuals, with an emphasis on curriculum integration. I have seen the pendulum swing from concern for the whole child to concern for accountability. I'd like to see some swing back and I think it has started to happen. The Board and Superintendent have come quite a way. It takes patience.

Stake: In which direction is the pendulum headed?

Nelson: In the last ten years our attention has been on standards. Standards are extremely important but we can go too far. We have to allow flexibility for teachers and students. We have to be involved in the processes of change. Objectives change, so does subject matter, so do parents. And in trying to understand it all, we simplify it all. I believe we have lost the power to integrate different topics. It is time for a reintegration of the curriculum.

Stake: Is that what the community wants?

Nelson: Generally we are well accepted by the community. We are moving toward a grades 6-8 middle school. Our views are somewhat liberal compared to the surrounding communities. But we are sensitive to many growing, or at least potential, problems—problems such as personal safety and substance abuse.

Stake: People are unaware of kids drinking?

Nelson: We get all kinds of objections. Acknowledging Halloween gets us complaints of embracing demonology.

Stake: (I failed to follow-up here on this problem of sacrilege, a problem seen by some to deter ambitions to bring the contemporary out-of-school culture into instructional assignments.) Is the school calendar holiday oriented?

Nelson: There isn't a lot of pressure for it. We just had a St. Patrick's concert. Some cultural education is holiday oriented.

Stake: What emphasis is there on the arts in the seventh grade?

Nelson: It has changed over the years. We now have "unified arts." We teach some of the cultural arts in social studies, English, and writing. We have a mentor arrangement. Every seventh grader must have at least 1/6th of their courses in the arts.

Stake: How prescriptive is your arts curriculum guide, *The Fourth R*?

Nelson: The activities there are only suggested. But the SLO's (student learning objectives) listed for grades K-6 are compulsory. Elementary teachers decide which activities to use to satisfy the objectives. Some junior high teachers use the exercises too.

Stake: Is testing influencing what is taught?

Nelson: Testing is not changing *what* we teach but perhaps the emphasis. We look at the reading test results, for example. If they are low we ask the teachers for perspectives of what is wrong.

Doug Dore's Unified Arts Class

Back in the middle school, Doug Dore is teaching ceramic glazing. The students are 13-year-olds, good looking, alert, clad in jeans, sweat shirts (proclaiming TKE, Sunshine Co., Life's a Beach, Adidas, Blue Moon, and Hanging Out) and canvas shoes. These seventh graders have gathered in the annex, a well lighted art studio aside the main building. They look over their bisqued pieces, ranging from fish sculpture to Tim's double-mouthed vase. Dore is saying:

> You started with clay fresh from the earth. What is it called? 'Plastic.' You followed instructions and it became 'leather,' then hardened until it was completely 'green.' You gave it the ring test. Listen. No cracks, right?
>
> I wish we had more time on the pots. We will do just one glazing. It is your choice whether to glaze the outside or just leave it bisqued. For water-proofing there must be glaze inside. Now, this would not turn back to clay even if I left it outside 10,000 years. Everyone should waterproof your pot inside. But not on the bottom. You may have noticed your ceramic dinnerware at home is not glazed on the bottom. The glaze would stick to the kiln.
>
> Tim has agreed to let me glaze his pot. For color Tim has chosen the jar marked 'Sand'. Note that you cannot tell that it will become sand color by looking at the liquid. As a liquid this glaze is dark blue. Look at the tiles here. These are color chips. See this blue. This one has cobalt in it. When fired it turns blue. Pick the color you want from these tiles.

He pours the glaze into the pot, then shows how to pour it out to cover the inside surface. He talks about making a mess, about taking a brush to spots missed, indicates choice of 0, 1, or 2 glazings. "And in my opinion it's best to get the glaze down into all the texture." Students are completely attentive. "And you must wipe your bottoms!" They respond comfortably to his style. The boys speak out more than the girls. All appear to be considering the requirements and options he puts before them. After leaving the demonstration, many work on tessellating designs.

Doug does not speak directly of aesthetics in this group scene. It seems to be production that counts. Planning is implied, but not pushed. In half an hour the demonstration is finished. Later he tells me he discusses color limitation as it relates to clay's earthen origin.

A Math Class

The Washington state K-12 Curriculum Guidelines (Figure 2) call for "infusion of the arts into the general classroom experience in a variety of ways including use as a means of communication." If this is happening we should find in non-arts classes occasional attention to the aesthetics of pattern, texture, and design as well as to examples of art processes, products and performances. I decided to look for infusion of arts and aesthetics in a math class and a social studies class.

The math teacher had grown up in Anacortes where his father before him was a teacher. The son attended two years of college, then transferred to Western Washington University where he majored in political studies. He did not take art or music in college. Presently he is teaching math and career education. He takes pride in developing student skills, including inquiry skills. In today's class he makes no reference to the arts, but experiences some pleasant involvement in mapping and graphic design. As do most people, he considers it important for all students to learn measurement skills.

In the class I visited the students spent the near-hour converting English measures of length into metrics. Twenty-four twelve-year-olds, more or less, worked text and worksheet items, with the teacher at the chalkboard talking them through difficult and unfamiliar exercises. Frequent references were made to the textbook, an Addison Wesley math text. Subject matter was presented as something essential for practical computation. Student activity level was high, on task; of course occasionally twos or threes diverged into nonmathematical whispering. During this session nothing about the subject was presented as artistic, elegant, or deserving of esteem. It was math.

Ray Stebner's Challenge Class

The social studies class I visited seeking integrated arts was called a "challenge class." Here we have a group of some 20 seventh and eighth graders, "a cut above the average." Most were identified by their sixth-grade teachers as especially good students, particularly hard working. For a *three-period* afternoon stretch they meet to advance their knowledge of history, social studies, and English language and literature.

Stebner has the room arranged in long vertical rows of tables with chairs. He maintains station at both ends. Posters and paraphernalia draw attention to matters of political and historical moment. Today is the second day back after a five day class trip to Washington, D.C. Stebner starts the day by scheduling for tomorrow a "fact quiz" on the excursion and for Friday an interpretive writing assignment. He gets many requests for clarification.

They talk about "muck-rakers." Stebner calls for an identification of Ida Tarbell. Several identify Tarbell's exposé of Standard Oil. Earlier, a few comments about how recent oil spills in the harbor had threatened wildlife and beachside property and marked growth of the community's multinational industry. It occurred to me that the two oil stories were related but the connection was not brought up.

Throughout the afternoon student hands are frequently raised. Stebner asks, "What do we know about Teddy Roosevelt?" Hands go up, but voices seize the initiative: "Teddy Bear." "San Juan Hill." "Youngest president." "Square Deal." When given the chance the students, particularly the nine girls, expand on the symbolic labels they've tossed out. For example, Tom tells about the image created when big game hunter Roosevelt spared a cub and an enterprising toymaker named a bear doll the "teddy bear." Stebner draws them out, corrects them, adds an occasional comment of his own.

He says, "We have a surprisingly short section on Teddy Roosevelt in our book but that's okay since one of you will be making an oral report to the class." He is referring to their textbook, the Scholastic Company's *A Nation Grows: Since 1877*. Well, *all* chapters are short. They are peppery factual, nicely illustrated, with wide-ranging reference to social topics. Chapters have titles such as "The U-Boat and the Lusitania" and "The Coming of TV". What in these chapters draws attention to the arts? Not much. Somewhere in the book is the paragraph:

> Some people called the 1920's the Jazz Age. Black musicians had brought jazz from the South to the big cities during World War I. Enthusiastic crowds flocked to Chicago's South Side and New York City's Harlem to hear Bessie Smith, Louis Armstrong, and many other black musicians singing and playing the blues.

Elsewhere there is a section on the coming of television, and still elsewhere references to dance marathons, movie palaces, rock and roll, the San Francisco Opera House, and Elvis Presley. Important all, but only a brush. This story of the social system swirls occasionally near the arts. In this book, society is not shown to be influenced by the arts.

Stebner augments their textbook with an eight-page reading list running from William Bradford's *History of Plimouth Plantation* through Louisa Alcott's *Little Women* to Sarah Woods' *A Russian Story*.

In this room we have—in contrast to many classrooms nationwide—a collection of students not opposing what the teacher is up to. Possibly they are on good behavior in the presence of a visitor (but in many other middle schools the presence of a visitor fails to deter unrest, dalliance and diversion). Here, when reading or writing time came, it did not take youngsters long to locate books and sharpen pencils. Stebner's students vie to tell what they know about Panamanian President Noriega, the stock market, the oil spill, and presidential primaries. Although but 12 and 13 year olds, they are considerably on their own and only occasionally needed prodding for more productive behavior.

Upon reading my early draft, Stebner corrected my view of the course by writing to me: "The class is composed of three basic segments: humanities, English and literature. Last year [they] studied American history, literature, politics, social systems, music, art forms, etc. Before your visit, and subsequent thereto, students developed oral and written reports on American art forms as a reflection of society's values, philosophy and change. These research reports began with the 1600s and concluded with the 1980s. Students presented architecture, painting, sculpture, dance, music forms, poetry, prose, religious tracts. These reports included representations of the art along with an analysis of the art for the time period. What was the artist trying to say or convey? Why did he choose the particular approach or media during this period? How did it address the society and its values? Etc."

Stebner's teaching is serious, sensitive to the developing minds of able young people. He treats his own learning and theirs with respect. The activity is a beauty to behold. Beauty however did not appear to be a focus. At least in the session I observed, the group showed little attention to beauty in the cultural phenomena under scrutiny. Perhaps the youth culture resists it. Perhaps school people have trouble defending time spent on beauty. Not just conventional beauty but any recognition of the exquisite. Even with Stebner's fascinating "challenge class," I saw little to persuade me that middle school social studies includes an aesthetic sensitivity.

Stebner objected to my drafted summary (much of which remains above), saying: "I must take umbrage. You are so wrong in your assessment. You made judgments and conclusions on little to no information. If we observed a music class and they were practicing Sousa that day, could we extrapolate [that] the class only learns and plays march music? We observe a drama class where the students are making masks. Do we infer that drama class only deals with costume design and development but not stage performance?"

This is not a typical class for Anacortes youngsters, nor typical for those who do take band or choir or engage in writing projects. When the school district is responsible for arts activities, most are production-oriented, with attention sometimes to analysis and critique but seldom to history or aesthetics. In terms of the whole school experience even for members of this challenge class, these art education activities are expected by most observers to remain peripheral, only occasionally integrated into the mainstream of coursework. Rarely is the study of art presented by a teacher as enhancement to thinking and communication. My brief experience with Stebner's social studies lesson made me think again but I remained persuaded that America's middle school social studies classes seldom manifest an aesthetic sensitivity.

Bill Love's Intermediate Band Class

The middle school students in this class travel several blocks by school bus to meet at the high school. Today about 44 students have gathered here in the band room. Seats are arranged in orchestra formation. After individual warm-up (with an insinuated tribute to Clementine), Love puts them through five minutes of scales. Then come make-up exams. At least once every two weeks each student is expected to play a dozen bars solo. The student chooses the piece, it is played by all, then while the group remains reasonably quiet, the examinee plays his/her part. Love makes a few diagnostic, suggestive comments. The students are aware that the best and worst performance gets criticized about equally gently.

Then together the band works on special passages. Today they play "A Technic Tune." They repeat it several times. Love stops them to review concepts and notations. Articulations: slur, staccato, accent, tenuto. A few youngsters are able to identify them. On to "That's Where the Money Goes." More technical terms, particularly about syncopation. Bill Love demonstrates the different syncopations. Then he redirects the snare drum so as to change the presentation, explaining his reasoning to whomever cares to listen. Conceptualization is important, but—if the two are separable—it seems aimed more at bolstering performance than at enhancing understanding.

On to "American Patrol." "Yaaaay!" The rendition is spirited. The second trumpet section has a fit of giggles. Then "Blue Rock." Love muses later: There's never enough time. Important to get in these exercises." Paraphrasing Love:

Should music be a part of everyone's education? Folks in Anacortes agree with folks elsewhere: it should be. But how to make it happen? Many do not enroll when music competes with so many other electives. But when made a course or graduation requirement, the classes fill with students having little interest who undermine the quality of learning opportunity for others around them. Requirements are probably not the way to go.

What about music history and music literature? It appears a mistake to force it. Many teachers have no such inclination, often little knowledge. They might agree that all youngsters *should* encounter intellectually the role of music in our history and culture but they already have a full slate. And, again, in a permissive and protest-voicing society, music lore appears to have better chance as an elective, within or in addition to regular music teaching. Performance and history probably should be taught together. Though no one in Anacortes appeared to, it would be a mistake to underemphasize performance. Most would agree that all the kids should know what it is like to put themselves out front.

The Young Authors Conference

A group of 13 eighth graders were invited to join over 200 other elementary school youngsters at a Young Authors Conference arranged by Educational Service District 189 at the campus of Skagit Valley College. During the morning the forty-some eighth graders attended a session on writing and illustrating presented by author Robert Gordon and professional illustrator Dan Lane. Starting with the sentence, "Jan's older brother is a jerk," Gordon drew the students into describing how a "jerk" looks and acts. Lane followed by getting everyone to draw Jan's brother. During the next hour Gordon had the students write interpretations of one of Lane's illustrations. The students were thoroughly engaged, asked an occasional question, seemed under little compulsion to discipline their efforts. It was a fun day. The big message seemed to be, "You can create whatever you want to but doing it well takes a lot of work."

During the early afternoon in small age-groups, each student read a previously selected work of their own aloud. The students responded to the opportunity in different ways, but most listened carefully and seemed pleased. An English teacher moderated; his comments social and celebratory, not intending to raise questions of quality, not asking, "How might that piece be improved?" Anacortes students had been coached to respond to questions about main characters, theme, inspiration for writing, etc.—but few questions were asked.

During the afternoon's large-group session, which closed early enough to allow return to home districts by schoolbus time, non-fiction author Ron Hirschi described producing his children's wildlife books, e.g., *What is a Bird* and *Who Lives in the Forest*. Such production the students discovered was a rather tame affair. Audience interest waned as the program neared its end. Hirschi's request for questions drew only a couple, but one girl took him on in earnest when the group headed for the door. Again the solicitation seemed to be, "Success is there for the asking—if the asker is a very hard worker."

The Cultural Education Planning Committee

At 3:30 on Monday in the Middle School library at my request, this committee met to discuss its function. Members made it clear that their primary function was to facilitate arrangements for the Artists-in-Residence program, partly to select artists compatible with teacher needs and to schedule various events, including hospitality for the artists in community homes. They spoke warmly of the program.

Susan Willet, English teacher, said, "The Committee does not really deal with curriculum issues. Mainly, it arranges for Artists-in-Residence. We look for ways of serving *each* building. We haven't been getting many requests from teachers for music specialists. Personally, I can integrate music into my teaching better than dance. Since our building has specific courses in music (band, chorus), music is not so often requested by middle school teachers."

Asked why they supported Artists in Schools, the members spoke of anticipated benefits for both student and teacher, including: encountering art production as personal endeavor, awakening possibilities of becoming an artist, having the experience of working with an artist, sampling the "smorgasbord of life," and beholding elegance. Sam Green, poet and bookbinder now working on a secondary certificate to teach English, added: "When I was in school I didn't know there were poets still living." The perception of the arts as creative experience was much more prominent than the arts as cultural heritage or medium of communication.

Asked to compare, in times of tight budgets, the contributions of artists and arts teachers to the arts education of youth, they seemed to feel it hard to imagine, at least in the circumstances of this community, how an arts teacher could make an equivalent contribution. "But we want both," said Roxann Meeuwsen, second-grade teacher: "We also want better training for us who teach the elementary grades." Phyllis Ennes said, "If I were in a position to hire an arts specialist, I wouldn't use that specialist as a supplemental teacher in the classroom but as a consultant—someone available to help teachers plan lessons, suggest or provide supplies, demonstrate teaching techniques and projects. We used Kathy Hastings that way through Cultural Education with great success. In some cases it worked as a team-teaching approach. But once funds are diverted from Cultural Ed to FTE, the district will exercise management rights and the arts will no longer be the real focus."

Later Ennes described the costs of the program. "We have a total budget of less than $20,000. Six thousand is from the state grant. With a per diem allowance of $35 per day we can buy 12 to 18 weeks of artists' time. 'Community housing' allows us to save the per diem allowance and plow it back into the program, buying additional artist time."

Kathy Hastings, Consultant in Art Education

At her home outside Snohomish, Washington, about midafternoon, I asked: "When did you first work in Anacortes as an Artist-in-Residence?"

Hastings: 1981. Since 1974 I've worked as a self-employed artist in Washington, Colorado, Oregon. I no longer work in the Artist-in-Residence program, though I continue my work in the schools.

Stake: You negotiate your own arrangements with school districts?

Hastings: My long range goal is K-6 scope and sequence, an art curriculum that builds from the kindergarten up. It is hard to find a district that will fund development of such a program. I had a good start in Anacortes but after *The Fourth R* was published the district decided not to rehire me. The [state] Artist-in-Schools program did not accept my application to continue in 1984. I think they weren't quite sure what to do with me. I guess in their eyes I was more artist educator than artist.

Stake: How did they come to see you as an artist educator?

Hastings: I have always been very interested in teaching. Since I couldn't get a teaching credential from the professional art school I was attending [Art Center College of Design in L.A.] I spent many hours at the university elementary school at UCLA. Madeline Hunter was the principal. I offered to teach filmmaking to upper elementary students so I could sit in during her teacher training classes. I have strong feelings about putting artists into classroom settings without teacher training but I never vocalized them to the commission. I think in their minds I wasn't spending enough time doing my own personal artwork.

Stake: I have formed some ideas about the Anacortes situation. I would like to see how they sound to you. Obviously this is a community with extensive resources in the arts. There is a working connection between community and schools. The superintendent is interested in keeping his community happy. He recognizes the interest in the arts. He wants a strong arts program, yet does not have a deep understanding of what a strong arts program is. He wants to take credit for the program and is not opposed to funding it but, as chief bookkeeper of the public trust and the taxpayers money, he wants to be accountable. And so he calls for curriculum specifications, not only in the arts, but across all subject matters. The specifications are rather simple and, though difficult to demonstrate, this straight-forward accountability approach is actually an obstacle to the kind of integration you are talking about, having teachers work together with arts resource people. The breakdown occurs partly because not only he, but all of us, lack the technology and language for representing how a teacher can teach five or six different things at the same time. So we have a problem defining the arts program.

Hastings: So far you've got it.

Stake: In this community, and maybe lots of places, people see the arts more as object than pursuit. Arts education is more something to have than something to use. The *stated* purposes of arts education are afterthoughts more than preselected intentions. Art exists because it is good. Art education is for art education's sake. It is good to have those activities. When educators are forced to defend the curriculum, they feel they have to say the result will be knowledge and skill. After the fact, people can come up with reasons—one favorite is that art is a useful experience.

Hastings: I'll tell you my purpose. It comes from my belief in God. We are co-creators. We are created in the image of God, the ultimate creator. So we have a creative urge—we have to create in some area or we die inside. Every suitcase-maker in every factory has to be creative in some way, maybe not within the monotony of his job, but perhaps in his garden, in his cooking, the way he designs his house, or the way he dresses. Somewhere this creativity has to come out. Or else we're not fully alive. That is what drives me to teach art. It's a vehicle for teaching creativity. I don't expect more than 2% of the students to become visual artists, but all of them will grow up needing to be creative. So when I give art lessons, I set parameters in which the kids can explore. The kids are free to look, select and rearrange within those limits. I don't want 30 little penguins up on the wall all looking the same. I want thirty right answers that all look different.

Stake: Is that your staff development message?

Hastings: Part of it. We've been training kids to give us the one right answer to questions—the date of the event, the answer to the equation. But there can be second and third right answers. Big businesses want off-the-wall, flexible, creative solutions. Art can be a problem-solving activity. This is a new concept for many teachers. Many have been content with egg carton and glitter activities on Friday afternoons. Many think coloring in the lines is it. For many, the idea that art can be taught sequentially, like reading or math, is a totally new concept. Many have no idea you can teach horizontals, verticals and angles linked with prereading activities in kindergarten or patterning linked with math in first grade.

Kathy Hastings reinforced several of my observations about arts education in Anacortes but she was not at all persuaded that the purposes those people express are rationalizations. Kathy Hastings had her purposes; Phyllis Ennes had hers; and the Superintendent had his—and she expected to find their purposes in their words.

Case Bound Writings by Young Authors

Issues

School and Community Interaction

Anacortes, Washington is a Puget Sound waterfront city located on Fidalgo Island in Skagit County. Its 1988 population is estimated at almost exactly 12,000 people and growing, largely thanks to its attractiveness for retirement. The largest industrial employers are Texaco and Shell Oil. Unemployment for 1985 officially was almost 13%. Some 22% of the people are senior citizens. The climate is mild, ranging 35-45 degrees in the winter and 62-75 in the summer, with 26 inches of rain in an average year. Most of the visitors to Anacortes are passing through, many en route by ferry to the San Juan Islands or to Victoria, British Columbia. Some come for tourist pleasures, many to take advantage of the 2500 moorings at local marinas.

Cultural activities and special events include the Anacortes community theatre, the arts and crafts festival, the art gallery, the barbershop quartet, the boat race, the Christmas boat parade, the Christmas street parade, the concert series, the Croatian festival, the salmon barbecue, the salmon derby. Facilities include Washington Park with 75 campsites, Storvik Park, Causland Park, Mt. Erie Park, the Anacortes Museum, Fidalgo swimming pool and fitness center, and the W. T. Preston sternwheeler.

Anacortes has four public elementary schools with a combined enrollment of 1205, the middle school with 277, and the high school with 636. There are 145 teachers. There are no private schools or colleges here. A fine auditorium, Brodniak Hall, sits adjacent to the high school.

To learn more about the arts of the schools and the arts of the community I talked with Walt Vonnegut, formerly a drama teacher at the high school. Vonnegut lives in a fine bungalow on a street projecting to the Puget horizon where an equinocturnal sun sets—when it isn't raining. Since retirement he devotes many a long day to the community theatre. Just now he is putting together a performance called *Broadway Melodies Too*. He is troubled by the infrequency of connections between the schools and community theatre. "Occasionally a student plays a part, but it is not seen as or credited as formal education." Vonnegut indicated that there have been joint productions twice, school and community joining in 1985 to present *Fiddler on the Roof* and in 1986, *The Music Man*. "But the intent, as it should be, is performance, not education," Vonnegut adds.

"What happens in theatre is highly specialized—acting, lighting, getting props. It's good experience, challenging, but not much for the people who are not actually doing it." When asked about theatre arts as enrichment to imaging and conceptualizing, Vonnegut said, "Well, I'm primarily interested in the performance. It's hard to do other things when production is so demanding. What the kids who are interested have to have is opportunity to participate. Participation is the thing."

From this point of view it is almost impossible for the schools or community to assume responsibility for all the arts for all the youngsters. With emphasis on deep participation, there are not enough roles, band uniforms, studios and mentors to give more than a few a big chance. Right now, the number of youngsters "just busting" to take advantage of those opportunities is small. So it is only a quiet problem, a problem of lack of education where there is little perceptible want.

Similar sentiments were expressed by Nancy Stark, special ed teacher, former director of Anacortes Youth Arts and present president of Anacortes Arts and Crafts Festival. She described a vigorous community arts program, adding: "Nowhere is disciplined art, the Getty approach, the combination of art history and technique, catching on. One teacher at Fidalgo tries. If we have teachers oriented to 'enlightened cherishing,' it is because they were so when they were hired. Occasionally a principal acknowledges their value. Personally, I care about the student, not about education. Education is a business, without time for cherishing."

As Phyllis Ennes put it, "Originally Anacortes was a blue collar town, a fishing village. Then came the oil refineries. And then, out on the island, a tremendous community of professional artists. And elsewhere in the county as well. As to support for arts education the mixed reaction in the community is reflected in the faculty. We have some superb teachers who have never invited an artist into the classroom. Our principal is extremely supportive, but arts and unified arts are electives, and underenrolled. Doug Dore is a particularly good art teacher, but gets too few students. His graphics compete with band, choir, crafts, home economics."

Here we have a town with a handsome supply of artists as mentors. The number of students interested in immediate and intensive involvement in arts education is smaller. More could be accommodated. The number of students interested in minor or incidental involvement in the arts is large. Their appetites are not presently satisfied by the school program. "All the arts for all the children" is not a priority of this school district.

The majority of people in the community do not find this deficit particularly troublesome. Other goals stand higher. It would cost big money. The perception of the Superintendent is that taxpayers do not want more of a school arts program than is now available. (They are getting, of course, more than they are paying for. A large number of activities are supported by special fund raising efforts, including parent purchases.) Whatever the reasoning and rhetoric, the arts as general education is not presently a serious goal.

Some voices do speak out for more. Peter Heffelfinger, director of Anacortes Youth Arts and curator of the Anacortes Museum, recently completed an oral history of children's books as seen by local librarians and kids. A transplanted New Englander himself, Heffelfinger related some of the Anacortes arts situation to the stream of new faces in town, "This is not a settled community. It's a settling community." Heffelfinger's aim for youth arts fits into a philosophy of general education: "I think the most important thing is to expose a broad range of kids to the arts, not just the kids who just seek it out, not just the kids whose parents encourage them."

The number of community members who assist with regular school programs is large, probably not different from other middle class, rural communities. What is different here is the number of persons caring a lot about the arts. Advocates succeed in keeping alive various youth activities, involving a minority of students in arts performances out of town and an Artists-in-Residence program—but cannot entice the community to provide a program of arts as general education *for all*. Those kids who want it are reasonably well taken care of. Those who do not get much less.

The Curriculum

The seventh-grade courses are:

- language arts (spelling, composition, grammar, punctuation, speech, literature, penmanship, and keyboarding);
- social studies (history, Eastern hemisphere geography);
- mathematics;
- physical education & health (life science); 1 semester of each;
- reading or speech and drama; and
- living skills, shop, crafts and fine art (referred to as unified arts) or band or choir.

The eighth-grade courses are:

- language arts (expression and mechanics);
- reading development;
- mathematics;
- U.S. history;
- physical science;
- physical education & health (life science); 1 semester of each;
- art, crafts, shop, and foods (referred to as unified arts) or band or choir.

Such are the courses: plenty of opportunity for the arts, yet some students take as little as 1/10 of their middle school coursework in the fine arts. What is the minimum arts a seventh or eighth grader might take? My estimate was: visual arts 3%, literature 7% of total load. Perhaps another 2% should be added for attention to the arts in crafts and other non-arts classes. And the children avoiding involvement here are also the ones getting less of the arts out of school.

The average is considerably higher. Charlie Kiel and I estimated that, if we include creative writing, literature, chorus, band, drama, and visual arts all as fine arts, on the average the middle school kids were spending about 25% of their enrollment in arts courses. If we also were to include some portion of their enrollments in speech, crafts and domestic arts, the average would run higher. That is an impressive involvement, comparing favorably with the national average of 17% (an estimate reported by the National Endowment, 1988) and by far the heaviest arts participation during the K-12 school experience in Anacortes.

Middle school students may join interscholastic sports teams that compete in the north division of the Sno-Co League. Opportunities in girls and boys basketball, wrestling, girls volleyball and track are part of the school sponsored program. Intramural activities include girls softball, boys weight training and boys and girls swimming. A variety of clubs and activities such as drama, Math Olympiad, journalism and Young Authors are open to interested students in addition to band and choir. Students may join Suzuki violin classes offered before and after school.

High school graduation requirements include 1 credit in fine, visual, or performing arts. Students are encouraged to fulfill this requirement from courses with Fine Arts designation, but may use any combination of courses.

Management Targets. Several years ago the School Board sought to raise educational standards by providing targets more difficult than the conventional high school diploma. As boards in many districts have done, it established three "endorsements," each recognizing additional achievement along specified lines. The "Academic Program" (featuring college preparatory work), "Occupational/Technical" and "Basic Skills" endorsements were defined by the Board. Candidates for the first two endorsements were finding themselves with but one elective per year, that is, with limited opportunity to take arts courses. Unique interests and desire to explore special topics such as business and agriculture were also constrained by the Board's emphasis on standardized programs. The educational merits of flexible and individualized programs officially was little acknowledged.

District management objectives for 1987-88 comprised ten items. Partly because there appears to be general satisfaction with the curriculum, only one dealt with the curriculum. The eighth item called for attention to K-12 social studies instruction. As with the other nine, this target was essentially to find a plan, to create a statement, to package something.

The K-12 arts program exists on paper and in fact. It is programmatic in that aims are specified and responsibilities identified. Sustained curricular coordination is missing. A few courses are sequential, but many only in that students have matured since the previous course. Students have far too little contact time to even schedule pursuit of National Endowment goals such as integrating the arts into general education, arts history and media studies. Both the somewhat autonomous Cultural Education Committee and the Curriculum Coordinator have little prospect of targeting the combined arts for full academic standing.

District administrators take pride in a decade of effort to stabilize and standardize teaching, referring to an olden day when teachers teaching the same course might overlap little in what they aimed to accomplish. These administrators spoke of community pressure to continue the effort to reduce classroom-to-classroom variability. The same administrators were quick to acknowledge that teaching is a professional responsibility which includes recognizing: individual differences in children, propitious situations for teaching specific ideas, and the particular styles of teaching at which as individuals they excel. They acknowledged that both standardization and teaching autonomy can inhibit professional responsibility.

In most school districts a large proportion, often a majority, of teachers speak favorably of further specification and reduction of instructional scope and sequence, saying for example, "We are tired of being expected to teach more than we can under present circumstances." Here in Anacortes, middle school teachers were aware of an administrative idealization of conformity, but gave little indication of feeling any pressure to conform. Teachers showed little support for further uniformity of teaching. There wasn't a battle but they appeared not to agree. Obviously teachers and administrators operate in different arenas and with different expertise but the difference in viewpoint also reveals different purposes of education. Low priority on ordinary maintenance of the formal curriculum may not only signify satisfaction with what is being taught and not being taught but recognition also that people hold widely different views as to how much teachers should conform and as to which teachings should dominate.

Arts in Elementary School

Many arts teachers believe that what can be accomplished during middle school is dependent on how much good instruction kids have had in the elementary grades. According to district promotional literature, arts education is an ongoing and highly valued component of elementary schooling and arts activities are integrated into all instructional areas. In addition, teachers undertake various other art and music projects. In addition to a weekly music class with specialist Pat Rein, elementary children have opportunity to take Suzuki violin and, in the sixth grade, introductory band. What is offered in drama and dance, other than what the classroom teacher might volunteer, comes from the artists-in-residence.

Teacher discouragement is easily found. One longtime educator said, "There still are strong negative feelings—now more an emotional drain—about poor support of School Board and Superintendent for the arts. Many [teachers] miss the specialist. And they did not like the way it happened: one July, no advance notice, elementary teachers were left with responsibility for which they had little training. We had drawn up a plan for using resident artists. The Superintendent didn't go for it, saying, 'Teachers could teach their own art.' The teachers appealed to the Board. We were told to run it through the Cultural Education Committee. We used an artist-in-residence, Kathy Hastings, to make materials for classroom teachers to use. Ultimately we produced our guide, *The Fourth R*. It's a valuable resource. The Superintendent is not reluctant to take credit for it. He wants it disseminated nationally."

The Fourth R. Most elementary school teachers in Anacortes as elsewhere are not trained to teach the visual arts. Yet the official schedule dedicates a few minutes each week to that end, and since the early eighties no one else has been available to do it. When the arts specialist resigned, no replacement was hired. Teachers were increasingly irate, not only with the unexpected responsibility but with the loss of a weekly 45 minute planning period. They confronted the Board, won promises of help, but not much more. The Superintendent decided that the artist-in-schools program should be used to develop instructional materials for these teachers but program rules prohibited it. Kathy Hastings was put on special retainer to coach the teachers and to organize lessons that could be used to integrate the arts into other instruction, a manual that came to be known as *The Fourth R*.

According to Hastings: "I had 20 wonderful teachers taking a first course in water color, clay, anything. They were saying, 'Show us.' OK, fine. A great team of teachers, really creative, hard working. I said, 'Let's take it a step further. I'll show you the techniques, but you link up with something else you're teaching. Link your water color with map making, your patterning with Pueblo Indians.' And they did. They came up with wonderful lessons. I said, 'Let's make them available to the whole district.' I asked the Superintendent to hire me for five months to write curriculum guides.

"I saw *The Fourth R* as a beginning, not an end. Once it was published the Superintendent could pass it out to the teachers and say, 'There you have a resource. Quit complaining about an art specialist.' I saw the book as the beginning of an art program that could teach art elements and principles in an interdisciplinary way. I saw it as guide to developing the program, *not the program*."

Curriculum Coordination. Without coordination, an instructional program is not a program. In Anacortes, low priority is given to the responsibility for coordinating arts instruction in elementary school and on through the senior year. The district has a strong Cultural Education Planning Committee, but its attention is largely limited to the artists-in-residence program. The committee takes formal responsibility neither for scrutinizing curricular offerings nor for inservice support for classroom teachers. If indeed the latter is a pressing need, as I believe, the combination of artists-in-residence and *The Fourth R* may be a weak link in the Anacortes curriculum chain. Few advocates were ready to fight for it—but I began to conclude there is more than small need for professional coordination of the arts, K-12.

On leaving the site, I asked Kathy Hastings about the choice between hiring a halftime arts coordinator for Grades 4-5-6 and extensive participation in the artists-in-residence program. She responded, "The two ideas are really different. There shouldn't be a choice, they should have both."

Stake: Of course, but for the same amount of money....

Hastings: Yes, where is the person to unify what's happening in the classrooms, giving teachers input, reminding them how to do it, finding out-of-the-ordinary supplies? Sometimes all they need is to hear, "Hey, come on, you can do it." In Anacortes there isn't such a person.

Stake: Should somebody say, "Let's take this artist-in-residence money and spend it for a half-time teacher?"

Hastings: A halftime person wouldn't cost that much. They could bring in a half-time consultant and still keep the artists-in-schools program.

Stake: During my stay I didn't hear people say they need an arts coordinator for elementary teachers. Charlie Kiel mentioned it and Phyllis Ennes quickly said, "We have used our artist-in-residence that way."

Hastings: With our workshops we did.

Stake: I thought maybe Phyllis was thinking, "Let's not talk about this any more. It's difficult to talk about it, it's been so personal, so many disappointments." So when I raised alternative possibilities, I thought I heard, "Let's draw attention to the children. Let's not talk about the curriculum. Let's not talk about philosophy. Let's not talk about teacher talents. Let's keep looking at what the kids are doing.

Hastings: Deep ones.

Stake: As curriculum coordinator Phyllis Nelson talks about an integrated arts approach. She emphasizes that teachers teach a number of things at the same time. For example, "reading isn't all language arts, but also socialization, communication skill, and art." Nothing Phyllis Nelson told me sounded like an integrated arts approach is being held back.

Hastings: Phyllis Nelson has been groomed by him.

Kathy Hastings' dour view of school arts in Anacortes was not entirely shared by anyone I met in town. Her disappointment that the district did not continue her consultancy probably colored her views but the troubles she spoke of are an important part of the discussion. In various ways, a number of teachers confirmed these differences in priority and inadequacies of arts teaching in the elementary grades.

Artists-in-Residence

According to a survey conducted by Gina May (no date), state supervisor for visual and performing arts, about half the Washington districts have not participated in the artists-in-residence program. In Anacortes the desire to continue participation was strong. From various interviews came these statements:

Phyllis Ennes, cultural education director:
> In most years we have had more than one artist but we are moving to a single in-depth residency, for something up to 12 weeks. This year we have Diana Lim for twelve. In '87 we had a poet, a theatre person and a dancer. The year before we had a visual artist for scenery design, a poet and a bookmaker. The year before that we had a video artist.

Charlie Kiel, middle school principal:
> We do use our artists-in-residence as consultants. Our teachers look for help in integrating the dancer's offerings with regular studies.

Duane Lowell, superintendent:
> We need better ways of showing teachers how to integrate the arts with regular teaching.

Sue Reynolds, primary teacher:
> Each of the buildings has a "rep" on the Cultural Ed Committee. We ask people in our buildings what they want. It was through the residency program that we developed *The Fourth R*. Teachers put in many of the ideas.

Pat Rein, elementary music teacher:
> For cultural enrichment I'd like to bring in musicians. There don't seem to be many available.

Sue Reynolds:
> I don't know why our teachers have not shown more interest in musicians for our residency program. We have had a composer and an instrument maker. It fits nicely into lots of subject matter. I am not as comfortable doing dance. Maybe musicians are not as interested in general education. But other artists too concentrate on performance, not arts education.

A total of 72 teachers responded to the request of the planning committee for participants in the 1988-89 program, some making requests for specific artists or art forms as follows: jugglers, magicians, Asian arts, centennial projects, puppetry, storytelling, Tim Noah, Teo Morca, Diana Lim, cooking specialist, playwright, and book illustrator.

The artist-in-residence is a tried and true contributor to arts education in Anacortes. Thorough review and cautious selection have contributed to almost 100% satisfaction in what the artists have done. Many offer assistance to classroom teachers either with arts projects or in integrating aesthetic, design and performance ideas with regular curricular content. The artists offer. Teachers take what they will. There is little obligation to take more than what the teachers see themselves needing. (To obligate them to take more would seldom be wise. Already the ones most needing it feel harassed.) Arts education is an area of curricular responsibility in which few teachers or artists have scholarly inclination. Thus the more complex goals of arts education, e.g., studying human activity through art (Feldman, 1970) and artistic imagery (Eisner, 1979), only infrequently are pursued.

Staff Development. There is little expectation that colleges of education will play a major role in helping to retrain classroom teachers. Half the state's school administrators indicated (on Gina May's state survey) that more support for inservice education was key to improving arts education. (They called even more for equipment and supplies.) But our Anacortes experience indicated that there is little real support for other than conventional in-service sessions and consultancies, such as with Kathy Hastings. Hastings told me how she worked with the elementary teachers here:

> I came to their classrooms primarily to teach the children. Some teachers used the time for preparation, some for coffee. They were expected to team with me, but many chose not to. Many are timid, frightened. Others will jump right in and work along with the kids. The kids think it is so special, so neat when the teacher works along. But maybe a quarter of the teachers won't do that.

As indicated on earlier pages Hastings perceived school arts as opportunity to develop creativity. There were few claims that Hastings' inservice education purposes were wrong, that studio skills or that history and criticism should be emphasized more. *The Fourth R* ideas she collected from the teachers and developed were generally seen as fitting what people expect of school art. Most involve creativity, imagery, integration with other subjects. The message seemed to be, "It is not important which particular purposes teachers are taught, just to get them into it."

Purposes of Arts Education

When Duane Lowell became superintendent, he asked for a formal statement of objectives of the Anacortes Cultural Education Program. The following were set forth:

1. to develop the aesthetic sensibilities of students;

2. to develop students abilities to express themselves creatively;

3. to provide students with training in life-long understanding and enjoyment of the arts of their culture, to include appropriate audience behavior;

4. to extend career awareness through artist residencies;

5. to identify gifted and talented students in the arts;

6. to provide inservice resources for teachers;

7. to assist in meeting the cultural needs of the community; and

8. to provide an opportunity for artists to develop professionally while contributing to their communities and the education of youth.

After spending two weeks in the community, I saw these eight aims to be reasonable representations of what ought to happen as a result of the many and diverse efforts to provide arts education in Anacortes. Each of the eight has a turf of its own, something important that would be lost if it were not mentioned or pursued. But the list is an artifact, a scant footscrape on the passing instructional scene.

Lists like these are used everywhere as part of the legitimation of educational programs. They are a representation of something, but they serve little to guide the practice or stimulate discussion about the teaching. When I talked with teachers and others, except when directly asked, they seldom mentioned such purposes. Furthermore, they did not seem to be differentially activated by them. Is the religious music chosen because it contributes to creativity or because it provides students with life-long understandings? There may be some difference of that sort, but that music was chosen because it is simple and accommodates a higher range of voices. Was *Tartuffe* chosen because, more than other plays, it extends aesthetic sensibilities? No, but because it will be produced this season by the Seattle Repertory Theatre and it's good to have students see professional productions. Teachers make choices for tactical reasons far more often than for strategic reasons. Almost incidental choices contribute to profound determination of what arts education is—all so indirect, seldom pondered, and seldom going "by the book."

If it is not the syllabus, what is the ultimate curricular authority? To what authority do teachers appeal when planning a course or faced with a choice of what to teach? It is not the curriculum theorist at the university nor the museum curator nor writer for the magazines. Those who study and write about the arts or education have faint voices at Anacortes Middle School. Neither more robust is the union leader or the elder teacher. Custom decides. And when experience does not suffice, a teacher reaches down into his or her own moral sense for authority. In *Habits of the Heart*, Robert Bellah and colleagues illustrated the lost authority of the professional organization, the university, the church, the political party, and the family patriarch. We follow the crowd but we are individualists. Our greatest trust is in ourselves.

From an earlier generation, I found a different voice. Ruth Kelsey, retired arts educator, once Phyllis Ennes' mentor at Western Washington University, told me: "I am a follower of Professor Henry Schaefer-Simmern (1948) who believed that if given the right encouragement, in each human being there will be an unfolding of artistic expression. That doesn't mean that arts students can't be lazy. I kept them on the move, even starting a new project every day."

Saying our teachers are individualists is not to say they are nonconformists, given their disdain for guides and organizational authority. In the sixth grade in Anacortes, arts activities are to be checked off against learning objectives listed in *The Fourth R*. It helps to show an administrator or a visitor that the teacher is accountable. In most American schools we expect syllabi to drive instruction only when check-off activities are monitored. In Anacortes it is not a monitored check-off and probably shouldn't be. Teachers are expected to adapt instruction, to work away from formal requirements as circumstances require.

Part of the reason there is little concern about the working value of goal and objectives statements is that such are not part of any dialogue, especially not that between educator and citizen. To many parents the language of the curriculum coordinator or testing specialist is obscure. Good conversations seldom follow. The citizenry, if choosing to converse at all, has learned to stick to particulars. According to Scott Gorman, newsman, Anacortes American: "The reasons for having arts education are seldom discussed in the community." Pat Rein, the elementary music teacher, agrees: "The community gives us little feedback." Some American school administrators are heard to say that absence of comment from the community is the best evidence that things are being done right.

The formal statements of purpose are foreign to the culture of the classroom. What works is the intuitive feeling, what a classroom feels like. I asked Ron Jones, math teacher, if there is anything he does in his classroom that is aesthetically pleasing. He said, "Quite a bit, I think. Take this triangle. The ancient Greeks called it a Golden Triangle. I had the students do these worksheets. They measured angles and lengths and found nothing elegant about the numbers, but noted how pleasing the triangle itself. Much in our math textbooks is aesthetically pleasing. Look at this 1898 textbook. Orderly but pretty grim. Nothing like the illustrated versions today."

In the classes I visited, personal expression, beholding of elegance, cherishing did occur, but incidentally to arts experience more than direct purposive outcome. Credit the educators with more than simplistic notion of purpose. In Anacortes, I sought to understand why arts teachers did one thing rather than another. I found few linkages to "ultimate purpose." The activity of the classroom was a part of a complex conception of what constitutes good teaching and learning. Creating that activity itself was the operative goal. Attaining it in order to accomplish an ultimate state of learner sophistication seemed seldom the way the teachers conceived their responsibility.

I was particularly interested in seeing if teachers were drawn to the aims of "discipline-based arts education" as advocated by Harry Broudy and supported by the J. Paul Getty Center for Education in the Arts (1985), aims pursued through art criticism, art history and aesthetics, as well as art production. Manifestations of aims of many leading arts educators (such as Rudolph Arnheim, Laura Chapman, Arthur Efland, Jerome Hausman, Suzanne Langer, Bennett Reimer, Ralph Smith, and Brent Wilson—all cited in our references) were discernable in the daily work of Anacortes teachers but to me the dominant impression was that the arts program existed as a part of life, not as a determinant of life. Existentialism more than instrumentalism. Being more than becoming.

Barriers and Opportunities

Anacortes Middle School was a good site for examining some of the barriers and opportunities for arts education in the American school. It was blessed with competent teachers, susceptible students and a community handsomely endowed with artists and arts activities. Abundant for the students who seek them out were two key ingredients identified by Howard Gardner: a nurturant atmosphere and a judicious blend of exploration opportunity and informed guidance. As enrichment, the arts opportunities here were impressive.

But beyond middle school enrichment[1], the arts program is not so handsome. Officially, the district places arts education in an inferior position. By treating the arts as less than full partner in education, the district goads its arts advocates into extraordinary extracurricular efforts to provide instruction and settings for the students with arts interests. The aims of the cultural education program are aims for all the students but aesthetic education is vigorously pursued in only a few classrooms, many of them elective or special admissions classrooms.

Thus, over the years, many students become knowledgeable, a few move toward a life of intense involvement, the rest remain more or less ignorant. Many are overexposed and vulnerable to the vulgar in ordinary life. In artistic experience, as in other regards, there may always be, as the Bible assures us, the poor. The best of arts education programs cannot overwhelm the vulgar around us. All too few programs will even analyze it. In the school of our dreams we aspire to immerse all youngsters in the meanings, experience, and creative spirit of the arts.

In Anacortes, the principal barrier is not money, scarce as it is, but lack of conviction. A few people would put the arts in a more esteemed and interactive place in the curriculum. Most teachers, citizens, and students would not alter present priorities. (It would be unreasonable to suppose the community could be of one mind about its educational goals, and perhaps would be dangerous to wish for it.) But there could be a quite different popular expectation of the role of the arts. The stated aim of *The Fourth R* is to integrate artistic idea and moment into ordinary instruction, a vital contribution to be made by the classroom teacher. The expression of intent is present; with exceptions here and there, the personal conviction is not.

Leadership. Especially in the formal leadership of the school system, the conviction is lacking. The School Board is not persuaded to place the fine arts anywhere near the station assigned the language arts, or even that assigned to computer skills. As I saw it, the Superintendent supports the arts, goes beyond the reluctance of the Board, acquiesces to many pressures to keep specially advocated arts activities on budget lines, but does not see the arts as a universal need in "being educated." He did say, "The arts are one important way of seeing things," but his role is regularly that of finding the compromise between the advocates and the unpersuaded. He does not appear to be reexamining the curriculum so as to assure instruction in those "ways of seeing things" in whatever courses the students may be taking.

The Superintendent designates a Curriculum Coordinator to do that. At one time such coordinators were primarily chosen to support the teaching faculties, to provide continuing professional education not only by arranging study opportunities but by working directly with individuals and groups, helping to refine the

---

[1]See Junius Eddy's views on comprehensive community school programs (1980).

question, "What shall we teach?" As superintendents were drawn more into financial, organizational, and promotional responsibilities, they increasingly drew the curriculum coordinator more into the Central Office to prepare and verbalize proposals, requirements, and justifications. The work became less the study of curricula and assistance to instructors, more the composing of standards, routines and, in the classical sense, apologies.

The district curriculum is described. It always includes the arts. Sometimes courses in the arts are required, sometimes elective. Teachers in Anacortes and elsewhere prefer elective courses, partly because the presence of conscripts often undermines the learning environment. Crafts courses are often an attractive form of arts credit, a respite sometimes for intellect and a regenerator of self-esteem. The titles of the course do not tell. Little challenge is raised to the stated goals partly because in their sweet and broad formulation the implications for instructional time to be spent, curricular enrichment, staff development, and selection of new faculty are not apparent.

In Anacortes, the Curriculum Coordinator has had wide experience both in faculty roles and with the uniquenesses of this community. Her philosophy of education in general and of arts education specifically are sophisticated. It is my view that she does not have an important voice in many decisions which affect the curriculum. When the Superintendent, acting for the Board which acts for the community, decided that college preparation is top priority, that classroom teachers in the elementary school will teach the visual arts, that the Artists-in-Schools program will be supported or that computers will win major increases in curricular budgets, the rationale for aesthetics and fine arts as a component in all education for all youth apparently was muted. I found little oral or documented allusion to an arts rationale in the artifacts of decision making, though I knew that both the Curriculum Coordinator and Superintendent were knowledgeable about such a rationale. They appeared not persuaded that the arts are underrepresented in the school program. That lack of persuasion is the major barrier facing arts education advocates in Anacortes.

A visitor for but two weeks, I speak of that with which I became barely acquainted. I have no evidence that there is personal shortcoming in the work of this superintendent and this curriculum specialist. I was not seeking to evaluate their work. I see lack of arts education persuasion in most district offices elsewhere. From sea to shining sea, the American school administrator is neither leader in curriculum study nor serious advocate of the arts nor auditor of instructional decisions checking implications for the arts in general education. Administrators weigh their own perceptions of what in our heterogeneous culture most needs preservation, what needs implanting. They hold their own views up against pluralistic views across the community, seeking compromises among the advocacies and indignation to which they are constantly exposed. Superintendent Lowell and Coordinator Nelson did that, and even more, to enhance the quality of arts education in Anacortes.

Leadership for arts education was much more apparent at the Middle School, partly because the district had established requirements in both seventh and eighth grades for participation in unified arts, elective opportunities for band and chorus, and a calendar of special events. Principal Kiel was an active participant in the work of the Cultural Education Planning Committee. He was troubled by tendencies to overemphasize and oversimplify the school's basic skills commitments. Through his own interests in photography he contributed to the personalistic and aesthetic environment there.

His faculty also was strong in leadership and advocacy. He claimed little credit for drawing talented teachers, noting how seldom he had a choice in teacher selection, but teachers have ways (not always) of getting to a place where their talents are esteemed. The special leadership of Phyllis Ennes needs summary acknowledgement. As librarian, chair of the Cultural Education Planning Committee and teacher of speech and drama, she raised expectations of the quality of artistic work and experience to be found here. She helped answer in the affirmative Les McLean's (1975) question, "Is this a place where the arts might thrive?"

When asked what is the most important thing to say in this report, Ennes responded: "That we persevere. That we try to keep attention on children's actual accomplishments. Many people do not understand what we do. We persevere. The economic constraints on arts education are only a small part of it. We cannot anticipate the objections a few parents will have. And we try to honor them. But we need trust, freedom not to specify what we will do. We can anticipate only partly where learning will take the children—and us."

Unlike many other charismatic organizers, her style was not of exuberance and bonhomie, but of quiet, even sometimes of austerity. She organized the informal system, enlisted and encouraged, responding with frowns and strategic protest when expectations appeared to be softening. My point here is that stereotypes of leadership can be misleading—more than one role or personalistic style can succeed. In almost every community, among lay and professions both, there are a few with vision, fortitude, tenacity, who will labor for arts education. Finding ways to increasingly gear them into the regular operations of the school system is challenge and opportunity for every administrator.

Formal and Informal Education. In March, 1988, whenever Anacortes middle school students were engaged in an arts activity, in school or out, chances were high that it was a high quality experience. The teaching was very good. The students were ready and willing, making arts learning socially acceptable. Whether in music, visual arts, drama or dance, the middle-school opportunities were impressive.

I spent little time in the primary grades or at the high school. Specialist teaching after middle school looked and sounded good, but not many students were taking part. Diploma requirements had caused at least some diversion of students away from the arts. Advisors were discouraged from directing students into arts courses within school and teachers in other subject matters seldom extended assignments to include aesthetic factors.

In the primary grades, sophisticated arts teaching occurred only occasionally, spruced up by visiting artists, but not, I would say, something for a district to be proud of. Peter Heffelfinger, director of Anacortes Youth Arts, estimated that the number of elementary school pupils who could have been signed up for music activities would be large, were the programs available. "Many parents are quick to agree to bring kids in after school." Unfortunately, most would be the kids already taking advantage of local activities. Heffelfinger expressed special concern for the many kids who seldom get into the arts.

So, good arts experiences in Anacortes schools are happening frequently in the middle school. But as indicated in the section on curriculum, even there some youngsters had very limited involvement in the arts. The goal of all the arts for all the youngsters is not met. The goal of good arts for those who want it is being met. Superintendent Lowell said about academic achievement generally, "We do well, but we want to do better."

As members of the Cultural Education Planning Committee are aware, further opportunity lies in informal, out-of-school experiences, engaging students in under utilized arts in town, in the nearby cities, and on television, assigned not just as encounters but as studies, with analyses reviewed by teachers and other students. Teachers are aware of this way of teaching but especially when pursued on an individual student basis, it can be lots of extra work.

To improve the quality of science education, the National Science Foundation (as reported by SRI International) has increasingly supported museums and science programs on television. Anacortes and America already have a bountiful system of concert halls, museums, touring groups for the classical and popular arts. But American teachers, overloaded by syllabi, troubled by public criticism, turn away from instruction using the cultural opportunities of the community.

Charles Kiel predicted an easing in the drive for basic skills scores. Examples of middle-school teacher use of community resources already were easy for me to come by. Ray Stebner had students find examples of art forms that reflected society's values. Ron Jones had students look for golden triangles in local architecture. Phyllis Ennes had students analyze the story development of television they watch. Teachers know kids are immersed in a complex popular culture. Kids analyze it all the time but lack an intellectual discipline their teachers could help them develop. Short of funds for powering up its own instruction, arts education might best hitch up to the engines of popular arts, not to race, but to move kids toward aesthetic sensitivity.

This is what I found in Anacortes. And what a mixed-up portrayal it is! Pressed by brief but thought-provoking experience at the Middle School, I have said that arts education there was excellent and inadequate. How can teaching be simultaneously excellent and inadequate? I remember what Phyllis Ennes said to her students seeking clarification. She said, "Think about it."

Chapter 3:
Washington and Prairie Elementary Schools Danville, Illinois

■ *Liora Bresler*

I began my study by looking at instruction in the arts, then interviewing teachers, students and administrators about what they did, why they did it, the meanings they attached to what they did. Soon the scene expanded to non-arts classroom lessons, to performances and concerts in and out of school, in and out of town, to skating parties, to Sweet Adeline chapters in which teachers participated (I almost enlisted...), to press meetings between superintendents and journalists. Interviews evolved to conversations and chats in corridors, school buses, cars, coffeehouses and restaurants, and early school breakfast meetings. Introduced as a dreaded imposition from the top, directed and announced in advance, teachers eventually welcomed me to visit and drop by their classes freely.

I spent 12 days between November, 1987 and May, 1988 in two elementary schools. I visited 30 different classes—4 music specialists, 15 classroom teachers—sometimes just once, often three or four times. I talked with classroom teachers and aides, former and current music teachers, students, principals and higher level administrators, the band director, social workers, secretaries, parents, grandparents and other "community" persons. I filled five spiral notebooks, 30 hours of cassette tapes, and 60 computer files.[1]

Violating the traditional non-participant role, I found myself, toward the end of my visits, helping the principal and school staff load students into buses, playing Israeli folk songs on the piano and writing the teacher's name in Hebrew (right to left!) on the blackboard. When the time had come to finish (an artificial ending—my natural inclination pulled me to stay on, to explore the many threads I had not pursued), I felt genuinely sad. I was frustrated with the incompleteness of it all, knowing that I would never enjoy a site as much as I enjoyed this one.

There are many stories to be told. This report is an attempt to highlight what seems, at this time, to be the most pressing themes and stories about arts education in these schools. I learned a lot about the complexities of teaching the arts in our society, about the important role that the arts play in teachers' lives, about the power of institutional values and support on teaching, about opposing goals and conflicts in making decisions. I learned a lot about my own biases and subjectivities. Time

---

[1] My Toshiba Laptop fulfilled the dual role of clever typewriter and facilitator of conversation with young admirers of technology.

and fate led me to incidents I had not foreseen, questions I had not thought of asking, issues I had not anticipated. I am deeply grateful to all who enabled me to do this study.

The Site

> If you were to say to the grown-ups: "I saw a beautiful house made of rosy bricks, with geraniums in the windows and doves on the roof," they would not be able to get any idea of that house at all. You would have to say to them: "I saw a house that cost $20,000." Then they would exclaim: "Oh, what a pretty house that is."
>
> —Antoine de Saint Exupery *The Little Prince* (1943).

Free Associations About Danville

"Nice community. Climbing back from major economic problems. Warm people. Nice place to live."
—Bill Handley, Director of Community Relations and Food Services.

"Blue collar. Rough. Small townish."
—Louise Moore, a music specialist and former resident of Danville.

"My home. Good school system. Much better place to live than many say. Great changes due to the industry decline. Good community. People are discouraged but we recruit industry from outside. I am optimistic."
—Matt Dole, principal at Washington Elementary School.

"Groundswells of idealism. I could have taken my cats and moved there."
—Eloise Fink, an-artist-in-residence from Winnetka.

"Shopping in Danville Mall. Good baseball for kids. Palmer Center for entertainment. Friends."
—Betty White, secretary at the University, resident of St. Joseph.

"Blue collar. Rust belt. Democratic. On the road to Indianapolis. Bad memory: I had a flat tire right on Main street."
—Robert Stake, Professor of Education.

"Community is supportive of humanity, supportive of fine arts. Conservative. Racially isolated."
—David Fields, Assistant Superintendent for Instruction at Danville.

And some numbers:

38,985 people; 7134 students; 457 teachers; 10 elementary schools; 2 middle schools; 1 high school; 5 parochial schools; 1 community college; 18 parks; 7 movie theaters; 1 symphony orchestra; 1 community theater; 2 music groups; 1 museum, built in 1855; 10.2% unemployment rate.

For the travellers passing on I-74:

Formerly the site of a Painkeshaw Indian village where several trails converged, Danville was discovered by French explorers in search of salt, a precious commodity... Named for first settler Dan Beckwith, the town was platted in 1827; it was incorporated as a city in 1869. Once a major center for the production of coal and clay, Danville now supports a diversity of industries.

Danville's summer opens with the Vermillion County Civil War Days Festival, held on the weekend following Memorial Day in Kennekuk. Annual events include Balloon Classic Illinois and the Labor Festival, featuring 20-30 bands. The Little Vermillion Fall Festival, a traditional harvest celebration with craft demonstrations, takes place on the third weekend of September.

—The American Automobile Association Guide (1988).

***

It is here our story takes place.

The Schools

I observed two elementary schools—*Washington* and *Prairie*. Washington, founded in 1961 as a junior high school, was converted to an elementary school in 1987. One of the larger grade schools in the state, it houses 820 students in grades 2-5 and most of the special programs in the Danville district, including the gifted, the hearing impaired, and the emotionally and mentally handicapped programs. There are 120 staff members, including aides, janitors, cooks, and 60 certificated faculty—principal, vice-principal and teachers. Minority students comprise 42% of the school population. Blacks are most populous at 28%, followed by Hispanics at 10% and Asians at 3%. At poverty level, 65% of the students are entitled to free lunches.

Prairie Elementary School was founded in 1953 and converted to its K-1 form in 1987. The school houses an early childhood special education program, Chapter 1, and a bilingual program for this age group. There are 440 students and 50 staff members, including 18 classroom teachers. Similar to Washington, 60% of the school population is below the poverty line and minority students comprise 42% of the student population.

Overture

Glimpses (Potpourri of themes to be developed later)

A freckled third grader, approaches the music teacher standing in the corridor and hands her a bunch of notes. "36" he announces proudly. Back in her office Louise Moore[2] puts the 3x5 cards in an envelope, on which she writes neatly: "Daniel Wang, 36," and hangs it on the wall, near three other envelopes. This is Daniel's entry to the Composer's Facts competition, this week featuring Aaron Copland. To the curious reader, the cards contain information about Copland's birthdate and other significant dates, names of compositions and books he wrote. The winners get musical handbags, musical rulers, musical items, which Louise orders (and pays for with her own money) from a mailorder firm specializing in music items.

Lily Metzer, a second-grade teacher, pours glitter, yarn, cotton balls and other stuff into little plastic bowls and arranges them neatly on a back table between scissors and pine cones. Laura makes green stems from yarns and cones. Christopher glues cones on a newspaper. Allison glues glitter on a cardboard. Mark and Sara fold paper for a magnificent lamp, each fold separately. Metzer looks at Allison's artwork: "Ooh, how pretty," then summons Allison to help assemble more bowls on the table. Jacob accidentally hits a box and the water colors spill out. Metzer: "Just clean it up, please."

A group of six children is sitting on the floor. Violet Green, beaming and animated, sings from the piano and accompanies herself with vibrant harmonies: "Hello, hello, hello, how are you?" and immediately translates it to sign language, for this "hard of hearing" group. The children take turns tapping the beat on the tambourine. Betsy's is a bit too fast, David's too slow, but the faces are intent. After all take turns, Violet asks them to stand up and march around the room to the rhythm. A focus of attention, the music accelerates and slows down, stops and starts again, and pale, proud, and dedicated Bernadine is leading them all in a row.

The third-grade gifted class is crowded into the center of the room, where the teacher, Mary Rose, is holding a large sized art book. "Now look at that picture. That is really unusual, isn't it? It's done by Marc Chagall. Do you know what he painted?" Dana: "His dreams." Teacher: "His dreams [with emphasis, she continues in a mysterious tone]. He would dream things and then he would wake up and just had these visions. Have you had these dreams when you remember just a little bit of it and you think: 'Ooh, it's driving me crazy.' Well, Marc Chagall painted his dreams. Different painting styles appeal to different people. My mother would buy only landscapes. She did not buy anything that did not have a barn in it." High, excited voices: "My mother is the same way." On to the next page.

More glimpses of a principal hanging children-framed pictures in the corridors; of children's excited "Oohs" and "Aahs" at a dance performance in a nearby cultural center; of gifted students looking through a frame and drawing an extraordinary

---

[2]Except for teachers who explicitly wanted their names used, names have been changed.

jungle with a colorful parrot in the middle of greenery, all carefully pre-arranged by the teacher; of dozens of pictures, collages, poems and some cassettes, strewn on the library's carpet, waiting to be judged by a team of three in the school contest.

Music

Song and Play

Christmas Time: 12/18. 9:30 in the morning. Twenty-five third graders are singing in a choir, holding pages (words, not music) in front of them. Louise Moore, the music specialist, is at the piano accompanying them, bringing out the pleasing harmonies. The loudness is just right: not too soft so as not to be heard, not so loud that it covers their voices—so right that one is not even aware of it.

The children choose the songs to be sung. Almost everybody has a suggestion. This is preparation for the Christmas party at the gym. Louise sings with them. She encourages them to sing at the party, but cautions to do only the songs they know. There is a need for voices in the celebration, but a smaller in-tune group is preferable to a larger one. And, like so many other situations, a few can spoil the work of many. Donna raises her hand, suggests a new song she has learned in church. Other children opt for familiar, well-loved songs. By the end of the lesson, they stand in two lines outside the room and sing in canon: "Season's greetings, happy holiday." An artistic contribution to school ambience.

Fourth Grade's Encounter With Copland

11:32. "Today we have one other work that we need to listen to." Louise holds up a picture of a bespectacled, pensive Copland and passes it around. "His name is Aaron Copland. You can read about him here. He was born in 1900. He is alive but very old." A girl calculates quickly: "He is 88." Some children swing in their chairs. Louise: "He is the first great American composer, the first *recognized* composer." The restlessness gathers momentum. Louise: "You are going to have a *test* on this. I want you to remember this. He tried to show something about American life and American history. What part of the country does he portray?" Children try: "Texas." "The South." Louise: "The Southwest." She comments that there are four sections of the piece, talks about the cowboys depicted in the music. "What kind of things do cowboys do?" "Dance." "Shoot buffalos." "Ride horses." Louise repeats the right answers. The level of noise builds slowly but surely, as a Bach fugue.

11:45. The listening is done in preparation for tomorrow's concert. Copland's work, along with Sousa and the others, is featured in the program. Louise starts a tape. The sounds flow, energetic, picturesque. A girl in the front row makes horse-riding movements. Most of the boys in class have a good time, laughing and talking with their friends. Louise: "Hear the horses? Now the shooting," and makes shooting gestures with her hands. Copland's picture, an added source of distraction, is still being passed around. A boy bumps his head against the picture. Another, in his turn, plays with it, turning it in all different directions. Jeremiah forgets himself in the noise, stands up and gets sent to the last row. Change of location makes little difference: he is active and restless still. Finally, the first section is over. Two girls clap their hands in applause.

11:51. "Now, Choral Nocturne. You will get the feeling of a wave. Do not make noise because it is very soft. We won't have time to listen to all of it." (A cautious warning?) The poor recording and low-fi are harsh, scarring this soft piece. Louise sits in a chair and swings to the played aural waves. Not for long though. John disturbs the whole group (who obviously do not mind being disturbed) and is taken out.

11:53. The waves are stopped, a waltz starts. Louise delivers a dictionary definition of waltz, pausing for emphasis before the "3/4 time." She gracefully demonstrates the movements of the dance. Then she goes over the conducting motions. Soon all are conducting. The class is quiet and attentive. Even Jeremiah. Louise notices a girl who conducts in very small movements and explains that the movements need to be larger. She conducts, demonstrating how conducting can reflect soft and loud sounds, staccato and connected notes, and asks the students for the respective qualities of the music. Students express concern that the conductor's arm may grow tired during the long concert. I notice the regular teacher, Jason Clements, who just came in, standing quietly at the back of the room, listening. Louise's last remarks concern tomorrow's performance. They need to be good representatives of Washington. And a word of caution: "It's not going to be a basketball game." In a grim voice, Mr. Clements adds that not everybody is going. Two children have not yet brought permission signatures from their parents. It's a public reminder. This is the last chance.

History, Appreciation, and Production: A Balancing

The balance of production and general musical skills, appreciation and history varies from one music teacher to another. Some scarcely teach music history at all. Louise was among the teachers who taught it more. This year, 13 out of the approximately 40 music lessons of her classes were dedicated to music history and appreciation.

> I probably have done more this year than ever before. And I won't probably do this much again because I am not able to teach the other skills that I would really like to teach such as sight-reading and playing [recorders].

> You've got to *talk* about the music. You can play it and say, "That was by Bach." So what have they learned? They're just learning a piece to recognize. When we did the Bach invention, I talked about the fact that it had two parts [humming the two parts]. We talked about the synthesizer playing it. I talked about what Bach did during his life and where he lived. It takes time to do that if you're to teach anything about it other than just listen to it and recognize that it's sad. A lot of them can't remember the name of the piece. A lot of them know the name Bach now. They'll say: "Oh, that's the Hardee's Hamburger piece." You've got to start somewhere, I guess. It's more than they probably would have done on their own.

Louise Moore and many other teachers comment about the fact that children are not good listeners. In school life, inattention is particularly irritating when it comes to following instructions. Teachers complain that they repeat instructions many times, only to have students ask again. When it comes to "purposeless" activities such as listening to music, there is even less motivation to be attentive to the sound and to hear instructions.

Difficulty in listening concentration is typical even when the class is relatively sophisticated and well trained in music. Bill Handley, former district music director, tells how, when the high school symphony played Mozart's 40th symphony, he brought a recording of the piece to class. Even though the students knew the piece well and the recording was "fantastic," in Bill's words, students found it hard to concentrate on the music. Our culture promotes activities. Music is typically heard as background. As a focus of attention, it is often accompanied by body movement and dance. Our concentration span as listeners is short. The teaching of active listening is difficult and, as in all teaching, takes not only a motivated but also a well trained learner. Here, as in many other instances in school life, we observe gender differences. According to my observations, boys were more disruptive, girls quieter and more cooperative. Are these indications of different degrees of interest? of compliance?

Teacher practices and beliefs (specialists and classroom) are reminiscent of the practices of the beginning of music education in the U.S. in the first half of the 19th century. Music was seen as an expression of the needs of the people, the common man, rather than a product of an artistic elite.[3] The roots of music education are in the singing school of the early days of the nation when Lowell Mason, William Billings and others responded to the desire of communities to improve church singing by organized instruction in music fundamentals and note reading. There were two primary aims of instruction: to read music and to sing acceptably. Later, vocal and instrumental performance were added to these and performance became the major focus of music programs. Music history and appreciation were added much later, though in many instances they never quite made it into the curriculum.

Use of Materials

Piano was prominent in all the music classes I saw. The four music specialists seemed comfortable playing the piano. Violet Green played by ear. Louise relied on music sheets. The consequence was not so much a difference in the quality of performance in class. All played correctly, with clear communicative sound but Louise needed more preparation. Violet, on the other hand, had less experience with and knowledge of Orff instruments, on which Louise was proficient. Consequently, Violet used them rarely. Voice was by far the most popular instrument. Talking about pitches, intervals and Kodály notation, teaching new songs, giving direction in song (e.g., "stand up" in an ascending major triad, where the body gesture illustrates the musical line). All music teachers had clear, pleasant voices. Louise sang without nuance or expressive device (e.g., dynamics, rubato, vibrato),

---

[3]This is in contrast to other branches of music study like musicology and string performance, the roots of which can be traced to clerical origins or to aristocratic societies which produced a cultural elite.

realized it, was concerned about it. Singing in relatively straightforward style was perceived by all as appropriate for this age group (first grade to sixth grade) and level of sophistication. The record player was used as much as the piano, exposing the children to a variety of instruments.

There was no one official textbook but a variety of music books from which teachers could choose. Silver Burdett *Music* was the leading series. The books in the series contain numerous songs (music and words) arranged in an attractive format with bright pictures of musical instruments and children of all races playing, moving and singing. The songs in the books covered a variety of styles and types, from Christmas and other holiday songs, through "Roll an' Rock" and "Brother Noah and The Ark of the Lord" to songs from different countries and continents—African, Mexican, Israeli and Japanese among many others. Each book contained several lessons on the different arts—dance, poetry, visual art—exploring concepts (e.g., direction, rhythm, patterns) and their unique manifestations in the different arts. The organizing unit was a single lesson or a cluster of lessons that could stand alone. The modules are the building blocks from which the teacher structured the curriculum.

The books functioned almost exclusively as sources for songs. I never saw a teacher use the "analytical tools" or the rich, visual material presented in the book. When asked about it, teachers maintained that the material was too advanced for the children. When, after the lesson was over, Louise and I were looking at a specific example (the concepts of leaps and steps in "America the Beautiful") she mused aloud saying that she could have used that concept in class. Why didn't she? Clearly, that material was not beyond their knowledge. All music specialists had advanced degrees in music education and, as reflected in their interviews, a wide knowledge base of music theory. Using analytic tools just did not fit into what they thought of as curriculum in music classes.

Grading and Evaluation

At present, there are no standardized arts education tests in Danville. This situation is scheduled to change in 1994 when the State of Illinois is to administer state-wide tests for music and the other arts.[4] Occasionally music teachers distribute their own tests on art history and appreciation, calling for memorization, recall and application of knowledge. Items include listening to a musical piece and identifying it; identifying a playing instrument; providing definitions for musical terms; translating notation from staff to Kodály signs.

There was no testing of playing an instrument or singing. In fact, there was little opportunity for hearing individual performances. Louise told me that sometimes other music teachers commented that a certain student had a beautiful voice. She wondered how they hear him/her in the midst of other voices. She tried to walk around and listen to the individual voices, but found it very difficult. Occasionally she asked somebody to sing a solo and for the rest of the class to do the refrain. Individual performance was hard to assess:

---

[4]More about teacher reactions to these tests in a later section.

Occasionally, if we're doing echo clapping, question and answer, you can do it so the kid does it after you and they do get a chance individually. When I play recorders, I sometimes have the kids play individually for me, in the class. It's not a very good thing to do, especially in a larger class. In a smaller class, with 15 or 16 students, it's not so bad. But it is when you get up to 30, because there are so many kids that can't play very well. If I try to give them time to play it, or try to help them a little bit, it takes too much time and the kids get all antsy and they stop being polite and listening. In the smaller groups, it works okay. They're pretty good about it and they like to do that, some of them.

It's a problem for me and I think it's got to be for everybody else. If I'm actively involved, I can't sit back and assess it very well and keep records of it. We can spend time and I can sort of remember in class who does what, sort of. But I can't remember exactly how well each person did. Sometimes if all learn the part, I'll tap three people. I'll have three kids play and then I'll try to keep track if they can play a certain part. But it's different, playing while everybody's performing and playing just by itself. A lot of kids can play a part and keep a steady beat but then when they have to put it with what they're accompanying, that's a different thing. They get confused. They can't do it as well. But it's hard for me to keep all that going and then be able to go back and keep track of it. So grades are kind of a silly thing for us at this point.

There are times that I wish I could take certain kids and listen to them and work with them. If I find that they're not singing well, then I'll stop and say: "Hey, you're not singing, you're shouting." That usually gets some improvement in the sound of the whole group. I don't know if the ones that are singing so loud just stop singing or whether they actually sing softer. To single somebody out in front of the group, I don't find that being very helpful.

Moore reminds us of some important issues in evaluation of music in classrooms. The logistics of music evaluation are different from the logistics of evaluation in academic subjects (or of evaluation in the visual arts, for that matter) in two respects: (a) Music is temporal; to evaluate the activity you have to be present; with pen and paper assignments, one can read the product later; and (b) Music involves sound; in order to evaluate, one needs to listen; but it is impossible to listen to 30 different sounds played simultaneously and be able to differentiate among them. As to having children play individually, the problem is mainly that of keeping children engaged while others perform. These same problems exist, of course, in a band or in choir classes; their different goals and priorities determine different time constraints and solutions. Consequently, feedback on *musical* skills in the elementary level was minimal and, when given, was usually directed to the group as a whole.

Grades in music (as well as in art and physical education at Washington) consist of E(xcellent), S(atisfactory), and U(nsatisfactory). What is the percentage of students getting the two extremes of E's and U's? Averages vary from class to class. Most gifted students get E's, other students typically get S's. When children excel in written assignments and participate willingly in class activities, they get an E. Few students get U's. One has to be disruptive, unwilling to cooperate to receive a U. "If unable to keep a steady beat but still appearing to do one's best, it is still an S," says Louise. "Why make people feel they are not good enough?"

Interestingly, the heart of the music curriculum—singing and playing recorders—was not being formally assessed. It was the secondary activities of music history and appreciation that were assessed. Music teachers said that grading is "silly," "subjective" and "unfair" since they can't assess individual performance for the musical skills taught in class.

Grading, or the lack of it, is closely related with teacher concerns about *attitude* to the arts. Attitudes affect achievements. "Why make them feel bad about their music abilities?" asks Louise, as do the other music teachers, when I ask if they ever give U's. These views stem from teacher beliefs about art as enriching and enhancing life. Abilities are secondary. Often, music lessons—a relief from the prevalent pressure of accomplishments and accountability—allow the teacher to reach a person. Violet Green, the second music teacher in the school:

> Something has to open there [points at her heart] before you can pour anything here [points at her head]. That's why I feel so lucky to be the music person. It allows you to reach them without having to worry. "Did we do our language arts today?" Hopefully, we can go back and now Johnny will do his language arts. Without "You've got to do this." Kids have to have that [relief]. We've lost that. Not every teacher can do it. Classroom teachers don't have the time. You've got all this stuff. Next week they have a test and everybody has to show that he has progressed. How can you show the child has progressed from "was not loving and caring" to where now he is? I can do some of these things. I don't have to show that he has increased in knowledge. Hopefully, with what I can do, he can go back and the teacher can see some increase in knowledge. Something is lacking in the other subjects and we can try to bring it in.

Pressure for Academics

At what grade level does the pressure for academics start? I started a search for the transition: from nonpressure to pressure. I began examining the lowest grade level—kindergarten, expecting only minimal pressure, if any. I asked Mary Harwood, a kindergarten teacher, if she ever senses pressure for academic performance. Mary's answer came as a surprise:

> We are told that we are responsible for the things that are in the Curriculum Guide. The Kindergarten Curriculum Guide will give you a list of things in each subject that the children are supposed to have covered. That's district-wide. In that way you get some pressure through the administration, through the superintendent. A big deal is made about test scores. There is much emphasis on math this year because math achievements were low last year. Then you get pressure from some parents who hear about other kids that can do something and they want to be sure their kids are getting it too. They call the school or they

call the superintendent or they talk with the child. A lot of pressure you put on yourself because you want to be sure that your kids are really good and ready.

And then you get some pressure when you listen or talk with other teachers. Sometimes it's comforting to hear about other people in the same spot but at the same time, there are always a few who like to stick it at you. "My children are on page such and such and my children do this and my children do that." Kindergarten teachers get pressure from first-grade teachers. When they get your kids, they put you down. They say, "I want to ask you about Joe Smith. Didn't you have him last year? Well, he does not know his letter sounds." So I think about Joe and I think about all the behavioral and socialization problems Joe had last year. The big thing for Joe and Joe's parents and me was when I got to send them a note saying "Joe had a good day." And they celebrated and I celebrated and Joe celebrated. Joe was all smiles because he had a terrible time getting along in school. It took us a long time to work it out. The test happened on the first week of school. One of the other teachers said: "What happened to review?" Joe has been home for three months. Because some of the teachers have so much pressure, and some of them are so academic, they start the year with full force. They want the kids to know all that when they get to nouns. And no matter how I feel or what I think about Joe, it puts pressure on me. It makes me feel, "Oh, my gosh. She thinks I should have taught him." I feel the pressure because I know that Joe has a real tough time because he does not know his letter sounds. I feel so sorry for his parents because they were so cooperative last year.

The extent to which kindergarten teachers teach art and music varied. Mary, one of the more accomplished and musically inclined kindergarten teachers, tried to teach music for 60 minutes per week. Kay, on the other end of the spectrum said that *maybe* she taught a total of 30 minutes all last year. Different teachers have different inclinations and talents and react differently to the academic pressure, depending on how strongly they feel about including the arts and how self-confident they are about their teaching.

Music was not the only "victim" of that pressure. The things that did not contribute directly to measured achievement were diminished, sometimes eliminated. Such was the fate of building blocks in first grade. "The less distractions we have, the more work we get done," said a first-grade teacher. Such was the fate of the visual arts. Not having a specific place in the curriculum, visual arts suffered the most. Judy Cervantes, a second-grade teacher:

> I integrate art with the subjects as much as I can but with the elementary age level, here in school, it seems that the time you spend with reading and math seems to take up most of your day. And so, you really have to make a special effort to get the art subjects in. It's very difficult at times. You almost feel pressured to keep the children advanced enough in their reading and math. At the same time, [they must] meet their other needs, needs that they have to express themselves in other ways. And so, you have to integrate it or just take special time aside to work

on art. I know a lot of teachers like to work on Fridays especially, because by this time, their brains seem to be draining and it's a good way for them to relax and end the week.

Or Nancy Dawson, a second- and third-grade reading improvement teacher, who said with emphasis:

> We slack off on the arts and sciences, especially in the primary grades. We have to read, read, read, read.

Mary, Nancy and Judy lamented the lack of arts in the curriculum. Some teachers felt that teaching art in the school should not be a priority, considering what students need to know in life. Jason Clements, a fourth-grade teacher, describes the pressures and agrees with the institutional priorities:

> There is not enough time in the school day to teach the basic subjects. I have a hard time finding time to justify teaching art because art is not tested on an achievement test. Art is not a grade parents are concerned with. Art is something that children enjoy doing but it's put to a back seat because right now we're pushed, pushed, pushed to get through the curriculum guidelines. Each year we keep adding things. Now we're going to teach about drug abuse, sex abuse, personal safety, along with reading, writing, science and math. I feel personally that those areas are more important than art. So art really takes a back seat in my classroom I feel there are too many other things that need to be covered.
>
> I think the pressure comes from our school board. I think the pressure comes from the media. I think the pressure comes from parents. Knowing what my students are facing, they will not be properly prepared if we don't let them know the basic concepts of geography and science or at least get them used to them. If they are not well-prepared, they will fall farther and farther behind at every grade level. I do tutoring on the side and every tutoring job I have I see the results. Like I said, something has got to give. There's just not enough time in the day to cover everything. Art is going to be one of these things that is going to be discouraged. Music is another.

Drama: School Productions

The conventional, acceptable organizers of the academic subjects—textbook, tests, grading system—were weaker for music and art. The music teachers and the curriculum director in the district developed a curriculum guide for music. It provided teachers with goals, objectives and specific skills. In an earlier section I discussed the role of the textbook in the music class. Productions used to be important events around which drama teaching revolved.

> We usually had a, well, we didn't usually call it a *Christmas* program, but a Winter program and a Spring Program. Sometimes it was just for the

PTA. The schools were getting to be pretty large. You almost had to have two programs because there would be so many parents coming. You couldn't fit everybody in at the same time.

Typically, resources for productions were minimal. The whole operation relied exclusively on school talent.

Mary Rose [one of the teachers] writes plays that are really good, so we did "Santa for President." That's hers. It's been printed, got rave reviews, and was pretty important. Bob [another teacher] got parents to come in and help. He designed the scenery and they built it. Sometimes we get the classes to be responsible for certain parts of the scenery, like Mr. Smith's fifth-grade class. It was after school and the rehearsals were twice a week. Sometimes they asked the teachers to have their kids make decorations for the gym.

Many teachers talked with nostalgia about these programs. They remembered and narrated in detail what the students did and how much fun they had. They stressed the importance of the *experience* of performance for these children. For some children, they said, "This is the only experience they will ever have. In junior and senior high school they have to beat out some pretty good competition to participate in a program." They talked about the importance of experiences in school lives. Why then are there no more programs?

Two years earlier there had been financial cuts. Instead of the ten music teachers that used to teach in the area, only six were teaching currently. With one exception, all music teachers travelled among 2-3 schools each day. That had a great impact on the presence of the music teacher in the school. It meant there was less time (and less energy) to work with students on special projects in recess time or after school. It meant that the children received a music lesson every *three* rather than every two days.

How did the cuts affect the music curriculum? Talking with music specialists, it seemed that the curriculum did not change that much. The effect on curriculum and pupils is gradual, they say. It is the new generation which would not receive as much music. The primary classes would suffer more than the upper grades students who had had more music training. One of the first things squeezed out of the curriculum was productions. There was simply not enough time for production, music teachers said. In informal conversations, some said that eliminating productions was also a demonstrative act. Since productions and musicals were about the only visible products of a music curriculum, cutting productions carried a message. With the new curricular emphases the message was that music programs would not just diminish, they would wither.

The outcome, however, was not simple and clearcut. Pressures to do productions remained. At Washington these were initiated from the top (principals), the bottom (classroom teachers) and the outside (parents in PTA). At Prairie, the principal let it be known that she expected productions. Said one of the teachers:

In the past, music teachers would bring their chorus to PTA meetings. It was good for increasing the number of people attending. More parents would come because their kids were going to be in it. The music teachers got together and decided that they no longer were going to prepare programs for PTA because they had double the schools to be in. It was just expecting too much.

The kindergarten never had music services anyway. We offered to do some things at PTA meetings. Right after that it was said that every grade level would be expected to have some kind of performance for the PTA meeting. Well, naturally this is going to include some music. The principal decided it was a pretty good idea to have all grade levels doing it. Oh, teachers were complaining and grouchy. The principal worked around it. She took what we had been doing and *used it*. We had the best intentions in the world. Well, the year after, Mrs. Smith was very upset because she was going to be PTA president and there were no music groups for PTA meetings. And I know she talked with Louise about "couldn't they just bring somebody anyway?" and Louise told her "No!"

The expectation was that parents would protest and that the top administration would back down. It did not happen (with the exception of the PTA president, who directed her protest to the wrong source). There was disappointment in parent reaction:

People could adjust to anything. A lot of parents who enjoyed those programs didn't just say: I think we should call the superintendent and tell him that we want more of these programs. A lot of them never approached the superintendent.

Eliminating the productions was a "solution" not without its costs. At least some classroom teachers felt strongly that by not including music, they deprived their students of extremely important experiences. They found themselves in a bind: when they did go out of their way to substitute for the missing experiences, they were confronted by other teachers who thought this was disservice to the music teachers. In addition, they felt that, in the long run, providing productions was a disservice to the students. With no protest and no change with productions, the administration would not restore the music lessons.

If you do productions, that shows that we can make the music program work. And you *can* make it work. But it shouldn't work that way because it is not the best. It is not fair to anybody concerned. So what do you do? Do you go ahead and make it work? Or you pull back to make it not work?

The dilemma involved more than the actual productions. It involved teacher relationship, loyalty and support as well as conflicting beliefs in what children should get in school and how they should get it. The resolution was problematic. Here and there I found some "minor programs." The gifted classes had a Christmas party. High-heeled mothers showed up with bright clothes and babies. Less elegant fathers took off in the midst of work. They came to enjoy their children reading poems, singing and acting in short, self-written plays featuring Santas, Christmas trees and presents. In the spring, the Honors Program featured all third graders in the school performing a few songs and a dance. With the principal's sanctifying presence, the enthusiasm of the children, and the pleased expressions of parents, the performances radiated a festive flavor. Still, teachers say that they are pale shadows of previous events.

Support from the Administration

An underlying issue in this drama was administrative support of music. Music enjoyed a special place among the arts in Danville elementary schools, being the only subject among the arts taught by a specialist. In 1970, the music program received a boost when the school district, having passed a tax referendum, invested money in the music program. It hired music specialists and bought equipment. Instead of one music coordinator, the district hired 10 music specialists for elementary classrooms. It bought some 20 pianos (at least one for each school), 18 sets of Orff instruments and other musical instruments.

The people I talked with—classroom teachers, music specialists, the principal, the former music director of the district—described the circumstances by which music received this special status. It was the teachers who spoke out in favor of hiring music specialists. The several stories are strikingly similar. Mr. Dole, the principal:

> Seventeen years ago homeroom teachers taught everything: Art, PE, Music. Most of them were not trained very well in these special areas. They did not always do a very good job. Some felt uncomfortable. Some could not read music, did not play a piano. Basically it was just a Sing-a-thon. One of the reasons that we've gone towards more music instruction—and this needs to be told—is to provide planning time for teachers. I feel that music is very important. But make no mistake about it, some people here don't care as long as they have their break. But most people do care.

Bill Handley, a former music director of the district, sheds more light on teachers' motives in choosing specialists:

> A lot of this came about not because the public or school board were clamoring for music education but because the teachers' union thought elementary teachers had a right to planning periods, like high school teachers did. So through the use of music and PE specialists, elementary teachers were getting planning periods. A questionnaire was sent out to the elementary staff asking which of the following areas they would like to have specialists: music, PE, art, counseling and library. Music was the top of the list. Teachers were afraid to teach music.

The principal has an important role in setting a tone of encouragement. Principal involvement varied from school to school. Mrs. Johnson, from Prairie, demanded more programs for PTA meetings. She told me explicitly that she did not promote the arts. They were certainly not a priority, often a hindrance. Ron Davison presented a picture of the high school situation:

> The administration knows we're good [in performance] but I don't know if they know *how* good we are—in comparison to other programs. There could be a hundred times more encouragement for everyone. You know, there's nothing that's better than someone slapping you on the back and saying "that was real nice." We finished in the top five in this state in marching band and in symphonic band in the last four years now. I felt like it was appropriate for the administration to acknowledge the kids at least but they tend to be lacking in that area. I think that's something that would really raise the morale and the image of the school and the students involved. Especially since they've worked so very hard. They've achieved a standard of excellence that is really laudable for their young ages.

At Washington, Principal Dole was a supportive force behind many artistic activities. He went out of his way to solicit funds for out-of-school performances, encouraging teachers to participate in the activities. He required that student art work be framed and displayed in public areas. He set an example by hanging the pictures himself rather than delegate it to secretaries. He was an important role model in the eyes of teachers and students. He initiated a special fund to help send interested teachers to conventions and music conferences. Music teachers told me that whenever they needed something, tuning the piano, a record player, replacing a missing bar in the Orff instruments, he found the money. Classroom teachers commented that he found ways to get needed art materials. Not least important, he acknowledged teachers in private and in public for doing the things they were doing, orally and in writing (e.g., sending a letter to the two teachers who organized the inservice in the arts, noting the excellent job they did).

As to "the people high above," the general feeling was that music is the lowest priority on their list. The cuts of two years ago affected several other areas but most of these other cuts were restored. Additional money was spent on hiring skilled teachers and monitors to solve "plan time problems" for the kindergarten teachers who did not have special music lessons. Music, many felt, was just not important enough for the people "up there." Expressions of anger about the cuts in the music program in the elementary level were heard not only from music specialists but from others, too. Earlier, we heard Mary Harwood and other classroom teachers expressing concern about cuts in the elementary program. Ron Davison, the high school band director:

> They cut our elementary music staff in half. We have one teacher teaching 700 students a week. I sense a lack of understanding in the district. They feel that as long as the high school maintains a great quality program, it would not hurt to not have it in the lower levels. And that philosophy bothers me because if you want to kill a tree you usually cut its roots. Oh, when I first came to Danville we had phenomenal elementary music teachers. They created in students at a very young age a real appreciation of music. There's nothing more valuable. I would rather see them cut out the high school marching band than cut out elementary school teachers.

Ron Davison's views about the effects of the cuts were reiterated by many other kindergarten and classroom teachers and by music specialists.

State Goals

The same theme of mistrust and frustration towards the people up the administrative ladder was voiced strongly against the State Department of Education. Public Act 84-126, effective August 1, 1985, amended *The School Code of Illinois* to include, for the first time in state history, a requirement that the goals for learning be identified and assessed. Six primary areas were identified: language arts, mathematics, biological and physical science, social science, fine arts, and physical development and health. Local school districts were required to develop and submit for approval by the State Board of Education, local learning objectives which met or exceeded the State Goals. The district level objectives were to identify the learning outcomes expected for students in their schools. The broad goals included understanding the principal sensory, formal, technical and expressive qualities for each of the arts; identifying processes and tools required to produce visual art, music, drama and dance; demonstrating the basic skills necessary to participate in the creation and or performance of the arts; identifying significant works in the arts from major historical periods and how they reflect societies, cultures and civilization, past and present; and describing the unique characteristics of each of the arts.

Standardized tests in grade levels 3, 6, 8, 10, and 12 were scheduled to start statewide in 1994. Classroom teachers held the main responsibility for teaching most of the arts curriculum since in most Illinois schools there were no visual art, drama or dance specialists. Even in music, some of the test coverage was not part of the music curriculum and classroom teachers were expected to assume responsibility for the discrepancy.

The prospect of these newly mandated tests aroused much anger and frustration. It was expressed by music specialists, classroom teachers and principals alike. Among the main complaints were lack of time, lack of empathy to teaching within present constraints, lack of responsiveness to teacher concerns, and lack of financial support to help the teachers learn new skills. Matt Dole, principal at Washington:

> It is not fair for the State to dictate this. I saw some of the art tests on ballet and dance. It's not realistic unless they send teachers to teach us how to teach these areas. No-one in this school is knowledgeable in ballet, for example. Nobody knows it. I don't know it. I would fail that test. You can't just legislate improvement. You can't just say we are going to raise test scores. You've got to build the groundwork. You've got to provide the resources and the leadership. You can't impose change from the top. You've got to ignite the interest of the staff to do that. People in the State Department of Education say: "You have to do this, this and this." But we have no money to do it! We were not asked if we wanted to do it! We were not asked how we could do it! Many times when we have been involved, we worked for years to do something and then funding runs out and nothing further happens. So people are discouraged. I know the intents of the legislators are very good, very admirable, but. . . [shaking his head].

Nancy Dawson, a second- and third-grade teacher, Washington representative to the committee writing District goals:

> [In the committee] we're having a hard time trying to scale the State Goals down for the child. We have one representative from each school. They are all elementary teachers with no background in music or theater. We have no expertise. We asked for art specialists to come in and help us. I know they would rather that we do it ourselves. No reasonable explanation given. That's the way it is, accept it. And we are all frustrated. They were talking about the different trends in art. I have no idea what they're talking about. So we have to try to figure out, how does this belong in kindergarten, first grade, second grade, etc. We've already had three meetings, and each time the group is getting smaller and smaller because the teachers are just getting frustrated.
>
> The State has just been pushing everything. All right, we're now teaching drug abuse; we're now teaching sexual abuse. We're now going to teach the arts. We also have to teach reading, language, spelling, social studies, PE, health, music and writing. They keep shoving more and more onto you. It's really getting bad. You can't get through anything. You're always behind. And teachers are getting very frustrated. Very, very frustrated. We were told that the people who sit on the arts curriculum council for the State are all from the university. There is *one* teacher there. They don't understand what its like to be in the classroom! Some of them have *never* been in a classroom. That is what is frustrating to us. How can they dictate what should be done in a classroom when they have no idea what it is like there. Let me tell you, every year it is becoming more difficult.

The concern that classroom teachers will be required to teach lots they do not know was a general one. It was the subject of every day talk among teachers. Michelle Little, who like almost all other classroom teachers, had not seen the State goals, said:

> I don't think I want to [see the State Goals], from what I've heard; because I don't teach a lot of things like how to draw, because I feel inadequate at it myself. . . I don't think that a classroom teacher can teach it in the way that they want it taught. I am not trained to teach the arts.

Mary Rose complained to the other teachers (while we were all driving to school in her car from an early breakfast meeting at Ponderosa) that exposing students to music was far more important than "learning all these irrelevant facts," many of which she did not have. It was clear that were State Goals to prevail, Mary, a leader and knowledgeable person in the arts field, risked losing that position within the school. These were the feelings of "leaders of the arts": Little, who volunteered to prepare an inservice art program for classroom teachers, and Rose, the artistic spirit of the school. It is not surprising that other more "average" teachers were even more reluctant and resistant to teach the arts.

The Hidden Curriculum

> 1:30. The RIP (Reading Improvement Program) second and third graders return to their classroom from recess. Ms. Dawson stands near the door: "Everybody, I want you calm and quiet." At their desks, they rest their heads on the table. She puts a record on the record player. 1:32. The sounds of *American in Paris* fill the room. The two aides correct papers. Ms. Dawson talks with another teacher who just entered from the adjacent room. 1:34. Teacher leaves. Ms. Dawson walks around the room. The juxtaposition of uniformly leaning heads and a classroom reminds me of a *Sleeping Beauty* scene. 1:36. Synchronized in Authentic Cadence, she lifts the handle from the record player. Time for Math.

As Mr. Handley remarked, most teachers did not feel comfortable teaching music, lacking formal background and experience. That did not mean that there was no music in the regular classroom. Nancy Dawson played Gershwin to "calm the children down" after the excitement of recess. Joe Herbert, a second-grade teacher, played taped orchestral music, Rachmaninov, Dvorak, and other Romantic composers at the beginning of the day:

> We listen to a lot of music. It's not always tied in to anything. It is just that during math time, if they are doing seat work there's music on. It just seems to go easier that way. If they have something to listen to, they won't talk. They'll concentrate on their work and let the music kind of wash the mood in. And during the seat work, after we set up an art lesson and they are coloring it. When they are finishing up, they will listen to music.

Mary, the kindergarten teacher, often plays Vivaldi's *Four Seasons* for the children. She shares with them her reactions to music. Her short introduction sets a special tone:

> Let's turn over on your tummies and relax. You don't have to go to sleep. We just need to relax for a while. This is listening music. It does not even have any words. There are no words to think about. We just listen. It just makes you feel so good to listen to that nice music.

To some, listening to music was a daily activity. Implicit were assumptions about the value of exposure, the feeling that enjoying arts was for everybody, that one did not have to have special education to enjoy the good things in life. Nancy Dawson:

> I don't have to know a great deal about the arts to appreciate them. I appreciate good music a great deal, yet I don't have to know a lot about it. I want my kids to understand that they don't have to know all of the great terms. It's nice to know all of this about a painting, but it isn't necessary to be able to appreciate it. Also, you don't have to be wealthy to enjoy the arts. I think a lot of times our society says to people [that you do]. You can enjoy the good things in life without being rich!

Sometimes there were problems involved in playing music. Jim Gholssen mentions "volume" as a source for debate. "Volume" can represent deeper issues of authority and student participation in decision making in class when the clear line of school rules and conventions is being changed:

> When we do our art classes, I play the radio. But what happens is, kids are used to listening to really loud music. At home they listen to rock and roll and it is loud. So when you play it in the room they want to have it loud and then if they want to talk, they have to even talk louder. So what happens is, you just fight it, it keeps going up and up and up.

Even more prevalent than listening to music was active singing. Mary Harwood coveted and obtained the second piano in the school, accompanying the children's singing when school day started—mornings and afternoons—as well as before holidays. She often sang with them a-cappella, "just for fun. Songs I felt they need to know and songs that fit with what we learn in class." Ms. Rodesky and Ms. Perez sang and did rhymes with their kindergartners and first graders. Occasionally, music was accompanied by dance. Lily Metzer, a second-grade teacher, started her day with 10 minutes of Muppet songs and dancing.

These were not part of the planned or formal curriculum. In fact, when I first asked teachers and principals about musical activities, these activities were not mentioned. Music was also not included in the lesson plan because, teachers explained to me, lesson plans need to be as explicit as possible and include all relevant materials, so a substitute could carry on the activity. The music materials were often part of aural tradition not documented. In most cases, teachers did not have the music for the songs, they just remembered them. And substitutes, of course, were not expected to know how to read music. As in the accountability theme, what can't be fully articulated isn't acknowledged formally.

Informal, regular, or scattered as these incidents were, they were part of the hidden curriculum. On occasion, teachers shared with their students things that sustained and nourished them emotionally. The time for these activities was typically "transition" time from curricular to non-curricular activities: starting the day in the morning, coming back to class after recess, before holidays. The objectives were affective: to set a certain tone, to get in touch with feelings. Typically, listening did not involve conceptual thinking and talking about it. Teachers did not have the appropriate education and background and did not apply a cognitive mode to listening. Thus, Nancy's students who listened to Gershwin, Bach and Tchaikovsky day in and day out, did not know what they were hearing, were not conscious of the instruments, textures, rhythms, and lines. Nancy herself was not aware of these parameters. A sensitive, intelligent and caring teacher, she explained the role of music for her: relaxation.

The lower the grade level, the more music and art there was. Thus, most kindergarten and many first-grade teachers engaged in some music activity in their classroom; few fourth- and fifth-grade teachers did.

Dance: Informal Curriculum

9:15 in the morning. "Lily Metzer's children are flying all over the room," comments Ms. Denny with a half smile (did I detect some criticism?). The second graders start their day, as they do almost every day, to the sounds of Muppet Songs. The record player is on, sounds flow, and without further prompting, the children start moving around. The pace and gestures follow the mood of the song. Energetic in the first, slow and soft in the second, lively in the third. Without being aware, Metzer follows an Italian Overture form (fast-slow-fast). Boys use the full space of the room, crossing from one end to another. Girls tend to stay at the same place, with smaller and subtler movements. Within different phrases in the same song, couples transform to 5-6 children groups, then back to couples. Sometimes Metzer joins, floating gracefully around the room. At other times she sits near her table. There is little feedback (one "very nice" in three 10-minute observations) and little monitoring. The children seem intrinsically motivated. 9:25. The music ends. Next to rows and reading.

Metzer was one of the few teachers who incorporated movement into classroom routine. Dance occupied a more regular place within music lessons. I observed Jingle Bells and Hora in two (unplanned) visits to music classes. These lessons consisted of rehearsing movements, concentrating on the more difficult ones and on the transitions. Most of it was done in silence. In the last few minutes of the lesson, music was added. Typically, the whole class participated as a group but sometimes the teachers called for volunteers or enlisted specific students.

Music teachers said that square and folk dances are the most common. The extent to which dance is incorporated into the music curricula ranges across all grade levels. Ms. Pedicord, a retired music teacher in Danville, remembered when dance had a greater role in the curriculum. Diminished time for dance, agreed the music specialists, is one more effect of the financial cuts.

The role of dance in music education is an established and recognized one. Along with movement and rhythm, dance is acknowledged to be basic, embodying beat, meter and articulation. Dalcroze (1865-1950), the famous Swiss music educator, claimed that unless the learner experiences aspects of music by body movement, the music he will perform will be mechanical, without feeling. The expressive responsiveness essential to genuine musicianship may never develop. A side benefit acknowledged by all was that it is unnatural for boys and girls to sit quietly for long periods of time. Movement can reduce tension and fatigue.

The more sophisticated forms of dance (e.g., ballet, jazz) are absent from the school curricula. Most classroom teachers report having little formal background or professional background in dance. Among the exceptions, Angie Perez, a first-grade teacher, used to be a dancer in a Mexican dance company in St. Louis. Nancy Dawson, a second- and third-grade RIP teacher, told me about a ballet course she took a few years ago. Matt Dole, the principal, mentioned a dance course he took in college.

Outside the school, ballet and dance courses were being offered in the community by trained teachers. Children attended and enjoyed. Forty miles away, Krannert Center featured dance performances. I joined the Danville and Champaign second and third graders in the Fables performance there. The children seemed to enjoy the graceful and humorous dance and the interviews with dancers between movements. Moments of fascination, judged by the general "oohs," occurred with falling of confetti and dramatic lighting effect. Was there a follow-up in class? Classroom teachers told me they asked the children what their favorite pieces were. Sometimes children noted such details as the dancers' outfits. Longer term effect? Liza and Debbie told me after the performance that they wanted to be dancers. The more assured and prosaic effect (and the one advocated by Susan McDonald, Krannert Director of Audience) is that the children will remember a performance as something positive, worth going to. Some may become future consumers of dance. A first step in building a connoisseurship.

Visual Art

A Winter Day in Ms. Little's Class

On a freezing winter day, Michelle Little's fourth graders are cutting paper penguins and colorful scarves, hats, pants and boots. Little gives detailed instructions on cutting. "If you keep your eyes on me, you can cut this." Four children help distribute materials: paper, crayons and glue. With classroom arrangement in the usual rows, Little assures that everybody is on task. She lingers a bit with the less accomplished pupils. Some of the scissors are in bad shape. David's are barely functional. Little asks David why he did not get a new pair of scissors. David, sullen, mutters that his mother did not have time to buy them. As we walk on, Little explains to me that his mother is separated from his father, busy with work, and scarcely spends time with her children.

Some penguins are more accurately cut than others. The pace of working is different from child to child. Some are already gluing boots, others still struggle with the outline. Ms. Little takes her shoes off, steps on the table to hang the "exemplary penguins" she had prepared on the window. Down again, she notices that Mary uses a different color from the prespecified ones for a scarf and redirects her.

What they don't finish now they will finish on Monday, she reassures them. With five minutes before the end of the lesson, some children have already finished and are sitting quietly, math books open. Most of the penguins, though, remain at least partly naked when the math lesson starts. But by the following Monday the penguins are lined up on the window, entitling their creators to a prize of five dollars. Ms. Little calls them the "best classroom in the fourth graders' pod."

A Winter Day in Ms. Metzer's Class

Lily Metzer (second-grade) pours glitter, yarn, cotton balls and other materials into little plastic bowls and arranges them neatly on a back table between scissors and pine cones. Laura makes green stems from yarns and cones. Christopher glues cones on a newspaper. Allison glues glitter on a cardboard. Mark folds paper for a magnificent lamp. Sarah helps. Children visit with each other and are interested in what the others are doing. Metzer summons Allison to help assemble more bowls on the table. Jacob accidentally hits a box and the water colors spill. Metzer: "Just clean up, please."

Children are scattered all over, in natural patches, which brings to mind the arbitrariness and artificiality of straight lines. Lily, young and graceful, slides from one group to another: "Now what I can do is I can cut that out, I can put glue there, and I can glue the paper, then it will be a little Christmas tree. And if I wanted to, I could glue it and it would be an ornament. Would that be an idea? Why don't you go for it?" "What are you doing? Ooh, that's nice. Do you have lots of paper to put them on or do you like them like that? Are you going to glue them to this paper? Why don't you do glitter on one side?" "Do you need some help? Are you going to put some glitter before you finish that? Why don't you paint this and wait on this for a little?"

Looking over Natalie's shoulder, she says: "It's not a telescope anymore. What is it now?" Natalie: "A pole, maybe?" Metzer: "Hm, maybe it is a pole." Natalie: "I don't know. Maybe it's a statue. Maybe it's a piece of art." Children crowd around. "I want to see it. I want to see it." Jeff complains about Santa's eyes sliding down. Metzer: "Yeah, it's kind of tough to make eyes on cotton balls. Look at all the Santa Clauses here. Cottonball beards. Pretty neat."

The freedom seems to confuse some students who just stand there and look at Mrs. Metzer. A boy approaches and asks for help with the glitter. As I look at his artwork, he tells me he does not like glitter. When I ask him why he chose it, he explains that he did not know what to choose, so he chose this one, encouraged by the teacher and by other students. Metzer encourages the self-conscious guy: "Your things look a lot better than you think they do. It looks fine. O.K., now you are ready? Is that what you wanted? Is that how you wanted it?"

Mrs. Metzer explains to me:

> These are their own art projects. They can make anything they want. What I told them at the beginning of the week is to bring any supplies they want to, anything that they would like for art. Somebody makes a computer out of cardboard boxes. We have many Christmas trees from magazines. The others do whatever they want. They pick up from three items over there (motions to the table with supplies) to start and then they can come over there later after everybody had their chance. Those are my art supplies.

She takes me over to two big drawers on the side of the room. When they closed two schools in Danville, Metzer tells me, "Nobody wanted the supplies and I just took them." I sense her pride in her special supplies and her enthusiasm as she shows me the shelves.

Metzer: "It's time to start picking up. Start cleaning up." (murmurs of disappointment). Jeff: "Where do you put this?" Metzer: "Let's find a place. How about one of the shelves? Oh, Adrian, you did a good job [expressively]. There are very creative people in here. Very neat. Jannele, I like your reed. Oh. That looks very nice. Throw it away. You don't need that."

Lou comes and wants to give her his artwork. Metzer: "I think you should go home and put it up on your Christmas tree. Put it by the light and all the sparkle will shine. Won't that be pretty?" He insists and she accepts. I hear from a number of teachers that many parents throw away the children's artwork. By giving it to the teacher, these children get, at least, an acknowledgement of the gift.

Metzer's and Little's were two different classes. Two different teachers, differing in tone, pace, pedagogical styles. They range from teacher-centered to student-centered style, from a didactic approach to an open-project approach, through a combination of styles. There are also common patterns. Length and frequency of lessons (45 minutes every one or two weeks), time of day and week (typically Friday afternoons). The projects were one-time projects, with no continuity, development, or sequentiality. Craft objects prevailed. There was little guidance to explore and experiment with materials, even less with ideas and aesthetic qualities. The absence of aesthetic qualities such as lines, textures, and forms in the curriculum, both in the production and in the evaluation, was prevalent. Evaluation consisted mostly of checking that directions have been followed and the expression of personal likes or dislikes, with no reasoning or attempts for justification. The great majority of products were oriented to craft and schematization (e.g., bearded Santas, glittering trees), with little attention to expressivity, little reaching for new meanings. School art taught by classroom teachers was much different from the discipline of art.

Grading

In art, as in music and physical education, the grades were Unsatisfactory, Satisfactory, and Excellent. What were the criteria for these grades?

> As long as they try, I give them an S. I feel inadequate in trying to grade art.

> I give all my kids S's. Satisfactory. Tia who is exceptionally good has gotten an E. Art should not be graded. It's a personal thing. Who am I to say? No one is going to tell me that my artwork is lousy, it may be great for me.

> I give Satisfactory to all students unless I think that they absolutely didn't [try]. If they really tried to be neat in what they did and they put it together as best as they could, then I say, "It's satisfactory." And then if I see that they really go out of their way to think about what they do, to be creative, then I say, "That was excellent."

> I don't know how you can evaluate art. If a child is following directions, then he will get an E. If he has completed a project, he gets an S. If he

> won't do it, then he gets a U. They have to experience some degree of creativity. It's not that this is wrong and this is right. It's a matter of how you want to do it. And that's fine. I try to avoid kids saying, "Whose looks better?" because art is a very personal thing. And if it's good enough for you and if you enjoy it and you're pleased with what you've done, then that's all that really counts. Especially when most of the students have no background in art. I myself do not have much of a background in art and I know I couldn't give a fair evaluation of it anyway.
>
> I have a bad time with E, S and U. If you have some natural ability, of course, your work is going to look better, isn't it? That probably isn't fair. If it satisfied you, if this is what you wanted to produce, then it's art. I don't mind giving them an E in handwriting when you can actually *see* that they form their letters very well. But in art I just give everybody an S.
>
> I am not critical of anything they do. I don't give any U's. I give E's to many students, because they produce terrific art.

The concerns about grading expressed by teachers are repeated with slight variation across different grade levels. With a purportedly accurate, objective grading system in academic subjects and in a competitive school environment, teachers manifested a strikingly egalitarian approach. Everybody who tried (note the emphasis on *motivation* rather than on *product*) was graded "satisfactory." Students who tried harder, who showed that undefined, unmeasurable extra, were graded "excellent." Students who did not try were graded "unsatisfactory." Teachers' beliefs that grading was unjust, teachers' concern about the effect on child's *personality* and attitude, and teachers' acknowledgement of their lack of qualification to evaluate creativity are remarkably nonauthoritarian, humble and humanistic. How different the approach in academic subjects where everything is assumed to be measured accurately with authority and rigor!

The reservations and barriers to grading art carry back to the teaching of it — the denial of criteria regarding children's works of art (the criteria can't be fully specified *a priori*; many teachers claim there are *no* criteria), the lack of conceptual approach to making, evaluating and thinking about art. The result is the well-intentioned but unfocused art lesson, where teaching is equivalent to presenting materials and directions.

Successful Students in the Arts

Who are the Tia's, the exceptional students of art lessons? All teachers I talked with emphasized the distinction between the good students in academic subjects and the good students in the arts. Nancy Dawson, RIP teacher:

> A good student is not necessarily a good writer. I have had "academically gifted" children before. They are about as creative as the door. I have a couple of children really good in art and academically very low. Linda, for example. Her parents have seen to it that she is being

expanded. She is the one who listens to Mozart. They go to the ballet. Her knowledge is a great deal more. She is good. She can draw beautifully. She thinks a lot, puts a lot of thought into her writing. She likes to write. And she does very well. I have another child who is very low in academics. But somewhere along the line someone has taught him to trace. He will put the paper over the picture and trace and trace. Somewhere along the line someone patted him on the head and said: "Good job, Jamie." And that's the only thing he has been successful at.

Nancy's words remind us that the low achievers in academic subjects are not necessarily the low achievers in art and the low achievers in art are not necessarily the low achievers in academic subjects. Verbal and numerical skills are irrelevant in the arts. As we heard in teacher interviews, motivation is primary. Art provides an arena where students with verbal disadvantages can succeed. Oftentimes, teachers say, art is the only place in school were they will get positive feedback. Judy Cervantes, a second-grade teacher, discussed the differences between the success in art versus academic subjects, touching on the different intelligences children possess and the importance of encouraging expression in different modes of presentation. Her compassion for students who don't succeed in the academics is evident:

> I don't think there is correlation between success in academic subjects and the arts. If they are very good students, they tend to take a little more time, be a little bit neater, but not necessarily to be more creative. I would say the ones who are the most creative are the ones who have problems expressing themselves verbally. I said to them this morning in science: "Now, I want you to draw me a picture." I thought Brian did pretty good. I could tell what he meant, even though he didn't say it with words. He has trouble expressing himself: he has problems reading. He tends to be a little on the shy side. And I have noticed that the bilingual kids are very expressive in colors, the bright and brilliant colors.

Perseverance and motivation are recognized as essential in both academics and the arts. Besides verbal and numerical skills, academics also require following directions and getting the right answer (or at least, the one espoused by the teacher). The arts, on the other hand, involve a dexterity that isn't taught. Teachers claim they don't know how to teach it. They also require creativity, originality, an ingenuity that transcended the mere following of directions. That "extra mile" teachers sometimes called it. It could not be prescribed *a priori*, but was recognized once it was there. Success in academic subjects appears not to require this creativity and originality. This is somewhat surprising in a society that celebrates these qualities. Who are our successful people? Is success in academics correlated with success in life? How do we define success? Old questions, but as relevant as ever.

Another important issue that came up in teacher interviews was acknowledgement of the variety of modes of expression and representation. Unfamiliar with Gardner's theory of multiple intelligences or with art education theories, teachers recognized children's drawings as pictorial devices that represent reality and reflect thinking. Validating children's achievements in art is recognized by teachers as an important educational goal. The research literature supports teacher intuitions. According to Silver (1982), children with inadequate language are deprived of many opportunities to represent their experiences. Without language, children lack a major device for constructing models of reality. When children's visuo-spatial capacities are intact, they may be able to construct visual models of reality and represent their experiences nonverbally through drawing.

Student Incentives: Contests and Prizes

What motivates students to learn or at least to comply with the requirements? The obvious thing, of course, is a dynamic common to all subjects. The teacher, even if kinder and gentler in art lessons, is still a figure of authority. Assignments are required and pupils comply with requirements. The mechanisms of the institutions, grades (even if they are not as specific or as valued as in the academics), detentions, and the like still exert a controlling force.

But at least for some students the arts, more than other subjects, stir a sense of pride, of ownership. Judy Cervantes told of choosing the pictures to be hung in the halls. Even though she was the one who chose the pictures, said Judy, children asked her to go see how the pictures looked framed and hung. Even when she hung the pictures in the classroom, students were sensitive to change of location. Other teachers told similar stories.

Self-criticism was prevalent too. Students were very conscious of the merit of their work. Students occasionally complained to me that their art wasn't any good or covered their artwork with their hands so I could not see it when I passed by. (Withdrawal, of course, could be related to their general level of confidence rather than purely to artistic abilities.) Others showed their artwork with a sense of pride. With or without teacher feedback, many formed their own judgment about their works.

External incentives consisted of hanging the better pictures on the walls of classroom and corridors. Interschool competitions bring money for the winners. For students looking forward to high school someday, participation in band and symphony carried a certain aura. There would be trips to faraway places. Ron Davison, the band director:

> I give them [first band] trips, like our marching band trip to Arizona. Those are rewards for hard work. We spent 9 days in Texas. I took them to the Houston Ballet, on a Riverboat ride, and to NASA. So we did a lot things besides marching in a parade. Those are things that kids will always remember. It's a reward for working hard all that time and for achieving that excellence. That's my way of rewarding the kids and I think the kids reward *me* by doing well.

Contests and prizes played similar roles in drawing public acclaim. Students and teachers dedicated time, thought and energies to produce a well-presented contest. The high school contest in Vermillion County drew students and their families to look at the winning works. Teen-aged students came with friends and large families (grandparents and parents, siblings) to show their own works of art and enjoy others. The organizer tells me, though, that every year there is a smaller crowd. Consequently, the organizers stopped distributing prizes at the contest site.

Teacher Beliefs About Art

We expect teacher beliefs about art to be intimately related to practice. Bringing these beliefs to light should help us understand what they do. I found several major beliefs to be repeated by almost all teachers.

Art as *Experience*:

> I think that anything that you do, that makes you think and makes you react, is art. Anything that causes a response in you. If you look at a painting and it makes you feel good, if you hear a song and it makes you feel happy, if you write a story and you are pleased with yourself. For me, art is a reflection of the inner self, it's yours or someone's else.

Art as *Personal Satisfaction*:

> If it satisfies you, then it's art, isn't it? That's always been my feeling. If this is what you wanted to produce, then it's art.

> We don't tell them that what they do is ugly or "not right." Because it's whatever they want to make of it.

Art as Promoting *Self-esteem*:

> I think it helps them feel better about themselves especially at this age level. I think it builds their self-esteem. It makes them feel positive, that they were able to do something on their own.

> I teach patterns so every kid can feel successful.

Art as *Self expression* and *Uniqueness*

> I try to teach my kids that they are unique human beings. And what they have to offer, no one else has to offer. You can do that through the arts.

These statements are consistent with teacher views regarding the grading of art, with their views of successful students in the arts. Prominent are the primacy of process (whether experience or release), the centrality of expressivity, the dominance of emotions, and integrity regarding the quality of the work. Implicit in what teachers said is the belief that creativity and expressiveness are natural and undirected. The artist's inner world is the *only* factor leading the activity. Most teachers did not refer to art as hard work, perseverance, and struggle, nor to the role of learning skills and experimenting with materials and ideas. These views fit with the lack of evaluation I observed in classrooms. If art is a *direct* expression of the inner self, based only on intentions or inborn talent, then it is indeed unfair to critique and judge.

Art education administrators should be aware of the consequences of this disavowal of cognitive skills. If there are no cognitive criteria, then it follows that there can be no intellectual progress, no learning. There was the inconsistency of teachers' recognition that we have better students and better works of art, yet they found it difficult to articulate criteria. The inconsistency lay in the two different contexts in which they used the word "better:" the perception of quality versus the articulation of what made it a quality work. That brought up a third context—expressing judgment without grounding it in how it could have been improved. When "better" is not an attribute of learning, teachers do not teach tools. Making art is seen as equivalent to art education.

There were exceptions to the themes I just presented. Joe Herbert, a second-grade teacher and professional artist himself, was only too aware of how much work and perseverance making art takes. In his classes he taught his students specific skills: how to look, how to draw. His second grade's bears looked and slept like bears.

Another exception, Martha Gaffnes, a third-grade gifted teacher with a rich background in the arts, stressed the importance of experimentation with materials. Occasionally, other teachers referred to skills in art, lamenting their lack of ability to teach them. "I feel inferior to teach them how to draw" said Michelle Little. And Nancy Dawson confided: "I would like to do more along the lines of true art, you know, about lines and depth. But I don't know. So I have to teach what I know." Most teachers did not know very much about art. Their college studies had not prepared them to teach art in the classroom.

Lines for the Gifted

The gifted program was different from most other classes in that teachers encouraged exploration and regarded process as the key. Unlike most other classroom teachers, gifted teachers expressed disdain of crafts. Mary Rose who claims to "hate dittos," told me, a gleam in her eye, that for Thanksgiving Day she relents and gives her children dittos of turkeys. The children are "in heaven" but she cautions them that this is not the way to do art. Martha Gaffnes elaborates on products versus process in art classes:

> When I do art, I try not to make it crafty. I don't like to make one and then have everybody copy what I do. Art is not making a cute little thing that the teacher made first or that she gave you a pattern to trace around. That might be fun. It might be following directions. I am not saying that these things are not worthwhile. But I think art is something else. I like the kids to *explore* a medium more than to have a product in art, the process is the most important thing to me. If we get something to put up, that's great. If we don't get anything put up, we've had this wonderful experience.

Jim Gholssen's art class for a fifth-grade gifted group exemplifies some of these explorations. While reading Jim's words one may imagine a background of fresh, attentive faces, pursed lips and concentrated expressions, the noises of crayons, an occasional giggle, a car passing outside, a secretary's voice popping in through the loudspeaker to announce a faculty meeting.

In the next few days, we're going to talk about lines, how lines make art. How lines make things other than art — writing, math — we make lines in everything we can think of. Look around this room for a minute. Look at all the different lines there are. This is a line, but it isn't straight. There's a line on that fish hook over there. Look how jaggedy this line is that makes up the set of books...

Today we are going to start experimenting with the different kinds of lines that we can make. I would like you to get out a pencil, a crayon (you only need one, preferably dark), a marker if you've got a marker. It can be flat or thin or both. And I am going to give you a craypa. We're going to experiment in making lines with these different colored craypas as well as our pencils and other things.

Now let's talk about these lines. There are a lot of different kind of lines. There are two basic groups of lines. There are lines that are *controlled* and the ones we *draw*. You guys draw lines every single day. What kind of controlled lines do we use every single day? Adam? When you write, exactly. All it is is a controlled line. Now, there also are free lines. Those are lines that don't follow a set pattern. They are not drawn with as much finesse or control. When you write in a minute, when you try to make controlled lines, you will probably be drawing like this and your wrist is going to be moving. But when we work on making free lines, I want you to kind of let your elbow, let your upper arm make those lines. You will feel the difference when you make them. No, no, no, don't stroke that fast. Try to draw one slowly and then quickly. Draw those. Do you feel a difference with the pencil? How does it feel differently to you? The crayon has a tendency to slide a little more than the pencil.

This lesson was unique in several aspects. It encouraged perception and thought, an awareness of the different qualities of lines. Jim related perceptions to technique, noting how one produces certain kinds of lines. The teacher presented a *guided* exploration. The exploration centered on a quality—lines—rather than on objects (e.g., turkeys, penguins).

Art History and Appreciation

Third-grade gifted students are sitting around a big art book, gazing at a reproduction of the Mona Lisa. Rose is the teacher.

Rick: Whenever I hear about painting, I always hear about the Mona Lisa. I think it is the most famous painting in the world.

Rose: It is very famous. I told you about the Louvre, this huge museum. It is very dark there. Well, in the Louvre, behind glass, they have the Mona Lisa.

Donna: The *real* one?

Rose: The real one.

Nancy: How much does it cost to get into the Louvre?

Rose: Oh, you only pay 2-3 dollars. That was to get to see the museum. You walk miles to see the Mona Lisa. But she is behind glass. And you will find this interesting [her voice rises]: you cannot take snaps.

Boys: Why not?

Rose: Why do you think?

Bob: You might, like, snap the Mona Lisa, and grab it, and sort of paint it, and people won't know what was what.

Rose: [Laughing good naturedly]: No, that won't do. If I would paint the Mona Lisa they would know it in two seconds.

Anne: You could not see it because of the sunlight.

Rose: No, that's not the reason either. It's not because of the glare of these pictures. They could probably care less about that.

Lauri: Because it might break the glass.

Rose: No. First of all, the light is a form of what?

Boys: Heat, heat.

Rose: [With an emphasis] A form of heat, of energy. Now, anytime you expose anything to energy, something changes. If I would take a picture and lay it in the sun, what would happen in two months? What would it be?

Nancy: It will look exposed.

Rose: What is the word I am looking for?

Some unsuccessful trials.

Rose: It will be *faded*. Everybody wants to see the Mona Lisa. If they let people take pictures, they estimate, put yours pens down, it will be an average of 60 flashes a minute. Now over the course of one week, how much of that light will go into the Mona Lisa? Quite a bit. It is precious so they are protecting it.

Now let's get to the next page. We are out of time. We talked about some of the things you can paint. You can paint still life, you can paint an outdoor scene with a landscape, you can paint portraits, you can paint themes from history and mythology. Long ago a lot of paintings had to do with religion. Now look [points at Van Gogh's *Starry Night*]. Here is the piece. We talked about artists painting barns and yards. Now look at this. This artist tried to show us an emotion. You know why we do art? Emotions are hard to see, you can't paint them. How would you paint Love? How would you paint Fear? How would you paint Sadness? Everybody would have a different way of painting; you don't know in advance. That's not how *I* would paint it. How would you paint Fear?

Linda: I would do eight different versions, all original.

Rose: How did the painter paint this? Isn't that pretty? And yet it would probably sell only for eight or ten million dollars. [leafing to the next page] Who is my favorite artist?

Five different attempts to pronounce Renoir's name.

Rose: This is a very, very famous painting by Renoir. Oh, listen, I saw this painting this summer. It is beautiful. The colors are still beautiful. No, let's look at the last one.

Oohs and ahh's. They look at a reproduction of a Degas.

Rose: Remember the man I told you about who was fascinated with ballet? He made sculptures. This is Edward Degas. Now what is that?

Voices: Impressionism.

Rose: You get the impression. Now, look how beautiful that is. He painted those ballerinas in reality. If you want to see the full difference between a *traditionalist* and an *impressionist*, how would a *traditionalist* paint?

Bruce: They painted very strict. The lines have to be perfectly straight. And they have to be perfectly in position. No curves.

Rose: Well, they painted it like it is. They painted exactly like it is. O.K.

Brian: Traditional painting is like realistic.

Rose: Impressionism means that this is *your* translation of the painting. I am going to take you kids to an art museum. I cannot imagine taking you to an art museum and saying: "Here is what you should see." I can tell you, here I see the technique, this is an Impressionistic painting, so you get the idea that this is what it is. That is *his* [the artist's] impression of this chapel. Your reaction to the painting is your impression. Everybody looks and see things differently.

Mrs. Rose was one of the teachers well known for her interest and involvement in the arts, described by Mr. Dole as "practically living in Krannert Performing Arts Center." When talking about "artsy" people, she was the first one to come to mind. She shared with peers and students her excitement about art, about museums and operas. Her class, too, was exceptional in that they were gifted students, the gifted and the motivated. Other teachers often commented, with a trace of envy, that gifted students were interested and enthusiastic about *everything*.

Not surprisingly, Mrs. Rose was the only classroom teacher I observed who included art history and appreciation in her lessons — not on a regular basis — now and then. Students seemed genuinely engaged in learning in this class, sharing reactions and thoughts, applying content to their personal experience. Children were exposed to great artists and diversity of styles. The notion of museums was made accessible and attractive.

The relativism in viewing and evaluating art that we encountered in studio art was manifested in Rose's room too. Rose said, for example, that she could not imagine telling children what to look for in a picture in a museum, confusing perhaps the personal reaction to a picture and the tools to scan it in terms of form, content, and skills. A second, related similarity between production and appreciation was the lack of cognitive tools with which to view and discuss a work or art. Teacher and students did not venture beyond the specific subject matter—church, dancers, fear—to *how* it was conveyed. They did not discuss how the painting expresses what we, as members within a culture, know about fear, dancers, and churches. There was no reference to technical or formal qualities of the artwork.

A Look from the Outside.

There was no reference to "aesthetic effects" (e.g., suggested effects and tricks).[5] In this lesson we observe students' misconception of concepts and ideas and teachers' lack of formal background which results in occasional inaccurate information.

Aesthetic Manifestations in the School

I talked with teachers about their classrooms. A Washington teacher:

> Look around this room. It's ugly blue paint. You know, when you look at our buildings, they are not very aesthetically pleasing. This school is not as bad as some of the others. Have you been in Danville High School? It's one of the ugliest buildings you would ever want to go in. They painted the hallways a sickening brown color. There is very little artwork put up. Utility: to make something that serves a function. You know what the hallway is for? To get kids up and down. It's not to display art work. And a classroom has windows in it because the State says so much light has to come in and so much fresh air. But it's all for utility. There aren't many designed to be pleasant.
>
> In the old schools, they tried to get across the idea of Gothic architecture. A lot of the older buildings in the United States are Greek or Romanesque. They tried to keep the classic types of architecture. We don't do that. Everything is very stark. There is no classic movement. If I were to design a school, I would make everything outside look classical because it conveys an idea. This is impressive. This is important. This is a special place. *This* school does not do that. There's nothing here that's special. It's just a long, flat box. Even the furniture is ugly. I think they could design children's desks and chairs to have more color. When the school board buys something, they want it to last 35 years. Maybe they could slap a coat of paint on it and it would be all right. If you could get something that was made to look attractive and in a few years it started to wear. ... Mr. Dole has tried to do a pretty good job here. I've worked in several other schools. He's made more of an effort than any other principal I know.

Joe Herbert, second-grade teacher:

> My room is in a state of confusion. It usually is. I have animal pictures and pictures of plants and things that we use in our art work. It's a colorful room. It's probably more eclectic than aesthetic. It's a conglomeration of things. We've got our fish. The dragon [points at a

---

[5]Suggested effects refer to "moods" and "motion" of inanimate objects and background. Tactics intensify an effect without really having anything to do with the effect. For example, the artist arranges light so that the shadow falls upon the face of a sad person. A specific kind of tactic is reinforcers, where features of the work that are not on the object being discussed, reinforce, by contrast or concordance, an effect of that object. For example, a bright background might intensify a figure's sadness by contrast, or a dark one intensify it by concordance (Perkins, 1983).

magnificent dragon crawling all over the walls] has been with me for about eight years. It goes wherever I go. We did bears last week. I put items up that students can use for reference. But otherwise I tend to keep them halfway organized and somewhat bare because I don't want a lot of distractions. Everything here is more or less functional. And everything in here is in a state of motion. Every month things move out, are sent home. Throughout the month we build up the new room. With the exception of the reference pictures.

A Bank in Danville

Aesthetic manifestations were revealed in the interior design of a classroom or library, in a well-arranged set of plants, more often in teacher dress.

Occasionally, I observed well-developed dramatic form in a lesson, like Joe Herbert's language lesson. It had a nice introduction, development to a climax, and then resolution. Nancy Dawson's poetry lesson was an aesthetic beholding. Michelle Little called children's attention to the snow settling on trees; Mary Harwood, to feelings evoked by Vivaldi's music. Mary Rose shared enthusiasm for pictures and museums, bringing to class the artistic calendars she had purchased. Occasionally, a teacher would refer to a television show (the Winter Olympics was referred to several times; Masterworks was mentioned). These aesthetic manifestations were the exceptions rather than the rule. Beauty was not a regular part of school routine. In all my observations, teachers rarely drew attention to beauty, in or out of school.

On two occasions, teachers drew my attention to Danville's Credit Union bank, insisting that I should visit it, mentioning the delicate china and pictures displayed in the entrance hall. The difference between the schools and other public buildings is striking. Wondering about the scarcity of aesthetic experiences in the schools, I asked teachers about aesthetics in their own lives. Two were among the "artistic" teachers in the school, the rest professed little or no background.

The Arts in the Lives of Teachers

Judy Cervantes, second-grade bilingual teacher:

> I don't have enough music background. I do sing in church. I do sing in choir, that type of thing.

Elizabeth Wilson, fifth-grade:

> I draw. Mostly in the summers. We hung one of my etchings, but most of the time I just throw them away. I just thought that they didn't have any great value. I like to draw. It's more like doodling with me. Pictures are important to me. In Indianapolis, the library rented paintings. You could rent them on your library card just like a library book. And keep them home for a month. That's why we never purchased any, because we would just get them from the library. We would look at it for two or three weeks and then trade it for another one. I would pick scenic and subdued colors. That's just what I like.

Nancy Dawson, second- and third-grade:

> You know, as a little girl I wanted to be a ballerina. When I was 30 years old I took a ballet class with a friend of mine, because we were never able to do it as children. It nearly killed us but we enjoyed it so much. It was something that I always wanted to do. [I asked her why she stopped.] Oh, time, money. I love museums. Sometimes I drive to Chicago. I get lost, I escape in them. Art museums and other types of museums. Any kind.

Joe Herbert, second-grade:

> I listen to music first thing in the morning. Mornings for me—I am up at 5—are a fairly tense time. I have a lot going on in the morning. It relaxes me to have the music easing the mood. I have paperwork to set up, I have lesson plans to set up, at home I have my animals to take care of. And, I don't know, music just seems to make things easier. Most of what I like is either 50s or 60s rock, Elvis, the Beach Boys, Iron Butterfly, Beatles. I am not picky. But my preference is classical.

Many teachers were involved in a variety of art activities, drawing, making crafts, performing in community theaters, singing in churches, in local chapters. Mary, a kindergarten teacher, for example, had been in Danville "Sweet Adelines" for 14 years. A single mother raising three children and working full-time, she still found time to go every Monday and sing. "How were you able to do it?" I asked her. "That was the only thing I did for myself," she answered. And when I saw her performing in a vocal quartet the following Monday, after a long day at school, eyes glowing, I got a sense of how nourishing and nurturing music is for her. A number of classroom teachers told me that when in college they wanted to major in drama or in art. At some point they realized that their drama/art skills were not exceptionally good compared with others or that teaching was a more dependable way of making a living.

Equality, Values, and Compartmentalization

I sensed a clash in Danville, a clash between the aesthetics in the classrooms and the aesthetics in teachers' lives. It puzzled me. It continues to intrigue me. Towards the end of my observations, I prodded this issue. Why, for example, didn't teachers talk in class about their favorite television programs? Teachers said they didn't feel comfortable talking about programs that not all students can watch. Some parents, they explained, did not let children make viewing decisions. I sensed a concern for equality, a concern about not giving to anybody if one can't give to everybody. And a concern about not provoking parental anger. We talked about drawing on other resources — the performances which everybody had watched, like the Opera and Dance in Krannert. Follow-up class discussions centered on personal preferences. The "I liked that" comment sometimes touched on content or effects such as costumes or confetti. Rarely, if ever, did form, rhythm, or expression enter the commentary. Teachers and children did not have the vocabulary and the appropriate conceptualizations needed for arts education. It struck me that teachers might not even be aware that they didn't have it. Sharing enthusiasm and love, reading poems, talking about favorite books and television shows were not seen as important. They ran counter to the pressure for academics, the pressure for achievements. It seemed that the system pulls towards compartmentalization— of personal life versus the curriculum. In the absence of analytic tools to help bridge the gap, teachers are more reluctant to cross it.

A related issue is the issue of values. A few teachers claimed they felt vulnerable in bringing up controversial matters in class. Fear of parental anger is a restricting factor. Few venture beyond what is accepted by all. Bringing up the controversial engages personal beliefs and vision. It also has to do with one's role and self identity in the classroom and with the way that administrators, parents, the larger community see the role of the teacher. The risks are large.

Even though many teachers do have rich aesthetic experiences outside the school, they seem not to influence what happens in the classroom. In my observations, I tried to find examples of school and society values on the one hand and teacher skills and conceptualizations on the other hand interacting to create arts education. The many themes in this case study are related: overriding institutional priorities on academics and good behavior reflected in the reward system of the schools, the pressure for academics and grading, the detachment of arts from academics, the distancing of the various arts themselves and the compartmentalization of art and life. Teachers learn to compartmentalize their "extracurricular" life and their professional roles. The pressure for academics and the "prizes" and rewards are important in determining what teachers focus on and what they choose not to focus on.

We should marvel at the exceptions. Joe Herbert's language arts lesson, guided by aesthetic principles with a dramatic structure, introduction, development, climax and ending, is one. Even though everything around him tells him to go for a simple fact-response, staccato form, Joe created a meaningful artistic lesson. He did it intuitively. When I tried, after the lesson, to elicit from him goals, rationale, purposes for what he had done, he said little about any of these. There were the teachers who provide a few minutes per day or per week of quiet and not-so-quiet time, allowing students to experiment, whether with movements, sounds or lines, exposing themselves to potential criticism of others for being different, for not conforming to direct, pre-specified goals. The school seems to be a place of measurable achievements and their evaluation—a work place *par excellence*. Perhaps, and I emphasize the *perhaps*, the compartmentalization of work and life isn't as necessary as we make it. Perhaps that future versus present-oriented approach isn't all necessary.

Coda

This study attempted to portray *what was*. At the same time, like quantum mechanics, it influenced to some extent Danville's arts education. The more superficial, universal and ephemeral instances occurred when teachers who knew in advance that we were coming would specially prepare and do the best things they could think of. All of us want to appear at our best when someone special is watching. Examining what people see as their best can be as instructive and illuminating as examining a "typical" behavior.

But I want to talk a moment about profound, longer term influences. Take one incident: when observing Jim Gholssen's class, he stopped to point a finger at me, saying:

> It's a good thing that she [the researcher] is here this year, because she is forcing a lot of us teachers to think more about art and to do some things which we sadly neglect.

Another instance: Friday morning. Passing in the corridor, I decided on impulse to drop in Nancy Dawson's class, even though I knew well that I wouldn't find anything related to art. I was greatly surprised to see Nancy and children in the midst of a Frost poem. Nancy told me two weeks earlier that:

> I am really weak in the poetry area. I myself am not really interested a great deal in poetry. Maybe because I've never had a really good appreciation of it.

"What's going on?" I asked Nancy, puzzled and baffled. She explained that after the interview (in which I asked her about the activities she conducted in class—no suggestions on my part, just listening), she started to think about what she *could do* in the class. She found this book of poems that she liked a lot, tried it the following week, and it worked. Children loved it, she loved it.

The mere presence of somebody who is interested in the arts and the names of the NEA or University of Illinois carry a special weight, providing a catalyst for thinking and for trying to do one's best. This presence, so small compared with the other pressures for achievement in the academics and problems of discipline, was enough to motivate some teachers to reflect, to design, and carry out that design. I find this immensely encouraging. The resources are so often there: many motivated teachers who are personal witnesses of the special power of art; an abundance of materials, ranging from quality television programs, through museums, festivals, community performances; children that are receptive, even enthusiastic, when given the opportunity to engage with art in a meaningful way—when there is legitimization to stop, to smell, to listen, to explore.

And so, we examine our dreams. What do we value mostly in ourselves? What do we want to become? We try to have a glimpse of the riches that life has to offer us: to hear more, see more, perceive more, feel more—an aesthetic experience which touches the subtleties and beauty beyond the simple boxes of numbers and other useful categories. In this report, we looked at what's current, at some of the barriers and the problems. This is not an ending. Hopefully, it is a pause to think of what all of us can do—and what to do next.

Chapter 4:
Armstrong Elementary School Chicago, Illinois

■ *Liora Bresler*

The Arts in a Chicago School

Chicago came after Danville. The differences between the town and the city were glaring. Chicago: rich in cultural events, a population of poor children over-represented in public schools; teacher-caring amid the isolation and alienation of the crowd; the sense of belonging and community of the multitude of ethnic races, living along and beside each other. Much of this richness and poverty was reflected in the school in arts instruction.

As with every other site I have observed, Chicago had much to notice and study. But here the voices seemed louder, more urgent, insistent: the voices of participants as well as of events. In Chicago, I sensed tension that I did not feel in Danville; tension, unfocused but sustained. It edged a large expression of welcome, invitation. It seemed too unconscious to be a product of the (then) recent Chicago *Tribune*'s sensationalized "Worst Schools in the Country" report (1987).

Teachers were of all types, covering the spectrum, but with more outliers than in the small town: the inspired and artistic, the drained and hopeless. There were many of deep commitment, in the school reality day in and day out, enduring and fighting frustrations with little positive feedback from outside the building.

Altogether I spent 12 days at Armstrong Elementary School—the first in October, 1988, the last in June, 1989. I observed 23 classes taught by 22 teachers, two artists-in-residence, and a group of student teachers from a neighboring college. With the children, I attended a variety of performances including school programs and their rehearsals. Principal, teachers, performers, parents, artists-in-residence, janitors, cooks, and students switched hats of interviewees, hosts, and colleagues for the moment. The distance from my home affected the data collection. Whereas Danville was within an easy 45 minute drive, Chicago was 3 to 5 hours (depending on traffic) each way. Staying overnight released evenings for leisurely, sometimes wee-hour conversations with teachers and community people, complementing the hectic pace and rapidly changing foci and activities of the earlier parts of the day.

As different as Chicago was from Danville, I found myself on a sequel, continuing where I left off. Danville's emergent themes — conflicting paradigms of teaching, discrepancy between arts as a discipline and arts education—gained weight and substance. I increasingly became more concerned about the implications of what I saw. With the widening scope of vision came a more pressing urge to portray as many realities as I could, as well as to arrive at some over-arching interpretations, continuing the quest for meanings and possibilities in education.

"Arts curriculum" is often said as if the term stands for one entity. I found that even when we took one art form (and the differences among the varied arts in the school are great), there existed a myriad of curricula and activities. Because it did not conform to the "academics," there was more freedom in regard to required content. Traditional curricular organizers—curriculum guides, textbooks, tests—scarcely existed. As in Danville, music textbooks were to be found. They were infrequently used, a source of songs to sing, some technical nomenclature, seldom used for cognitive development or music appreciation. There was little official consensus (and, so far, little effort invested in arriving at such consensus) on what should be taught, on what should constitute the core of art teaching. From a distance as well as close, thinking about the arts promoted diversity. As a result, the school system offered little guidance and imposed few constraints on teachers to conform to some agenda. Arts' instruction territories were open for teachers and artists to navigate and explore.

Armstrong School

Armstrong Elementary School is one of 471 elementary schools in Chicago. Altogether, there are 595 public schools housing 28,675 teachers and 419,537 students. The city is divided into 21 school districts. Many differences among the 21 districts of Chicago are rooted in socioeconomic differences. There are parallel differences in student achievement as conventionally measured.

Sociologist Robert Havighurst (1964) divided the Chicago schools into four types: high status schools, main-line schools, common-man schools and inner city schools. The common-man type, in which Armstrong fits, shows a great internal diversity in student body, parental cooperation and home background. The student population tends to be less academically oriented and less inclined to identify with the school and its personnel. The school is attended by a large percentage of first or second generation foreign-born and/or Spanish-speaking and Afro-American children.

Teachers considered Armstrong—unlike many common-man schools—a desirable place to work. High on teachers' priority lists in choosing a work place is the proximity to home. Located on the north side of the city, Armstrong School is conveniently close to the suburbs in which many teachers lived—Skokie, Park Ridge and Lincolnwood among others.

Armstrong was average in size for the district, housing 780 students in grades K-8. There were 37 certificated faculty members—principal, vice-principal and teachers. Out of these were 11 Afro-American faculty members (including the vice-principal), nine Jewish teachers (including the principal), two East-Indian and one Hispanic teacher. Minority students comprised 74% of the school population. Afro-Americans were most populous at 40%, followed by Hispanics (the most rapidly rising population) at 20% and East Indians at 13%. Fifty percent of the students were entitled to free or reduced price lunches. About 70% of the parents were single parents. I heard teachers talk about a family unit sometimes consisting of mother and grandmother living together.

The school was founded in 1913. Veteran teachers remembered more glorious days of over 20 years earlier when the school population consisted mostly of neighboring Jewish students from affluent homes. School reputation was high. The past 21 years were declining years for the school. Student population underwent dramatic changes. Many of the better educated and more affluent moved to the suburbs. Private and magnet schools attracted many of the rest. Now in 1989, average and below average students predominated. When, after 21 years, the previous principal retired, some of the veteran teachers left with him. His replacement, Dr. Arline Hersh, became principal in the fall of 1987.

Although Chicago Schools had been admonished as "worst in the country," Armstrong School was currently shown to have student achievement test scores at national norms. The principal initiated a variety of special programs in an effort to recruit more of the "better students" of Chicago. In her "Going Beyond Average" program, for example, each grade level had three ability levels. The highest level, housing approximately one third of the students in the school, was the local equivalent of the "gifted" program. To be included in that category, a student had to be at or above grade level (on Iowa test scores) and recommended by the teacher. A related initiative, the "Option Program," consisted of two special teachers (one for "creative language art," the other for "critical thinking") who taught in the "high tracked" second through sixth grades once a week. In addition to providing "enrichment," the specialists released the homeroom teacher to teach another class in her/his specialized subjects: social studies, music, art, or math.

As far as art offerings are concerned, Chicago was different from Danville in its in-school as well as out-of-school resources. One of the first things to become apparent was the wealth of possibilities Chicago has to offer—performances as well as curricular programs. Many were free, others required special efforts. Writing proposals and making telephone calls, Hersh actively drew on these resources. Whole classes were bused to museums, operas, and theater houses. Chamber ensembles and artists-in-residence from a variety of institutions regularly came into the school to perform and present workshops.

That wealth of programs and opportunities of the big city contrasted sharply with the absence of music or arts specialists in the schools. Danville had music specialists and classroom teachers who were "expected" to teach art and contribute to the "hall exhibition." At Armstrong, classroom teachers were expected (expectations being rather loose) to integrate music and art into the curriculum. Whereas in Danville's Washington School, music and art lessons constituted the majority of the arts that school children were exposed to, in Armstrong the outside resources shaped students' art experiences.

As indicated in the introduction, the division between inside and outside school resources became an important conceptual organizer of this case study. That difference, I believe, carries beyond performers and artists-in-residence to researchers, scholars and administrators in national foundations, state departments, research and teaching universities. The question of which type of resources is a better investment depends on whether we espouse an Archimedean model in which things can be easily moved from the outside or a Michanhausen model, which emphasizes movement from within. In this case study we see the unique and essential role of both.

Music

Spring Time is Playing Time

9:12 a.m. The school day has just begun. The freshness of a new day is punctuated with the Pledge of Allegiance and the National Anthem. The 22 kindergartners seat themselves in semi-circled rows on the soft carpet. It's song time, and the song today is about spring.

"What is the season we have right now?" asks Gail Lowenfeld, the kindergarten teacher, from the piano. "Spring" resonate the 22 children. Lowenfeld: "I am going to sing this; we'll sing it together; and then I want you to put in your own words." Accompanying herself with simple, sturdy tonic-dominant chords, she sings: "Springtime is garden time." The short four lines completed, she motions to the class and they all join. The melody is clear and accurate. The piano, a bit on the loud side, nearly covers the small voices, but there is energy and rhythm as they chant.

Lowenfeld: "What else is springtime?" Joseph volunteers, "Rain," and another chord precedes the next version: "Springtime is rainy time." The next suggestions include "Hot" and "Cold." Lowenfeld cautions, "Let's not only talk about the weather. What do we do in the spring? What do you see kids doing outside?" "Planting time." "Playing time." And they sing, "planting time," then "playing time."

Joshua offers, "Swimming." Lowenfeld: "I don't think swimming. What season is swimming?" "Summer." "Summer. It's not quite summer yet." Chris suggests "morning." Lowenfeld: "Don't we have mornings in other seasons? Winter? Summer? Fall?" An awkward moment for Chris, but attention soon drifts elsewhere. "What do we think of when we think of spring?" "Springtime is sun time." [Lowenfeld with emphasis] "Sunny time! Right." And there goes another verse. "Julia." "Sunny time." "We just mentioned that. Jason." "Snow." "No, what season is snow time?" A chorus of voices: "Winter."

"Okay, what are some of the activities you do outside when you're playing? Springtime is park time, isn't it?" With children nodding, they go for another verse. The next suggestion is "riding bikes." Lowenfeld: "Well, we mentioned parks. What else do you do besides ride bikes in spring?" Lynn suggests, "Visit friends." Lowenfeld: "Springtime is visiting time? Okay." (More singing.) Carlos suggests, "Ball time." "Ball time, right. Now, some places you can go in the spring, summer, winter, and fall. You don't go to the park in those seasons." Brittany suggests, "Picnic time." Lowenfeld: "Picnic time. That's a good one." (More singing). Phillip: "Springtime is real hot." Another suggestion of picnic time. And so on, for 5 more minutes, until 9:25, when spring gives over to the alphabet.

In-School Resources

There is much repetition in the description above. There is much repetition in classroom life. And in music. As we read classroom descriptions, we are confronted with the fact that our tolerance level for repetition in real life situations is much different from repetition in text (granted its two dimensional nature, lacking expressions, sounds and movements). Music, perhaps, lies somewhere in between. The nine repetitions of the musical verse, identical in all planned aspects (melody and rhythm) and nearly identical in the unintended ones (articulation, loudness, agogics) are within our tolerance limits. It is the *words* that need some change. And here it is that children are invited to add their own input, to insert a travelling adjective into the song.

Remember, Lowenfeld is a kindergarten teacher, not a music specialist. The music educator in me notes that the children are ready for further development: their second and third verses of the song sounded secure and accurate enough. The teacher could have added some complexity by including contrasting elements of dynamic (loud versus soft), offering an alternative phrasing (breathing points), adding some instrumentation (such as clapping hands or thumping feet) or harmony (a different chord). She could have added a simple variation to the melody or the rhythm. The fact that she did not do any of these things at any point, that day or during the year, that she did not mention them as part of her goals and future plans, is a manifestation that her sensitivities were oriented to the verbal more than the musical domain. Thus, the pedagogical focus of the springtime song came from a framework other than music.

The kindergarten class received more music by far than any other class in the building. It came at a time of the day when the children were fresh and alert. Gail Lowenfeld was one of the "musical forces" in the school. She could play the piano and, thus, was an important asset to school performances and programs. She provided her class with an accurate exposure and production to basic levels of pitch, melody, rhythm and harmony. In kindergarten, music activities were a common starter for many school days: singing familiar songs, learning new ones like the one we have just heard, or doing movement songs (e.g., "Ring Around the Rosie" or "Hokey Pokey"). Teacher skill was one reason for the almost unique presence of music in kindergarten. The fact that even Lowenfeld was not conscious of the many musical possibilities is an indication that attention to musical parameters is typically not part of thinking, of education, even for those with musical background.

The legitimacy of nonverbal (visual, kinesthetic and musical) activities for this age group was a second important factor. In a later section, we will talk more about the pressure for academics and its influence in preempting the arts even when teachers are skilled and interested, legitimizing the lack of art when they are not.

Mostly listening. Little music found its way into the regular school schedule. Most teachers said that they did not teach music because they could not sing or play. Trudy Garfield, a first-grade teacher:

> Music? I don't sing. We play records once in a while but that's it.

Molly Leonard, a seventh-grade teacher:

> We can't have the classroom teachers teach music because they don't have the background and they aren't interested. Unless they have a beautiful voice, they're like the little child that can't function.

Few teachers include music as part of the regular curriculum. But there are bits here and there, "fun songs" at the beginning of the day or on Friday afternoon in Shari Jacob's fourth-grade class, "when she feels like it." Listening to music happens occasionally. Molly Leonard:

> We have music appreciation, listening, in the classroom, by way of the radio. I try to include it during lunch time when they are eating. It doesn't always work because they want to talk. If the radio is on, they want to turn to *their* favorite music. Sometimes on Monday, Wednesday and Friday, the last 15 or 20 minutes of the hour is for recreation or reading. I try to include some classical music at that time.

Listening to classical music had been institutionalized earlier. At one time, music was piped in during lunchtime from the office throughout the building, classrooms and halls. I asked, "Why listen to music?" Leonard:

> I think it's good. It just adds. I enjoy classical music although we know that young people don't appreciate it. They don't really know its importance. They say music has a way of soothing the beast in man, so I try to think in terms of soothing the beast in man at that time. Lunch time is such a free time. That's the one time you don't say, "Don't talk," but "Keep it down, keep it low." Listening is kind of difficult.

Although there had not been music and art specialists in Chicago schools for many years, teachers still felt it was "taken from the school." Most teachers agreed that music should be part of the curriculum but contended that it should be taught by specialists. The music that occurred was typically done by people with specialized musical backgrounds, as we shall see in the following section, or by student teachers expected to include music in their activities, as the following case shows.

Integration of Music and Art. *Integration* was a word often used around the school, mostly meaning integration of the arts with the academics but sometimes integration of the different arts among themselves. The following lesson was presented by a student teacher, one of several who visited the school during the academic year. In this lesson, effort and pre-planning were invested in doing something special, something festive. The messages conveyed about the content of music and art and the kind of integration between them are typical to many other arts lessons taught by classroom teachers.

Friday, October 14, 1:00 pm. Trudy Garfield's first graders are back from lunch. Garfield, in the center, announces in a beaming voice: "Ms. McHenry has something *fun* that we don't usually do in school." Ms. McHenry, the student teacher, takes over the central place: "How many remember the Columbus song from last time?" Eagerly, all students raise their hands. McHenry closes the door so the singing won't disturb other classes. A chorus of "Autumn leaves are falling down" follows.

Now to the new project. "In order to do this, everybody has to be quiet. Heads on hands. I just want you to listen." The tape runs, bringing noise of ghosts, wind, then screams. Towards the end, McHenry distributes a "ditto" featuring a dainty, sad-looking ghost flying amidst Halloween pies and a simplified-sketch house. The tape announces that the lights are off, then ends abruptly with a shriek.

McHenry: Where do you think we were?

Children: Haunted house.

McHenry: How did you know that you were in a haunted house? I want you to picture it.

Children volunteer: Trees, screaming, wind blowing, rains, vampires.

McHenry: Let's pretend we all went into this haunted house. Use the sheet in front of you.

The light is on. They start the next song. It is short—four lines—and relatively simple, revolving around a major chord with a span of a seventh at its widest. Composed by McHenry's music teacher in college, the words go like this:

> *Spooky shapes, cats and owls,*
> *Listen to the wild dogs howl.*
> *Witches fly, in the sky.*
> *Tricks and treats and pumpkin pie!*

McHenry sings it twice in an off-pitch tune with correct rhythmic patterns. A group of four chosen children echoes, then several other groups, each with correct rhythmic pattern and off-pitch. The children are chosen on the basis of good behavior—thus, singing is presented as a prize of sorts. Jack, disruptive, is the one exception. It works. Jack straightens up and looks more alert for the following few minutes. Singers are asked to stand up, their posture in accordance with their central position. With five repetitions, the song gains familiarity.

Integration with visual art occurs as the students are asked to color the ditto sheet. Slowly and patiently they work, careful to stay within the lines. Red, for blood, is the predominant color. McHenry's "Oh, Beatrice, very nice" (when the girl comes to show her finished product) contrasts with the flat intonation in which it is uttered. A few more children approach and are praised similarly. No feedback for the ones who stay in their places. Interestingly, most students do not solicit feedback for their music activities. I hypothesized: Either because they are not used to it (few music experiences in the school) or because they may identify less with the product because it's a group product.

There are points of similarity in these two music classes. In the hands of the non-specialist, music is taught in a transition period—beginning or end of the day, after lunch. The content consists of learning to sing a simple song. Teacher skills and the availability of materials (e.g., piano, record player) shape the content as well as the quality of music provided. In the kindergarten lesson, the piano functioned as a pitch corrector. In the Halloween lesson, the teacher's untrained voice was the major teaching aid around which the activity revolved, with the tape for additional effects. Lacking the more sophisticated musical parameters of the kindergarten class, the problems in McHenry's class concerned the basic parameter of pitch. The question of high quality musical content for students remained in both classes.

Halloween was treated in a schematized manner, centering on widely used symbols (the same symbols that provided the basis for integration) whether on ditto sheets or in songs. Such treatment was typical of most arts activities. Seldom did I hear, from parents or teachers, other expectations or visions of what arts education could and should be.

Integration With Other Subjects. Teachers often said they did not have time to teach music separately. The principal and teachers talked about trying to integrate the arts with other subjects. Molly Leonard, seventh-grade teacher:

> Music and art are part of the curriculum all teachers are expected to teach. You don't always have time to do it. If you want to teach music or art, you have to teach it included in another subject.

When I asked her for specific examples she said:

> Sometimes (it depends upon the curriculum) the writer or the illustrator has depicted music or art as a part of that curriculum, perhaps as a culminating activity. Then you can work it in.

Even when pressed for clarification, she gets no more specific than that.

Edna Rice, an eighth-grade teacher, integrated music into social studies. Hers was rather sophisticated, prodding cultural and political contexts:

> Every week, I try to do something with music. It may not be a 40-minute period of time. I try to integrate it. What I try to do is incorporate information about composers into the period of time. We discuss what people were doing during this particular period of time. "Why do you think this music came about?" This was very revolutionary. In this modern electronic time it's hard to understand that in the past we didn't have Moog synthesizers. You can't just study historical events without knowing what comes before, during, and after.

Rice had a reputation as an excellent and firm teacher. Her musical background and interests were above average. "All the way through my life, music has been of vital importance to me." She tells me she went to a high school that was outstanding in music. She had a very good piano teacher who taught her about composers. Her parents had a great love of music.

Classroom Teachers with Music Background. The lack of music education was acknowledged by the principal. She had assigned two classroom teachers with specialized background in music to teach several other classrooms. We will now visit two classes taught by these teachers, one a third-/fourth-grade group in the teacher's homeroom, the second, a sixth-grade class.

Wednesday, 1:13 p.m. Mary Ann King's third graders and Eve Gratton's fourth graders are assembled in Gratton's room, decorated with Miro's *Child and Dog* and other bright pictures. On the piano, in the far left corner, an assortment of music sheets and textbooks: *Discovering Music Together* by Charles Leonhard, Margaret Fullerton and others; the teacher edition of Richard's *Music;* and Silver Burdett *Music,* (all for third graders); a record by Pete Seeger; *American Folksongs;* the *Readers' Digest Children's Songbook.* Arranged in rows in the one room are 63 children now. From her place near the window, King watches her class. There is no need to say anything. Eye contact is enough.

Gratton is at the piano, playing "Remember That," to quiet attentiveness. The two eighth graders who enter with printers and a computer withdraw to the background after the first few seconds. As Gratton is playing, children are humming the melody. Then they start with full force. Obviously, the song is well-known and much loved. Gratton's accompaniment, always from the music sheet, is soft (all the better, I write in my log, because the piano's sound is rather poor and many notes are missing). The singing is a bit chaotic. They start again, this time more slowly. Gratton conducts with delicate movements, her accompaniment is barely audible, more a reminder of pitch. She commands: "Second time, a little louder," and they repeat five times altogether. By now the singing is musical, there is articulation, change in dynamics. The sixth time, it is sung in canon, a round, with the children divided into two groups. The harmonies get more sophisticated. Gratton sings the refrain: "Please, oh, please, don't make me go to school, I never thought of you as cruel." It is a long song, well beyond the four traditional lines. It is well done.

Occasional disruptions occur—another computer coming in, children needing to go out for speech class, a janitor entering, a disciplinary remark here and there ("Erica, if you put your necklace down, I will be real happy.")—but seem marginal to the concentration of the singers.

1:23. Gratton opens her bag and takes out a new music book for a new song. In a small, delicate voice she sings in a C major key: "Hello, hello, hello. We welcome you today. We'd like to sing a song or two. . ." With the exception of a few in squeaky chairs, children are quiet and attentive. Gratton repeats and now it's the children's turn. Few are silent, most are singing. Gratton: "May I make a suggestion?" and goes to Jeff in the first row, makes a Kodály movement and says: "A little softer." Another repeat. Children's voices are clear and energetic. Gratton repeats the difficult passage with the high notes. Some students are saying the words rather than singing them here, four students are gazing at their fingers, one at the wall, but almost everybody else seems to be involved and singing. When they sound comfortable with separate lines, they try for the whole song.

1:28. Gratton: "Let's do something old." Children jump up, wave their hands. All are eager to suggest names of songs. Gratton: "Let's start with 'Chickery Chick.'" From now through the rest of the lesson she provides an anticipatory chord, then it's *a cappella.* They sing with relish. She conducts faster and they get excited, their singing a bit out of control. Gratton: "It really sounds like a lot of chickens." In the next few minutes, Gratton chooses different songs from the small library on top of the piano, at one time consulting with King. The next song is "A Spoonful of Sugar" from *Mary Poppins*, the piano adjusting tempo and phrasing to the lively mood. "All night, All day" is followed by the quieter "Pray the Lord." There is variety and contrast in the choice of repertoire: quick and slow, lively and mellow. At one point, Gratton demonstrates the difference between two musical sentences. In each new song, the children's singing is somewhat cacophonous but with voices quiet and cultured, the effect is not jarring. At 1:40 it is time to leave. King's 33 students take their chairs with them to their room. Until Monday.

* * *

Eve Gratton—a second generation American from Italy—holds a baccalaureate in Music Education (piano) and a master's degree in Education. She decided she did not want to be a music teacher because there are no music specialists in the Chicago elementary schools. She did not enjoy teaching the older age group as much as the younger. Gratton is teaching music to this group half an hour twice a week. The collaboration with King was going well:

> We started out with an assembly at Christmas. We work on things together. I would not want to [work with 63 children in one room] without another adult. We both have our classes trained pretty well. It wouldn't work with all groups. With music they have to *want* to participate.

Gratton also teaches music to a second grade and another third grade, each once a week. Not all the teaching is successful:

> It works beautifully in one room but in the other room I really can't teach music. Too disruptive! I have tried various things and I have used the VCR. I'm bringing stories on the cassette player and filmstrips. The last time, I taped part of "Peter Pan." They were even chaotic watching that! Now toward the end of the year I can't teach music in that classroom anymore. They need so much training that in 40 minutes it's impossible to do anything. It's really very defeating. I want to go in and do music but I can't. Also, there isn't a piano in there. You could do a lot of things with note reading and even listening. But you have to have a group that's behaving.

There is a correlation between tracking and discipline. The second-grade children to whom Gratton is teaching music, as well as Gratton's own, are high tracked. The troublesome third grade was low tracked. The special relationship between a class and its homeroom teacher was an important factor in the quality of music lessons. The availability of a piano was still a third. All play a role when we try to understand different lessons by the same teacher.

Talking about goals and practices, Gratton highlighted enjoyment, appreciation and exposure to a variety of styles, including classical:

My goals in music are that they enjoy it, that they have an appreciation of music, and learn that they *can do* it. Also, to expose them to opera and orchestras, so it won't be strange. You don't have to like it but you should know about it. Without knowledge, there is no love, as they say. It takes knowing to like something.

I start with my own songs, songs that are appealing to them, fun things. I *ad lib* it. About halfway through the year, if I feel that the group is pretty good, I'll try some part singing, starting out with rounds. Just two verses, very simple. I teach it by rote. Everyone learns one melody, then I teach everyone the second melody. I divide the room in half and have them try this line and the other try that line. It isn't the easiest thing to do. You can try it with a tape recorder, let them hear how the harmony sounds. What they have to do is concentrate on their own part and not try to listen to the other part. It is a good experience. If time would permit, I would like to go into music where they start learning notes. With 60 children in the class, it is too hard to pass out worksheets and do that.

Gratton's practice reflected that of the professional music teacher. Even with popular songs, she evidenced a high level of sophistication regarding musical form, harmony and tone. Her background was not unique. Since music education jobs were being cut, many music teachers with general teaching credentials found themselves homeroom teachers. It is interesting to note that the music specialists in Danville had general teaching certificates as well as advanced music education degrees. They all told me that if their positions were cancelled, they could still be classroom teachers. Their specialization, though, comes in handy, especially at Armstrong where the principal assigned them to teach music to other classes. Lessons were guided by musical goals and attention paid to musical parameters. Two related issues—teaching art to "low-track" classes and the role of the regular classroom teacher when an in-school or out-of-school specialist comes in—will be dealt with later.

The second music specialist brought in advanced aspects of music—theory and jazz. These aspects are less common than those we have just observed. Let us now go to the other side of the third floor corridor where Charles Brophy, a sixth-grade teacher on weekdays, a percussionist in a jazz group on weekends, is teaching music to a sixth-grade class other than his own.

Jazz and Theory for Sixth Graders

1:52 p.m. Brophy enters with a boy carrying a heavy record player. Brophy: "Last time we listened to some Indian folk music, some classical music. Today we are going to listen to some jazz music. At the same time, we will do a little review."

A boy comes in, in break-dance movements. A bunch of students are throwing papers at the waste basket. A tall girl hits her neighbor with a package of posters. Brophy walks over to the blackboard and chalks a staff, then writes assigned exercises which he copies from the "Ready-to-Use Music Activities Kit" in his other hand. The exercises on the blackboard require the drawing of a series of treble and bass clefs, naming the line and space notes and writing letter names for specified notes. This is the first time the bass clef is introduced. Brophy's clefs lack a bottom. What is being taught is the visual shape and name (bass clef), but not including the clef's role, meaning or origin. Some students are busy making lines, others are copying the clef; most are conversing among themselves. Brophy puts a record on the record player. His soft voice, the sounds of jazz music and student murmur get tangled. To hear better, I move from the back forward to a vacant seat. (Under the desk I notice a pencil, three pennies, an orange social studies textbook, pieces of tissue paper, and a book, *Sex and the Stars*, worn with use.) Brophy notes that they are hearing an album by Charlie Parker called "Swedish Snaps":

> Charlie Parker is one of the most famous jazz musicians. He is responsible for changing the style of jazz back in the 40s, changing from Swing to what is called Bee Bop. Let's listen to a couple selections. They recently made a movie about him called "Bird." That was his nickname.

Brophy walks around, showing children how to draw clefs, reminding them of the formula for the note names ("Every Good Boy Does Fine" and "Empty Garbage Before Dead Flies"). After 4 minutes he goes back to Charlie Parker, then talks about a concert at McCormick Place in which he participated the previous night. He mentions names of other participating groups. Some children ask about ticket prices for the performance. Many are talking among themselves, laughing, moving around. There is a clear lack of focus and direction. At 2:15, Brophy begins another record. 2:20. Lesson ends. Brophy goes back to his classroom.

***

Charles Brophy, a friendly, mellow person, has been a percussionist since 1956, when he joined the Air Force. Initially, he did not want to be a musician because he thought it involved "being on drugs and all of that stuff." But, "When I found out you didn't have to do that to be a musician, I said okay." Music runs in his family. His grandfather was a tuba player in a Dixieland band. Brophy is teaching his son to play drums. He characterizes himself as a "weekend musician":

> I worked quite a bit around Chicago. I played in the Grant Park Jazz Festival. I play with two or three different groups. I'm working currently with a group called "Spaceship Love." It's sort of Latin jazz. It's composed of a singer, myself, bass, a guitar, and a saxophone. I get a lot of jobs from the Musicians' Union. Basically, I'm a weekend musician. I try not to take too many jobs during the week because it's hard getting up to come to school in the morning.

He sees it as difficult to make a living as a full-time musician:

> It's not impossible, but it's difficult. Especially if you've got a family. Some people are very successful at it, but they've been, you know, the name people. What you have to do—you have to go to New York, because that's the center of everything that's happening jazz wise. There's not that much work here in Chicago. Most of the musicians

> that are here are weekend musicians and have day jobs. They work with the telephone company or post office. Except for the young guys that are maybe going to school and don't have the responsibilities of a family and homes to take care of. So that's a big drawback for being a musician. If you are out on the road, you can't be with your family. It's pretty difficult to make it.

Our schools are revolving around job opportunities. More prominent at the college and secondary level, jobs are definitely a concern at the higher elementary grades. Seventh- and eighth-grade students commented to me about their parents', as well as their own, concerns about their future careers. Brophy presented a realistic (and not too rosy) picture of a role model as far as a career in music was concerned.

Making a living out of music was one important aspect in career choice. Enjoying music was another. When talking about performance, Brophy's eyes light up as he tries to express the experience:

> It's indescribable, the pleasure you get out of creating music and playing. You can't beat it. It's hard to describe. It's so wonderful and enjoyable to create and to play for people and see that they like the music and that they are happy and that they dance, they tap their feet, they clap their hands. You get a big kick out of it.

Why didn't Brophy choose teaching music as a profession? Brophy mentions the lack of piano skills.

> My piano playing is nil. To do a really good job of teaching music one would have to play the piano real well. These kids, they get restless, and they have to turn around and look and see who's doing what. And see, when I'm playing the piano, I have to look at the keys to see what I'm doing. So I could not do that. That's one of the reasons I've been reluctant to go too far into teaching music.

As we talk, it becomes clearer that Brophy's musical background in performance did not prepare him for teaching music. Student receptivity and expectations of music, too, are different from audience receptivity. Contents and pedagogies are quiet different. Goals, though, are similar to the ones articulated by music specialists in Danville with perhaps some greater intensity when it comes to the music that Brophy holds personally dear:

> I want them to know something about music. I want them to know how to listen to music and how to enjoy music, how to appreciate music, *all kinds of music*, from classical to jazz. They know about rock. That's the greatest thing, they think. But I would like them to know that there is other music, folk music, music from other countries. I'd like them to enjoy it, as well as be able to sing and perform. Also, to give them the basics of music theory and music appreciation.

Many classroom teachers emphasize the open-ended, creative aspects of the arts. Brophy is well aware of the crucial role of discipline, especially when it comes to group performance:

> Let them know that even in music you've got to have discipline. You can't fool around. Things have to be done *on time,* notes have to be sung in tune or *in key.* So it's not just getting up, singing, opening your mouth, dancing or fooling around. If you're going to do it as a group, everybody's doing the same thing.

Looking at music appreciation versus production in Danville, it became clear that student interest and concentration levels were higher in the latter. Here, too, Brophy says that students find it "a lot of fun to sing. They get a kick out of that," but that "they don't like the theory part because that's too much like academics. You've got to take your paper and you've got to write." Students' performance is visible as much as it is audible and receives the principal's as well as other teachers' appreciation:

> In the Black Gallery of Honor Week, the principal had everybody open their doors in the classroom. I had about 70 or 80 kids, I pulled the best kids out to be in the program. We sang in the hallway here, "Ole Man River." Then during lunchtime, we went down to the second floor, and we sang there too, sort of a serenade like.

Concentration and effort are necessary for every subject matter. Because the arts are regarded as easy and open-ended, teachers need to override such expectations. Brophy reiterates Gratton's complaint about the difficulty of maintaining discipline with the lower-achieving students. All these are issues that keep coming back in different classes, in the various arts.

The most striking issue in this class was the disassociation of music *theory* (or the acquisition of the music symbol system) from musical *experience.* I found the disassociation even more intriguing because Brophy does include both aspects of the curriculum in his class. (Sometimes music is neglected in music theory classes.) Even though they occur simultaneously, there is no bridging between. Theory remains at the level of learning names and shapes. At no point did the lively jazz music in the air connect with the clefs and signs on the blackboard. Thus, students were explicitly taught formal definitions, but have not been taught to connect the formal definitions to what they were experiencing at the moment or to their other musical experiences. Moreover, it has not been indicated that this was possible to do. Students' different reactions to theory and performance become more understandable. The perceived unrelatedness of music theory to students' real life is an important factor.

Brophy did not talk of the discrepancy between the domains, of the need to do things differently. This is even more puzzling given his strong commitment to performance, his emotional reaction to musical experience, and his outstanding qualification as a musician. Obviously, the skills and commitments required of a performer are very different from those of a teacher. Classroom settings, too, promote different communication styles from the ones in concert halls. This contrast of skills and ambience is illustrated in the next section where we encounter out-of-school performances.

Why is the theory part purely analytical, with few references to real music? Part of the answer lies in curriculum organizers—textbooks, testing and grades. "Fairness" is an important concept in tests. It is more problematic in music, as musical skills are often regarded as inborn talent rather than educable. How do you resolve the fairness issue? In this class as in many others, test items do not require musical skills, so that any somewhat motivated student can succeed. They are also easy to generate and measure. The lack of testing of "auditory" skills is apparent. Grading and testing reflect goals and curriculum contents. Says Brophy:

> I give them a little test, have them draw a clef, a staff, a bass clef. Ask them to name the space notes and the line notes, little things that are music theory. I try to stress to them that even if you don't know anything about music, even if you can't sing, you can still write the notes on the lines and spaces. I try to stress to those who are not good singers or who can't carry a tune that they can still get a good music grade, because if you can add, subtract, multiply and divide, music theory is the mechanics of it, and doesn't require any musical talent to do that.

Singing, an important part of school culture, belongs to special occasions and to after school, voluntary activities. Though listening takes the better part of the music period, its content and presentations do not invite an aesthetic experience or an intellectual challenge. The fact that auditory skills aren't being tested, conveys clear messages and shapes students' attitudes to music as "frills" in a world where the untested is marginal.

Brophy teaches three music classes in addition to his own class. By May, each class has "maybe ten lessons," perhaps less, depending on the day of the week allotted to them. The lesson occurs at the last session of the school day. Subjects like drugs and sex education compete for that time slot. Other things often pop out.

As in so many academic (but not music) classes, the textbook is the hub around which the curriculum revolves. Here the "Ready-to-use Music Activities Kit" advertises itself as "Over 200 fun-filled classroom activities to build basic skills." In "Learn a Few Basics," the basics include analyzing the staff, drawing line and space notes, naming the notes, drawing clef signs, ledger lines. Each page has a name, date, score and class sections to be filled in—ready-made for homework assignments. The information is divided into small segments, illustrated in a clear manner. Student assignments consist of items like: (complete the following) "The third space is _____ (higher/lower) than the third line," or "The letter names of the spaces spell the word _____."

Emphasis is on clarity—providing specific manageable tasks, drawing on facts that pupils will be likely to be familiar with (e.g., in the treble clef, the instruments mentioned are voice, guitar and the right hand of the piano, rather than flute or violin, for example). Brophy's satisfaction with the textbook corroborates his espoused goals for the music theory part: "That's a very good book. I ordered that when I first came to this school. That's got quite a bit of theory and stuff in it."

Classroom deportment is a problem in this room. That is not necessarily a result of its being a "foreign" class. Brophy's own homeroom is as unrestrained. In this class (as in all of Brophy's classrooms), one student (always a boy) was assigned to stand near a blackboard and write the names of disrupters. The list of names grows long, but the turmoil is undisturbed. Music does not affect disciplinary problems.

Armstrong Elementary School, Chicago, Illinois

Outside Resources In Music

Armstrong students are exposed to a variety of opportunities to attend art events. Among the events offered this year were the opera, the Imagination Theater and the Art Institute. This wealth reflects principal enthusiasm for art consumption. It also is a manifestation of the variety of programs and possibilities that exist in Chicago, available for the interested.

Transportation goes both ways: some productions, like the Chicago Symphony Orchestra Quartet, the Nola Trio, or the Puppet Show, come to the school. Brophy's words sharpened our awareness of the differences between a live performance and classroom learning. Let's peer at Armstrong Assembly Hall/Gym, filled with intermediate and upper grades (4-8) on a hot, early June afternoon. Sponsored by the International Music Foundation: the Nola Trio.

The Nola Trio

12:55. The stage features marimba, drum set, and a double bass. The children, already seated in their chairs, many with heads half turned to see who is coming, talk with their friends. A giggling girl hits a boy in front of her. The acoustics of the hall are poor. The decor familiar and uninspiring. But there is anticipation in the air. The three players, wearing informal clothing, stand in front of their instruments. The vice-principal makes a brief introduction. And they start. The music—a Brazilian bossa nova—is lively, rhythmic, communicative. The double bass player is smiling, the marimba player is hopping to the beat. It's catching, makes you join the fun. The clapping at the end of the piece is spontaneous and hearty.

Ron, the bearded marimba player, assumes the role of the spokesman.

> This music was from South America. Another kind of American music you don't normally get to hear is Ragtime. This was written 100 years ago. Does anybody here remember their great grandparents? When your great grandparents were going out on a date they might have gone to the movies. But the movies have something now that they didn't have then. Anybody know what that is?

Students fill in: "Sound." Ron tells them about "the musicians who play music behind the movie to set the mood. The trick to it is you have to play a kind of music that reflects what's going on onstage. For instance if it's a love story, you get [imitates in a melancholy, high pitched saxophone-like voice—the 'love-story theme']. Or if it's an action-adventure you get [imitates the dramatic, mechanic theme of a famous TV show]. We don't have a movie for you today so we're going to ask you to make one up. We're going to play a tune for you. And when we get done, we want you to tell us what kind of movie it would go to. Think you could do that?"

Children nod. At the end of the three-minute Ragtime, featuring many diminuendi and crescendi, they come up with "an action movie," "a mystery," "Star Wars." Probably more an indication of the kind of movies they see than a reflection of the music, as it contained little dramatic or mysterious qualities.

Judy on the double bass features the next item, a Dixieland Jazz tune. "Dixieland was very popular in the 1920s period." The next one features the marimba; the one after that, the drums, creating a balance among the three instruments. As Mancini's sweet and mellow "Days of Wine and Roses" flow, children sit with their eyes closed, a concentrated gesture. A girl listens with a rapturous expression, her eyes intent on the stage. More Swing, followed by "Anna" from Trinidad and a reggae from Jamaica. The next one features a different set of drums—steel drums. "Steel drums were among the few instruments invented in the 20th century in Trinidad."

1:30. The music is still going on but distractions increase. A girl gets angry and her voice raises, for a dozen long seconds, above the music. A chubby boy is seen walking across the aisles, accompanied by the vice-principal, looking for the boy(s) who hit him. Now the marimba player invites questions. A boy asks how much the drums cost ($2000); another asks what the steel drums are made of (the drummer turns the drum upside down, and demonstrates the different sounds that go with the different materials). From the back row Bob, the janitor, asks how much the bass player practices every day. "About 2-4 hours a day," says Ron, mentioning calluses and making an analogy to sports. The next question, by a third grader, is barely heard. After a second failed attempt, Bob approaches him and repeats in a magnified tone: "What is the lowest note on each of the instruments?" "Good question," says Ron. He checks the marimba and asks the other players for their ranges. Another child wants to know how long it takes to be a professional drum player. The drum player tells (in a sentence) about his own history, summing up: "Lots of practice." The stream of questions continues.

After 10 more minutes, they play again, finishing with a short and lively African tune from Mozambique. The marimba player's dancing is even more excited, the drummer gives full rein to his skills and imagination. The music gets louder, more sweeping. The applause is loud and warm.

After the performance, the musicians have a few minutes before they move on. The drummer is surrounded by many young people. I ask Judy and Ron about the experiences of playing in the schools. Ron, sweaty and limp, is still enthusiastic. In contrast to Brophy and Gratton, the emphasis here is on cultural and racial heritage:

> The best thing about performing in the Chicago Public Schools is that I went to Chicago Public Schools when I was a kid. I know that there's a lot of things lacking in the school system. So it's nice. It's especially nice for us to be able to come back and give them a sense of their own culture, something that they don't get everyday. They all listen to WGCI, a Black punk radio station. That's all they ever listen to. They don't know anything about their own heritage as Hispanics or as Blacks in American cultural history. So it's fun for me to be able to come back and feel that our performances are doing some good. What I want to give them is a perspective that there's more than one kind of music. We often talk about the United States as an immigrant country and how the various immigrant groups bring their music and their culture. That makes the United States art scene so vibrant. There are so many different kinds of stuff you don't get in other places. I also like to give them a sense of the history. When these tunes were played, it was your grandparents time. They can feel for themselves when these tunes were

popular, that they're not out of a book. And then to spark their interest with the steel drums. These instruments, except for the drum set, are not the kind of instruments these kids get to hear. Even some of the teachers have no ideas about them.

We get letters from the kids. They actually remember some of what we said. They come up and ask, like these guys here [points at the stage where six children examine the instruments, striking up a conversation with the percussionist and the double-bass player], they're up asking questions. It sparks their interest. That's hard to do to a kid, to really get them going. It's wonderful musically because you feel like you're working for an audience that can really gain something from what you're doing. I remember being a kid in these schools. It wasn't easy.

We haven't gotten any letters from teachers. Teachers usually come up and say, "that's great but you should have played a Polka or something like that." But generally the teachers are pretty responsive. Anything to keep the kids happy, anything to make their day.

I ask about children's behavior.

Children vary from good as gold to a royal pain in the butt, depending on how much sugar they had in their lunch, what time of year it is, how hot it is. We've had schools where they're like swaying wheat. They're moving and talking the whole time. And we've had others, like these guys, who were good. And it's after lunch, so they're a little quieter, because they are a little sleepy.

There is an intensity in a good live production—the combination of sound, the visual dimension, the experience in real time—that is missing even in the best of recordings. Hi-fidelity is costly and schools (Armstrong is no exception) are notorious for having low quality musical equipment.

"Meeting the artists" had other educational implications. The discussion of hard work and perseverance in making music on the one hand, the joy and glory of playing and performing on the other, carries messages rarely communicated within the school. It takes performers in an elevated time-slot to communicate them. But they are very important parts of what it means to be an artist.

And there were the goals of extending children's listening repertoire and knowledge about instruments, countries, styles and eras. Few children might remember exact names and dates, but many grasped that music can be conceptualized in different categories, that musical styles evolve over time, and that they themselves relate to a variety of styles. Most important of all is perhaps the intensity of the musical presence. For a brief time, sacred and elevated, music is central in student experience. Unlike other background listenings, while students relax, eat, draw lines and answer drills, listening becomes a primary focus. I saw manifestations in students' body-language. I heard them in student conversations.

A Day at the Opera

Tuesday morning, a chilly, spring day. Ms. Gratton and I (today in the role of chaperon, and not a very experienced one...) are sitting in a half full bus with a group of third and fourth graders on the way to the Civic Center to hear Humperdinck's *Hansel and Gretel*. I count 30 students: 15 each from two different classes whose parents were interested and willing to pay the $4.00 admission. Going to the opera requires some initiative and administrative work on the part of the teacher: sending letters to the parents; collecting money; arranging for another teacher's class to participate so transportation expenses would be reduced; going to the library to pick up the video of the performed opera so the children could see it in advance. The Lyric Opera provided some information about the opera. Gratton read the synopsis in class but does not remember any of the other information provided. While the students watched the video, she graded papers and did not watch carefully. She did a fast forward when children lost interest. Whatever experience she provided for the children was not powerful enough to hold her attention. Perhaps the daily pressures were too strong.

Twenty minutes have elapsed and the bus has arrived at the Civic Center. Children unload and align themselves with lines from other schools. We enter, greeted by four elderly ushers standing in a row with a distinguished look, ties and all. We are seated in the last rows of the main hall. The teacher just behind us gets a special welcome and a poster. Some teachers, obviously, are regulars here. The hall is decorated with masked faces, the orange lights serving as hats. There is a piano in front. Gratton, dressed in an elegant dress, talks with the children, suggests that they take their coats off. At 11:15, 45 minutes before the performance, the main hall is two-thirds full, even though the letter said that doors will be *opened* at 11:30. Children talk, seeming cheerful and happy without being disruptive.

Seating is gender-segregated. The girls' section features many dresses, much lace, brooches and glittering stones. There is a variety of colors in garments, and also of people—as in the school, but in different proportions. It is a festive day. The girls next to me, one freckled, the other with a white bow, tell me they went last year to "The Magic Flute" and loved it. What did they like about it? "Well, they explained what was going to happen."

Energy abounds. I wonder how it would be restrained during the performance. This is also a time for reunion: one sees teachers in the aisles, hugging each other. Two boys bolt out of their seats, tapped gently by the teachers, and resume a good sitting behavior. Children point at the elaborate ceiling. There is walking back and forth to the rest rooms. At 11:57 there is still considerable movement. Doors are closing, the spreading clapping is transformed into a mock clap.

12:00. A blue light comes on. A series of Shhh.... The chaos subsides in an intense diminuendo, with some uncontrollable giggles as leftovers. Then silence. The stark silence makes me uneasy, seems to invite a reaction. But no. The light goes down. The piano starts.

Today's performance is a shortened version of the opera, 60 minutes rather than the original two hours. The cast consists of the junior group of the opera members. The production, too, is reduced. The orchestra's part is transcribed for piano—an accomplished young woman who plays the difficult virtuoso part flawlessly, rhythm and notes. Enter Hansel and Gretel. Hansel, a taller girl with a soprano voice, is dressed in boots and a peasant brown outfit. Gretel, a feminine looking girl attired in laced dresses, provides a dramatic contrast. There is much humor and jest as they tease and chase each other. Children laugh *with* the singers, a legitimate laugh. A good channel to release the tension of the unfamiliar. With diction clear, it is easy to understand the singers. Another hearty laugh when Gretel hits Hansel on his head with a broom. The scene of teaching the dance feels a bit long. The games that follow are similar to contemporary children's games. The tension rises when mother enters, blaming and chasing, getting angrier. In the midst of the chase a cup of milk is broken. End of act. Children clap, some whisper.

The next scene brings a change of scenery: a green mysterious forest. "Ooh's" and "Aah's" express general enthusiasm. Enters a blonde fairy. Excitement peaks with the movement of the trees. The stage, designed in good taste, is minimal and economical. So is the casting: six personas are portrayed by five actors, with mother and witch acted by the same person. When it all ends, the boy in front of me shouts repeatedly with great gusto, "Bravissimo." I make a mental note that at least one of Armstrong's students is used to operas and public performances.

It's 1:04 and we are on the way back. Unloaded from the bus, Gratton comments on Alia's pretty dress and is concerned about Joseph not having a coat. On the way to the classroom, two girls tell me that they did not like the opera, it was boring. The one nice part, they comment, was the Gingerbread House.

When I asked Gratton a week later if she discussed the opera after the performance, she answered in the negative.

***

The information the Lyric Opera sends to schools includes a double-sided, one-page information sheet. One side has a synopsis and a picture. The other, titled "Background," provides information about the composer and the opera. The opening reads:

> The music of Engelbert Humperdinck (1854-1921) bridges the gap between German romantic opera and modern times. Grounded in traditional musical procedures and inspired by the kind of folkloric atmosphere summed up in Weber's opera *Der Freischütz*, Humperdinck was transformed by Wagner's influence into a precursor of Richard Strauss and lived to see the latter eclipse him as Wagner's heir in German opera. His first opera, *Hansel and Gretel*, is important in the history of opera for two reasons. First, this lovable fairy-tale opera is one of the high points in the luxurious but mostly sterile production of the followers of Wagner. Second, it was an effective counterbalance to the *verismo* style, which had taken over in the opera world.

The extensive references to different musical styles and composers, (e.g., *verismo* style, German Romantic Opera, Weber's *Der Freischütz*, and Wagner's influence) and the language (words such as "eclipse," and "precursor") indicate that it is written for an audience other than children, more for music connoisseurs well familiar with music history and jargon. To assume that a child could extract the "kind of folkloric atmosphere summed up" in the opera and to summarize it as "one of the high points of the followers of Wagner" is unrealistic. The authorless sheet seems to be copied from an encyclopedia. Though initially I was critical of the teacher's choice not to read the information, after reading it, I concluded it was the right decision: it might have had an alienating effect.

Dance

Dance appeared infrequently under a variety of categories. Carolyn Lutgen's spring project for the high-tracked fourth graders was one. An occasional part of school performances was another. The physical education teacher did some simple dancing in January and February with the lower grades. In the spring, a student teacher came every Friday to the kindergarten class to teach a dance session. Most successful perhaps was using dance to illustrate ethnic differences and legitimate diverse cultures, a cherished school goal. The dances in the "Ethnic Week" were referred to by many long after the event, as were the special foods and costumes. Some productions such as the opera we have just attended had dance parts.

Not surprisingly, dance adapted to the context in which it was presented. The spring project had the quick, alternating foci and activities that Lutgen's other "language arts" lessons had. Within a few weeks, the high-tracked students watched a video "Dance Theater of Harlem," wrote a review on one of the dances, listed types of dances, went on a field trip to see *The Nutcracker* ballet (in which one of the students was performing), learned Indian Folk Dances, taught the teacher how to "House" dance, constructed original dances (writing and diagraming instructions), watched and reviewed the video "Choreography by Balanchine", and performed original dances. Venturing away from the safety of textbooks, Lutgen learned with her students with much eagerness—a role model. For one class it was a good winter of dance.

Another instance of dance, the choreography of the "Bunny Hop" in the Spring Frolic program, is representative of many others in the school:

> Kick right leg to the side two times two. Kick left leg to the side two times two (two times). Hop forward, hop back (four times). Hop forward three times.

It was easy, utilizing everyday movements, accessible to all, with little emphasis on kinesthetic or aesthetic awareness, little awareness of conceptual organizers like space, rhythm, line or form.

Dance did happen but had a marginal role in the school, not because dance had a lower status than the other arts, but because dance education had even fewer qualified to teach. Like music, dance involves a different symbol system. Unlike music, dance education is a rarity in college. Apart from the athletic domain which has a fundamentally different set of goals and traditions, "enlightened" kinesthetic awareness is not part of our culture. When dance specialists came to the school they were greeted as warmly as their colleagues in other media: welcomed for relief from teaching, often enjoyed, but rarely looked at as sources from which teachers could learn. Teachers typically used these sessions to do other things, like correcting papers and grading, part of school necessities.

High Art, the Popular and the Vulgar. I often witnessed the separation between high and popular arts in the school. *Sex and the Stars* in children's desks versus the Steinbeck and Hemingway in the class library; Jazz versus Rock; Classical versus Jazz. Implicit, sometimes explicit in teachers' talk, was acknowledgment that not every sound, color or movement should be elevated and considered art. In dance, using the body as the main tool, the distinction between the "elevated" and the "vulgar" was perhaps even more distinct. Arnold Porcheddu, the bilingual teacher, tells about his unhappy experience in preparing his students for the ethnic lunch:

> In my class I had some girls who knew some Mexican dances. We were to perform them here at school this year at the Ethnic lunch. They were not strictly national dances; they were the dances people do in the dance halls. The principal didn't like it. She said, "These are bar dances," and she cut short their dance.

Indian Folk Dancers

As in the other arts, the loud and vulgar were banned, the classical honored.

Drama

Carolyn Lutgen, the Creative Language Arts teacher, was a major force in the school's theatre productions, often single-handedly, sometimes collaborating with other teachers. In this section, we will observe two programs: the Spring Frolic and the Christmas program.

Spring Frolic

The Spring Frolic, initiated by Sandy Henson, inspired by Schaffer's magazine, and brought to life by Carolyn Lutgen, was the second grade annual program, hopefully strengthening school and home ties. Today is Monday, May 1st, one of the last rehearsals for tomorrow's frolic. A big poster reads:

Springtime Frolic: A Spring Program
Time: 2 o'clock
Place: Sunny Meadow

1:54. Lutgen is in constant motion, explaining the merit of audience laugh in a performance (*with* performers, not *at*), reminding them of the text, directing them to their respective locations. Once in place, they recite the poem, their gestures illustrating content: imitating wings (moving hands), rest (head on hands), then the climactic sentence: "Good Morning, Good Morning, The Little Birds Sing." Henson, the classroom teacher, is watching another class but enters periodically to observe. Lutgen examines the reciters, then suggests: "A little further apart so when you do the wings you don't get squelched." They try again, this time allowing space for the flutter. She compliments full movement which starts from the shoulder, then attempts to polish coordination: they need simultaneous, identical movements. Again, they chant happily: "Good morning, Good morning, The Little Birds Sing."

Raza marches to the front, solemnly acknowledges anticipated clapping ("Thank you"), and announces, "Bunny Poem will be our next poem." Lutgen motions silently, a cue to start jumping ("hop, hop, hopping"), then (on "started to run") to run in place. Another repeat of the poem ("Two pink eyes, about that small"), where children are making small circles with their fingers; more hopping and running. Lutgen checks that everybody has bunny ears, a carrot. "Not too many movements," she cautions.

The next song, "Did you ever see a bunny?" starts with feeble voices. Lutgen ("This is pathetic") emphasizes togetherness. The second time is more talking than singing. Lutgen ("You guys look as if you are all dead") conducts again. This time they sing louder, with more confidence. Henson, peeping again, reminds kids they will be wearing their bunny hats.

At 2:18, the people on buses have to leave, reluctantly. But some do stay. The Frog's mother, a young, athletic-looking woman in T-shirt and jeans is carefully drawing a large, red clock. Lutgen discusses logistics with Henson.

The Springtime Frolic—eight reproducible pages in Frank Schaffer's April-June 1984 issue of *Schooldays* promises active participation for everybody:

> Bring out the hidden talents in your little actors and actresses, dancers, singers and artists. Every member of your class, from the shyest to the most outgoing, will make an important contribution to this delightful program for spring.

Instructions and suggestions are specific: where and how to present the program ("plan a Mother's Day Tea, perform for other classes as a spring vacation treat, or divide your class into groups of six and perform for each other"); goals ("whichever way, it will be a worthwhile and memorable experience, improving communication skills and developing poise in your students"); assigning roles ("28 parts are designated, but you may add"); dress ("keep the costumes simple"—festive apron for Fluffer, baseball cap for Jack Rabbit, colorful scarf to drape as wings for Cherry, two pairs of dark socks for hands and feet for Cuthbert, and so on). The professor is featured with a briefcase, a vest and bunny clock. There are directions for making bunny hats and tails, for designing the scene, choreography of the dance. The magazine also provides an illustrated program and the poems to be learned.

The play is about a bunny with a problem: all ready to go to the Bunny Hop, he does not know what time it is. Asking for help, the answers his friends are able to provide are "wrong": "This is the time to feed my baby." "Time for me to wake up." "Lunch time." That won't do for our bunny. It is Professor Long-Ears who tells them "what time it *really* is." They plead a lesson ("Professor Long-Ears, kind Professor Long-Ears, may we have a math lesson? Please.") The professor explains about time, that is, how to read the clock. The day is saved.

I think about the grand themes of this play: *Chronos*—mechanical time of schooling, versus the *Kairos*, the time of experience. I think about the need for chronos teachers, and schools inculcate its value, the attitude of students, humble, ignorant, being saved. Bunny's eagerness to learn math is as stereotypical as the belief that the content of math is learning to tell time, function in our society, not experiencing life as much as planning for life. Looking at the sourcebook I ponder the pedagogical clarity—the detailed, clear directions to teachers, about the difference between aid to teachers and recipes for teaching.

The play is a success for the parents, siblings and neighboring classes who gather in this crowded room the following day. Everything turns out all right. Students did not forget their lines and their was enough space for the flutter. Jones bows. Another memory for the children.

Holiday Programs. There were many more, mostly centered around holidays and special events, some, like the Animal Program, the result of teacher's cherishing. The three Christmas programs for the different grade levels featured colorful program notes prepared by students in their art classes, festive clothes, and ushers (wearing diagonal sashes, white shirts, and gray pants) who directed parents and grandparents with professional courtesy and efficiency.

Gail Lowenfeld, at the piano, plays popular Christmas songs from the music sheet. Santas are prevalent, one on stage, another peering from a huge sock hanging from a basket, still a third, this one real, slimmer and less jolly than the painted ones, with a white puffed beard that he keeps tugging at and sneakers visible below the black boots. Announcing the next skit, his mumbling voice does not carry past the second row.

The highlights—circus and tumblers—are repeated in all three shows: tiger, lion, and elephants, as well as two magicians who put in and take out pink bunnies in black hats. Ballerinas in leotards and dance outfits are dancing. The circus procession continues. Older children hold younger children's hands. Santa consults with Lutgen. Classrooms come and go on stage. Teachers supervise and conduct from their place. I am conscious of rhythmical thumps behind me and turn to see a one-year-old kicking. The song ended, my newly-acquainted neighbor, Fakra Imam, tells me that her son has been practicing the song for the past two weeks.

Next comes the after-school instrumental music teacher, holding a guitar. His class—three young violinists and one guitarist—sit in front. They play one phrase of "Twinkle," then "Jingle Bells." Next is "Song of Joy." The simple arrangement omits the one interesting rhythmic pattern in the song. The last song, "The Yellow Rose of Texas," is sung professionally by the teacher, accompanied by feeble voices of the students. The performance elicits a "Bravo" from one mother.

The next item is a simple-movement dance, to the background of recorded music. Then come the tumblers, with graceful movements, ending their *stück* with a pyramid. As the tumblers somersault, Laura, a somewhat heavier girl, falls with a clumsy movement. Children laugh. As the next round reappears it happens again. Again, a third time, and Laura bursts out in tears. Carolyn Lutgen follows backstage to comfort. Christmas parties are not a happy event for everyone.

An international flavor is present in the intermediate and upper grades' Christmas parties, featuring Christmas in different parts of the world, as well as other winter holidays: Hanukkah in Israel, the Chinese New Year. Each room honors a different holiday or state.

Christmas in Mexico features piñatas, some useful information on Mexico (altitude, size, natural resources, cities), and a gorgeous native outfit worn by one of the girls. The Mexican episode ends with a dance and the singing of "Felice Navidad."

The Israeli sketch on Hanukkah features the national colors (white and blue), an accurate historic background of the holiday, and some facts about Israel's temperature and climate, major exports, geography and demography. After a popular Israeli Hanukkah song, we move to the Chinese New Year. The

Chinese sketch features Chinese hats and golden dragon. The dance is rhythmical. The long green paper dragon, making a round then collapsing on the floor is as impressive and attention-getting as the noise of the fireworks.

Christmas in Germany is represented by a full-laden table, as well as information about German states, cars, chemistry, music and philosophy. The ceremony ends with some Christmas songs. Edna Rice conducts in graceful, articulated movements. There is energy, a sense of direction, aesthetics in the gestures, in the sound, in the rhythm and harmonies.

The ceremonies end. Teachers congratulate each other. Principal Hersh acknowledges the decorations prepared by teachers and students; she acknowledges parents' presence ("We are delighted. How meaningful it is for your children.") Matt's mother kisses him with obvious pride. A bearded father hugs his son, Jason, then pats Lutgen's shoulders and tells her how happy he is to meet her at last. An elderly woman with a fur coat approaches her grandson. Raza joins his mother and younger brother for an approving comment.

***

Arline Hersh captures the communal feelings as she talks about the performances, part of what makes school life memorable:

> I enjoy doing these things. When I used to go into the school and see the classes and the kids working on a mural or doing this or putting on that show, see the parents, their faces shining, even though they couldn't hear a word those kids said through the paper-bags [at the animal show], I really get off on it. I enjoy it. I think it's wonderful for children. I think it's terrific for the adults. It's just a real positive kind of thing. When you look back on the things you remember about school and about growing up, it's this kind of stuff that I remember. I remember standing up at an assembly and doing songs of history. I think they really made me a more well rounded person. I think if we want our children to really develop, just teaching them to read and write is not enough. They have to be able to appreciate and then share. Who knows, maybe one of them someday will contribute to art and make everybody a little happier.

The Wonderful World of Puppets

Outside Performances: It's summer time. The primary grades, K-3, are assembled in the gym. Today is "the wonderful world of puppets" with recorded music as background. A man attired in black stands in front of a beautiful red curtain. Lights dim. Puppets resemble Muppets. There are jokes about mispronunciation of words ("I have to say sausages because I can't say sausages") and a story about a 400-year-old baby who gets thrown through the window by an impatient father. The guilty father escapes punishment from both the police and the devil. The next story, about an ambitious stonecarver, portrays the cravings of power. Good and Bad are presented with two brothers and a predictable ending. The diction is often unclear, the literary quality uneven, but the assortment of puppets—string puppets from India, marionettes (with some etymology), shadow puppets, rod puppets—is truly magnificent. The stories hold children's interest, the gold and silver and shining cloth elicit "Oohs and aahs" from the audience. When it all ends after 53 minutes, the puppeteer follows the first graders on their way out and he pats several young shoulders.

Coda

Drama centered around performances, mostly school holidays and festivities, occasionally an initiative by Lutgen about a topic important for her. Sometimes small variety shows, within or across classes. The plays are a collection of short skits rather than a development of theme or characters. Content was popular, accessible, easy to comprehend. Inculcating the mores of culture, holidays and seasons and important values to be disseminated, drama was typically regarded as entertainment, a necessary accompaniment to ceremonial occasions, not so much an art form with depth and meaning, nuances and subtleties.

After-school clubs included drama as well as music and the visual arts. Inter-school competitions brought an occasional discovery of unexpected talents. Going out provided opportunity to see bigger productions. Driving, almost like making a pilgrimage, to the grandiose halls with their special decor and ambience elevated a performance. In both in- and out-of-school performances, the greatest impressions for children and teachers alike, were often created by technical effects. When I asked about lasting impressions, Nancy Pielot, a special education teacher, told me with awe about the transformation of Sendak's "The Wild Things" bedroom to a jungle. It is the visuals that elicit children's "Oohs" and "Aahs."

Funding. Some performances, such as the Puppet Show and the Nola Trio, are free, organized and offered by local institutions. Others, like the opera, call for individual payment. Sendak's play was made possible for children by a concerted effort of parents who baked and sold cakes ($99), a senator's contribution ($48) and some volunteer work ($50). Fund raising is a common activity in the school. Principal and teachers comment. Many parents don't have money for workbooks, but have money for potato chips. High culture is rarely a value for most families. For many children, going to these events is an opportunity to be exposed to something different.

The principal refers to cultural events as "lots of goodies." The direct connotations between candy and events—the direct, easily enjoyable experiential element—is emphasized by the school. The cognitive and historical are marginal, even though they may be featured in artists' agendas or in program notes.

Performance arts have traditionally revolved around holidays and school programs. Parents and teachers remember these special occasions—part of school and culture, meaningful rituals. The more activist principals, such as Hersh, helped organize these programs. Drama and music were important parts of such programs. Typically, the content considered suitable was light—short sketches, a variety of sorts. The repertoire—literary, musical, kinesthetic—was never beyond the simplest, its function marking a festivity of that special day within a school framework.

It is in the more chamber performances of the after-school clubs that content could get deeper, moving. It is there that Lutgen could venture into nuances and subtleties, into some essential dramatic elements. It calls for a different kind of text than the larger, "symphonic" performances require, a different kind of concentration. Because Chicago is a big city, because such institutions as the Lyric Opera and Imagination Theatre exist, children get glimpses of professional performances, of real drama. Their presence helps create expectations of what drama can and should be. Isolated, without preparation or follow-through, most audiences missed messages, the full power of the medium.

Visual Arts

Bunny Hats for the Spring Frolic

9:26 pm. Today's project is bunny hats. The second graders are preparing for tomorrow's "Spring Frolic," an annual play for parents and guest classes. Betty Jones takes out crayons as students move chairs to form horizontal lines facing her. She holds her bunny hat high above her head.

"Let me show you what were going to do." She motions to Johnny to stand up and places her hat on him. "What do you think you look like?" Johnny, switching from leg to leg: "I look silly." Teacher protests: "You're not looking at yourself. Trust us, you look cute. [To the class]: Do you want to do one of these? [approving voices] I already traced the pattern. First you need to put some eyes on it. I'm going to give you a choice. You can have pink eyes or blue eyes."

With heavy demand for pink, Jones gets more pink paper from her desk and hands it to Matt to distribute. Ears, eyes, nose and whiskers are to be constructed in that order. Jones instructs: "Okay, I want you to hold it so that the ears are going down on your paper. No, turn it around, put it flat down, so that the ears are down. Now, where do you think the eyes should go?" Lucy suggests right in the middle. Jones cautions: "Don't put them too high. Put them about half way, about like that. You can make them as big or as small as you want. Now we need a nice, big pink nose. Then you're going to cut the black paper in some skinny strips and make some whiskers. If you have your scissors—Remember? Yesterday I reminded you, I said you need scissors and glue—if you got your scissors, you may start cutting your pink, your blue and your black. How many whiskers do you think you should cut?" Matt says three, other voices echo. Michael says six. "Why six, Michael? Everybody else is saying three, how come you said six?" Michael: "Three on one side, three on the other." Jones: "That's right. Maybe you could do eight. But don't do any more than eight because then it will be all whiskers."

Bunnies proliferate as children cut, glue and paste. At 9:45 Jones reminds them to put their names on the back of the hat. Passing from one student to another, she checks that things have been done correctly, compliments ("I see some real nice bunny ears here") and—the final sanctification—staples the hat. Now she holds the finished product high: "Okay. Our *first* bunny. Yeah!!!" Josh, the creator, smiles. "And here is another bunny." Children put their bunny hats on, showing their bunnies to friends. Small groups of children are talking softly. For those who are finished, the math lesson starts like a stretta. The teacher addresses both subject matters similarly: "When you start the math, do it sidewise. Would you settle down, Mark? Brian, I like the way you did your [bunny] eyes. I still see scraps on the floor. Everybody get their scraps out." There is some tidying up. Most students, though, are doing math at this point, with bunny hats on.

***

In many ways, visual arts offerings in Chicago were similar to what we had observed in Danville. Pupil skills consisted mostly of coloring, cutting and gluing, manual tasks that in themselves had little to do with art—with essentially no guidance about aesthetic qualities, about expressivity, about broadening associations, or about experimenting with materials and ideas. The teachers were craft-oriented more than art-oriented. Interpretation was not an aim. Most lessons could be summed up as pleasant experiences, the product as "cute." (The relationship between a "cute" product and its attraction to girls more than boys is another interesting issue.) The choices (pink or blue eyes, six or eight whiskers for the bunny hat) remained technical, not for broadening one's understanding. The discussion ("Where shall we put the eyes?") did not address an aesthetic problem. The acknowledgements did not refer to a particular quality in the work. Ongoing evaluation of student work consisted mostly of checking to see that they performed the task at hand, that directions had been followed.

The curricular unit was a single lesson, with no apparent attempt at sequence or continuity. In the early grades and especially kindergarten, non-academic activities were legitimized because of the short concentration span for academics' and arts' acclaimed contribution to hand-eye coordination. The amount of art activity varied with teacher background and personal interest, typically once every 2 or 4 weeks. Seventh and eighth graders at Armstrong had few, if any, art lessons.

Exceptions are important because they indicate what is *possible*. It is revealing to look at possibilities. Whereas many teachers complained about constraints, some created different realities within these very same constraints. The exceptional instances illustrate how specializations, commitments and teaching ability interact among themselves as well as with student tracking and age level. An important factor was teacher preplanning combined with readiness to transcend schematic thinking, to improvise, and to invite others to invest their personal visions. The larger reports (Bresler, 1989) provide a more detailed description of Eileen Rosovsky's sixth graders' and Helen Brahos' first graders' art lessons. Let us step in for a quick look at Brahos' class.

Painting Summer as Spring

9:30 am on a hot summer day. Helen Brahos, a first-grade teacher, carries a thoughtfully-arranged bouquet of flowers—a variety of colors, textures and forms. Placing it in front of the blackboard, Brahos inserts blue paper as a background, then squints her eyes and adds a pink tablecloth for contrast. Standing at the side of the vase, Brahos prompts the children to look at the shapes and colors, to perceive, then to "recreate":

> This morning we're going to try and capture these flowers on paper the way they look today. They are fresh flowers and they won't live very long. We will start this morning with four children. I want those four children to study how the flowers look. You're probably not going to have as many flowers in your picture. Let's take *one* flower. Now, we've talked about flowers before, haven't we? [She motions toward a group of pictures near the blackboard, products of a previous project.] We will make the vase not quite as large as the vases we did outside and inside. We want the *flowers* to become more important than the vase. So we are going to make the vase just a little smaller.
>
> Now, I've brought two old tulips from my garden. I know they are dying, but today we want to paint a spring picture. You can make the tulip look more alive, can't you? You can use a bright red. You're an artist, so you can change your colors around. But we also like to stick as much as we can to the color and shapes of the little flowers here. Now remember, you can put in the flowers you want and leave out the flowers you don't like. It's not important that you put in every flower. You can create your arrangement of flowers. I want you to pick certain ones that you think you would like in there.

As Brahos presents her own picture, Bryan points at a flower on the side and observes, "That one is not real." Brahos agrees:

> That one is not real, that's right. I had to give the picture balance. But first let's have the Good Morning Story. I'm going to ask one person to read it and then we'll start. [The middle and right side of the blackboard are filled with an assortment of assignments: math problems, words to spell, and the Good Morning story.]

Later, Brahos explains to me that she chooses assignments which are fairly manageable for children to do on their own. Amanda is assigned to read the Good Morning Story. Reading in a clear voice, her unit is a sentence (rather than words or syllables): "May 30, 1989. Good Morning. Today is the 30th day of May. It looks like a beautiful summer day. . ." After three fluent readings by other pupils, it's the whole class' turn. Next, Ida, Dwayne and Debbie read the spelling words. Three more minutes for further directions on assignments, and at 9:41, the class is on its own to do the right-blackboard assignments, except, that is, for Rashni, Ashtar, LaDonna and Angela—one East Indian, one Iraqi, and two Afro-American girls who are assigned to the art table. A quick change of clothing: Angela puts on a carefully designed apron made by her mother (an art teacher). LaDonna wears tight black pants with white dots and a colorful expressionistic shirt. The two others choose among the stained shirts lying in the corner.

Brahos picks up 4 of the 30 blue-painted sheets of paper and places them on the table, explaining to me that she was "cheating": "The children painted the paper last week, so today they can start with the "real activity." The four girls arrange themselves around the table, all four facing the bouquet.

Rashni works her chalk across the blue paper. Brahos stands behind her, supervising closely, making frequent comments, giving her and others ideas for translating what they *see* into what they *do*. She helps them with strokes, ("Very light now. Not heavy, because you are going to paint over this. You just want the *shape* of this flower.") She guides them in their planning ("I want you to *plan* your flowers. The tulips are way up at the top, right? Then take a step down, like a step coming down the stairs, and put in these blue flowers. All right. And another step down and welcome to the daisies. Get the clump of daisies in there. Then we come down another step and down here is our lonely daisy, so there is a white daisy here and there are some daisies here.")

Choice is an important issue: "In art, you can make it come alive. Also, you can put in the flowers you want and leave out the ones you don't want. We can see it anyway we want to. An artist can change the way things are. If you came up close you'd see it star-shaped but our eyes make it look roundish. Because we're artists we can see it any way we want. It doesn't have to be exactly the way we see it. If I wanted it to be exactly *like that* I'd take a picture of it. All right. Let's look at the next flower because we are almost there."

In a few seconds, the black of the board transforms into a blossoming bouquet. Brahos adjusts the vase to give them a better angle. As the girls draw shapes in chalk, Brahos continues to arrange materials. She pours "Thick Paint Tempera Gel" into plastic containers, brings in an assortment of brushes. In the next hour and a half, she is in constant motion: to and from the art table and blackboard; supervising work, dipping brushes, opening more colors, carrying from the outside a heavy brown pail filled with water, papers and computer materials, stopping for a moment to smell the flowers.

In the first 20 minutes of the session, some children in the "non-art" group wave their hands and socialize. Two take the initiative to approach the teacher, ask a question, complain about others who disturb. Brahos ignores the hands and shoos the two away: "Mrs. Brahos is not there. Mrs. Brahos has gone off to lunch." This works! Some giggling, but from now until the end of the session, at 11:30, the scene remains relatively quiet. Most of the children work diligently. An exception, Michael, to be transferred to a special education class next year, wiggles in his chair, then yawns and stretches. For the next 20 minutes he is sitting, to all appearances doing nothing, his hands supporting his head.

By 9:54 all four artists have outlined vases. At 10:25, in full progress of color, they are in the midst of a yellow core of the daisy, discussing the tension between details and overall design, design and product, Brahos goes over to the other, "non-art" children, to answer some questions. Back to the art corner, the search

Armstrong Elementary School, Chicago, Illinois

for techniques, colors and visions continues. At 2:30, there are eight magnificent flowered vases hanging on the blackboard. By the following week, it's all 28—a colorful garden in the midst of summer.

Work in progress.

For the While Art Comes First. There were many messages communicated in this class. The artist's role was central: learning to look and see, capturing as vividly as they possibly could, changing reality, consciously and skillfully. That power to modify colors, create forms, shape foreground and background, was not arbitrary but brought out through pre-meditation, reflection, consideration of aesthetic qualities. Seeing was neither automatic, nor given. It required effort, concentration, awareness and thought. Equally important were technique and skills with materials. Painting was done with appropriate materials and involved specific techniques. While there was room for improvisation, spontaneity and personal preference, that also had to be conscious. Technique was a tool to convey aesthetic concepts: Color, shape, balance were central in the design of the painting. Aesthetic concepts provided lenses and guidelines with which to conceptualize and construct. Brahos introduced the thinking in stages, moving step by step to perceive a picture, to design, to draw. Evaluation of the technical, the formal and the expressive was an integral part of the lesson, made on a continuous basis. An intentional paradox was the sharpening of senses to see what exists juxtaposed with the recreating of reality through aesthetic lenses. Implicit messages about mistakes in the process of learning refined; the interplay between plan and product. Each "chamber group" got special instruction while other students did their academic work.

Making art takes a long time; it needs more than the traditional 45 minutes of class time. The need for students to concentrate means that mornings rather than late afternoons should be allotted to art sessions. Only four people produced one picture in two hours (not counting the time for preparing the background paper). Doing lessons that way meant extra work for Brahos. To teaching art, she applied the same principles she applied to her own art work. She recognized the need for prolonged periods of work and uninterrupted concentration, the importance of continuity and sequence. The many pictures around the room—flowers, trees, earlier experiments with paint—reflected a sequence of arts activities. Brahos emphasized the combination of vision and imagery on the one hand, meticulous work and attention to detail on the other. The mechanism of production was necessary to reflection, providing schema from which deviation and uniqueness could be meaningful.

Brahos' baccalaureate in studio art and active involvement in the arts are far above the average for classroom elementary teachers, but not so unusual in this school. The wealth of art centers in Chicago—the Art Institute, museums and galleries, opera and theatre houses—attract and nourish people with artistic interests. Clair Hirsch, Mary Ann King and Rivian Simon were other teacher artists at Armstrong.

Deviations: Special Populations

The pressure for academics that characterized the majority of classes was felt to be less oppressive in bilingual and special education classes. This was due to a combination of interrelated factors: students' perceived inability to succeed in academics; recognition that these students can succeed and gain a feeling of self esteem (regarded by teachers as crucial for these populations) through non-academic activities. Class size, too, was a factor. Special education groups were considerably smaller, ranging from three to ten. As it happens, the teachers in the special education classes in this school were among the more "artistic." Clair Hirsch made collages and other art projects with her small groups of five mainstreamed students. Rivian Simon taught a special education class of ten students with a variety of learning disabilities, mostly severe dyslexia, bused from different parts of the city. That great variety (in ESL and bilingual classes, as well as in special education) necessitated tolerance of differences—of processes and products. Rivian Simon:

> My curriculum is every curriculum. If a child is working at third-grade level, that child is working on a third-grade curriculum. I find these students have wonderful imaginations. In other classes I see, especially in the primary grades, there's a cut-out. All children color the same bunny rabbit. If I show my students a bunny rabbit, I'll get ten different bunny rabbits. They love to use their imagination. So I find projects where they can use their imagination. I give them examples and go from there.

Simon shows me some of the artwork in her class, going over individual children's difficulties. Technique can be extra difficult and coordination problematic but the students' products are impressive. They communicate freshness of idea and design. Like Brahos and Hirsch, Simon is a practicing artist.

> I'm a wood carver. I carve as much as I can. I take lessons with two different teachers twice a week. I go out to Algonquin, Illinois on Saturdays. It's far away. You really have to enjoy what you're doing to travel that far. I won't sell my things. Nobody could pay me enough money. It takes too long. For example, I am making a flying pelican. Each wing took me about 90 hours. More than that. I work so intensely. Every line is put in separately, every feather, every little thing on the feather is separate. It takes a long time. My concentration is so intense. I wish I had put that much effort into anything else in my life.

Like Brahos, the projects that Simon did in class were inspired by things she cherishes. She was moved not by ideas of behavioral change or opportunity for personal expressivity so much as her desire to share understanding important to her. She promoted artistic production. She recognized the time and commitment art projects take.

Debbie Plotkin, the ESL teacher, did not have an art specialist background, but was interested in the arts. The less formal structure in her class (children were pulled out from regular classes rather than from a homogeneous class) helped to promote art-related activities. Plotkin taught a wide range of ages and abilities. The children were less subject to testing, and didactic teaching was less prevalent.

Plotkin loved opera. She taped *Carmen* and brought it to class. The children loved it. The Creoles understood the French libretto, the Latin-Americans responded to the Spanish-flavored music. One child borrowed the video for the weekend, to show his parents. If art needed to be justified to parents or administrators, Plotkin said she would do so under "reading the subtitles" or art appreciation of cultures. At another time, she brought a video of *Swan Lake* to class. Occasionally, the class ventured into visual arts projects. Lacking visual arts training, Plotkin called to her colleagues for help. Said Plotkin:

> We read a story about a sculpture. It turned out the kids had no idea what a sculpture was. We looked at a couple of sculptures in the building. They wanted to know if they could make a sculpture. I said, "That's terrific. But I'm no artist. I don't have the faintest idea what kind of sculpture would be good for you to make." So I talked to a couple of teachers, Mrs. King and Mrs. Hirsch, both very artistic. They suggested junk sculptures. The children brought paper rolls, empty cans, pieces of string, paper, yarn, and doll clothes. I told them that this had to be *their* thing. (I brought scotch tape; that was my contribution.) For a while my room looked like a junk heap. My roommates [the two bilingual teachers] commented about it. After the children designed the sculptures they wrote stories about the characters. This took a long time. It wasn't just a one- or two-day project. Then they were exhibited in the District 2 Multicultural Art Fair.

Plotkin did not allow a weak background to keep her students from experiences in the arts. When teachers let go of authority, children's creativity and initiative may surface. Here among Plotkin's children, a sense of ownership promoted enthusiasm:

> Sometimes teachers make things first, then show the students saying, "this is what I'd like you to do." I could never have done something like [this sculpture]. I was so proud because they did it all themselves. And they had so much fun doing it. That was the best part. It was something they wanted to do and they had fun doing it.

Colleague support contributed not only at the initial stage, providing the idea and tolerating the mess, but also in recognition: "When I showed these to my colleagues, we got a lot of acknowledgement!"

Out of School Resources

As in music, the out-of-school curricular activities constituted an important part of the visual arts offerings. During the 1988-1989 school year, Armstrong had six artists-in-residence, each visiting two to eight times. In a larger Chicago report, we presented three artists-in-residence, as well as a group of student teachers, each with distinct goals and pedagogical styles. Here we follow Graham Stewart from Urban Gateways—an artist and muralist, spending five 75-minute sessions with the three fourth-grade classes. His was one of the few obviously sequential art activities in the school. Each lesson built on the previous one and contributed directly to the final mural.

Since a major goal for these programs was supposed to be staff development for the teachers, let us pay attention to the teachers in the classroom milieu during these sessions. Now not the soloist in the classroom nor the conductor, the teacher is asked to assume a *"basso continuo"* role, providing support and structure.

Mural Making With An Artist-in-Residence

In the midst of the second of the five-session art project in an "average" fourth-grade class, Graham Stewart, young, agile, in white shirt, black jeans, moves about inspecting student work. The theme is "Nature." Pigs, horses, giraffes and elephants are being glued to construction paper prairies. Children are cutting mountain peaks and green trees in a variety of shapes—round, oval and triangle. Stewart walks from one child to the other, helping, showing them what to do when something does not quite work. Children constantly call for his attention, show him the work. Stewart responds with a distinct British accent: "That's very good." "I'll draw it. You cut it." "That's a wonderful piece of work." Often enough, there is need for disciplining: "Somebody's voice is too loud." "You are getting rowdy!"

The back corner of the room is increasingly populated with a multitude of black elephants in different sizes, as well as a dog in motion, cat with curled tail and a grazing zebra. "Make his back longer," advises Stewart. At another table, I watch as Stewart transforms a small, orange rectangle of paper into a horse. At the far end of the group, Lisa had misunderstood the assignment and is making a city instead. Stewart legitimizes it, Lisa brightens up, cutting sky scrapers and windows with confidence. With "two minutes left" they will "have to put the stripes sometimes between now and next week."

Attention centers as Stewart, holding some finished products, announces from the front: "Sit down, please. Put your scissors down. And your glue. I need your undivided attention. I picked these works." His voice is counterpointed with the principal's via loudspeaker: "I want to remind you that recess is a privilege. We will not tolerate rough behavior." As it subsides, Stewart points at the one animal on top: "Hard work. Good in detail. Good in shape. Good sense of composition. Not finished yet." Then, pointing to a second one: "That's mature work. I haven't helped him at all!"

With five minutes to go, the regular classroom teacher enters the room. Looking at the teacher's sample, she exclaims: "Oh, my goodness, this is beautiful! Gorgeous!" Stewart is still in motion, walking around, talking about scaling, pointing out that they have to make it larger. The session twilights as he collects his pink, purple and white plastic scissors. The children clean up, then move to Reading. Stewart walks to the next class.

High-track. His next class, same grade level, is Mary Ann King's class. Here the theme is "Careers." The teacher, always present, is sitting behind her desk. Not an ordinary desk, this one features, along with crayons, tissue box and pocket fact-finder, the series "Art for Children," a collection dedicated to Rousseau, da Vinci, Picasso, Van Gogh, and Michelangelo. Beautifully designed, the book focuses on the scanning of pictures. King listens attentively to Stewart and helps with materials and advice.

Stewart talks about background colors and variety. The problem of cutting shapes to match a drawn design needs attention. For representation of careers, the boys' artwork features grim physicians with stethoscopes, basketball players, pilots, farmers, astronauts, and policemen. Girls have featured teachers and nurses. (As I am finalizing a judgment about stereotypes, I discover a veterinarian and an army officer, more done by two girls; however, none of the women teachers gesturing and scribbling numbers on blackboards was done by boys.) Here, too, there is much attention to details: how to cut pockets, eye lashes, the hands of a clock, a nose. When asked to help with a hair design, Graham enquires: "Does the hair come this way or that way?" then cuts a wavy, energetic ponytail in the right direction. The shape of a face is declared to be "not really round, more the shape of an oval." "Everything should be made out of paper, no crayolas, please." There is frequent reminder that all this work serves the ultimate goal—the mural. Children seemed absorbed in their work. The principal's voice breaking in to announce that the social room is closed accentuates silence. Children cut and glue: red curtains on an orange background, a yellow door; plenty of clocks in classrooms and in physicians' room; an occasional sun. Stewart is everywhere, commenting, asking, helping out with his pink scissors. As the lesson progresses, the constant low hum, like the buzz of bees, becomes more noticeable.

Today the fourth graders will continue the fourth lesson. Drawing and cutting completed, individual compositions merge into "The Seasons." On large sheets of pressboard primed with a base coat of flat white latex, Stewart is gridding 64 squares. The grid is alphabetized horizontally and numbered 1-4 vertically. Stewart shows how to locate squares on the grid. He emphasizes teamwork: "The mural is a whole piece of work, it belongs to everyone. You have to do it carefully, because if you mess up, you are messing up everyone else's work."

Mary Ann King helps with mural work.

Artist, teacher and children are taping the gridded pictures on the pressboard. He measures with a pink ruler, shows them, step by step, how to measure. "You have to multiply everything by two because the board is twice as large as your mural. You made a mistake. Don't worry about it. The important thing is to learn from your mistakes." King participates actively, asks "How many remember how to enlarge?" (16 hands): She reiterates messages, demonstrates how to measure; multiply 1/4 by 2; helps pupils practice drawing figures in proportion. She makes a mistake, transferring the wrong picture, then talks about the mistake so others can learn from it.

The mood is serious and attentive. As Stewart leaves, King voices a concern: Stewart's last visit is next Monday. "We need him. We need the professionals!" she says in an agitated voice. She complains that the mural project should have taken nine sessions rather than the five they can pay for. "Who wants to continue work on this today?" Many hands wiggle with excitement. The gridding continues.

We are in Abrahams' below-average class four weeks later. At her desk, Abrahams is correcting papers. Children work silently on their workbooks. Occasionally, Abrahams interrupts the silence to clarify matters such as the difference between wrappers and rappers. At the back of the room, four girls with brushes surround a huge white cartoon on a large table—mural in process. The original drawings are hanging on the wall, carefully glued and gridded. The mural includes all four seasons but features the warmer ones. An image outstretches her hands on a green landscape—trees and houses; two taut bodies dive into a swimming pool; girls jump rope. Each of the four girls is painting a different corner of the mural. They group and regroup surrounding greenery. Except for some conflict over mistakenly smeared windows that have now become a wall, work is silent. Glancing around, I discover bright, captivating colors in another mural, already finished—white clouds, yellow lightning sparkling from black clouds; more swimming pools, birds, suns and moons in a variety of sizes and shapes; in the midst, an elaborate baseball player. This one had been done earlier by Shelly, the teacher's friend, just helping out.

Abrahams expresses enthusiasm about the new mural and the artist. Her priorities concerning the lessons were slightly different—hers were directed to mural completion; his, to techniques of construction.

> He [Stewart] was patient, he was wonderful, very outspoken. But he left. He didn't do anything but start us on the first mural. That was as far as he got. I thought he could have taken one of the lessons and made it shorter or eliminated it altogether. [We really needed to finish at least one mural.]

***

Graham Stewart got a Studio Master's Degree from the University of London, then a Master's in Architecture from the Art Institute in Chicago. He had been staying in the United States on a Fulbright scholarship. An artist and muralist, Stewart was doing commissioned murals—he had done murals in legal and medical offices as well as exhibiting in the Chicago galleries. Mural-making, like teaching children, provided enough money to do what he enjoyed most—painting.

As we talked, it became clear that his philosophy, goals, visions and daily concerns were grounded in the artist's purview. Though he had just completed a successful educational project, it was from art that he received his satisfaction and nourishment rather than from the interaction with children. Teaching was temporary, almost marginal, in his world.

In the longer version of this case study is a description of five art lessons by Mirentxu, an artist-in-residence from ART, an agency which arranges artists' visits to the Chicago schools. Both artists-in-residence, Stewart and Mirentxu, were professional artists in the visual arts; both were visiting schools for 5-6 once-a-week sessions. Their similarity of context accentuates their differences, illustrating how school art can be enriched and expanded in a variety of ways. Mirentxu stayed with the individual children's work. In Discipline Based Arts Education spirit, she addressed art history and appreciation as integral parts of the project. Other differences appeared in presentation modes (didactic versus facilitator role), and pedagogical approaches (cognitive, eliciting ideas from students versus specific skill oriented).

Finale

The paths of arts in the school are many. Curriculum organizers in the arts are fewer and less canonized than those in other subject matters. Their agents (specialists and classroom teachers and others) are extraordinarily diverse in training, commitment and aspiration. Contexts, too, are widely different: from classrooms, studios, school auditoriums, to museums, opera and theatre halls. With few demands to standardize or to increase test scores, productivity and cognitive skills, teachers are left to draw on their own resources, personal beliefs and visions, yet they draw upon a small array of customs and precedents.

The scope of teacher training, as well, is wide. In a later chapter, we will examine teacher belief about art and a certain dissonance with school environment, structure and goals. The relationships are far from simple.

Schools, by definition and custom, are highly structured institutions, emphasizing discipline, and "right" answers as defined by authority. Across the curriculum, the current emphasis is on isolated skills, clearly measurable achievements and standardized test scores. Experience, meaning and a feel for the whole, are often neglected or suppressed. Teachers and principal alike sense the loss, sometimes lament the imbalance. The arts, for many people, symbolize the essence of experience and intuition and are regarded by many teachers as unique to the curriculum. Introducing more of the arts into the school should restore some balance. Using talents of specialists in art, music, dance and drama, a small aesthetic experience and understanding occur. For many teachers, both classroom and specialist, the school's prevailing mode of teaching is too strong. They tell children what to know and what to do. What results is an infrequency of profound experience and opportunity for creative expression, a bare-bones knowledge of the classics and skills needed for critical review. It takes great effort to change pedagogic practice and prevalent classroom dynamics, especially when knowledge of subject-matter is limited and opportunities for reflection on aesthetics in schools and our culture are few.

Goals in Arts Education: Cognition and Expression. The concept of art as providing experience plus cognition is acknowledged by arts educators (Broudy, 1972; Eisner, 1982; Langer, 1957; Olson, 1983; Perkins, 1983) and art institutes. Phrases like "allowing interpretation of life experiences and continuous reconstruction of the self" are common (see Goodlad & Morrison, 1980). These goals are not restricted to arts education circles. The Department of Superintendents of the American Association of School Administrators (AASA, 1965), for example, stated:

> It is important that pupils, as part of general education, learn to appreciate, to understand, to create, and to criticize with discrimination those products of the mind, the voice, the hand, and the body which give dignity to the person and exalt the spirit of man.

More recently, the Association for Supervision and Curriculum Development (ASCD, 1989) adopted a resolution on the arts as essential in the school curriculum:

> With recent focus on specific subject matter, academic achievement, and a series of reform efforts/movements that emphasize raising test scores and graduation requirements, a balance of curriculum offerings is not being maintained. Dance, drama, music, and the visual and performing arts are disciplines with aesthetic, perceptual, creative and intellectual dimensions. They foster students' abilities to create, experience, analyze, and reorganize.

Even though acclaimed by a wide body of advocates and authorities, artistic experience and aesthetic thinking are in many schools only rarely part of school life. Even when technically elegant and educationally complex, many teachers and administrators continue to treat them as entertainment. Preparation for concerts and exhibits may be demanding but even they are not seen to need the best of intellectual and emotional investments. The educators already converted, those with artistic background draw best on the outside resources—artists-in-residence, museums and performances—to expand and to learn from. Not surprisingly, the majority of others have little interest or ability to capitalize on those resources. Exposure to the fine arts, when there is exposure (these teachers will be the ones to grade papers when the artist-in-residence comes in and the ones not to apply for tickets to arts concerts), does not fit with their paradigms of knowledge, experience and expectation. It takes a change of paradigm to look for aesthetics in life in everyday situations as well as in the more elevated ones. Such a change is not part of most teacher training programs.

I started this case study pointing out the richness and diversity of arts curricula vitalized and enduring so that many teachers and parents believe them universal. Within the diversity, "interpretation of life experiences" and "criticizing with discrimination, products of the voice, the hand, and the body" happen in special places in every community but they vary in most. Even with zeal and with able students, most teachers with little personal art background do not and perhaps cannot address these goals. The cognitive side of art is not part of the ordinary conceptualization of arts education. Hence, students in art classes are typically not engaged in formulation and expression of ideas, feelings and images through materials. Rather, they create some specific object—be it bunny hat, simple dance or song—by imitating a teacher's model. Procedures are simple and unambiguous. Opportunities for exploring imagery and broadening associations are rarely pointed out. Resource materials delimit rather than empower an exploration. With the exception of music, resource books accept where teachers are, largely falling within the category of "200 exciting one-page projects." Whether in the visual arts, music, drama or dance, specialist books and magazines provide lists of instructions for teachers on how to organize activities. Much of the mood is entertainment and fun. Continuity and sequence, skills, sensitivities and gooseflesh are foreign concepts to these projects.

High-Track, Low-Track and Special Populations. In most classrooms, we found continuation of the "Back to Basics" movement, pressures for academics and deference to standardized tests. The populations getting some relief from this pressure were the two extremes—the aptitude-scoring "high-tracked" at the top, and the bilingual and dyslexic at the "bottom." The latter typically have smaller numbers of students per class and often individualized curricula. For arts education these are favorable factors. The children, unfortunately, are not expected to compete, let alone succeed, in the academic market place.

In contrast, the high-track children are released from some of these pressures because they are already successful. More importantly, the goals and traditions for this population are different. University of Pittsburgh psychologist Lauren Resnick (1987) commented that American schools, like public schools in other industrialized countries, have inherited two quite distinct educational traditions—one concerned with elite education, the other concerned with mass education. These traditions conceptualize schooling differently, with different clienteles and different goals for their students. In the last 60 years or so, the traditions have merged to the extent that most students now attend comprehensive schools in which several educational programs and student groups co-exist and intermix. Resnick argued that the continuing and as yet unresolved tension between the goals and methods of elite and mass education produces much of the current concern about teaching higher-order skills. Intellectualized fine arts education, with its emphasis on holistics and problem solving, requires higher order cognitive skills. The required sense of ownership, exploration and need to redefine questions and rules are typical of elite education.

Another important issue is behavioral orientation in the rhetorical schools. In high-track classes, teachers find it easier to attend to the academics. It is in the low-track and average classes that the sophistication of behavior becomes a serious problem: to gain all the support they can from the system, teachers often feel the need to increase the behavioral orientation, with the academic orientation subordinated. Many Armstrong low-track teachers and the principal expressed concern about the control and change of student behavior. Even though "high" in Armstrong is "average" in the suburbs, different goals for the high and low tracks are evident. Artistic teachers are more frequently assigned to high-track classes. The kind of opportunities each track gets reflects school attitudes as well as different codes of behavior. A social issue rather than merely artistic, it assumes importance because many teachers comment on the importance of the arts for lower-achieving students. Teachers often claimed that the less scholastically accomplished students are the most creative and able in the arts, emphasizing that these students need the arts in order to express themselves and increase their sense of accomplishment.

Even extracurricular opportunities such as some artist residencies are different for the high versus the low track. According to my observations, low-track teachers have been present less often to help in classroom management, to model attentive attitudes, and to learn from the experience. Artists-in-residence (typically knowledgeable) find discipline a problem in these classes. Teachers' attitudes affect student motivation and success. (While this is true for art within the curriculum, performances do allow students from all track levels to participate and enjoy. Performances still fulfill their role as enriching experiences and as a a starting point for critical discussions in class.)

Summing up views of teaching art, resources, and teachers' roles at Chicago Armstrong and Danville Washington, I recognize particularly the differences between *in-school* and *out-of-school* people. Artists by definition are more likely to draw on art ideas than teachers. As visitors, they may also be more enthusiastic and fit into the charismatic "performer" role. Teachers, on the other hand, have a continuing, daily contact with the students and daily communication of content and attitudes. Striving for improvement, we need both inside and outside resources. And we need them to work *in cooperation*. We need good, communicative artists to inspire and show the fundamentals of their fields. We need teachers to precede and follow what artists do, assisting in acquisition and interpretation. Good teaching requires a personal witnessing of the powerful role that art plays in life.

Training in the arts is inadequate. Teachers find arts education a difficult assignment because arts education taught right is so different from what they themselves have been taught. For students, major advances in the understanding of arts need to occur in middle school and secondary school, but also in the elementary schools. As Howard Gardner (1973) pointed out, if the opportunity to develop artistic competence is not available before adolescence, children are unlikely to acquire basic literacy in using artistic tools to capture their ideas and feelings in artistic ways and appreciation of the ways others capture their experiences in art forms. If this task is not taken up by the elementary schools, it may, for many, not be taken up at all.

Chapter 5:
Alexandre Dumas Elementary School Chicago, Illinois

■ *Linda Mabry*

Chicago!

The windy city: home of the wealthiest neighborhood in America, Kenilworth, and the poorest, Ford Heights, according to a 1989 Roosevelt University study.

The Magnificent Mile: A kaleidoscope of historic and ultrasleek architecture adjacent to a china-blue expanse of Lake Michigan. The hubbub of pedestrians and traffic. The Art Institute. The Museums of Science and Industry and of Natural Science, the Shedd Aquarium. Wrigley Field and Comiskey Park.

The Southside: How many people are crammed into those blocks of mammoth, fire-scarred apartment buildings? The people waiting for the el on open-air platforms—why are they all black? Do the kids who live here ever see the lake and the museums?

Chicago Public Schools: Between May 15 and 29, 1988, *The Chicago Tribune* (as noted by Liora Bresler in the previous chapter) printed a series of articles resulting from a seven-month examination of the city's public schools, schools which U.S. Secretary of Education William Bennett had called "the worst in America." Published as a volume, the collection of articles included the following information:

Politics: Schools were an instrument of racial politics in the late 1950s when the school board provided mobile classrooms and scheduled double shifts at crowded Afro-American schools rather than bus. Caucasian children were a majority in the schools then but, in the 1960s and 1970s, parents of tens of thousands of children transferred them to private schools or moved to the suburbs. Middle-class Afro-American children also left, leaving the public schools with the toughest children to teach.

Poverty: Of the 419,537 children attending Chicago Public Schools (CPS) in 1988, 68% lived in poverty, coming to school "with a background of deprivation that would make learning difficult under the best of circumstances." Sixty percent were black. Impoverished, needy, and difficult to teach, these children had no option but to depend on inner city public schools. CPS enrolled about one-fourth of Illinois' schoolchildren but more than half of the state's low-income students.

Dropouts: Chicago's drop-out rate in 1989 was 48%, compared to Houston's 40%, Los Angeles' 34%, New York City's 31%, and Miami's 30%. At some

Chicago schools, fewer than 15% of students graduated when expected. A 1964 study regarding the difficulty and necessity of teaching children from low-income families declared that until the Board of Education, community resources, and citizens "are willing to give more than lip service to the idea that education is an investment and that it is better to spend now than pay later for social misfits, we will continue to pay the cost of our failure to educate the majority of our culturally deprived children."

Personnel: The *Tribune* reported a teacher-pupil ratio of approximately 29 to 1. The social worker-pupil ratio was 2151 to 1. The psychologist-pupil ratio was 2268 to 1. The truant officer-pupil ratio was 2715 to 1. The bureaucrat-pupil ratio was 123 to 1. One-fourth of the teachers (7,294) in classrooms were substitutes. State-mandated teacher certification was circumvented by classifying 4,350 substitutes on FTB (full-time basis) and placing them, in lieu of certified teachers, in charge of classrooms. Of those certified, nearly 20% failed or declined to take the National Teachers' Examination.

Unions: The Chicago Teachers' Union contract made it so difficult to fire an incompetent teacher that, of 139 teachers whom principals tried to fire during 1983-88, 99 were still teaching at the end of the year in which their principals tried to fire them. CPS went broke in 1979 after former Mayor Richard Daley, to avoid strikes, repeatedly ordered the school board to grant teachers pay raises with money the board did not have. Principals were not represented by a union. Their authority was seriously undermined by the plethora of union contracts of other CPS employees. To function at all, they selectively followed and ignored board policies, took duties that contract employees could refuse, and cultivated personal persuasiveness.

Tests: "An overemphasis on reading and math scores on the Iowa Test of Basic Skills, combined with tight finances and priorities skewed to benefit bureaucrats, has pushed science, art, music, and literature out of many classrooms, especially in low-achieving neighborhood schools." (*Chicago Tribune*, 1988, p. 166)

First Impressions

In the six months between October 1988 and March 1989, I drove the two and a half hour stretch between Champaign and Chicago many times. The farmlands changed from autumn reds and browns and golds to wintry gray and white—even the sky is gray then, a spare Andrew Wyeth watercolor. Tentative greens erupted in early Spring sunshine. Sometimes, the drive seemed long as I brooded over the overwhelming obstacles one little school faced, sometimes bright as I marvelled at its success.

I-57 to the Dan Ryan Expressway and its clotted urban traffic even in off-hours, then off on 71st Street and east into the Southside neighborhoods. The streets were not well-maintained. Cars lined curbs, rusting gas-guzzlers mostly, not the trim fuel-efficient models gleaming from television commercials. Billboards with black faces advertised cigarettes and liquor. Aging storefronts were barricaded behind bars that offered no pretense of decoration. Afro-Americans waited for buses, bundled against the Midwestern cold. Their eyes caught my attention: stoic, wary, defensive, suspicious of hope. In warmer weather, those who would return the smile of a Caucasian female seemed somehow too friendly; others seemed affronted.

At Cottage Grove Avenue, a concrete wall dominated the busy bleakness. The wall separated The Oak Woods Cemetery from the neighborhood. Behind the wall, a world apart, curving drives ribboned through shade trees, monuments, small lakes.

Across a narrow street stood a three-story school, its windows facing crowded Ellis Street. Amid small apartment complexes, both curbs of the street were jammed with cars, requiring delicate maneuvering by school buses. There was a small fenced parking lot but no playground. Alexandre Dumas Elementary was a nondescript school building hidden in low-income housing.

But there were flowers planted out front.

Alexandre Dumas Elementary School
Chicago, 1989

A security guard controlled admission to the school. He was young, short, inexpensively overdressed, and flashed a smile of recognition to familiar visitors,

"How ya doin'?" From a student desk at a strategic intersection of the two first floor halls, in view of the school's three exterior doors and two staircases, he worked crossword puzzles as he watched.

A single step into the foyer and I realized that Dumas didn't fit. It didn't fit the neighborhood. It didn't fit the *Tribune's* generalized description. It didn't fit the expectations I had tried not to preconceive. An inviting redwood and wrought iron park bench was flanked by potted palms. Brilliant red foil apples burst the edges of a Fall bulletin board; in Spring, storybook characters along the walls would climb into clouds. Colored paper with book titles and authors hung from a section of the ceiling. A fabric banner proclaiming "Creativity" stood near the stairs. A table displayed an Ashanti royal bench and hand-woven African fabrics; a glass display case enclosed more artifacts. Toward the cafeteria, a series of student murals emblazoned the hall walls—a basketball, a ballet dancer, theatre curtains, a piano in vibrant colors. In fact, all of the hallway walls of the school were brightly decorated, mostly with student work: portraits and essays of famous Afro-Americans, illustrated stories and family anecdotes, Halloween witches and pumpkins and ghosts in many shapes and sizes, charts showing attendance percentages.

Principal Sylvia Peters pats shoulders and straightens student lines in the hallways near a chart showing one grade's high attendance percentages.

Children were in the hallways, classes taking a restroom break or going to library or gym or cafeteria. When not walking, each child stood on a foot-square floor tile, separated by one tile from the children in front and in back. Most stood with arms folded across chests but small fingers slipped out and waved greetings accompanied by smiles as passers-by were recognized.

When Principal Sylvia Peters was in the halls, she patted shoulders, straightened lines, bent low to offer comments. Younger children whispered, "Mrs. Peters!" and affectionate hugs were sometimes exchanged. A few words and a smile were likely to pass between principal and teacher, a few words of praise or admonition offered to or about the class.

On many days, students were away on field trips or visitors were in the school: artists presenting music or dance programs, anti-drug speakers, Project CANAL (Creating A New Approach to Learning) representatives observing classes as the school moved determinedly toward shared management.

The Seven Principles Ceremony. On September 22, 1988, my two colleagues and I were invited to an assembly in the Dumas School gym, where folding chairs seated the entire student body, the faculty, and a few visitors. Ushered into a sea of attentive black faces by two girls in white blouses, wine-colored cummerbunds, and black skirts, I was suddenly aware that I was white, as were my companions and a very few, seemingly unselfconscious teachers.

Music was being played. With no verbal direction, just a vigorous cue from the piano, everyone rose, respectful of a procession up the center aisle. In formal step-pause-step-pause progress, the principal and assistant principal led children carrying seven banners—depicting Unity, Faith, Creativity, Perseverance, Integrity, Purpose, Self-Love, and Respect.

At another cue from the piano, students in crossing guard belts quick-stepped in to audible "Left, left, left-right-left" commands. They stood the U.S. and Illinois flags in stands. Voices pledged allegiance, heartily sang "The Star-Spangled Banner" and, even more enthusiastically, "Lift Every Voice and Sing" before the color guard retreated. The piano sounded a few notes and everyone sat.

An eighth-grade boy, identified in the mimeographed program as Rahsaan Foster, stepped to the microphone and, in ringing voice, spoke of the philosophy of the school and the contributions of Afro-Americans to U.S. society. A girl, Sharrell Howell, then spoke of the Seven Principles depicted on banners and "embraced" by the faculty. Next, Assistant Principal Charlotte Gray gave the reason for the morning's ceremony—to honor eighth graders, beginning their final year at the school, for their "dedication and commitment to these Seven Principles for young black adulthood."

The stage curtains opened and a grades 4-6 gifted class, standing on three tiers of risers, sang three songs *a capella*: a parody of Shaker song "The Lord of the Dance," an African melody accompanied by clapping, and a beautiful round. Then Assistant Principal Gray reminded eighth graders of the Biblical warning that from those to whom much is given, much is expected. She exhorted them to continue

Afro-Americans' struggle for freedom, dignity, and justice. A woman next to me quietly intoned, "Mmm hmm!"

A girl, Tasha Kelly-Thompson, lit a candle, then stepped to the microphone. With barely a reference to the notes in her hand, she initiated a series of speeches on the seven principles, proclaiming in a sure, strong voice, "My classmates and I commit ourselves to the first principle of young black adulthood," Self-Love and Respect. The assemblage applauded. Wendy McCall declared the class' commitment to Purpose, and listed as practical applications of this principle higher education and choosing a spouse. Heather Scott softly extolled Integrity. Another girl, Jauri Bullock, was awarded brief but thunderous applause when she defined Perseverance as "to be, to do, to act, to agitate if necessary . . . to survive in an alien homeland, the only home we know." Four candles lit.

Creativity is "ideas and notions that go beyond basic living, that are as important as eating and sleeping," said Jefferey Holloway. This principle "has sustained black people for generations," he claimed, citing Duke Ellington, Langston Hughes, Charles White. A pause lengthened; he began again, reading from notes. The bobble was ignored by applauders. A girl, Domini Moore, forcefully and gesticulatingly spoke of Faith, "the ability to do and believe all that we want to become." The final boy, Crofton Whitfield, in oversized white sportscoat with hemmed sleeves, urged "the challenging job of motivating our black youth" beyond personal concerns in the interest of Unity. Seven candles lit. Everyone stood and promised to uphold the principles.

Finally, a trim, well-dressed woman stepped confidently to the microphone. "This is my fifth year as the principal of Dumas School," Sylvia Peters smiled. She pronounced the school's name doo-MAH in proper French. "And today's my fiftieth birthday—some of my family has traveled here and is sitting over there. And I've lost fifty pounds!" She introduced themes: the school as extended family, personal concerns as school concerns. Black pride was important. "The only place where I learned about my blackness," Peters told them, "was at home. But not you. All our staff—black and white—care enough about you to tell you about blackness."

To parents, "We cannot believe when they say that the black family is falling apart," she said, both offering and asking support. She invited parents' involvement in the school: "We need you." She spoke of the school's movement toward shared decision-making, giving a voice to parents, staff, and students.

To students, "It's my job to know everything about you," Peters warned. "And I expect perfection. We expect you to become winners so you must understand your roots and mainstream culture and yourself." It was a conscious and emotional extension of the principle of *in loco parentis*. "It's nice to see you dressed up and, as always, well-behaved," she smiled again.

She mentioned the school's two-year association with The Oak Woods Cemetery across the street. An Ashanti royal bench from Africa, draped with African cloth, stood on the stage, a gift from cemetery administrator Bruce Holstrum. "We will probably be one of only a few schools in America to have an African art museum," Peters announced, referring to the bench as an important first exhibit.

When Peters finished speaking, seventh and eighth graders formed a candlelit procession out of the gym, piano cues directing movement. Perfect attenders were applauded and followed. Classes left last, becoming chatty toward the end.

Peters introduced some students to her relatives, who hugged them. The clan recalled that many of their forebears were educators, that Dumas had been a "dump" a few years ago but was a "miracle" now. Peters remembered that there hadn't been enough chairs for an all-school assembly when she arrived. As older students removed audio equipment and the Ashanti bench, a youngster lagged behind his class to ask the principal, "Can I sit on the king's stool?"

Two Research Foci. After the first visit to Dumas, our research team decided to stray from our original plan to study one Chicago school. Studies of both Dumas and Armstrong Schools, we felt, would contribute to our broad goal of understanding arts education in ordinary U.S. settings. Armstrong better typified arts education practice but Dumas offered insights into the potential contributions of arts education in an inner city setting. When we selected Dumas for our National Center case studies, it appeared to be little more than a ghetto elementary school with an aggressive principal getting their act together. By the time our study was completed, Sylvia Peters had become recognized across Chicago and introduced to a national television audience as an arts education spokesperson. Although the vision and commitment at Dumas would encourage an idealized view of arts classes for the impoverished, a portrayal of daily classroom difficulties would also obviate why Dumas' hard-won success was rare among such schools. The exception would illustrate the rule.

After a second visit to the school, a double focus for a case study at Dumas was determined. First, as in all the studies in this book, I would try to learn *how* the arts were taught here, aims and approaches, philosophies and methods, resources. I would observe and interview. I would try to figure out what worked and what didn't. Second, I would inquire: *Why* does arts education work here? If it was working well, why here? What was the impetus, the motivation for arts education at Dumas? What contributed to or impeded success? How strong was the momentum?

How the Arts Were Taught at Dumas

The first research question: How are the arts taught at Dumas? The short answer: (a) by integrating the arts and academics in classrooms and (b) by taking advantage of arts in the city.

Integrating the Arts and Academics. Integrating the arts with academic subjects rather than teaching the arts as separate subjects is a matter of trading off advantages and disadvantages. Integration suggests connectedness across subject areas, encourages holistic perspective, offers opportunities to synthesize information often presented as exclusive domains. Integration offers more time for arts instruction than would otherwise be possible. Integration may help teachers with limited arts backgrounds; knowing how to teach history or English already, they may find it easier to add art or music or drama than to prepare separate lessons in these less familiar subjects.

But integration usually also means that the arts are subservient to academic masters. Maps are drawn in social studies; science experiments are documented *via* illustrations; the alphabet is sung. Much of what passes for art is therefore prescribed by academic content with little opportunity for creative expression. There is little engagement in art for art's sake, or appreciation and critique, or art history, or aesthetics. For these reasons, the Getty Center for Education in the Arts has opposed integrating the arts and academics.

Before Chicago's reform movement, elementary schools had no arts specialists prepared to teach the arts as separate subjects. There was little time in the daily schedule for either music or the visual arts, had specialists been available; no time at all specified for theatre or dance. At Dumas, efforts to expose students to the city's impressive array of arts offset some of the drawbacks associated with the absence of arts teachers and with the integration of subject matters. This exposure was a vital component of arts education at the school, fully recognized as such by school personnel, even when the efforts were exhausting.

Observations and interviews at Dumas indicated a variety of practices and opinions regarding integrating subjects.

Sandra Henderson's Kindergarten

The worksheet resembles an oversized roadmap, covered with curvilinear purple lines. The names of colors are printed in the odd shapes formed by intersecting lines. If all the shapes marked "blue" are colored, a kite will appear on the page. Coloring those shapes blue is the current task of about twenty five- and six-year-olds.

Sandra Henderson, the bespectacled young teacher, moves cheerfully and purposefully about the grouped desks in the room. Several months pregnant, she bends low over a quiet, round-faced girl. The child smiles, her head dropping shyly.

"Mildred, do you know what that says?"

Mildred hesitates. A forefinger tucked into her mouth comes out and points to a patch marked "blue." Her eyes widen as she turns to her teacher and softly offers, "Red?"

"No, you've been listening to Erskine," Henderson replies. "I told you not to listen to him." Henderson explains the directions softly and asks the child if she understands. Mildred nods. Looking up, Henderson announces generally, "I want it neat, folks. Stay in the lines. We're going to end up with a pretty picture. What are you going to do, Randy?"

As if reading, Randy responds, "I'm going to color it blue where it says 'blue.'"

Henderson nods approvingly, "Color it real nice like you did that banana for me." She continues walking among the clustered desks, cajoling the youngsters into attending to task. To a group beginning to squabble over shared crayons, "If you have a blue of your own, go get it." The school-supplied blue crayons from the plastic bucket are too few for the number of students in the room.

The room is colorful with both teacher-made and commercial materials. An alphabet crowns the chalkboard, each letter learned displayed, letters unlearned facing the wall. It is early November and A through H are visible. Cupboards line one wall, coathooks and a sink another; windows overlook Ellis Street.

"Oh! Oh, Stevenson!" Stevenson is coloring his entire paper blue. Recovering, the teacher calmly asks him to repeat the directions. He is silent. "You're always good at this," she coaxes. "What's the problem?" She brings him to her desk where they can talk privately. A few girls tease, "Oooooh, Stevenson!" He hangs his head.

"Leave Stevenson alone," Henderson comes to his defense. "Thomas, you'll be able to see a pretty picture after you color in the right spaces," she says *en route* to her desk.

Before the talk with Stevenson is over, several children have lined up to show her their progress on incomplete kites. Those whose coloring stayed within the lines are praised. Stevenson returns to his desk with a star sticker on his forehead and a hopeful expression on his face.

Sitting next to him, Mildred colors the proper shapes dutifully but not fully to the edges, so the kite fails to emerge. On those occasions when her eyes wander from the page, her fingers continue to move the blue crayon back and forth, rubbing thick layers of waxy color onto the paper. She decides to outline the shapes she is coloring, a productive move, then takes her paper to Henderson for approval.

"OK, Mildred, pretty good, pretty good," her teacher encourages. "You got out just a little bit but that's not bad." Mildred prances back with a smile.

Brandon declares that he needs a Band-aid. As Henderson washes his hand at the sink in the room, Brandon reports that someone broke someone else's nose last night. His teacher tells him she is sorry to hear that and that there are no Band-aids.

A girl is scolding Joshua for deliberately sitting at the wrong desk. Henderson seats him, then talks to him about his paper. At the next table, she hugs Mildred, "You're doing much better."

"I needa write my name," Mildred says.

A class of older students, visible in the hall through the doorway, is lining up. Each child stands on a foot-square tile in the asphalt floor, arms folded across his or her chest. Mildred and another girl wave silently to them. Natasha taps my knee and remarks, "My friend says you got yellow hair."

A kindergartner with a star sticker on her forehead has finished her paper and written her name on it. She glances around the room aimlessly until Henderson says, "Don't you have somebody to help?" Then the girl takes a wandering boy by the elbow and leads him to his desk. They lean over his paper and soon she is coloring it for him.

A boy finishes next and asks, "Who wants help?"

Back at her desk, Henderson issues a general reminder: "On the back of your paper, once you have finished, you should be practicing your name." Children bring papers to her desk and she writes their names on the back as models for them to practice.

Most of the kindergartners are sitting at their desks but there are always a couple up and moving, especially Joshua. With a big grin, he hops across the room on one foot; his teacher ignores this. Soon, a girl is helping him write his name. Henderson joins them, putting a hand on Joshua's shoulder.

"I wanna..." Joshua begins.

"You need to practice your name," Henderson interrupts him, then returns to her desk.

Joshua writes for a moment, then protests, "I can't practice my name." Soon he is up again.

"Joshua, you know what?" Henderson asks. "I'm tired of seeing you up." Her tone is not harsh. Joshua moves to his chair, stands behind it for a bit, then wanders again; he jumps; he skips. He catches her attention; she raises her voice; he sits.

Erskine says in dismay, "I messed up my name."

"That's OK," Henderson and another boy respond in unison.

The public address system crackles. "Everyone is expected to eat either in the cafeteria or something brought from home. Junk food is not allowed. We will be on our best behavior," Then a cryptic addition: "I think we have all learned a lesson and we know how to behave."

The bell rings. "Table one, you can get your hats and sit down," the teacher announces. The children take paper crowns bearing their names from a shelf and put them on. "Table two, you can put your papers in your book bags." She points to children who stood before they were called; they sit.

After all have put papers into book bags and donned millinery, children are dismissed by tables to wash hands with the teacher's help at the classroom sink. "When we finish washing our hands, heads down on desks and we'll listen to music. Stevenson, I'm going to have to take your hat back unless you relax like Mildred." Silence eludes the group until the teacher threatens, "I'll play *my* music again if you won't listen to *yours*."

"Their" music turns out to be a phonograph record of verses about trains sung by a soprano with children's voices chiming in for the chorus. Brandon and Dominique sing along. Joshua and Stevenson fidget with their hats. Most sit quietly, joining the singing sporadically. When the song is over, a few applaud.

Henderson goes around, collecting hats and replacing them on the shelf.

"I don't have a hat," Lawanda complains.

"I'll make you one today," her teacher assures her. "Stevenson, we just washed hands. Why is your hand on the floor? Joshua, I want you to be quiet."

"Zip your mouth," a boy chimes in earnestly. He moves a pinched thumb and forefinger across his lips.

"Yes, that's a good idea. Zip your mouth," Henderson confirms.

A girl now: "Zip your mouth."

Again, the teacher agrees.

The first boy unzips his mouth to offer an encore, "Zip your mouth."

"Don't open your mouth with any more zips," Henderson calls a halt.

Another song begins, "Snowflakes falling, falling very still. Sh! Sh!" The children become quiet. One girl has her fingers in her ears. Stevenson has moved his star sticker to under his left eye. Handwashing finishes during the next song, a Halloween tune.

The teacher asks, "Is that enough music for today?" Some children say "yes" and some say "no."

Excerpts from an Interview with Sandra Henderson.

> I don't have a lot of background in the arts except that I grew up in a neighborhood with a lot of after-school programs. And in the Chicago Public School system, we went to museums. The city has so much!
>
> I did my undergrad and graduate work in social service. Then I went to Chicago State to get certified for teaching. When it was time for student teaching, it was during the strike so I did my student teaching and a half year of teaching in a Catholic school.
>
> This is my first year here. I came to Dumas for a meeting once and I liked the way it looked and what I had heard. From what I can see, this school is different. Somebody's always going some place or coming in to present a play or something. We do a lot of theatre here. Also ETA, a black theatre group, does ten or twelve plays a year. Today, everybody on the first floor except the two kindergarten rooms went to the Museum of Science and Industry. Recently, the school got free tickets to take the older kids to see Maurice Hines' musical at the New Regal. My husband, my sister, and I bought tickets and went, too. A pair of

volunteers and a couple of teachers hauled the students there on Saturday.

In my class, I have 15 all-day kindergartners, who may not be as developed as the others, and ten half-day. I prefer they all go all day. The half-day kids need more art. I think the arts are important for kindergartners because they learn to manipulate their hands and their muscles. They all do the math and writing but sometimes half-day kids say, "We didn't get to color."

I let them paint sometimes and they make something wild. I need to do more of that. We do a lot of coloring and cutting and pasting. They like to draw. A lot of times, they'll ask, "What should I draw?" or "What color should it be?" I tell them to draw whatever or to color whatever color. If somebody colors a blue nut, I might tell them, "Nuts are usually brown but this is a pretty blue nut." I try to keep them creative and then bring them into realistic colors. One boy's stuff is so abstract and it makes perfect sense to him. I tell him that's OK but to follow directions, too.

We have paint and scissors and glue and plenty of construction paper—that's why we do a lot of things with construction paper. We get an allowance for supplies each year. A lot of things I buy—books with sheets I can duplicate, magazines the kids can cut out of.

When I teach, it's all one. We do math but it's art, too—counting, recognizing, writing numbers; coloring, cutting, pasting, drawing. The same for the alphabet. I don't know if it's better to mix art into other subjects but it helps to cover more things. There's probably not enough time for art except around a holiday. Kids might learn more because it's exciting. A lot of kids are so TV-oriented. If you don't have games or ways of keeping their interest, you'll lose them. I think it helps to have art integrated into other subjects but I always try to find some time for strictly artwork once or twice a week, like when we made penguins.

With the penguins, I cut out everything beforehand because that work was too fine for them. I gave them the parts and showed them one I had made. They glued the parts together. Of course, some of the penguins were all glue and some of the heads and mouths were in funny places but cute. The kids liked them. We walked around the room like penguins. Just to say, "A penguin lives on the North Pole"—big deal. But they'll remember they walked around like penguins.

Commentary. Sandra Henderson was a cheerful, caring, dedicated teacher. Despite little specialized arts training, she made the arts, especially visual arts, part of all her kindergartners' activities. Seeing the children loved art, she wanted that enthusiasm to motivate better learning in academics. She saw drawing, cutting, and pasting as activities to develop fine motor coordination. She used music as a behavior management tool. In her classroom, activities overlapped several domains at once; they served various goals simultaneously.

In addition to integrating subjects, Henderson believed there was a need for separate curricular space and time for art. She found that time and dedicated it to "making little things"—holiday or seasonal things like pre-planned, pre-cut penguins. In these ways, hers was not unlike other kindergarten classrooms across the country, Henderson not unlike other kindergarten teachers.

But Henderson's classroom did not match most Americans' concept of kindergarten experience. We do not expect every student to be Afro-American; we do not think of an inner city school as typical. Unless we look into a classroom like this, we do not comprehend the myriad difficulties of teaching the impoverished. More than other teachers, Henderson spent enormous energy training her charges to develop behaviors more-or-less taken for granted among the middle class: take turns; share supplies; stay in your seat; raise your hand; finish the page. Henderson's students did not focus easily on school tasks, did not conform easily to school behaviors but, under her tutelage, they were moving toward interaction patterns sanctioned by mainstream U.S. culture. Although the habits were difficult to acquire, kindergartners' attitudes were open and accepting, Henderson thought.

The school was different from most, too. "Somebody's always going some place or coming in to present a play or something," Henderson said. Through field trips and in-school performances, community arts resources were often engaged. Stu-

The accomplishments of Afro-Americans such as Chicago Mayor Eugene Sawyer are highlighted in hallway displays Nearby are student silhouettes.

Alexandre Dumas Elementary School
Chicago, Illinois

dents were introduced to Afro-American art forms to gain a sense of heritage, roots, pride. Western art forms were also in abundance as avenues to personal enrichment and mainstream culture. Although Henderson found it necessary to buy some art supplies herself, it did not seem, as the *Tribune* charged, that emphasis on basic skills and test scores, finances and priorities had pushed art and music out of her classroom. In the hands of a non-specialist, the range of arts experiences offered to children narrowed but, compensatorily, frequent exposure to arts professionals broadened children's experiences.

Down the hall, Laura Downey, one of the schools' few Caucasian teachers, also saw the arts as motivating and integrative.

Laura Downey's First Grade

In a "science experiment" to estimate how many seeds will fill a spoon, first graders are reminded: "Now, the first thing we do when we do an experiment," Downey says with a dramatic pause, "is to draw the things we're using." On the chalkboard, she draws and labels seeds, the dishes holding the seeds, the spoon.

The children read each letter as she writes, "P-U-M-P-K-I-N."

Of one sketch, Letitia says, "A peanut doesn't look like that."

"Yes, it does," Downey replies. "What kind of seeds are these?" she asks, holding a dish aloft. "British?"

British hesitates. The class squirms. "We're all going to respect British by being quiet so she can answer."

"Sunflower," British offers.

"Good. If *you* knew that, too," Downey adds generally, "give yourself a pat on the back." Several children take this comment literally.

Although the primary grades have art supplies (funded through the Educational Consolidation Improvement Act or ECIA) that upper grades do not, scarcity of supplies plagues Downey's classroom as it did Henderson's.

"I have some boxes of crayons but you'll have to share," the teacher says. Even when one box per pair is distributed, there are not enough of the small boxes to go around. When the children bring this to her attention, Downey looks unhappy. "I don't know what else to do besides share."

In this class, the arts seem less endangered by lack of materials and academic priorities than by the rambunctiousness of students. Downey is unfailingly courteous in her discipline, modeling the manners she tries to instill. An example of her style: "Thank you, William, for being so quiet," Downey says. A few others respond and are thanked. "Oh, I'm so glad that Nina and Kevin followed directions." But the management effort consumes most of the instructional time.

"Amber, how come every time I give you crayons, the box comes back half-empty?" Downey asks a girl. Amber blames another child for taking crayons but her teacher quietly replies, "I see them in your desk," and puts an empty box on Amber's desk for her to fill.

Pencils passed out to those in need are now collected. Richard gets up to give the teacher his. "Sit down, please. I'll come around to you," she tells him but it is when Ms. Sprat, the teacher-aide, says "Richard, sit down!" in a quiet but authoritative tone that he does so. From the perimeter, Sprat takes a more direct approach than does Downey, battling the noise with individual corrections.

Downey raises her voice to announce, "It's time to go home. I'll dismiss the *quietest* row first." There is silence, which she savors for two full minutes. Then she gives three awards for "working hard on assignments, not running around, being quiet, and doing a nice job in the hallways" to Charles, to Tiffany who is said to be improving, and to Malcolm, one of five students new to this classroom today. The trio proudly accept certificates, prizes, and applause.

Students in the quietest row are dismissed to get coats. In a different row, a boy anxious to leave silences the boy next to him with a stranglehold. The bell rings and the rest becomes bedlam. Sprat, giving up on silence, hurries along the dawdlers.

Excerpts from an Interview with Laura Downey.

> I got my undergraduate training at Michigan State University but I have no formal training in the arts except for one music theory class. I've had a little piano but not much. I dabble with drawing and painting, some water colors, a little oil. Mainly, I sketch with pencil and charcoal, nothing fancy. It's a relaxation mechanism.
>
> I'd like to have an art teacher in the school. It's not so important in first grade but, as the kids get older, they really don't get any formal instruction in, for example, drawing in three dimensions or shadowing or the difference between sketching and drawing, and different types of art forms. I do art with my students fairly frequently but I don't know many songs so my children don't get music as much as I would like. That bothers me. I can cover drama because I have some training in that. We do quite a bit of acting out stories and puppet plays during reading class. I don't think the kids realize when we're doing drama—they just enjoy it. Last year, we had a little Easter program for our school—costumes and everything.
>
> The Chicago Public Schools Board of Education requires each teacher to turn in time sheets indicating the number of minutes spent on each subject area. A prescribed number of minutes are required for reading, math, and the other subjects. There's not much time available for the arts.
>
> Also, standardized testing hurts the arts. Everything is ITBS [Iowa Test of Basic Skills]. The pressure we feel to concentrate on academics comes from our principal, who gets it from her district superintendent,

who gets it from parents, who get it from the media—all the rotten stuff they say about Chicago Public Schools. Teachers are evaluated by their principals and principals are evaluated by their district superintendents, primarily based on the kids' scores. Most of our children are behind academically, so we're under pressure to push academics.

Kids actually get academic concepts a lot better when they're acting or something else. I would integrate the arts into my teaching of other subjects even if someone told me, "I don't want to see you wasting time doing this again." It's definitely motivating and I think it helps socially and developmentally, too.

In the classroom, children are often limited to oral response as their only form of communication, unfortunately. To do any kind of arts gives them another mode of communication—drawing, painting, acting, writing. A lot of children communicate better given a different way of expressing themselves. I have children who wouldn't answer questions if I paid them but who will get up there and act like nobody's business. All of a sudden, you see this different person come out. They assume a character and they're no longer timid.

Mrs. Peters really encourages the arts here. She has a background in the arts. She allows the students to experience ballet, opera, tap dance, the art museum. She offers us a chance to go and actually experience these things. Four or five classes a year get to work with resident artists in theatre arts, dance—all sorts of different things.

That's encouraging but she always selects children who are excelling academically. I understand that it won't hurt the children who are doing well to be out of the class. But, unfortunately, it's the children who are *not* motivated in school, who are *not* doing well, who are *not* really inclined even to be here who keep getting left out. I feel those children really need the arts.

Commentary. As in Henderson's kindergarten, there were overlapping and conflicting goals in Downey's first grade. Downey recognized the benefits of self-expression in the arts but felt a competing pressure from standardized testing. Respecting individuals and modeling manners seemed to compete with—in fact, to overshadow—instruction including, presumably, arts instruction. Lack of specialized training also constrained classroom arts experiences. Downey worried that the enrichments of professional arts experiences were denied to the most needy; that, even where the arts were enjoyed in a low-achieving neighborhood school, that the neediest students were still denied.

Patricia Beckwith's and Grace Matthews' Second Grades

Two second-grade classrooms rehearse for a joint performance of *Peter Pan* in the Spring.

With a cheerful smile, Patricia Beckwith tells students, "OK, let's stand. Put your arms at your sides to control your energy and show discipline. Actors need a lot of discipline." She demonstrates deep breathing. "Stomach out on inhale and in on exhale," she directs. She has them inhale, hold their breath for six counts, then exhale; they droop and sigh with relief. "Discipline!" she calls and they repeat the breathing three times. After the third time, some playfully fall to the floor in mock asphyxiation.

After seating themselves in rows on the floor of an empty classroom, each child is asked to recite a line as persuasively as possible "so we can be the best we can be." The first row stands and turns to face the rest of the class. Each child says, "I don't want to share a room with my brother because he is too sloppy!" Many speak with natural inflection and good volume.

"Good," Beckwith responds to most but to the last boy in the row, "Good but I don't believe you." He sits dejectedly and holds his head in his hands. "Just be more convincing," she encourages him.

The next row stands. A girl virtually shouts, "I don't *want* to share a room with my sister because she is *too sloppy*!"

"I believe you!" Beckwith responds, impressed, as the children break into applause. When the fourth row stands and elocutes, many seated students respond, "I believe you" or "I don't believe you."

From persuasion, they move on to articulation, reciting a new line, "The fat cat ate the fat rat." One boy loudly proclaims that the rat ate the cat and the children burst into laughter. Some speakers articulate the letter T so precisely it sounds like tap dancing.

Grace Matthews comes forward, looking serious, and Beckwith leaves the room. "We're going to practice our songs. Let's warm up with the scales. Do," Matthews intones, placing a hand horizontally before her. The children join her, more-or-less on pitch, some raising their hands as she does when they move to "Re." They sing up and down a scale.

"Now, the first song comes when the lost boys are trying to convince Wendy to stay," she explains. "For the play, just the lost boys will sing this song but we'll all learn it now. I'll sing a line and you repeat it after me."

They try this. As she sings, Matthews draws out some syllables to emphasize certain words. Volume increases until, toward the end, some students are nearly shouting.

"Settle down," she says sternly and they begin the song again, line by line. "Stay with me," she cajoles. "Don't let it drag." A change in rhythm elicits confusion but she directs them with finger-snapping and her own determined singing. The singing deteriorates to chanting, then mumbling, only the teacher managing to maintain a semblance of melody. But today's practice is only the first and, at the end, Matthews compliments them on their effort, "All right. Not too bad."

Alexandre Dumas Elementary School
Chicago, Illinois

Excerpts from an Interview with Patricia Beckwith. A teacher of fifteen years, three at Dumas, Patricia Beckwith trained in education and in clinical psychology and was gradually moving toward a doctorate. Having taken a few art courses, she declared, "I love theater. I love visiting the Art Institute of Chicago. I collect Oriental and antique art."

> I feel that this school is interested in the arts. Mrs. Peters tells us all the time, "Get the paints down! Mess up your room! Let them put their hands in the paint." Mrs. Peters is wonderful. She gives you free reign. Not only that—she wants definite concrete experiences every month, for instance, handprints with paint or making popcorn or soap bubbles—not necessarily the arts but stimulants that encourage creativity. Or taking the kids out on a Fall day to collect leaves and really looking at the beauty of the colors and textures. We're encouraged to awaken aesthetic senses.
>
> I think the importance of the arts here has a lot to do with the person at the head. What's important to the boss automatically becomes important to you. Mrs. Peters really motivates the faculty. She brings in articles on the value of artistic stimulation in the classroom. She's just such a verbal, artistic person herself. You have to admire her.
>
> I try to integrate the arts into everything I teach. It comes naturally because art is so much a part of me. I have students draw everything that they do—a science experiment, story illustrations, reading with expression. It personalizes things and incorporates an artistic angle. Having the arts as part of lessons enhances students' learning. They become more creative. They look at things more than one way. They learn more; they personalize it more; they remember more; and perhaps they have more fun.
>
> I think you should integrate the arts into teaching but I think also it should be taught separately. Some kids are truly interested and have a vocation in the arts; they should be encouraged. The others should be respected, too. I think there's time to do both.

Excerpts from an Interview with Grace Matthews. Grace Matthews had taught for fourteen years, three at Dumas. In collaboration with Beckwith's, her classes had celebrated Black History Month each of the previous two Februarys with student-made masks and jewelry displayed for the school. She extended Beckwith's feeling that the arts enhanced learning through motivation and personalization with her own feeling that the arts enhanced learning through improved self-esteem and classroom discipline. She acknowledged both the benefits and difficulties of field trips. Directly and indirectly, she noted lack of parental interest or involvement in the arts, Dumas School's default role as sole provider. Of her preparation in the arts, Matthews said, "I took some music and theatre classes as an undergraduate. I guess I'm a frustrated actress but I would *not* want to perform. I play the piano and organ." Like Beckwith, Matthews saw Principal Sylvia Peters as the school's inspiration and driving force for the arts.

We do lots of things besides the arts. Character education is very important. But the arts are a school-wide effort here. I think the arts are important because it's important for every child to experience success. Sometimes you can see in their eyes that they have mentally dropped out by third grade. The arts allow kids to draw on their experiences and to use their talents. Kids need to be proud to learn. We give lots of praise and recognition. We always have student artwork on display.

I integrate the arts with other subjects—draw experiments, act out reading stories, illustrate letters—anything to get the concept across. In reading today, for instance, I taught a song called "Over in the Meadow" to go with a story and, pretty soon, kids who weren't in that reading group joined in the singing. I often bring in songs.

I have more time for the arts when I integrate them into academic work because we have no scheduled arts time. So much has to be covered for the tests. Each quarter, we have criterion-referenced tests in reading and math from the Chicago Public Schools Board of Ed and Iowa tests annually. And the state requires writing as a focus; they have these manuals that list topics that must be written on. You have to squeeze the arts in. Sometimes you need a whole afternoon for art; by integrating, I can get a whole week.

I think discipline is easier when the arts are part of everything because the kids want to be involved. Their interest is contagious. They share materials and keep the noise level down so they can finish their product and get comments on it—especially from Mrs. Peters. It's very important to them to hear from her. You can see that she gets around to every room nearly every day but, if she doesn't come by, they send stuff to her or someone else in the office.

It all starts from the top. We have a principal who isn't afraid to stick her neck out. She has lots of energy, lots of stamina. She gets out from behind her desk. She gets the staff involved and then the kids. You've probably noticed that the kids don't mess up this school; there's no graffiti anywhere. You can see kids picking up litter without being asked. There's a feeling of pride. We let the kids do as much as possible.

We've had Urban Gateways here since before my time. It's a program the school buys that includes an artist's residency; one or two field trips, such as the one six classes took a few weeks ago to the opera *Hansel and Gretel*; and some assemblies at school. They brought African musical instruments into my room. Sometimes field trips can be rough. It can be so much responsibility that the teacher can't really enjoy the trip. But they're necessary because some students would never get to go to see an opera, to learn audience participation, how to behave. They need those experiences.

Parents rarely comment about the arts. They may talk to me about the computer lab or gym time. The Suzuki violin program does require parent involvement, however.

Under murals made by students during an Urban Gateways artist residency, Dumas Elementary students smile as they stand in line near the cafeteria.

Commentary. From conversations with these four teachers, three benefits from integrating the arts and academics emerged. For one, they all voiced strong belief that students learned more academically in response to interdisciplinary teaching. Downey said students "get concepts a lot better;" Matthews, that she used any kind of arts activity "to get the concept across." Beckwith stated this idea a bit differently: "They learn more;" and Henderson, "kids might learn more because it's more exciting." Henderson's phrasing brings up a second, closely related benefit these four teachers all noted: motivation. While these first two benefits of integration are enhancements to academic learning, the third favors the arts: these teachers found that integrating subjects allowed more time for the arts.

As the next interview reports, Lydia Mosley agreed with her colleagues that the arts were a motivating factor in students' academic learning but thought academics could also enhance arts learning. Mosley also shared Matthews' conclusion that the arts had a generalized positive effect on students' feelings of successful accomplishment and, consequently, confidence and self-esteem. Interestingly, Mosley described herself as less likely to integrate the arts and academics than the others, although she alone voiced the opinion that integration allowed students "more freedom about how to learn."

Matthews saw that integration improved classroom discipline. Henderson explicitly employed the arts in behavior management. Mosley talked about the arts having differential effects on student behavior considered holistically as opposed to deportment during a single arts-related activity.

Lydia Mosley's Second-Third Grades

On low cabinets under windows, blue- and red-painted turkeys made from oatmeal cylinders sport construction paper heads and tiers of fringed paper tails.

"Second graders? Third graders? Who would like to read your paragraph?" tall, fashionable Lydia Mosley asks. Hands shoot up. She chooses a second grader and calls for quiet.

A girl comes forward. "My turkey's name is Felicia. My turkey looks like me. Yes, it is friendly..." she begins. The class ponders the inclusion of the word "yes" in the third sentence. Whether to keep or delete "yes" is a choice left to the student.

A second girl is chosen and approaches the front of the room. "My turkey's name is Leon. My turkey looks like a dog..." she reads.

Mosley begins the discussion, "What did you like about her turkey? Her turkey's kind of different." The class wonders about a turkey that looks like a dog and the girl decides to delete that.

A third girl reads and a critique session follows. A fourth girl begins with apparent innocence, "My turkey's name is Piss..." Laughter erupts and must be quieted several times as the lesson continues.

Excerpts from an Interview with Lydia Mosley.

> I've been at Dumas less than three years. Before that, I worked at various schools FTB [as a full-time basis substitute]. I was not certified at that time.
>
> I have a lot of interest in art. I had several elementary art courses and also art history. And I have taken hobby courses such as ceramics. I go to art galleries.
>
> I think the arts are very important in education. It gives the child a chance to use his creativity. It gives him self-esteem, confidence, and a sense of accomplishment. We do have art in this classroom but not as much as I would like because, this year, I'm adjusting to teaching younger children than I have taught in the past. My energy is going to the reading program and phonics and handwriting. Our priority in this school is reading.

In this room, sometimes we integrate the arts with other subjects but sometimes we don't. Students have more freedom about how to learn with the arts in lessons; it's not as structured, not forced. They learn on their own. The motivation to do art is greater if it follows an academic subject. For example, we discussed the history of the Cameroons before we made masks and they felt more comfortable about making them.

Art is messy and kids get wild. It can be an aggravation. It takes time. I think that's why more teachers don't do more of it. Most schools don't emphasize the arts because of the time element. The stress is put on reading and Iowa test scores and math—that pushes away the arts. But I personally believe that art helps with reading and math by giving confidence.

I think the arts makes us more pleasant with each other. We have a more loving classroom relationship. There is a lot of movement in the room when we do art but, at another level, some discipline problems don't occur because people like school. Somehow it works that way.

Some kids have an "I can't draw" attitude. In my room, we don't use "I can't." We always try. That's my personal philosophy.

I have bought art materials out of my own pocket. Either you like art or you don't. If you do, you'll find materials.

The arts are contagious here—our philosophy, bulletin boards, beautification, the plants outside. The hallways throughout the building have art. It's part of the school and it becomes part of the child. No one wants to get left behind. It keeps expanding because we have so many good field trips. It's just like money—the more you have, the more you want. The field trips are very important.

The attitude starts with our principal. She will tell you her expectations on art. She wants art; she wants theatre; she wants field trips. She won't put you under pressure. She lets us discuss which field trips we want, which plays we want to see. She lets us brainstorm.

Lydia Mosley said of the arts, "It gives the child a chance to use his creativity." But her Thanksgiving turkeys were less an example of self-expression than of following directions. There were few creative options other than naming.

In Mosley's classroom, as in the others, the arts were closely associated with words. For Mosley, turkeys were made, then paragraphs written and read; for Beckwith and Matthews, lines were recited and lyrics sung; for Henderson, the word "blue" was recognized and colored. For people in Western, literate societies, language is easily accessible, directly taught. In classrooms, the arts, more esoteric than the word, may be in danger of being collapsed into more familiar verbal expression. In the next classroom vignette, an improvised drama precedes a written language exercise.

Karen Genelly's Fifth Grade

Two lines of fifth graders scurry upstairs from a lesson outdoors in the cool November sunshine. Wordlessly, they nearly run to the classroom door where they stop abruptly, conveying an image of a locomotive braking to a silent halt. With a brisk pace, Karen Genelly, tall and Scandinavian in appearance, catches up to her class and gives a key to a boy who unlocks the door. Students tumble in, quickly hang coats, and take seats. Points are recorded on the blackboard for good behavior outdoors.

"OK, social studies," Genelly announces in rapid-fire style. Leif ("Lav, not Leaf") Erickson's voyages are reviewed, students pointing out relevant locations on a map. Cristoforo Columbus is next, Genelly leading discussion with a rat-a-tat of "why" questions: Why did he go to the Spice Islands? No refrigerators—why not? Why didn't they use dry ice?

"OK, let's act this out," she moves quickly on. The children catch their breaths. The teacher chooses a girl who trots smartly to the front of the room, beaming. "Do you want to be Columbus or Isabella?"

"Columbus," the girl snaps. "No, Isabella."

Both girls and boys raise hands, hoping to play Columbus; a boy is chosen. A newspaper reporter rounds out the *dramatiis personae*.

"What newspaper do you want to represent?" the teacher inquires of the boy chosen.

"The *L.A. Times*."

"What's the problem with that?" the teacher wants to know.

"No L.A.," Isabella remarks succinctly. But disbelief is willingly suspended, as Coleridge would have it, over the appearance of a California journalist in a fifteenth century scene.

A brief search for Isabella's crown is fruitless, so there are no props. The "set" includes photos of Egyptian art and a chart of hieroglyphics, student-made monster masks from Halloween, and hand-drawn portraits of unidentified characters in tuxedos. But the show goes on.

Columbus: Your majesty, I need some boats.

Isabella: Why?

Columbus: I don't know.

Hoots of laughter erupt from the class.

"How are you ever going to find the New World?" Genelly wonders. "One more try."

Alexandre Dumas Elementary School
Chicago, Illinois

Columbus: I believe I can sail to the Orient by going west, around the world.

Isabella: No. (She crosses her arms and turns her head away regally.)

Columbus: Let's ask the king.

Isabella: I don't care *what* the king thinks!

Columbus turns to Genelly, stymied. "What do I do now? The play's over if she won't give me the boats."

Isabella retorts, "No! She didn't give him the boats the first time he asked. Five years later, he asked again and *then* she gave them to him."

That's right," Genelly confirms. Columbus exits briefly and returns to ask again but the queen seems adamant.

Columbus: Come on! I need your help!

Isabella: On your knees!

"Do I have to get on my knees?" Columbus pleads with Genelly, who shrugs. He genuflects but Isabella remains skeptical. He begs and she is persuaded.

The reporter enters the scene and interviews both actors.

Reporter to Isabella:
Don't you want to see the Indians?

"I think we have a time traveller here," Genelly comments of this anachronistic question, noting that there could not have been a reporter either.

Reporter: How do you like Isabella?

Columbus: I don't like her.

The class laughs again as Isabella screams for guards to arrest the petitioner.

"Get to the point," Genelly directs. "No personalities."

New characters are chosen for a scene in which Columbus' crew considers mutiny. "Make sure you can do this with *facts*," the teacher warns a prospective actor. She cues the cast with a few motivational comments, including the idea that Columbus is beginning to doubt the roundness of the Earth. Timing in this scene sags until a more aggressive sailor is added to the cast. He quickly foments an insurrection and is called a fool by a loyalist.

"Marcus, you gotta face *us*," Genelly interjects a bit of stagecraft.

Hostilities escalate and the sailors fight with relish, then sight land. Lots of facts have been recalled and the emotional vacillations of the historical figures have been explored.

Genelly is at the map again. "This is where Columbus *thought* he was and this is where he *really* was," she points. She explains why he was confused, why he called the natives "Indians." "The last scene is going to be from the Indians' point of view. This time, I want to see less silliness. It's fun but we want to see what it was like."

A new cast is selected to explore Native Americans' reactions to people with an odd skin color, big boats, different language, clothes, and customs. Tepees and pueblos studied earlier in the year are remembered before this third scene is haltingly enacted.

"What we saw was a dramatization," the teacher then explains. "Some better than others but it was OK. What you are going to do now is write a newspaper article. You have three choices: one, Columbus asking Isabella for ships. You should be able to tell me who, what, when, where, why, and how," she says and reviews a few facts. "Two, interview the sailors. Three, an account of how you think the Indians felt. Remember, the Indians did not know . . ." she continues. "Decide what your newspaper story is going to be about. Use your book and use your imagination. 1492 is the 'when' for everybody." She shows them how to calculate how many years ago that was.

Excerpts from an Interview with Karen Genelly. Karen Genelly, a docent for the Chicago Architecture Foundation, told me, "I really like the arts. Because they are important to me, the arts are part of my teaching."

After earning an elementary education degree at De Paul University and teaching amid Chicago's Robert Taylor homes, a low-income housing project, she found teaching at Dumas "almost like going to the suburbs."

> I think the arts are very much a part of the school. Younger students can take Suzuki violin lessons. We take students to dance and other performing arts. We have a lot of assemblies. We emphasize, "This is part of your culture, no matter who you are." These kids are segregated; this is a totally black school. A lot of our kids do not know about other races or cultures.

> There's an atmosphere here. Everything doesn't have to be quiet; just because somebody's quiet doesn't mean they're learning. It's OK if you fail here so you won't fail outside. The arts give confidence to a kid who might say, "I'm not good at reading but I'm good at *this*. I'm not a complete idiot." It lets each kid understand he's got a gift.

> The arts here depend on each teacher's initiative. I think you would find a lot of variation among teachers. There are some really outstanding people on staff. Others you have to bring in by the carrot, not the stick. People need confidence. You need a supportive administration.

It would be nice if we had more time for the arts. They don't get enough attention when they're integrated into the day. But so much is asked of us that, if I had to make a special time to do the arts, they wouldn't get as much attention as they do now. And integrating is a real good way to teach. It's more exciting, more fun, more human.

We don't have enough supplies. Somebody's not sending me paints—and painting is a crazy enough activity that, if I have an excuse to put it off, I sometimes do. Having murals on the walls and painting throughout the school is encouraging to the children.

Including the arts in my academic lessons gives me another way of looking at the child. And I think, too often, we don't allow kids to have enough input into their own education. This gives them participation and self-discipline. They're taking responsibility. Kids start seeing the arts as part of themselves. You don't hear our kids say, "Oh, opera—singing by the fat lady." "Oh, ballet—that's boring."

It's good that the school gets outside help. That is very important. Teachers have written for grants. Recently, we wanted to go to a ballet. We needed 63 tickets, $3 each. We couldn't find someone to fund that, so Mrs. Peters took money out of the school fund. We have Urban Gateways artists and programs coming in.

I had an Urban Gateways group teach dance. Coordination has never been my *forte* but I actually got up and danced with the artist in front of my class. At one point, the kids designed their own dances. A deaf girl in class got up, even though she could only sense the vibrations, and performed a dance. It was the most wonderful experience. I think every child left feeling it was important. But we had a quilt-making residency where the woman would come in and do things she should have done the night before. We never finished the quilt and that was bad.

To a certain extent, school has to be fun, has to be exciting. There has to be that kind of feeling to it. I think the arts excite you and connect you to something bigger. Children see the world in a different way.

Commentary. Karen Genelly alone explicitly stated that the arts were shortchanged by integrating them into the daily schedule pervasively rather than independently. Like others, she recognized as important the connection with arts professionals to enrich student experiences, acknowledging constraints of time, materials, and teacher initiative on classroom arts. Like others, she praised Sylvia Peters for encouraging and supporting such exposures, even to the point of juggling the school budget to purchase ballet tickets. Genelly saw a great need for expanding the cultural awareness of inner city children.

In this case study, only a few observed classrooms were chosen by the school principal. These vignettes illustrate the problematic nature of integrating the arts into academic instruction. Academic objectives impose severe restraints on student opportunities to explore media and ideas, to engage in spontaneous and creative self-expression. Lack of specialists or classroom teachers with specific training in the arts is a common situation in the U.S. Without professional preparation in the arts, teachers often lack the background to envision the full potential benefits of arts education in their classrooms. They rarely recognize the diminished role the arts are assigned when subject matters are integrated. They do see that the arts are important in schooling for lots of non-artistic reasons: promoting self-esteem, improving motivation, encouraging harmonious relationships and good discipline, contributing to knowledge retention. Some speak of creativity and self-expression. But the penguin parts were pre-cut; the turkeys were nearly identical to the eye; the lyrics to the songs in *Peter Pan* were set; Columbus *had* to ask for ships and Isabella *had* to grant them. In practice, the boundaries around creativity and self-expression were close.

Yet the arts were a strong feature of the school climate. Constrained as they were, the arts were part of classroom life. They were visible and audible throughout the school. They came easily and frequently to conversation and activities. The arts were brought to children and children to the arts, often at no small effort. Professional input was vital to the quality of arts education at Dumas. Appreciation was far from absent. Classroom teachers and others from the community, to be presented next, readily credited Principal Sylvia Peters for breathing life into the arts at Dumas.

Engaging Community Arts

My first research question at this site was: How are the arts taught at Dumas? As stated earlier, there were two important answers. The first answer was: by integrating the arts and academics. The second answer was: by taking advantage of arts in the city. In interviews, teachers often commented on field trips, artists' residencies, and in-school programs in addition to classroom arts activities. Two external resources to be discussed next, The Oak Woods Cemetery and a Suzuki music teacher, offered the school long-term contacts with the fine arts.

Excerpts from an Interview with Soubretta Skyles of The Oak Woods.

> The Oak Woods Cemetery adopted Dumas School roughly three years ago. Sylvia Peters came to the cemetery and expressed an interest in the adopt-a-school program of the Chicago Board of Education. As Oak Woods' Director of Community Relations, I became involved.
>
> It is unusual for a cemetery to have an art gallery in, of all places, a mausoleum but the long corridors lend themselves beautifully to that. We have been having exhibits for about three and a half years.
>
> One exhibit with the children was "Nubia," our black history exhibit for 1987. We worked with the Oriental Institute, which provided artifacts, some over 5000 years old. The children learned about a great African dynasty from a curator and his staff who brought slides and filmstrips and set up visits for the seventh and eighth graders to visit the Oriental Institute and its archives. As a part of their history class, they wrote essays on Nubia. We set up a children's gallery to display their huge

map of Africa and pulled it all together—art, history, social studies, science, language arts. We display our black history exhibits for a month to six weeks but there was such an interest in what these children had done that it was here for months. When the exhibit closed, some teacher-aides and parents and children created a mini travelling exhibit to take to other schools.

We like to include the Dumas children whenever we have a major exhibit. The seventh and eighth graders are part of the current 1989 black history exhibit, tracing family histories. Shortly after the death of Mayor Harold Washington, we had an exhibit in his honor to which the Dumas children contributed. Tomorrow a group of 50 children will go to the black rodeo. Black cowboys are a neglected part of American history.

The Oak Woods gave an Ashanti bench to Dumas to be the first piece for an African history one-room museum that we are going to help them develop at the school. The school has some other things, I believe some from Sylvia Peters. But we encourage more than the arts—history, science, even math when students create scale models. The science teacher will be here with his class this Spring as soon as the lakes thaw to get specimens. And they borrow a couple of our turtles every year and bring them back when the cold weather is setting in.

It's not unusual for youngsters to come in on their own and ask me to take them to visit an exhibit or to walk around in the cemetery. I know a lot of parents of the children now and they stop and talk to me.

Dumas School has a philosophy and a very nurturing environment. Sylvia Peters always has time to listen, to give a hug. It's not common for an elementary school to be involved in so many experiences and programs as Sylvia has brought to Dumas; I know because I was an educator by profession until I retired and was asked to come here. Students have to have basic skills but to hear someday beautiful stories about them as young adults—this is what we hope for. We intend to be involved with the school as long as they'll have us.

Commentary. Dumas students were enriched by the school's relationship with The Oak Woods Cemetery. Especially important enhancements occurred in the areas of Afro-American history and arts, areas in which ethnic heritage and individual self-esteem were promoted. Sylvia Peters' philosophy, alluded to by Skyles as that of the school, and her persistence in pursuing it provided the impetus for making such connections and the momentum for maintaining them. Peters' vision of the school's role in educating neighborhood children took in community resources as essential, not peripheral, elements. It was she who led the way in connecting with The Oak Woods, Urban Gateways, and a variety of other programs and experiences.

Another case in point was the Suzuki Violin Program, believed to be the first in-school Suzuki program in the Chicago Public Schools. As did many classroom teachers, as did The Oak Woods' Soubretta Skyles, strings teacher Barbara Farrell credited Peters for her leadership in bringing the arts to Dumas. And praise from a parent involved in the Suzuki Program went even farther.

Excerpts from an Interview with Suzuki Teacher Barbara Farrell.

> The Suzuki strings program includes only violins now but we're adding all stringed instruments because of the high level of interest here at Dumas. About 40 new children want to join the ten already studying. The kids enjoy it; we incorporate games in lessons. But the unanticipated high turn-out poses some scheduling problems.
>
> For additional lessons, these kids come to Sherwood Music Conservatory on Saturday, where I have my other program. This allows more students to participate in the program because it opens up more time and some parents couldn't come during the school day. With the Suzuki method, both a parent and a child come for lessons. Grant funds pay for the Saturday lessons.
>
> Mrs. Peters is incredible. The impression that I get is that the arts are here because of her, that she is the strongest single factor. I've only been here a few months but my impression is that she has motivated the whole school with her attitude and her vision. When I walked in the door, everyone was friendly—and it's an all-black school and I'm white; that is tremendous. Instead of "I don't know if I like this," parents and children seem to feel, "Let's try that. Wouldn't that be wonderful?" If we had more leadership like hers in schools, I'm not saying you'd have more Suzuki programs, but you'd sure as hell have more education.

Excerpts from an Interview with "Suzuki Mom" Peggy Bartlett.

> It's difficult for parents to join something totally unfamiliar but, last year, Dumas bought violins from a school that was closing its program and began renting them for $5 a month to pay for insurance and repairs—lots of strings break. Then the school told us, if we wanted our children to learn to play, it wouldn't be expensive. All we had to do was come. A lot of people heard and wanted to join but, even though the lessons are free, parents still have a difficult time because of work. I was excited that my child could take music in school.
>
> As "Suzuki mom," I help Barbara contact parents and I bring the children from their classrooms to their violin lessons. But I did not volunteer to be "Suzuki mom." When Mrs. Peters gives you a job, there's no such thing as "I don't feel like it." She told me, "You'd be best for the job. You can learn it; you're intelligent." That's the attitude. She thinks everybody should feel special. I'm new but people treat me like I'm part of the brick.
>
> Suzuki is just part of what's going on at this school. They're always doing something. My son is on a field trip to the opera today. I've taken him to plays but I didn't know that he would enjoy opera. Nobody had ever said, "Here, take these tickets and come see this opera." He got all

excited and made his lunch the night before, brushed his teeth and everything—I didn't have to say anything.

Mrs. Peters has enthusiasm, genuine warmth and kindness. Whenever a child says, "We can't do this," Mrs. Peters says, "Oh, yes, you can! If you can learn Suzuki, you can learn this!" With any program, she says, "I know that my children can do it." She hugs the kids; she's in the rooms; she knows exactly what's going on, who's doing what. She doesn't have to be told what's going on in 306; she's already up in 306.

The school needs a strong leader. She teaches me and I chug around to help teach other parents. We're into Project CANAL, school reform. We've been taught that the sky is the limit at those meetings. We can take responsibility for our neighborhood school.

Once when I went to the violin shop because my little girl had broken a string, the clerk was asking me where I was from. I said, "Dumas." She said, "Oh, yes! I heard about you guys." That makes you stand real tall to know that people are talking about the good things you're doing. And we are the first public school in the city to be teaching violin during

Suzuki teacher Barbara Farrell uses a hand puppet in teaching a violin lesson to a young Dumas student.

school time. That'll trickle down to the children. They're going to get that sense of pride and achievement, too.

Why Arts Education Worked at Dumas

My second research question was: Why does arts education work at Dumas? The short answer: because the principal made the arts feasible, important, and irresistible. Sylvia Peters called for integration of the arts and academics and for connections between the school and the city.

Excerpts from Interviews with Principal Sylvia Peters.

I became principal of Dumas January 3, 1984. I had been a teacher in the Chicago Public Schools system for eighteen and a half years. We have 658 students right now. We should have more but some don't have the required inoculations yet. And there are about 40 inoculated kids who are truant. Most of our classes have 32 students. We have 46 on staff here and at our early childhood center a few blocks away.

In the 1980s, a fiscal crisis wiped out CPS liberal and fine arts programs. I became disenchanted with the public school system and went to work for a publisher of educational materials, SRA. I got a chance to go to schools all across the country that were making a difference. I developed very clear standards for what it took to make a successful school. My husband encouraged me to interview for a principal's position but I couldn't get hired because I had no political backing. Dr. Preston Bryant, now in charge of ECIA, brought me to the attention of Charles Almo, a CPS official who saw to it I got this school. Deep inside my heart, I knew I wanted an inner city school because I knew I would be able to do some special things for an inner city school.

When I came to Dumas, it was a wasteland, dark and dirty. There were ugly, antiquated pictures on the walls—nothing that spoke of the children's heritage or culture, no display of children's work. The first textbook brought into the school in 1963 was still present; the first machine was still present. I found no consistent instructional program being used in any curriculum area. The school was supposed to have a Ginn basal reading program but there were seven versions of the Ginn program and materials from other textbook companies, too.

Staff attitudes were very depressing, sneering. Teachers could not stand the children and they told them so in a thousand ways. They talked about their color, their poverty. Some walked around with sticks taped together hitting children. I heard teachers cursing children, parents calling teachers names, children calling everybody names. It was a vicious circle. Some of children were involved with gangs, which added to the physical and emotional abuse. I felt sorry for the children who came on the first day.

I think I disarmed everybody. I looked like a nice, middle-class black lady who was not going to interrupt the *status quo*. But inside three months, I had changed the early childhood structure of this school. Then I brought in a computer lab through grant funds; I am great for writing proposals and grants. Then I started recruiting teachers.

There were rooms not being used because they were piled high with old books, ordered but never used. There was nothing here you would want to use—no paint, no brushes, no music, no copying machine. So the parents, a few teachers, and I started cleaning and throwing out. I was told, "You can't throw this out!" And I said, "Look, don't tell me what I can do. I'm going to do it." One evening I took down the old, scroungy prints and hung my own paintings from home.

I came from a family that revered the arts. I had been taken to concerts. I had studied classical dance. I went to the National College of Education in the middle '50s, a wonderful time for the humanities and arts, a wonderful experience for a kid coming from the inner city. I started bringing arts performances to Dumas. The International Music Foundation had just started and we had them give three concerts. But the kids didn't know how to behave at concerts. They had not had assemblies in this school for three or four years before I came. There were not even enough chairs for the children in the auditorium.

Very strong-willed people on staff set out to undermine me. They went to Superintendent Matthew Byrd and said, "This woman has got to go." One Monday morning, I was greeted at the door by a boycott of parents these teachers had organized. But the children were on my side and they saved me.

In the first year and a half, I lost nineteen of 39 teachers. They asked to go. Charles Almo arranged transfers. I almost gave up a couple of times. Once, with my sister, I broke down and cried. She said, "You are not going to quit." I hadn't understood it as political but, when they threatened to take my school away, I became very political. By that time, I had recruited my assistant principal, Mrs. Gray, and a few teachers who really loved kids. We'd meet until eight or nine o'clock at night to define appropriate professional behaviors and plan staff development. Around Christmastime, we had a staff breakfast and the teachers who were left cried. It had been that wrenching.

People say you cannot do things in the Chicago Public School system. That is not true. You can do whatever you *want* to do. We transformed this school. We decided what had to be done and we put all kinds of energy into doing it. We stayed late at night; we spent Christmas vacation working.

What our kids need is a nurturing environment. For our kids, school is where sanity reigns—not abuse and drugs. There's no cursing here, no corporal punishment. We've had three teachers arrested in five years for mistreatment of students. I'm in court with two of them now. If I hear crying, I get up and find out what's going on. Mrs. Gray and I counsel our children instead of turning them away and we go through some problem-solving. We also put our hands on children in an affectionate way. I get depressed sometimes over these little babies who come here and go through so much mess. I'd like to bring most of them home but I can't.

The children trust me. They feel I will listen and give everybody a fair shake. Children know, when they break rules, something's going to happen. But we don't have very many rules—five or six.

I am not the ultimate force in this building. I am one person who might have overriding opinions but others can give other opinions. Shared decision-making, participatory management of the school—I really, truly believe that schools are stronger when more brains are working toward a common goal. Everyone gets some responsibility. We're involved in the CANAL Project—Creating A New Approach to Learning. It's about school-based management. Their symbol is a little boat on a canal, like a gondola in Venice. School-based management is controversial, so I think the image should be a steamship on the high seas. Our core planning team includes twelve teachers, six parents, the lunchroom manager, the engineer [custodian], a secretary, and two teacher-aides—about 22-23 people.

My responsibility is to make sure that legal requirements are met, to maintain discipline according to the group's philosophy, to maintain fiscal matters, and to keep people well informed about the vision of the school. I believe that being a mentor is part of my responsibility as a black female in a public school system. I must nurture people, put their wings on.

The teachers are wonderful—I can't say enough about them. They come to school early; they serve on committees; they're at meetings. There's no power struggle. I give them lots of responsibility but I'm a very hard taskmaster. I don't understand "no" and I don't understand "burned out." When I have to redo someone's reports, they hear about it in a most emphatic way. If you can't get it done, I'll give it to someone else. The teachers get these maroon and white "MS" ribbons—that's for "movers and shakers." The staff gave me this orchid with an MS ribbon.

I have a vision of how school should be. This school may be in the ghetto but it is *not* a ghetto school. Other principals tease me for what they call my strong sense of righteousness but I do what I think I should do, even if it gets me in trouble. Other principals know that I'm interested in art, so they direct people in the arts to me. And I never say no. I think the reason why other schools don't incorporate the arts into what they do is because schools are test-driven. They're afraid to give up the time.

I feel depressed about one of the things I did: I wiped out special education. There were over 100 children, many boys, out of about 700 students classified as educable mentally handicapped, behavior disorder, emotional disorder, learning disabled, and so forth. That seemed too many. I gradually returned them to a normal setting. Now as I'm reviewing our achievement test scores, I'm going to have to give in to the pressure to do something so that we get a better academic picture of the school. I'm going to have a resource room for learning disabilities and send other children to good special education schools.

I think test scores are important to a degree but elementary school is just the beginning of becoming an educated, literate person. All elementary school does is prepare them to learn, expose them to things that will help them make choices and develop values. The strength of one's character or integrity—that's what we have to get back to; we have to make sure our kids know who they are. We're teaching our children to become independent thinkers, to understand and not be afraid to question. There are many ways to solve problems.

Last week we took some kids to breakfast at the Palmer House, a tradition in the black community, to kick off black history month. They were able to see first-hand some of our great black leaders. Everyone sang "Lift Every Voice and Sing;" we met some authors; we saw some paintings; they had things for us to bring home. I was so proud because my kids saw that we at Dumas are not the only ones who talk about black history.

With the arts, exposure is the start. So often in schools, there will be a concert every two or three months. Here, after initial exposure, we break it down into subsets. Once, we had a six-week session on how to make stringed instruments. There was another session on wind instruments. Then, we had ensembles come and play.

The other day, a boy said to me, "I've decided to play the 'cello because boys ought to play the 'cello." I don't care that he thinks boys ought to play the 'cello; I love it that *he* wants to play. With our Suzuki program, we are adding viola and 'cello. We'll have 49 kids on stringed instruments. It's so wonderful! Next Sunday, some parents and I are going to take a bunch of kids in our cars to Sherwood Music Conservatory. We're going to spend the day having fun; we'll listen to music and we'll play a little. It's exciting to see them grow from ignorance to valuing.

We have Suzuki violin pull-out lessons at the lower grade levels and classical choir at the upper grade levels. We do this without there being any music specialists in the Chicago Public Schools. The choir can sight-read. They sang gospel music when I came but I also wanted European music.

I think our kids are sophisticated in the arts. They appreciate images. In our society, we value things that are slick—television, beautiful colors. Here, the arts are subtle. Deep inside the children, there are the beginnings of real creativity, fragile and elusive. We have even big boys who want to sing in the classical choir. And interest in dance doesn't mean you're a fag—it's hip. Kids may discuss with adults a play they've seen, even if something in the show was a little risque. They're much more worldly than ordinary kids.

A group of kids and I were guests of the Chicago Symphony; we sat in box seats. A gentleman asked one of my sixth graders, "Who is your favorite composer?" The student said, "Well, I'll tell you the truth. It's Mozart." The man was in a state of shock and I was so startled I asked his teacher about it later. She said, "The children are doing reports on musicians and he does like Mozart very much."

Most of my kids keep journals and diaries because they understand that's a way to get their feelings out. Privacy, when parents read their diaries, is an issue for them. Ramona Hudson, a seventh grader here has a three-year journal. Harcourt, Brace, Jovanovich Publishing Company said it was excellent. She is writing a methodology section for one of their textbooks—how she began, how it became a habit.

We don't have arts teachers in the Chicago Public Schools. We don't have any trained artists on this staff. We don't expect to produce a Van Gogh from among the students. An arts background is not particularly important when I'm selecting faculty but I do want people who are receptive to the arts and to change. It's something you can develop. This oil painting on my wall of the Chicago skyline was done by kids. Their teacher had no arts training. We have winners at the arts fair.

We don't have any art classes as such but our arts go real deep. Instead, we integrate the arts into our curriculum. In my opinion, it is appropriate to teach through the arts. My children hear me recite poetry. When I first came here, they would crack up. Then they started reciting the same poems with me; they heard the rhythm and alliteration and thoughts. I would ask them what they thought it meant. That's how we got the whole school turned on to those cognitive activities. The arts also offer discipline, the most essential training. Discipline is how one shapes one's life, forms one's habits.

After school, we have classes in oil painting, drama, arts and crafts, singing, and Spanish. Students in grades 3 through 8 can sign up. About ten to twelve teachers are involved at any one time. These activities are funded by the board but we did them before we had funding. We raise money selling candy and T-shirts. We have to spend money for concerts and things. We buy Urban Gateways programs. We spend money on buses.

I'm a member of the Urban Gateways Principals' Coalition for the Arts. I think that the quality of the arts here has greatly improved because of outside influences through Urban Gateways. Right now, we have a lady working with us on an ancestors project writing wonderful, juicy stuff. And we're getting ready to put up an exhibit at The Oak Woods Cemetery. I would like to see a higher quality. That's the reason we need a written curriculum in art.

I would say that, because of our accomplishments in the areas of the arts and creativity, our children have a better sense of self. Parents who left the school are now coming back. A family returned yesterday after trying a private school and then a very good public school. The children had been begging for a year and a half to come back here so the mother moved back into this neighborhood at a financial sacrifice.

I think Chicago should allow parents to select schools for specific reasons. If they want a sit-down-and-be-quiet school, or a school that focuses on science and math and basic skills, or a school that addresses the arts and character education, they should have those options. I would like everyone to be in a school like Dumas but it may not work for everyone; I've transferred some children out of the school because, after three or four years, we hadn't helped them.

Our overall goal is to turn this into a fine arts academy. I want a brand new school, building and all. I want to be able to offer my children more fine arts experiences. I want them to be able to think well, to have some control and knowledge of what they're doing. It's very important for children to develop a sense of approaching life artistically. They need people around them who understand that. Fifteen years from now, I want these children to say, "There was a crazy lady in school who had us singing and all this kind of stuff. And we had fun." That would be a great legacy.

Conclusion

Alexandre Dumas Elementary School was a dream amid the nightmare of many of Chicago's all-Afro-American public schools. For many associated with the school, it was a dream come true. But its success is not readily repeated; to some, it may seem an impossible dream.

The Meaning and Context of the Arts at Dumas

As indicated, there were no arts specialists in Chicago's public elementary schools nor time in the prescribed daily schedule to teach the arts. Arts funding was nearly non-existent, although principals had some discretionary monies and the time- and energy-consuming option of fund-raising. For the arts to exist at all was for them to be taught by regular classroom teachers, usually in conjunction with academic subjects and with few supplies. At Alexandre Dumas Elementary School, there was the desire that the arts more than exist, that they permeate all aspects of the life of the school.

Teaching *anything* in the environment surrounding Dumas was a challenge. Prior to 1984, everyone—principal, teachers, students—seemed satisfied simply to survive school. The school's students were victims of neglect, abuse, poor nutrition, inopportunity, poverty, gangs, drugs, prejudice, bitterness. No one was surprised that these children came to school undervaluing education, with little real hope of college. No one was surprised that they knew as little about appropriate classroom behavior as they did about audience etiquette. No one was surprised by an initial absence of respect for each other and school property and authority. No one was surprised by a classroom's constantly changing population, where there might be five new students in one week. No one was surprised that a huge proportion of class time and teacher energy was expended in maintaining order. What was surprising was that, when Dumas teachers were asked to name the obstacles to arts education, not one mentioned the children, behavior, or discipline.

Children lived in neighborhoods familiar with poverty and drugs. They survived violence: feared, witnessed, experienced by themselves or family members or people they knew or had known. Caught in families' daily struggles to subsist, their needs for nurturing were neglected. Opportunities for healthy personal growth were relatively rare but introductions to prejudice, hopelessness, and cynicism were not. At Dumas, as at San Sebastian, Texas and Plymouth Meeting, Pennsylvania, children's exposure to the arts was valued as enriching because it was enjoyable and because it sensitized children to appreciation of the arts as adults. But here, there were additional, stronger imperatives. At Dumas, the arts were also seen as a way out, a way to acknowledge and celebrate being Afro-American as well as an *entrée* into mainstream culture, an opportunity to experience the good things in life inside and outside the impoverished community, an expansion of the range of imaginable goals. The arts enriched spirits in danger of becoming numbed and deadened.

The marriage of the arts and academics at Dumas, as elsewhere, had its conjugal ups and downs. Almost unanimously, teachers felt that integrating subject matter made academics more interesting, more memorable, more deeply understood. But even as they extolled the virtues of integrating subjects, they implied that the arts were being shortchanged and they repeatedly wished aloud that the arts could be taught separately as well.

Arts education in classrooms varied in quality. While an interest in the arts was clear in many instances, in nearly all integrated activities, the arts were added as little more than a motivational component. Sometimes they seemed an afterthought. Occasionally they were merely busywork. Many "strictly arts" activities focused on reproducing a paper craft. There were rare but notable occasions when children's independent artwork was admired to the point of changing a teacher's display policies and lesson plans.

Although there was little correlation between teachers' avowed personal interest in the arts and classroom arts instruction, most Dumas teachers said they relished teaching the arts. It was fun for them and fun for their kids. It gave teachers a chance to "see the kids in a different way" or "to try something novel" themselves. It gave kids a chance to do something different and enjoyable, maybe even encouraging them to stay in school when academics might not, teachers thought. Teachers remembered fondly arts activities from two or three years past. Some complained about meager supplies but most did not; a number of teachers supplemented arts supplies from their own means rather than have children do without. Painting, seen as messy and time-consuming, was avoided by only a few.

Dumas teachers were aware of their limits as arts instructors. Most acknowledged restricted backgrounds in the arts. Under pressure to improve scores on mandated standardized achievement tests, some attended to academics at the expense of the arts. A change in grade level or the collective personality of a class sometimes required adjustments that diverted energy from the arts.

Such natural phenomena as wind and rainbows are the subjects of student-written myths and painted illustrations.

Can it be claimed that the arts flourished at Dumas if this was the state of arts instruction? That is the claim. The flourish was consistently noted by outsiders. Newspaper stories about the arts at Dumas were displayed in the school office; other principals sold their stringed instruments to and directed arts people to Dumas; The Oak Woods Cemetery regularly shared exhibits and display space with Dumas children and gave them *objets d'art* for a planned art museum at the school. In my drives through the neighborhood, I found aesthetic views in only two places: the rolling, shaded grounds within the cemetery walls and the interior of Dumas School, its corridors emblazoned with children's artwork, its inviting foyer, the reproductions and original framed pieces in the principal's office, the prominently displayed artifacts for the proposed museum in the school.

Important to the arts climate at Dumas was the connection between the school and the myriad arts offerings of the city of Chicago. Students were bused and driven to plays, concerts, dance programs, museums, music conservatories during the school day and on weekends. They played stringed instruments and sang classical music. Through the Urban Gateways program the school purchased each year, some classrooms interacted with artists-in-residence for six-week periods. Students participated with artists in creating masks, murals, dances, interpretive genealogies. Programs and assemblies were planned. Field trips were taken. The Oak Woods Cemetery provided an ongoing interface with the artworld.

The well-spring for both classroom arts and the interface with the city was Sylvia Peters.

Leadership. If I asked the school psychologist who divided his time between this and other elementary schools why he thought conditions better at Dumas, he answered: "Sylvia Peters." If I asked the Suzuki violin teacher why Dumas was the only public elementary school in the city with such a program, she answered: "Sylvia Peters." If I asked parents why they were moving back into the Dumas catchment area at a financial sacrifice, they answered: "Sylvia Peters." If I asked teachers why the arts thrived at Dumas, they answered: "Sylvia Peters."

Sylvia Peters would readily concede she had a vision of what an elementary school should be and formidable determination but, if I asked *her* why things went well at Dumas—the arts, academics, organization, administration, purposefulness, respect—she answered: "We have a lot of good people here who care about children."

It is not unusual to find social programs blossoming because of the charisma and dedication of a leader; it is not unusual to find the same programs wither when the leader leaves. Such leaders are relatively unusual in the population and in education. Certainly, Sylvia Peters was a rare Chicago principal and, if the *Tribune* investigative reports were accurate, Dumas was unusually successful and humane among Chicago's all-Afro-American elementary schools. In saying that any school could incorporate the arts into its curriculum and its life as Dumas had, Peters understated the generative power of her own leadership.

How did she do it? How did she get eighth graders who had sneered at classical music to request the opportunity to sing it? How did she get kids who had thought she was crazy when she recited poetry to recite and write it themselves? How did she get teachers to believe that it is more important to offer children opportunities to grow through the arts than to bully them into submission? Three ways: she made the arts fun; she made them accessible; and she made them important.

Peters made the arts infectious. Although she could be stern, she smiled when reciting poetry. She sang vigorously. She draped her dress with handmade fabric and cheerfully told how it was made, invited appreciation of the colors and texture and craftsmanship. She decorated her office with framed originals and reproductions and flowers. She verbalized her admiration and enjoyment of plays and concerts and dance performances. She looked forward to the next event. She clearly had a wonderful time enjoying the arts. Her enthusiasm was relentless and, ultimately, irresistible. A few teachers caught the happy contagion from her and their pupils had fun. Ultimately, Lydia Mosley said, no one wanted to get left behind.

Alexandre Dumas Elementary School
Chicago, Illinois

Peters made the arts feasible. She found funds. She arranged for Urban Gateways' artists and programs to come to the school. She offered opportunities for teachers to choose field trips. She approached the Suzuki violin teacher and bought instruments for students. She approached The Oak Woods Cemetery, ushering in opportunities for students to appreciate and to exhibit their art. She encouraged teachers to get out the paints and get messy; cleanliness, also a virtue, was secondary. Gradually, she shared and shifted some of the administrative responsibilities of Dumas-style arts education as she developed leadership among faculty and parents, moving toward group management over many aspects of the school.

Peters made the arts important. Student artwork was proudly displayed. Accomplishments of all kinds were recognized in announcements over the public address system. Informal recognition of student artwork was given even more frequently. Precious school time was spent on assemblies, trips, artist residencies, and classroom arts activities in spite of heavy pressure for improved academic test scores. Peters shared journal articles with the faculty, letting them know that others also thought arts education important. Through modeling, immersion, enthusiasm, and expectations, Sylvia Peters communicated the importance of the arts in her view of elementary education. Teachers and others said that the arts were important at Dumas because they were important to their principal.

Chapter 6:
Colonial School District
Plymouth Meeting, Pennsylvania

■ *Linda Mabry*

Arts Education in Suburban Philadelphia: Earning a Home in the Curriculum

For the third of my case studies for the National Center for Arts Education Research at the University of Illinois, Bob Stake and I decided that an East Coast, affluent, suburban site was needed to balance our research project in terms of geography, socioeconomics, and urbanity. In November, 1988, at the suggestion of Dr. Harris Sokoloff of the University of Pennsylvania, I called Dr. Richard Creasey, superintendent of Colonial School District which serves the townships of Plymouth Meeting and Whitemarsh and the borough of Conshohocken, suburbs of Philadelphia. Creasey graciously consented to a case study focusing on two elementary schools in the district's wealthier neighborhoods.

At the start, I was concerned about the likelihood of my insensitivities toward such a site. In Texas, I had returned to my home town, wondering about the effects of economic decline and differential access to the arts by ethnicity. In Chicago, I had been awed and inspired by the successes, against overwhelming odds, of an arts-minded principal and faculty in an all-Afro-American inner city public elementary school. It was hard to imagine that I was going to care much about the well-fed, well-dressed scions of suburbia in their well-equipped and well-maintained classrooms with their well-prepared teachers.

Well, indeed. Arts education at Plymouth Meeting turned out to be an appealing case to study. Unlike teachers and principals in San Sebastian, nobody at Colonial School District seemed interested in anonymity or worried that anything I might see or report could cost his or her job, although a few requested pseudonyms after reading transcripts of interviews. Nobody asked me to turn off my tape recorder. People seemed to feel secure and, in terms of conducting my research, this translated into friendliness, interest, and candor. I found sincere educators encountering intransigent difficulties, many people confronting problems with resolve and creativity. Several issue-significant events coincided with my stay and the site itself offered an intriguing history.

Methodology

I came to Plymouth Meeting expecting to focus on two issues: (1) the sequentiality of the fine arts curriculum, and (2) the effects of proximity to arts opportunities in Philadelphia on school arts. But I soon discovered other matters which seemed to me more informative about arts education at this site.

The longevity of school personnel quickly emerged as a significant influence on arts instruction. Other formidable influences included the relative importance of the arts *vis-a-vis* academics, administrative support, class scheduling, and the professional assignments of arts teachers. The district's continuous curriculum development process also seemed important in understanding arts education at this site. Secondary to these matters were issues of curricular sequentiality, proximity to a cultural center, the tendency of school people to focus on needs and to overlook strengths, the increasing demands upon schools from societal problems, and the nurturing of student initiative and creativity.

I spent nine Spring school days in 1989 in Whitemarsh (K-3) and Colonial (4-5) Elementary Schools. I spent the intervening weekend discovering community context: visiting historic Philadelphia and dining on the Delaware River, driving in the rain through Valley Forge, admiring Wyeth paintings at Chadd's Ford, attending a performance by the Pennsylvania Ballet, and cheering the Seventy-Sixers to a basketball victory over the Cleveland Cavaliers—in response to the ubiquitous remark, "Sports are a big thing in this area."

There were plenty of after-school events during my two-week stay: a performance by the regional high school band, a middle school choral-strings-band concert, a Whitemarsh PTO executive board meeting, a meeting of district visual arts teachers at all grade levels, and a Board of Education worksession followed by a public meeting. School days included an assembly program by a member of the Philadelphia Folk Song Society and a Curriculum Council meeting. With Ruth Nevergole, a member of the local historic society, I also toured the Quaker meeting house for which Plymouth Meeting is named.

Mostly I visited classrooms and interviewed people. I interviewed Superintendent Creasey and the district curriculum supervisor, Harry Markley. I talked endlessly to Dr. Jim Capolupo, the newly hired fine arts coordinator, and even more endlessly to his tireless predecessor, Pat Iannelli. I interviewed Rachele Intrieri, Dr. John Mickelson, and Art Wood of the Board of Education. I talked extensively with Principals Al Erb at Whitemarsh and Bill Wilson at Colonial and met their staffs and several academic curriculum coordinators. I interviewed virtually every visual arts teacher in the district as a group at their curriculum meeting and interviewed Wilma Spangler at Colonial and Jan Canterbury at Whitemarsh individually as well. I interviewed music teachers Jeff Spangler at Colonial and John Fino at Whitemarsh and sat in on their classes and those of Teri Marinari, Carmella Quarry, and Jeanneane Bozzilli. I observed and talked with Thomas Smith, who teaches a dance unit as part of physical education at Whitemarsh, and his counterpart at Colonial; I exchanged a few words with high school drama teacher Bob Riley and watched a videotape of the previous year's production of *The King and I*. I interviewed two teams of non-arts teachers at Colonial and one at Whitemarsh and observed the regular classrooms of Sue Schiele, Elaine Notaro, and substitute Sue Prenchik. I interviewed Patty Zierow of the "Art Goes to School" program at Conshohocken Elementary and listened to the lunchtime conversation of the faculty there. I interviewed Counselor Mary Legette who used visual arts extensively in her work. I interviewed Sue Castle, president of the teachers' union. I solicited the views of four Whitemarsh parents Sally Brewster, Jane Evans, Chris Feorelli, and Linda Goldberg. I interviewed several second graders before and after watching them perform an original play, then fielded their questions about how much fame would accrue from a published account of their effort.

Documents to review and analyze were many and easily accessible. I reviewed visual arts and voluminous music curricular documents. Madeline Hunter's instructional strategies, used in the district, were shared with me. I requested and was given lists of the district's audiovisual resources in the arts, arts faculty assignments, a schedule of PTO assembly programs, ethnicity of students by schools, an organizational schema of district administration, budget documents and projections, state curriculum mandates, preliminary documents for an upcoming curriculum site review by the state, student remediation projections based on the previous year's standardized achievement test scores, inservice topics, teacher evaluation form, and a March/April 1989 copy of *Media & Methods* magazine featuring Plymouth-Whitemarsh High School students and staff on the cover.

Description of Site

Colonial School District served the borough of Conshohocken and the townships of Plymouth Meeting and Whitemarsh, which includes the village of Lafayette Hill. Immediately adjacent to and northwest of Philadelphia, these communities comprise about 24 square miles of the Delaware River valley.

Quakers from Devonshire arrived in 1686 aboard the *Desire*, naming their settlement after Plymouth, England. Soon lonely, they moved to Philadelphia, selling their property to Friends from Wales, whose descendants continue to be members of the Meeting. The oldest school still functioning in the township was established by the Friends in 1780, although it is thought that a log cabin school existed even earlier.

Whitemarsh, a township dating from 1704, derived its name from a "wide marsh," through which the Wissahickon Creek ran. Originally "Baren Hill" from the German word meaning "bears," then anglicized into the unpalatable "Barren Hill," Lafayette Hill was renamed by housing developers in the 1950s for the 21-year-old French general who strategized a brilliant retreat there in 1778. Conshohocken, named for an Indian word meaning "pleasant valley," was incorporated as a borough in 1850.

In the early days, local lime quarries supplied building materials to Philadelphia over roads still in use. The Corson family, descendants of early owners, still quarried limestone in 1989. Some overgrown kilns were visible. Built for quarry workers, two-and-a-half story houses with topmost "eyebrow windows" dotted older neighborhoods. Near a trading site established by a member of the Friendship Company for Protection Against Horse Stealing, sleek Plymouth Meeting Mall stood. Mid-twentieth century steel mills on the Schuylkill River no longer operated, giving Conshohocken a "rust belt" look.

Plymouth Friends Meeting House
H.C.P.

The Plymouth Friends Meeting House, built in 1704 by Quakers using local limestone and trees, remained in continuous use as a house of worship. Listed on the National Register of Historic Places, the building was also used as a hospital during the American Revolution and the property as a campground for Washington's army on the way to nearby Valley Forge.

Plymouth Meeting and Whitemarsh appeared middle to upper-middle class, partly self-contained and partly bedroom communities. Homes in the Lafayette Hill area were the most upscale: single-family residences in the $80,000-1 million range, most ranging between $200,000-250,000. In Plymouth Meeting, property valuations averaged slightly less. Conshohocken slid into lower brackets and included multi-family residences and greater ethnic diversity.

Plymouth Meeting centered a convergence of roads, including the Pennsylvania Turnpike and an extension of Interstate 76. Many, like Germantown Pike, a cart road in the seventeenth century, were historic. During my stay, many were under construction. There was concern that even these expanded roadways might not accommodate increased traffic to a proposed complex of corporate offices and hotels at their vortex.

Schools. In 1988-89, Colonial School District operated seven schools, whose enrollments are shown in Table 1. Because of our interest in curricular sequentiality, I requested access to Colonial Elementary and one K-3 elementary school. Because Whitemarsh Elementary had the highest socioeconomic standing among the elementary schools, it was chosen to suit our search for suburban affluence.

Table 1.
Colonial School District enrollment by location and ethnic grouping

School	Location	Total Students	Afro-American	Asian	American Indian	Hispanic
Colonial Elementary	Plymouth Meeting	521	40	19		
Colonial Middle	Norristown	784	58	37	1	5
Conshohocken Elementary	Conshohocken	177	39			
Plymouth Elementary	Plymouth Meeting	318	7	27		
Plymouth-Whitemarsh HS	Plymouth Meeting	1113	83	67		
Whitemarsh Elementary	Lafayette Hill	380	10	14		3

Whitemarsh Elementary School was a sprawling, one-story, many-windowed building which housed two kindergartens, five first grades, four second grades, and five third grades. Jewish, Protestant, and Catholic children, most of whose parents worked in Philadelphia, attended with fourteen Asian students—Korean, Chinese, and Vietnamese. Sixty of its 380 students were classified as gifted and given two and a half hours of "pull-out" instruction each day. The school also maintained a resource room for the "emotionally disabled." Principal Albert D. Erb presided over a friendly, outgoing faculty.

In its second year of operation, Colonial Elementary School was a three-story structure with few windows. Once a junior high school, the first floor accommodated the district's administrative offices, school cafeteria, band and orchestra rooms, gymnasium and physical education offices and, on a rental basis, a tax office and a day care center. Upstairs, eleven classes of fourth graders, ten classes of fifth graders, three learning disabilities classes, and two learning and adjustment classes were located. Instruction for the hearing impaired was also provided. The principal was William H. Wilson.

Known for high academic aspirations, the area was dotted with many colleges, universities, and private secondary schools. Seventy percent of Plymouth-Whitemarsh High School graduates enrolled in four-year colleges and universities, many preferring Ivy League schools.

A long-standing tradition of private schools paralleled the public schools. Some, such as the Quaker school, were operated by religious groups, some even by ethnic-religious groups, like Polish-American Catholics. Many were secular, expensive, and academically selective. Neither public school personnel nor parents thought academic standards different between public and private schools; many students attended both public and private schools before graduation. Everyone I spoke with said that social selection was the predominant factor for choosing secular private schools. Some families traditionally sent offspring to a particular school. Parents said that a child's personality sometimes indicated the need for a particular school environment. I detected no feeling of competition with or flight from public schools.

Private schools seemed to pose a problem for public school officials only in busing. Required by state law to bus to private schools lying up to ten miles outside the school district's boundaries, Colonial School District bused 1500 private school students. The district also had to match private and public school busing for field trips. This cost served to limit public school field trips to one per class, paid for by the PTO. And because of after-school transport, field trips were limited to the length of the school day.

At the elementary level, specialists taught music and visual arts with reference to locally developed district curriculum guides. A long-polished three-week unit of dance instruction was included in physical education in a K-3 school; otherwise, besides the hiring of a choreographer for the annual high school play, dance was absent. At the elementary level, drama was not taught specifically but dramatizations, puppets and plays, were readily apparent as activities planned both by teachers and by students. And usually, elementary youngsters were invited to participate in the high school play, the previous year as Siamese princes and princesses in *The King and I*.

Primary Issues

As one would expect, teacher interest, expertise, and philosophy greatly shaped arts teaching and learning. Naturally, differences in style and quality of instruction were evident. Student exposure to studio production, art history, art criticism, and aesthetics—the four disciplines widely promoted by the Getty Center for Education in the Arts—varied by teacher and topic. Still, there were common elements in arts education in the district. Four factors particularly seemed to contribute to the state of the arts at Colonial School District:

1. Longevity of personnel at all levels;

2. The district's centralized curriculum development process;

3. The relative importance of the arts in the schools and in the community; and

4. Leadership.

These became the primary foci of my study.

Longevity of Schools Personnel

At a team meeting at Colonial Elementary School, three fifth-grade teachers talked about demographic changes in the district.

Gordon Vitello:
    During the 1960s, we had a tremendous influx of students into this district. A lot of us were hired then. In the mid-nineties, a lot of us are going to be retirees. As the older teachers got up farther on the scale, a move to another school district would have meant earning less money.

Janet Gafner:
    It would be nice to get some new blood. Sometimes you need someone young to come in with a great idea.

Thomas Thies:
    A few years ago, at the beginning of the school year, they had the *one new* hiree—I think in elementary—stand up. We gave 'em a standing ovation as the first new, full-time elementary teacher for quite a few years.

Principals Bill Wilson and Al Erb, both hired in the 1960s, discussed longevity in the district.

Wilson: In 1971 when we started the decline in pupil enrollment, basically, people froze. We lost a lot of people and those that stayed were afraid to move any place else.

Erb: A lot of teachers retired early back then. The ones here now earn about as much as administrators or superintendents in other districts.

Wilson: In this building, we've been able to hire young teachers within the last two years. Most of the staff has fifteen years' experience or more. As far as the character of the school is concerned, you're getting an experienced staff but not the young kid who comes in with new ideas. We've inserviced the staff a lot. Everyone has gone through the Madeline Hunter instructional skills and computer education. And we have a mentor program in this district. I think the majority of teachers are pretty happy. We probably have one of the finest salary scales in the state.

Erb: And I think the Board of Education has confidence in us. For the most part, they're supportive of the staff. It's a nine-member board elected for three-year terms. It's not unusual for incumbents to be reelected."

Superintendent Richard Creasey was a confident, energetic man with a direct, open manner and an easy smile. Prior to his thirteen years at Colonial School District, he taught in steel and railroad towns; completed graduate studies at Penn State; and moved to superintendencies, first in Lancaster, "a first-quality suburban style school district, similar to this situation, where people generally assume a level of competence," then in rural Buck's County, "where education is not a priority and everyone thinks you're spending money like a drunken sailor." Arriving as the full force of demographic decline hit the district, he recalled:

> It's amusing now but, at the time, it hurt. The story went out that the board had hired an S.O.B. whose job was to close schools, lay off teachers, cut the budget, and force a teachers' strike. Within seven years, they were going to get rid of that person and hire a nice guy. I could hardly believe it but, within 30 days after arriving, I found the buildings and grounds budget had $1.4 million they hadn't known how to spend. With that plus borrowing $600,000, we were saved for a while.

> But within a year, I closed the first school, the first time this district had ever had that happen. We reduced our staff by almost 50% but we lost about 65% of our students. We had a strike in two years; there wasn't any way to head that off. So all the things that had been predicted happened except they didn't find a nice guy in seven years, which is the part I like to kid about.

> We did not chop out programs wholesale. We used fair and reasonable methods for laying off teachers. It wasn't comfortable but it was the best we could do. The constant suspicion that I have some devious motivation to stick it to teachers has been alleviated in the minds of all but a handful. We turned around dramatically without damaging the educational program. We improved our teacher-pupil ratio.

Aging faculty and administration suggested an impending loss of important personnel. But Superintendent Creasey and Curriculum Supervisor Markley did not think the many upcoming retirements, including Creasey's within two years, would hurt the district, given the quality of recent hirings.

Stable District and Community Relationships. New suburban development had moved farther away from Philadelphia. Plymouth Meeting was stable, populated with descendants of early settlers, post-World War II newcomers, and aging professionals. Everybody—parent, teacher, administrator—seemed to know what he or she was supposed to be doing, how to do it, whom to contact, and when. With familiar procedures and rich associational links, security was evident despite high expectations.

Community members seemed sure of themselves and each other, confident. Teachers were familiar with curricular guidelines, district policies and politics, and parental views. Parents spoke of ready access to school people, praised teachers and principals, pushed attendance at student performances to standing-room-only.

One clear example of schools' responsiveness to community was apparent in the work of Whitemarsh Elementary Principal Erb in the district's most affluent school. Earnestly, he described his and his faculty's interactions with parents.

Erb: We've been accepted by our community. I think we get respect. We have parental pressures and we need to respond to them. This is a professional community; people have a lot of ideas. There is also a time to say, "I'll have to think about that and get back to you," and then just do what you were going to do anyway without getting everybody offended.

Treated with respect and affection by parents and teachers and students, Al Erb was constantly alert to the myriad human and administrative details required for the polished functioning of Whitemarsh Elementary as "a pleasant place for children." He addressed immediately those difficulties he did not outright preempt—an exemplar of district practice in maintaining community relationships.

A second example of the district's responsiveness to the community was apparent at a Board of Education meeting. Some parents were incensed about safety measures on the first floor space of Colonial Elementary School. Jeff Spangler, who taught band to small groups and feared losing his specially designed first floor classroom, explained the problem.

Spangler: It's maybe 100 yards from the bottom of the steps to my classroom door. That's considered unsafe by some parents because this building is open to the public, with school district administrative offices and space rented to a tax office and day care.

At the beginning of the school year, two girls ran off the playground at recess and ended up at the Whitemarsh police station. They had wandered off the playground but the parents were furious and threatened lawsuits.

Principal Wilson suspected the angry parents had a more complicated motive.

Wilson: Conshohocken Elementary has the most one-parent families and low-income apartment housing in the district. Conshohocken was not in our school district until the state reorganized it in 1963. Well, the Whitemarsh parents don't like it that their kids mix with the Conshohocken kids in the grades 4-5 school. One of the ways they show it is by complaining about security in this school.

These parents appeared in force at the board meeting. Conciliatory from the start, the board president prefaced discussion with a history of the board's decision to convert Colonial Elementary to a grades 4-5 institution, the board's appreciation of parental concerns and efforts, and an offer to hear them out. The board heard speaker after speaker and then brainstormed possible solutions on the spot. Superintendent Creasey sought clarification as to the range of acceptable remedies for

Colonial School District
Plymouth Meeting, Pennsylvania

the problem and promised an immediate, perhaps temporary, hallway "watchdog." Parents and teachers, initially at verbal odds, pledged cooperation and support. Within three days, a controversial and potentially divisive issue had arisen, gained momentum, and been addressed and defused.

Controversial, even unpopular, decisions have to be made in schools and in school districts. Rather than shrugging off this reality with a you-can't-please-everyone attitude, Colonial School District personnel seemed eager to identify and remedy problems quickly and with as much consensus as possible. This seemed both a contributor to and evidence of remarkable social cohesion.

Longevity Influencing Arts Instruction. I found personnel stability to be an important and largely positive factor in the arts classes in the schools. Like classroom teachers, most arts teachers had been at their craft for a long time. They spoke of taking recent workshops. They knew where to get materials and information. They knew which requests were likely to get favorable responses. They were familiar with their students' interests, abilities, backgrounds. They were well acquainted with the district's curriculum guides. They were knowledgeable and confident.

A glance into a couple of arts classrooms at Colonial and Whitemarsh suggests how longevity affected instruction.

Observation of Wilma Spangler's Visual Arts Class

Wilma Spangler, visual arts teacher at Colonial Elementary School, is placing watercolors, newspaper, flat wooden sticks, paper and oak tag on tables. Her second-floor classroom is spacious and light; large, smooth tables and stools give a studio ambiance. There are sinks, shelves, cabinets, closets, countertops, and two glass-front display cases housing art objects, some by students. Student paper sculpture masks adorn cabinet doors; student watercolors are affixed to closet doors beside Impressionist reproductions; tissue paper "stained glass," the most detailed I have seen, hang translucently in the room's few vertical windows. On the wall, Spangler has displayed for today's lesson some Oriental fans, some postcards of Oriental subjects she purchased from the National Gallery in Washington, D.C., and teacher-made examples of today's project in various stages of completion.

"I wanted to watercolor with them and it's in our curriculum. But I find that these kids like to have some kind of finished product, something besides a picture, when they finish," she explains. "So, we're painting Oriental fans today. I'm not well-versed in Oriental art but I like to share some art history and some art from other cultures with them, so I'm adapting an idea from a conference I attended recently."

Four girls appear at the door, asking to come back later in the school day to spend extra time working on a class project. Spangler ascertains that they have approval from their teacher, then grants permission. "It's hard for them to finish sometimes in just one period a week," she sighs.

She has partitioned the room with shelves to create a small foyer at the door. Here she greets 27 fifth graders, "a large class." The children, about equal numbers of boys and girls, three Afro-Americans and one Asian, seat themselves quietly and, within two minutes, have spread the tables with newspaper.

"Did anyone talk to the school secretary about her watercolors?" Spangler asks in a soft voice. Three girls, barely audible, did. She draws the students' attention to a piece created by the secretary and displayed in one of the glass cases, saying, "You know, you don't have to be a professional artist to enjoy doing watercolor."

She reminds them of last week's preparatory exercise, an exploration of watercolor technique and, with the display of fans and steps listed on the chalkboard, explains today's project. The term *uchiwa*, meaning fan, is introduced. Paper is to be painted and glued to oak tag, wooden handles attached, and yarn glued to the edges of the fans and wound around the handles and pressed. Spangler talks about subject matter for the painting. Traditional Japanese motifs are pointed out and discussed. Five minutes at the end of class will be reserved for discussion.

"Tom, could you be a resource person on this?" Spangler asks the Asian student. "Could you suggest some subjects for people to paint?"

"Who, *me*?" Tom seems flabbergasted.

"I could," a Caucasian girl suggests. "My mom is interested in Oriental art."

Shirts to be used as smocks are available but no one seems worried about messiness. Spangler moves among the students with encouragement and suggestions. Mostly, the children paint representational subjects: ballerinas, butterflies, a *bonsai* tree. Some images are only stick outlines; some are fully colored. Some representations are stereotypic; some are individualistic. Some students use a dry point technique; some, wet-on-wet.

One girl has painted a flower on each side of her fan. On one side, the colors ran together and blurred the picture; it is a highly aesthetic accident imbuing the blossom with a dreamy quality. The girl smiles, "I like the messy side better. It has more life."

Spangler is demonstrating wet-on-wet technique to a boy. She encourages exploration and abstraction. "Don't worry too much about details now. You can add them later, if you want."

While Spangler helps him, students are coming to her. She advises, explains, encourages sharing. To a girl, "You might want to look at other people's work." To a boy, "Perhaps Matthew could help you put your fan together."

Free to move and talk, these children nevertheless concentrate on their fans. Every child is attending to his project and seems to know what to do. Nearly all are talking but the room is not noisy. Those coming to the teacher are not in need of repeated directions.

Colonial School District
Plymouth Meeting, Pennsylvania

Spangler circumnavigates the room. Tom, having finished a graceful dry point sailboat and palm tree on one side of his fan and a tree and mountain on the other, is told he may make another fan and begins immediately. She suggests that he try wet-on-wet paint application. After assisting a girl having difficulty wrapping her fan's handle with yarn, Spangler offers a general suggestion to make this step easier. With another girl, she suggests a different technique and discusses "good craftsmanship."

"I'll ask you to clean up in about three minutes," she announces. "If you have a little more yarn to glue, do that. But you won't have time to start a whole new painting."

A girl fans herself. "Aaah. It works."

Clean-up time is announced. Some students have already begun. A boy rolls around a big trash can lined with a plastic bag, picking up paper from the tables. There is an orderly crowd washing up at the sink.

From a chair at the head of the room, "Five and a half tables ready," Spangler observes aloud. "OK, everybody, let's talk about what we might use these fans for—something besides a cooling agent."

Decoration is quickly suggested. When dance is offered, Spangler reminds them about *noh* drama and *kabuki* theatre, with which they seem familiar. She brings up fan etiquette and nonverbal communication, "like semaphores," she says.

"How might men use fans?" she asks.

"Swat someone," a boy guesses.

"Very close," she tantalizes.

"Swat flies!"

"Close again but go back to people."

"War!"

Spangler nods. "Intimidation displays by *sumo* wrestlers, for instance."

A girl offers, "Females could use fans to attract males." Then, "Can we take them home?"

"What shall we do about that?" Spangler returns the question. "I'd like to display some. Maybe some could take them home and then bring them back for a while. Boys and girls, make your decision and line up, please." They line up immediately, some leaving their fans and receiving the teacher's thanks.

"Hint, hint." Spangler notices that one table is not clean. Two girls turn back to clean it. "Thank you. Maybe those from that table could help." They do. The two girls industriously scoot stools under tables, then leave a little after their classmates.

Excerpts from Interviews with Wilma Spangler.

We used to coordinate projects with academic teachers before we moved to the grades 4-5 school. We're new here. We've only been a faculty for two years but most of us have taught in other schools and know each other quite well.

As for integrating the arts with other subjects, a social studies teacher wanted some help in making a globe. I don't think you can be very creative about that; there are only certain ways you can make a globe—you can't make it square. And I don't think she'd want her globe to have yellow polka dot water. I think a lesson in fine arts should have more options, more choices. The teachers do have the option to ask me—the only thing is, I don't always have time in my schedule.

I don't have enough time with students. I'm not able to meet with them other than during our class period unless I can find a special reason. I would like to have time for children that are gifted or absent or that just need help. I would like to have some time with them to explore things more freely, to further their creativity.

I think it matters to have a room that is made for art because it gives a feeling of professionalism that filters down to the children. In this district, every school has a room for art—we're fortunate that way—but they were not all built as art rooms. Some lack cabinet space or a place for a kiln; mine is in a corner but some are in closets. Whitemarsh has a very nice art room. Conshohocken and Ridge Park and Plymouth Elementary have nice rooms but not sinks and flooring for spills, that kind of thing.

Faculty longevity does not guarantee student learning in the arts, of course. And longevity is not uniformly positive in effect, as interviewees' calls for "new blood" and "new ideas" attest. Nor does teacher longevity guarantee student arts experiences of an aesthetic nature, as Monroe Beardsley and John Dewey wrote of them. Many other factors—materials, community values, out-of-school art opportunities—influence classroom activities. But in many of the arts classes I observed, a sense of familiarity and confidence pervaded and enhanced the scene. This sense was frequent and strong enough to persuade me that, here, teacher confidence, born of longevity, was a prime determiner of student arts experiences.

Observation of John Fino's Music Class

A few miles away at Whitemarsh Elementary, Dr. John Fino, in suit and tie, prepared to teach music to a second-grade class. His windowless room was bright with neat bulletin boards: "Guess the Symbols" with music notation, "Let's Read Music" with fingering for recorder and a keyboard, and Easter decorations. He had an office off the classroom.

Fino's instructional emphases appeared, in my two observations, to include socialization—behavior in class and at music programs—and singing, mostly for enjoyment but inclining toward performance. Fino spoke familiarly of the correlation between student age and attitudes toward singing, of which ideas to try and which goals were reasonable. He acknowledged relatively low importance parents gave to music education in schools.

"Please come in quietly," he tells the children at his door. "We have a guest." Orderly, the students file in and sit, boys alternating with girls, in two rows of chairs along a wall perpendicular to the piano.

"We're going to have a treat today, a tape at the end of class, since it's close to the holiday," he tells them. "Before that, we're going to practice our songs. The first song today is 'Boom, Boom.' Do you remember that from when you were here last week? It's like a rap song," he passes out sheets of lyrics. There is a murmur of assent from the seven-and eight-year-olds.

At the piano, Dr. John Fino introduces a song to Whitemarsh Elementary School second graders.

"We'll need someone to play the timpani," Fino says and selects a girl. "Then we'll sing 'Baby Baluga' and see the film. By the way, there's a rap program coming on the Disney channel. Check for the time and watch it at home. I'll tape it so you won't miss it."

Children are looking at the sheet music and some are humming. "OK, quiet," the teacher directs. "Let's begin." He plays the piano and sings encouragingly, with volume but the children struggle. The timpani sounds hesitantly. "Don't you remember this?" Fino interrupts the song to ask.

"No," a staggered chorus answers. Up tempo, he has them try again but they drop out completely by the third verse.

"Can't you read this?"

"Can't we do 'A Girl from France'?" a girl asks, referring to the next song, "Baby Baluga," by it's first line.

"Let's do this one first, shall we?" Fino replies. He tries again but with little success. "I'm sorry," he says as he tries a recording of "Boom, Boom." "I thought you remembered this song from last week." The children listen, reading along.

Next he plays a few bars on the piano. "Who knows this song?" Many recognize "Down by the Bay," and sing along, enjoying a sequence of question-response style verses:

Question: Did you ever see a bear . . .

Kids' response: Wearing yellow underwear?

All: Down by the bay!

The children pass songsheets forward and, asking permission, move their chairs before a television perched atop a rolling cart. A boy wordlessly stations himself at the light switch, then flips it on cue.

"We'll sing 'Baby Baluga' next time," Fino says as folk guitarist Pete Seeger appears on screen. The children clap and tap their feet to the music. They join softly in a calypso chorus, to which Seeger adds some bluesy phrase endings. On screen, a seated girl about the same age as these students moves her upper body rhythmically; some of these viewers try that for a few minutes. The teacher motions two inattentive boys to come nearer to him.

"I think you know the next one from first grade—'Five Little Ducks,'" he says. When Seeger asks the kids around him to make the mother duck's sound, Fino's second graders readily join in. When, in the lyrics, more and more baby ducks fail to return to their mother, Fino says reassuringly, "It's got a happy ending so don't worry." Then, "What do you call that thing?" he points to the screen. A boy identifies and he confirms: a kazoo.

The next song is "Apples and Bananas." "That's the crazy one," he says. "You can help him on this one." The vowel sounds change in each verse to, for instance, "opples and bononos." Some wiggly boys twirl in their chairs as the tape ends.

"You were a good audience," Fino praises them as two boys vie to turn on the lights. "What if we went to a real concert? There's nothing more annoying than to go to a concert and hearing someone talking all during the performance."

Excerpts from Interviews with John Fino.

> I've taught music at all grade levels and English for four years. I have dual certification. I didn't think I'd like teaching elementary but I like it best. The kids are wide-eyed. They come in singing. It's in everything they do—math and poetry and stories. In upper grades, they want only rock music.
>
> This year, I've started an elementary choir, the first in the district. Fifty third graders, non-auditioned, come twice a week before school. We're singing "Bless the Beasts and Children" and some Gershwin. I won't try more than two-part harmony at this age. I see a tremendous improvement. It opens up their voices. I also work with a boys' church choir.
>
> Materials here are good. I have Orff and rhythm instruments, for instance. The videotapes are mine; I show them before holidays.
>
> But parents are apathetic. Music is not important to them unless it keeps their kids off the honor roll.

Other classroom vignettes will follow. This pair illustrates teacher longevity and suggests a range in pedagogic styles along several continua: teacher-directedness, encouragement of creativity, students' personal interaction with the arts, level of sophistication of arts activities, student initiative and purposefulness. Not atypical, this pair indicates that teachers here were knowledgeable and experienced, familiar with district and community. They undertook their assignments with confidence. Day to day, they worked largely in isolation from academic teachers and from other arts teachers.

Lack of Innovation. Besides Fino's elementary chorus, in its first year and more an extension of an upper grades idea than an innovation, only one new program in the arts was mentioned to me. That was Pat Ianelli's, then Jim Capolupo's, proposal for a dance artist-in-residence grant from the state of Pennsylvania. This school district had never had an artist residency. But because only one school would be served, district approval for the proposal had been delayed and funding doubtful. Such ideas seemed to be the kind that district personnel wished aloud that new people would propose but official receptivity evidently could not be taken for granted.

In school districts where funds are short or where societal crises are manifested in classrooms, a failure to innovate would be more understandable. At Colonial School District, knowledgeable and secure arts teachers and administrators did not push for new or expanded arts opportunities. Despite long acquaintance with colleagues teaching academic subjects, arts teachers rarely integrated arts and academics in joint activities. Perhaps they were reasonably satisfied; perhaps they knew which ideas would endure, dropping riskier novelties; perhaps the logical connection between new ideas and new people too readily excused them from trying new approaches and programs; perhaps scheduling prevented integration of subject matter. On the other hand, the district's process of continuous curriculum development provided a vehicle for incorporating new strands into the curricular fabric, potentially for weaving new cloth. Was this opportunity sufficiently exploited?

The District's Centralized Curriculum Development

For some years, Colonial School District had employed curriculum coordinators for each academic subject area. Officed with the central administration, each coordinator's responsibilities included: to plan and administer a budget, to evaluate teachers, to monitor instructional progress, and to ensure the continuous development of K-12 curriculum in the given subject area. A subject area was said to be "on cycle" when there was a coordinator and when these functions were occurring. Fine arts was the most recent subject area to go on cycle.

Local curriculum development I found to have a strong impact on arts instruction. Groups of teachers were periodically hired to take part in the process, a continuously repeating five-year cycle of development, implementation, monitoring, evaluation, revision, and reimplementation. Arts teachers were central to the development of art and music activities and to the listing of materials and resources—which perhaps helped to explain why every arts teacher with whom I spoke seemed familiar with his or her guideline, seemed to make adaptations and adjustments as deemed appropriate, seemed invested in teaching based on the art or music document. Both appropriateness to local conditions and familiarity to teachers seemed assured by this process of curriculum development.

Curricular Sequentiality. The district's faculty-developed K-12 curriculum guides showed sequentiality. In fact, visual arts guidelines were presented in a more linearly sequential format than content suggested. Faculty appeared to implement the guidelines faithfully, if flexibly. During Iannelli's long tenure as fine arts coordinator, execution of the guidelines was an important point in teacher evaluations.

Yet there was an uncomfortable pause at the visual arts teachers' meeting when I asked, "Do you feel that the students coming to your classes have been well-prepared?"

"That's a loaded question. Yes and no. We're all different personalities. The kids come from four different elementary schools. They have different socioeconomic backgrounds."

"You have to realize that, in the elementary schools, they have art once a week, maybe 40 minutes. How fast can we expect them to learn something well enough to really know it the next year?"

"We often touch upon the same topics at different levels of sophistication. Elementary is for learning to manipulate tools, then using tools to promote an idea—moving from the subjective to the abstract. It's quite possible to see linoleum block printing at elementary, middle and high school and for all those experiences to be worthwhile."

"In high school, less than 10% of the time, we get the precocious child whose parents are interested in the arts. The other 90% might remember two-point perspective and might not. Half won't remember anything; they're not even interested in being in the room. Some guidance counselor decided this was the only place to put them."

The unwillingness to criticize each other was tangible. So was the sense of working toward a common goal against common odds. Jeff Spangler, the band teacher at Colonial Elementary, explained: "They probably just didn't vocalize [the lack of student preparedness]. It is there. It is a problem."

Relative Importance of the Arts

Most teachers, administrators, and arts specialists would have agreed with John Fino's judgment that academics were far more important than the arts to parents but some parents would have challenged this view. Some pointed out that many parents exposed children to Philadelphia's cultural smorgasbord and to a wide range of private and after-school programs; many acknowledged that a large number of parents, perhaps a majority, did not. Conshohocken and Ridge Park Elementary students were thought least affluent and consequently least likely to have such opportunities. In contrast, local interest in college preparation and sports was uniformly acknowledged.

The value commitments of Colonial School District and those of the community seemed to be in harmony. Support for arts education, although strong in some ways, was limited. Arts teachers appreciated their plentiful materials and special classrooms; fine arts curriculum coordinators appreciated their equal administrative footing with academics; but arts personnel chafed at scheduling constraints, itinerancy of many specialists, and a perception that arts were less important than academics.

Community Interest in Arts. Sally Brewster, Jane Evans, Chris Feorelli, and Linda Goldberg, four mothers of Whitemarsh Elementary students, gathered in the school library and offered these views about parental priorities.

"Families here are interested in the arts. They support concerts even when they have to take kids to extra practices, even rehearsals at 7 a.m. on Saturday."

"There is so much divorce. Activities can run into big money, too much for working mothers. We know some Conshohocken girls who can't take gymnastics at $28 a month, although they are doing school-related things."

"With more than one child, different age groups and interests, distances too great for walking, it's a major commitment to get kids where they have to go. You have to keep up the enthusiasm and juggle the responsibilities to make it important. Sometimes, when I've had a day of work, I want to say, 'Can you skip rehearsal tonight? I just can't drive one more place.' But then my kids would get the sense it's not important and *they'd* skip it."

"There are competing interests in our family. When we went to see "The Nutcracker," my seven-year-old daughter liked it but my ten-year-old son fell asleep. We go to historical landmarks—you can't get away from history in Philly—and science museums and the planetarium. We took friends from Jersey to the Art Museum; of course, the first thing we said to the kids was, 'This is where Rocky [from the movie of the same name] went up the stairs!'"

"My kids are at the [Recreational District] Art Center right now. I specifically chose Thursday classes because a lot of kids come on Wednesday when the school district lets out early. I said, 'This is for you and your art.' We've talked to my son's teacher about recommending him for the art consortium this summer and I'm to start a portfolio for him. Of course, he might go and then say, 'This is the end of it.'"

"My kids will never see a piano except in school. I couldn't care less although I admire music and I'm glad the schools touch on it. My son wanted to play the saxophone but then chose not to."

"We have artwork all over the refrigerator; I think everyone does. My son's father is an attorney with a master's degree in electrical engineering but he's a frustrated artist. He denied his creative side and he verbalizes that. My son is very artistic and likes to draw pictures. His father encourages him and says that he wishes he had continued his drawing. We'd support whatever the kids wanted to do."

"When my son mentions becoming an artist, my husband, an optometrist, says, 'It would be real nice to get Daddy's practice and do art on the side.' I don't want him to starve, either."

"The main emphasis in the schools is learning 'basics.' At the K-3 level, a real effort is made to make art and music."

"I think our school gives good exposure to the arts—dance, music, creative writing, visual arts. I'm pleased. I'm really sorry we'll have to leave Whitemarsh for the new grades 4-5 school at Colonial, where they're still groping."

Teachers. Teachers from Whitemarsh and Colonial Elementary Schools offered these comments on the subject of local and district priorities for the arts.

Thomas Thies:
> I don't think the community views the arts as basic to a child's education. That would be one of the first give-aways in the schools. A majority can afford it outside of school. They never come to teacher conferences wanting to know how their children are doing in art or music or phys ed. There's a good turn-out at concerts but if it came to basketballs or horns, you'd have more basketballs around here.

Cindy Phifer:
: We have such extremes here—kids who go to Broadway several times a year and children who don't even get to a movie theatre. They've never seen a live performance.

Janet Gafner:
: I don't feel that the district supports the arts very well. If you can get it in during school time without extra resources, then fine—they'll take it and say they've done it. There's the summer consortium but they refused to fund it for a couple of years. Computer education gets lots of money but not the arts or guidance or psychological services.

Nancy Biehl:
: I think the arts are basic in elementary school. I think we use a lot of visual art in the content areas, like science and social studies. At higher grade levels, sports becomes more important.

Sue Pronchik:
: In the high school, the arts are more of an add-on in the curriculum.

John Sitar:
: I guess I would say the arts are basic to education from the standpoint of amount of time the schools devote to the arts. But I am feeling pressure to meet the academic requirements of the curriculum. We no longer put on assemblies and teach speaking and acting skills.

Shelly Schwartz:
: No one subject is more important than another. But the emphasis in schools has shifted. Now, there's a lot of pressure for standardized tests. I think that's destroyed the importance of the arts.

Sue Schiele:
: You can do some neat things in the classroom tying art and music in with academic subject matter. But can you live with yourself for taking the time to do them? Those are the things that make kids want to come to school. I think the skills and experiences that kids have in art class carry over into feelings of success in reading, visualizing, inferential thinking. Part of what we're doing wrong as educators is not conveying that message to administrators—or maybe they're not listening.

Schwartz:
: Three or four classes get together for one field trip a year, mostly to historical sites but once we went to the Philadelphia Museum of Art. If the PTO didn't pay for the buses, we probably wouldn't have any field trips because of the legal requirement to provide equal transportation to private schools. One year we had 125 free tickets to a Christmas play but we couldn't go because the PTO didn't have extra funding to bus everyone.

Betty Simon:
: Our PTO schedules eight or nine assemblies a year. Some are excellent. We've had fairy tales performed by seniors from Cabrini College, the

Philadelphia Orchestra, computer music, the Philadelphia Folk Song Society.

As in most American schools, academics were preeminent in the general curriculum here. Teachers and parents found the arts expensive in time, energy, money. It would be difficult to argue that academics should *not* be schools' top concern but the arts might be given more opportunity to contribute to students' overall development.

Administrative Support. Although academics and sports overshadowed the arts, there was significant and incontrovertible evidence that Colonial School District supported arts education. For one thing, arts specialists were retained even during the drastic decline in student population. For another, every arts teacher with whom I spoke declared satisfaction with materials, facilities, and supplies. Music and visual arts classes were taught in classrooms set aside for that purpose, many specifically planned and equipped for the arts. Several said it was difficult to obtain approval for extra expenditures but, given a sound rationale, the administration often granted requests. Also, the district was one of a consortium of three that funded and alternately housed a summer program in the arts. Finally, the district created the position of fine arts curriculum coordinator and put the arts "on cycle" in continuous curriculum development and budgeting, alongside all other subjects.

Three members of the Board of Education talked with me about board support for the arts. Art Wood quickly ticked off arts rooms in the schools, the summer consortium, Iannelli's promotion to principal "without any reservation whatsoever," and the hiring of Capolupo whom "we think will really enhance that position." An industrial arts teacher in another district since 1959, Wood observed:

> The board has made a financial commitment to the arts all the way through. We'd like to have fifteen youngsters in a program but there have been times we continued arts programs with less than fifteen. We'd like to encourage participation. Philosophically, I have no reason to think that would change.

Rachele Intrieri, mother of five students and a Conshohocken resident, said:

> I've been on the curriculum committee for about eight years now. One of our biggest concerns—and I feel we address it—has been to make sure that students have the opportunity to take courses in music and art. This community is very college-oriented; lots of parents prefer Ivy League. So we've always wanted to make sure that students weren't cheated out of the opportunity to relax and enjoy art and music. The state requires more courses in math, science, and English now, so we've had to be protective of the arts to keep them from being eliminated.

John Mickelson, professor emeritus of curriculum and instruction at Temple University, added:

> The change in state requirements made it difficult for art and music and some other areas in the secondary schools. This district has done a good

job of retaining arts activities. We just renovated the high school and we improved facilities for the arts.

I had watched the board address parents' concerns about security on Colonial Elementary School's first floor in a way that protected the band and orchestra classrooms.

Class Scheduling. At the middle school, many curricular and extracurricular interests competed for the daily schedule's "activity period." In the middle and high schools, scheduling the activity period was complicated by one-day options. Some science courses for instance, required as many as seven periods per week, two from the activity period. As a result, the band rehearsed with a different group each day; many difficult music pieces could not be considered. Other arts options also suffered. Arts personnel said guidance counselors encouraged students to take more academic courses rather than arts electives. New fine arts coordinator Jim Capolupo ventured:

> I think the middle school is hopping with things for them to do but too many things compete for the activity period. I think the high school may need another period to accommodate arts electives.

Arts teachers at all grade levels complained that too little time in the school week was reserved for arts instruction. In the elementary schools, a single period of 30-45 minutes per week in music and in visual arts was allotted each classroom. Set-up and clean-up absorbed precious class time. Visual arts teachers usually coped with this time pressure by presenting short-term, discrete lessons with easily communicated aims. Students were less likely to forget between segments of a project; storage and transporting of materials were reduced.

Elementary pull-out programs in band, orchestra, and chorus offered unique problems. Young students had to remember to bring instruments to school one day a week and, at the grades 4-5 building, to bear primary responsibility for getting to pull-out sessions on time. Student attendance and preparedness for lessons was inconsistent. Consequent slow progress may be understood in the following portrayal of Jeff Spangler's band classroom. Classroom teachers felt inconvenienced, as their comments, following later, indicate.

Observation of Jeff Spangler's Band Lesson

There are three children in a room filled with folding chairs and music stands, two Caucasian boys and an Afro-American girl. The girl, Janelle, is playing the "Marine's Hymn" on a clarinet. The notes are written on the board in a style developed by her teacher, Jeff Spangler, integrating note names and conventional notation from the *Ed Sueta Band Method* clarinet book. Janelle earnestly focuses on the notes. A squeak escapes her clarinet. She and Spangler stop and work on improving her fingering. When he asks her to write down the notes on the board for home practice, she does so.

Ricky plays the oboe next, sitting Indian-fashion in his chair, his elbows resting on his knees. Despite his informal air and his difficult instrument, he plays most notes with even timing.

Clarinet in hand, Brian asks, "Should I try to hit the high note?"

"Yeah, sure," Spangler encourages. Brian's clarinet playing is clearly that of a beginner but his teacher compliments the "good sound on the low notes." Then Spangler announces, "OK, let's play the 'Theme by Beethoven.'"

"Oh boy, I like that one," Brian enthuses.

"Goody, goody!" Janelle gushes.

In a unison rendition of the familiar "Ode to Joy," Spangler joins in on trumpet. Afterwards, he checks Janelle's fingering again.

"Is it time for your lunch?" he asks them. Brian says he must leave. "When are you two coming next week?" Spangler asks Janelle and Brian.

"What about me?" Ricky wonders.

"Don't you have a field trip?"

"Oh, yeah! We have to go to the planetarium, too," Brian remembers.

Spangler checks his schedule against their upcoming activities and times are arranged for next week's session but an air of uncertainty remains.

"Bye, Janelle. Practice!" he reminds the departing girl. "Bye, Brian. Have a good day." To Ricky, "How's your reed?" They examine it. Spangler glances at his watch. "I think it's time for English to start."

Excerpts from an Interview with Jeff Spangler.

> They are beginners, fifth graders. Normally, we start beginners in fourth grade but we allow them to start in fifth.

> Brian is doing extremely well. His parents have signed his book to verify that he has practiced. Ricky, on the oboe, also plays string bass in Ms. [Carmella] Quarry's orchestra. The oboe is very hard to play. He hasn't practiced much lately and it shows. He's a good musician; he has talent potential. He gets a lot of parental support; his mother is here at school a lot. But his teacher told me that he is coming out of class too often; she feels that too many children leave her room for lessons.

> Janelle is slowing down a bit because she lost her book. She is writing the songs down and trying to make it with that. She is definitely trying; she comes every week. I don't think she has much supervision at home but she must do some practicing because she can play the songs adequately. I'll have to try to get her a book.

Janelle borrowed her instrument from the school because she could not afford one. With lower-income families, Conshohocken was able to purchase some instruments through a federal program. When the grades 4-5 school was established, those instruments came here. I lend them to kids who can't afford to rent or buy their own.

I first introduce them to a few notes by fingers: G is so many fingers; A is so many fingers. We work on fingering, notes, simple songs like "Hot Cross Buns." I write notes on the board with their alphabet names instead of using the staff. Then I show them music notation in the book and they learn to read. Ms. [Teri] Marinari, who teaches music classes here, does quite a lot of music reading and it is noticeable. But it's amazing how much the kids forget from year to year. The middle and high school teachers complain that we're not teaching them anything.

I try to be skill-oriented and to keep it simple. With a half-hour a week, I really can't progress to musicianship very often. I can just barely teach fingerings, how to count, and prepare for concerts. At the high school level, maybe 20% of teaching is actually music instruction. The rest is academic problems, paperwork, arranging concerts, scheduling, writing drills for football shows—that kind of thing. It's a performance orientation.

There are two bands in this school. The advanced band is composed of second-year students in fifth grade. The beginners' band has first year students in both grades and is twice as large. There are over 200 band students in a school of just over 500. When you count the kids in orchestra and chorus, about three quarters of the school is participating in before-school music rehearsals. But a lot drop out between middle school and high school.

Classrooms accommodated the pull-out music lessons. As I observed a well-planned social studies lesson in Sue Schiele's fourth-grade classroom, I was astonished at the many wordless, independent comings and goings of students. Especially in the grades 4-5 building, pull-out programs seemed to work because of the initiative and motivation of students. They assumed responsibility to arrive at programs prepared to participate. At team meetings, teachers said:

Thomas Thies:
> We have a crammed curriculum. There are a lot of pull-out programs; I don't even know how many. Depending on your class, you could have kids out all day long and, I mean, they're everywhere. We're locked into half-hour blocks but we end up with a spare ten minutes here, twenty minutes there. It's very frustrating. There is just not enough time.

Sue Schiele:
> The daily schedule is packed with a required number of minutes per subject per week. Then we have to juggle time for a new health curriculum added into science, computer education which takes a large block of time, LD classes, hearing-impaired classes, remediation classes, resource room, English as a Second Language, swimming in addition to

gym class, bus trips to the planetarium. The district gives comprehensive tests in academic areas like science at the end of the year, covering each chapter that is to be taught, so that *has* to be done."

In non-pull-out programs, visual arts classrooms sometimes appeared messy and uncontrolled but there was underlying order and purposefulness. Directions were clear and concise; routines were familiar; children amicably formed lines and shared supplies. Chatter was enthusiastic but not disruptive; movement was casual, unchallenged, almost always task-oriented.

Observation of Jan Canterbury's Visual Arts Class

Jan Canterbury's visual arts lessons at Whitemarsh Elementary revealed the careful, step-by-step planning favored in the district for the single, short weekly lesson.

"We're going to have to settle down or we're not going to get these string prints done," Canterbury is saying as I arrive. "Spread the newspaper on your tables. I'll bring around orange paint. We'll stop at quarter 'til today because we have a lot to clean up."

Third graders happily create string prints under the direction of Jan Canterbury (not shown) at Whitemarsh Elementary School.

The third graders busy themselves spreading newspaper on the tables. Then they glue string on cardboard and paint the string orange. Paper is pressed against the string to create a print. They talk quietly as they work.

Painting, a girl singsongs softly to herself. "Dab, dab, dab, dab, dab,..."

"I'm putting this paint on," says another girl, "this is hard."

"You're supposed to dab," says the first girl.

"What do you think I'm doing?" the second replies.

Undaunted, the first suggests, "Try not to get too much paint on it. Your brush is too full."

Canterbury circulates among the students.

"Mrs. Canterbury, did that come out good?" a boy asks, holding up a clean, unsmudged print of his painted string.

"Beautiful," his teacher admires. Then, to the class, "If you want to be adventurous, you can paint again and print over your first print like we did with block prints."

Several try her idea. A girl pounds on her paper in hopes of a clear print. The children are engaged, enjoying the process and interaction with peers. On the whole, they seem more pleased with their products, mostly non-representational designs, than last week when I observed them tracing and coloring crayon resist Easter baskets.

Canterbury holds up a student's print. "Boys and girls, look at Andy's print. He made this by overlapping."

"I did that, too," another boy says.

"I'm overlapping mine four or five times," a girl tells a boy who is extending his design off the edge of his paper, requiring a second sheet.

The teacher comments on several prints, "That's neat." "I like this one." "That's a great idea, Paul." Then she directs clean-up: "Stack your prints on your resists. Put whichever is driest on the bottom. If you don't want your cardboard, raise your hand and we'll collect it. R.C., what are you supposed to be doing during clean-up?"

Class ends with a review and questions: Why is it called crayon resist? What is crayon made of? What was our other project called?

And praise is offered. "Boys and girls, you completed two lessons in one week and you did it beautifully. Clean-up was terrific." She gives them a fourth star on a chart listing each class in the school. This class is now tied for first place; they cheer. "The winning class could have popcorn and juice or do a tie-dying project."

When directed, they line up at the door. Andy, the only child in the district I will ever observe in a smock, is washing paint cups and stays behind. Eventually, it takes prodding to return him to his class. "Thank you for cleaning up but you have to go when I tell you." A pause. No movement until a friendly, "Scram!"

Professional Assignments of Arts Teachers

Former fine arts coordinator Pat Iannelli reviewed arts teachers' schedules, showing how it might appear on paper that arts teachers had plenty of preparation time.

> Look at this specialist's schedule: art at 9:15, 10:00, and 11:00, a preparation period and, in the afternoon, "supplies"—that means time to work with art supplies. In the beginning of the year, that will be a busy period but, after October, supplies will have been distributed to teachers. We block it out all year long to give the art teacher some flexibility to call kids together for extra help or something.
>
> I don't know that we need more staff so much as we need creative scheduling, especially at the high school. Frankly, I'd prefer full-time staff to sharing arts teachers among buildings and more flex time for interaction with the kids. But let's call a spade a spade—the administration has not blocked them into schedules that won't permit them to go to the bathroom. And the board can't see the arts teachers' point that they need more faculty.

A thorny problem, as Iannelli suggested, was the sharing of arts teachers among schools—"itinerancy." All but one district elementary visual arts teacher divided time between buildings, all but three elementary music teachers, and all of the high school music faculty. Carmella Quarry, the orchestra teacher, taught in four different schools. These teachers spoke of feelings of displacement and discontinuity. It was hard for them or for classroom teachers to see them as genuine faculty members. Travelling and transportation of materials could be inconvenient. Itinerancy reduced opportunities for interdisciplinary projects.

Iannelli explained the origins of multiple school assignments in this way:

> Let me give you an idea of what happened all over this district in '81, '82, '83. Let's say one school needs an art teacher for four days; that's .8 of a teacher. Another needs 2.1 and another, 2.4. Before you know it, an art teacher is assigned three days at one school and two days at another. And a school without enough students for even *one* full-time teacher has *two* art teachers and *two* music teachers coming at different times. The teacher being split between two schools asks, "Why do *I* have to be the guy to do that?" We solved that problem by deciding *everybody* would be shared.
>
> A lot of money is saved by doing that but we lose the integrity of the individual. There might be adverse programmatic consequences, as

well. It's not student-oriented and it's certainly not teacher-oriented. It's program-oriented and budget-oriented.

At a meeting of the district visual arts teachers, these feelings about intinerancy surfaced:

"I would like to see one art teacher per elementary building. We could give the children more time. There would be more continuity. And the teachers would know us better."

"Eventually that shows up in your attitude toward your job. We used to have a specialist in each elementary building. It worked. We had consistency. The kids and the teachers got to know us and we got to know them."

"It would be less disorienting not to have to jump between grade levels."

"The district doesn't like down time, time when we're not with students, even if we're doing displays and preparing materials. You can't really fault them because they get their mandate from the parents who say, 'Cut here; cut there.' It's never a personal thing; it's dollars and cents."

"But having to allow travel time is lost money, too."

"But otherwise, they'd have to hire more art and music and phys ed teachers and more librarians."

Art teachers also said classroom teachers considered them relatively unimportant but classroom teachers denied this. Principals were more empathetic.

Again, from the meeting of visual arts teachers:

"There are a couple of teachers whom I feel don't care what I do so long as they have their break."

"When I taught at the middle school, I didn't feel the difference. I was considered one of the teachers. At elementary, there's a different feeling. When a teacher loses fifteen minutes of her break, it's an issue. Attention is drawn to you personally, even if you had nothing to do with it. It's 'Can we make this up?' 'Can we change the time?' That doesn't happen at the middle school where you have the same class periods.

Classroom teachers said:

"I've never felt arts teachers just provided prep periods. A lot of children who don't like school at least enjoy art or music. Our art teacher [Wilma Spangler] had two degrees in elementary ed before she became an art teacher. She's very developmentally oriented."

"I haven't met any teachers in this district who've thought arts teachers were second class. I know the administration doesn't have that impression because we are told not to keep children out of specialist classes for any reason."

"It's an old argument that started when the union required prep time as part of teachers' contracts and the administration linked that to specialist time. Art teachers don't like to view their classes as covering somebody else's prep time. And classroom teachers raise a fuss when they miss their prep time."

Principals noted:

Bill Wilson: I'm conscious of prep time when I schedule meetings and programs. I have told teachers point-blank, "You wouldn't take reading away; you wouldn't take math away; why should you take the arts away?"

Al Erb: If I had to choose between reading and art, honestly, I would choose reading. But I believe that art is an important part of education and I think most teachers would agree. We have good specialists but I think some do not feel valued. Classroom teachers think that specialists have great schedules.

Leadership

Pat Iannelli was the district's second fine arts curriculum coordinator. Sharing the sentiments of many, Jim Capolupo, the coordinator at the time of the case study, described Iannelli's role in raising administrative support for the arts.

> Pat single-handedly did a lot for the arts program. She was a creator, a go-getter. She provided the momentum and she is one of the main reasons that the arts are OK here. It's a lot easier for me because she carved a great path.

She was short and assertive, with a stubborn chin, a determined stride, and a no-nonsense haircut. Her demeanor and wardrobe were thoroughly professional. Her smile was as firm and inviting as her handshake. She offered coffee and pastry if I arrived in the morning and the hospitality of the school cafeteria if I stayed for lunch. She leaned forward tenaciously when she made a point; she didn't blink. She cocked her head to one side and peered at me from behind her spectacles when I said something of interest—and many things interested her. Where student welfare or education were concerned, where community needs won her support, she took initiative and attended to detail. Pat Iannelli was an irresistible force. Her candor in describing arts education in the district was no surprise:

> We went through a period of decline about the time I became fine arts coordinator, about '77, '78, '79. We had to close schools and cut staff, some of our youngest, most enthusiastic arts people. Everybody in the arts had been full-time until then but we took people out of art or music and put them part-time in social studies or English or wherever they had dual certification. It was hard to tell a person who'd taught instrumental music to two, three, maybe five kids at a time all his life that he had to teach elementary general music—and he had to go back to school to find out how. The professionals lost their dignity. They were devastated. For a long time, I wasn't restructuring a program; I was restructuring human beings. In eleven years, I think I've hired three new

people—and that because of maternity leaves or something. They're all full-time in the arts now but they are not all in one place doing one thing.

Then we began to look at our curriculum. For the first three years, every time I asked for something, I had to go back and go back and go back. For example, at the time, the music textbooks were collections of songs, 20-30 years old. I had to ask four times to get them updated. I had to do a reading level evaluation, to project enrollments, to persuade them to buy up-to-date books. In contrast, the social studies coordinator could come in and say, "Our books are five years old," and they'd say, "OK." Sometimes in the early days, I would be told that the board didn't approve of something and I'd go to Superintendent Creasey and say, "Let me appear before the board." Usually if I took it to the board, I was able to turn it around.

It's interesting. We won a lot of battles in a period of decline. I think I was given a great deal of leverage as fine arts coordinator. I don't know that I built a lot of new things for the fine arts department but I think I maintained a great deal that was there—and one of them was the integrity of the department.

I don't think money was a real factor. At that time, minor subjects weren't on the five-year cycle, so we didn't have continuous curriculum development and a budget of our own. That first year, the arts people joined together and said, "Hey, put us on cycle!"

I've not really been refused anything. But I have to think a problem through; I can't wander in and dance around an issue and expect to get much. I think we have a rather substantial budget for our band program, for instance; we could always use more. We're not going to dedicate a twelfth of the school budget to the arts; I know that. But once something has been approved by the Curriculum Council and the board, it's as safe as it would be in any other subject area. I think that's saying a lot. I've heard of districts where budgets are approved but things get cut when the money runs out. I feel good about the administration in that way. They're not simply the purse-holders that some people think they are.

I've been compared to a terrier with a bone. However, all terriers are sometimes told, "Stay!" I was, vividly at times. But until I'm told to stay, I don't let go of the bone. The superintendent and others have said to me, "I know the arts are important to you but that's just a part of it." And it's a small part. I don't think we're equal to academics. Hierarchically, the coordinator is but we're not, in terms of time, staffing, or budget.

Iannelli described one of her final acts before leaving the coordinator's position to become principal of Conshohocken Elementary School.

> A few years ago, we wrote the first grant proposal for an artist-in-residence program in this district. It sat on someone's desk. This year, I made several calls to [the state Department of Education in] Harrisburg and was given a tip that demographics were important. Conshohocken is the lowest school, socioeconomically, in the district. I prepared a $3,000 proposal for a residency in Conshohocken Elementary. When I presented the idea to the Curriculum Council, the superintendent said he wanted the residency for all schools. I checked with the other principals, who weren't really interested. They preferred assembly programs; I wanted the dance residency. We have dance only as a very small part of physical education. Dr. Creasey said, "You can do this on half the money and it has to be shared with all the buildings." I said, "It won't fly that way," but that was the only way we could get a signature. I'd made my point and [new fine arts coordinator] Jim [Capolupo] was here. With forty-eight hours before the proposal deadline, he quickly rewrote it, cutting it by 50% and involving more buildings, and sent it to Harrisburg.

In my two weeks on site, I observed Iannelli obtain approval from both Curriculum Council and Board of Education for a state matching-funds breakfast program for Conshohocken School.

> The school was eligible but no one had ever drafted a request. People said to me, "We don't need it," but we'd needed it for 25 years. They said, "You won't get anyone to come in and chaperon the kids." I said, "Fine. Let me try." People are volunteering.

> The same was true with our arts program. I don't want to spend my time talking about what's wrong when we could be seeing what's working and fixing what's wrong. Our job is to create change. Maybe that has something to do with the creative nature of the individual.

Secondary Issues

A number of factors seemed to affect the type and quality of arts opportunities in Whitemarsh and Colonial Elementary Schools including:

1. Proximity to Philadelphia;

2. The tendency to focus on needs rather than strengths;

3. Increasing societal and curricular demands; and

4. Student initiative and creativity.

Proximity of the Schools to an Urban Cultural Center

Philadelphia and its environs offer a wealth of arts opportunities mostly unexploited by the public schools in this suburban school district. Field trips were limited by the expense of busing, a double-ticket item since, by law, equal busing was required of public schools for private schools. Although teachers recalled a few arts-related field trips, most trips had been tied to academic subjects, especially history.

The community brought art to the elementary schools through volunteers like Patty Zierow, who shared reproductions of paintings with each elementary classroom through a program called Art Goes to School.

Parents, through the PTO, offered exposure to professional artists by financing field trips and assemblies. Each school's PTO was a separate entity whose treasury reflected the socioeconomic status of its neighborhood.

One assembly, of a folk arts nature, occurred during the time of the study. A representative of the Philadelphia Folk Song Society performed at Colonial Elementary for only $20, the society's grants covering the remaining costs.

On stage in the school's spacious auditorium, with its carpeted aisles, an energetic young man in blue jeans sings a fast-paced song, accompanying himself on the banjo. Then in a friendly way, he guides students through an historical tour of musical instruments.

"Do you know the oldest instrument known to humankind?" he asks them. After savoring an expectant pause, he answers: "The human body." He solicits their participation in hand-clapping and knee-slapping, then chants, "Juba this and Juba that. Juba killed the yellow cat..." Familiar with rap, the kids clap and slap with him, getting more and more excited, as he pushes the timing faster and faster. He ends the chant with a resounding finger-in-the-mouth pop.

Then he talks about Zimbabwe drums, how to construct a one-stringed instrument. He rests a bow against his jaw and changes the shape of his mouth to alter pitch. He talks of Senegalese lutes, gourds covered with goat or snakeskin, as the banjo's ancestor, comparing Senegal's traditional oral history-telling to the Bible's "begats." Coming to this country, slaves duplicated these instruments with cheese boxes and "busted guitars," synthesizing a "truly American instrument" from African musical ideas and European technology.

He plays "Happy Birthday" on the jug for everyone born in March, ending with a deliberate, laughter-eliciting foghorn sound. "You brass players out there can all play the jug," he encourages. "It's the same technique."

Playing "Minnie the Moocher" on the kazoo, he explains the traditional call and response song of the American backwoods. He plays the song again, adding intervals of banjo, jug, and singing to the kazoo. It is an infectious song and the audience responds enthusiastically. The more the kids bounce, the more energetic the performer becomes.

"Charlie on the Board," a little wooden limberjack who hangs and twirls from sticks, is introduced in a bit of dramatic play. A rhythm instrument "from Germany or American Indians or who knows," Charlie is made to dance an accompaniment to "The Arkansas Traveler/Bringing Home My Baby Bumblebee." With a little ventriloquism, Charlie then displays his stubbornly mischievous ways by refusing to stop twirling.

Cued, the kids yell to him, "Come down, Charlie!"

"No!" Charlie retorts shrilly and continues his antic spinning. But finally, of course, he comes down, offering a little bow before he is put away.

The performer demonstrates Appalachian clog dancing, telling of its African roots. Then as the students clap time, he plays the banjo and simultaneously performs a high-stepping, heel-clicking dance.

Almost breathless, he takes out a stringed instrument. "What's this?"

"A mandolin?" a student offers.

"A dulcimer," he says. "It's easy to play. You play the melody on one string. See where the frets are missing? I took out the wrong notes." Few kids seem to know "Aunt Rhody" when he asks them to join in. Played softly and beautifully, this song elicits a calm response.

It's "Polly Wolly Doodle" on the spoons, with whistling and a little more clogging, before he takes questions from the group.

When did he start playing the banjo? At age fourteen.

Who taught him to play? Lots of different people. "I floundered for several years until I got started with a good teacher." He gives the name of a local studio that offers lessons.

Does playing the spoons hurt his mouth? He has to be careful.

Is it hard to clog? No, you just need loose knees and ankles.

Where did he get his instruments? The banjo, reconstructed from five different banjos. Charlie, repaired so often that he thinks of him as hand-made. The dulcimer, from a central Pennsylvania maker. The stringed gourd, from a self-supporting ex-convict in the western part of the state. The jug, just a jug of maple syrup. The kazoo, bought. The spoons, from his kitchen.

Wilson closes the program, saying he enjoyed it and hopes the students did, acknowledging their participation, and prompting another round of enthusiastic applause. He has the performer explain how one joins the society and directs the orderly dismissal of the students.

Colonial School District
Plymouth Meeting, Pennsylvania

The Tendency to Focus on Needs, Not Strengths

The most oft-repeated statement I heard was: "This is a good school district." I could see the statement was true. Yet every time I asked teachers, principals, or district administrators to enumerate the district's strengths, they looked at me blankly. Sometimes they mentioned a minor point or two. Usually they told me of problems or current tasks.

I came to feel that many important things—attending promptly to problems, developing curricula collaboratively, faculty experience, systematic preparation for lessons—were taken for granted. I was not likely to hear of—although I could plainly see—the district's solidity and accomplishments. On the whole, this tendency seemed to fuel dedicated efforts at every location. I found no one resting on proverbial laurels. Most individuals' efforts both supported and were supported by the efforts of the group. Sometimes, people seemed sorely tried but no one seemed overwhelmed.

Increasing Societal and Curricular Demands

A conversation with the two principals was informative about effects of social changes on their schools.

Al Erb: We're not getting the quality of school board member we used to get. We used to have a lot of professional people but they don't want the aggravation. Now we get politically ambitious people which never helps. And we're not getting the quality of child that we used to get. This district has changed socioeconomically. This isn't suburbia any more.

Bill Wilson: When Al and I moved here, this was true suburbia. Now the new housing is being built farther north. This is becoming a fringe of the city.

Here in Colonial Elementary, I have 555 kids. I would say without a doubt, about a third of them come from one-parent families. Ten or twelve years ago, the average IQ for kids in this district was about 116, 117; now it's down to about 108, 109.

Erb: My school is considered the highest, socioeconomically, in the district. But I have children from all over the district that come for resource room, mixed category special education. We have an English as a Second Language program in all the schools. Right now, I have four little boys who take up an unbelievable amount of my time. They're not bad kids but they are constantly causing problems. I work and work with them but I don't know if I'm getting anywhere. I've never had a kid like that before.

Mary Leggette was a K-3 guidance counselor at Conshohocken and Whitemarsh Elementary Schools. She talked about the kinds of children's problems she tried to address and the use of visual arts in her work.

> I do developmental counseling and also I'm there when kids have problems. If I were to give a 1989 profile of the kids I see, I'd say, first, that they're pretty stressed; second, that their concept-formation is pretty age-appropriate except for those who are victimized by dysfunction in families; and third, that some kids are really in crises. I try to get them to get out what's troubling them. Often it comes out in psychodrama—we call it make-believe—acting out a problem-solving situation on the playground, for instance. But the truth always comes out. I hope that, directly or indirectly, they get some insight into their problems.
>
> To appropriately relate feelings in context, we are drawing pictures in a feelings book. Whitemarsh children are very structured and performance-oriented; they want rules and models. At Conshohocken, there are more troubled homes; this is a mixed ghetto of poor whites and intergenerational blacks. Kids have trouble expressing their feelings; their pictures often show chaotic feelings and confusion. But both schools have problems: kids that have too many internal controls and demand more and kids that need controls but don't know enough to ask for them.
>
> I think it's a tremendous relief for children to draw. Teachers have said that kids are quieter after being here. Art is a way of seeing and knowing. It mirrors themselves and lets them see who they are in relation to other people and themselves. I've had kids make clay figures and give them roles, releasing some feelings of inadequacy.
>
> I get concerned about the overwhelming structure in these schools. The whole district is in lock-step. Everyone reads at the same time. At Whitemarsh, the kids are constantly compared. At Conshohocken, rules are needed but kids are told what *not* to do, which complicates the problem. We need to make more provision for individual differences; I think of art as unique to the individual.

The Board of Education also responded to social issues at a worksession, approving a free breakfast program, revising a suicide intervention program, and reviewing procedures for confiscating and reporting illegal drugs. Responding to social ills squeezed school schedules for time. Many thought the arts were one of the losers.

Academic pressures also constrained time for arts instruction. In many districts, mandated student assessment exacerbated this situation but Colonial Elementary teachers reported a different view of their district.

Mabry: How big a bite does student assessment take out of your time?

Teachers: Two mornings.

Mabry:	That's to administer the test. What about preparing students to take the test?
Thomas Thies:	Beg your pardon?
Mabry:	Teachers in Texas told me that they hadn't taught art or music in three months because they had been trying to prepare their students to earn good scores on standardized tests.
Thies:	(laughter) We don't have that time.
Gordon Vitello:	I think if it were discovered that we were doing that specifically, we would be severely chastised. We just hope they remember enough from last year and a little review in September to take the test in a reasonable fashion.

Nurturing Student Initiative and Creativity

In an incidental finding, youngsters in this district displayed dazzling initiative, independence, and responsibility. In schools, I noted that children were rarely given direct answers to questions. Rather, adults were likely to respond, "What do you think?" or "Where have you looked so far?" or "Did you ask Jack? He might be a good resource person." This kind of verbal interaction seemed both to expect and to promote initiative and responsibility. Three examples from Whitemarsh Elementary illustrate: first, a look at a first-grade classroom; second, a play conceived and performed entirely by second graders; and, third, the school's annual "hat day."

Observation of Elaine Notaro's First-Grade Class. It is St. Patrick's Day in Elaine Notaro's first grade. Last week, the children made and played with elephant finger puppets, index fingers as trunks, before writing fantasy stories. Today, the teacher returns the stories to brainstorm title improvements. "Two Elephants and the Swimming Monster" is too long and, after several suggestions, changed to "Elephants Meet the Monster." Soon this title is joined by "Trick or Treating Elephants" and "The Elephant's Adventure," each title scrutinized and abbreviated. Notaro explains use of the apostrophe and distinguishes the possessive from the plural, then asks, "Anybody want to guess how to spell adventure?" A boy does so correctly.

"Today is a special day, St. Patrick's Day," the teacher announces in a quiet, animated voice. She talks about legends, oral tradition.

Next they plan letters to Ace, a classmate who moved to New Hampshire. A short letter appears on the board:

> *Dear Ace,*
> *How are you?*
> *Love* _____

The class talks about what they might write to Ace, consider asking about his new home, his trip there, new friends, skiing, and sledding.

"Use super-kids paper," the teacher directs, "unless you'd like to use this . . .?"

The kids see the second option paper and one says, "Yeah!" So both kinds are made available. "You could write something about St. Patrick's Day," Notaro suggests.

Everyone seems to be working, all on different assignments, depending on what they have to do and their preferences of the moment. Most of the assignments are listed on the board. I wonder whether six- and seven-year-olds will manage to complete all of them independently but I perceive no confusion, no off-task behavior. Notaro confides, "This is the most motivated class I've had in twelve years. Nothing is work to them."

Observation of Second-Grade Play. Down the hall a few days later, a group of second graders performed a play about a leprechaun. "They conceived and wrote it," their teacher, Ms. Pupkiwiecz, explained. "I don't know what it's about."

A few children face the class, a girl in green pops out of a bookshelf, cue cards flash, and the play is over in less than five minutes. I can't figure out what it was about. But the performers are only too happy to tell me.

"Are you going to interview us?"

"Is that a tape recorder?"

"Will we get any money from this?"

Billy Guess, Mike Schaller, Amy Stern, and Michael Grodantz, words flowing and tumbling, talk about their play.

Billy: I'm the director and I wrote the play, too. I just sat down and thought about it and the words came out of my pencil. I started to write a story but, then, I thought I could make it a play and I did! St. Patrick's Day was coming, so I made one up for that.

Amy: We had a lot to do to get ready. I had to get paper for the cue cards. Mike called them booby cards.

Mike: Shut up, Amy.

Amy: I was afraid I might forget my lines. It feels funny being in a play because everyone's looking at you.

Billy: When I said, "Try to practice your lines," everybody always forgot. Then Mike came up with this great idea and said, "Let's make some cue cards."

Mike: Billy thinks all of us have to do *perfect*.

Colonial School District
Plymouth Meeting, Pennsylvania

Billy:	I was very, very nervous but it was a pretty good play. Me and the whole play agree we're going to keep on doing plays until Mr. Erb lets us do one for the whole school.
Mike:	He's gonna have to let us.
Michael:	We thought he might let us this time because *you* were here and because we were getting interviewed.
Billy:	We kept asking him and he said, "I'll think about it." Then he said it was up to our teacher; I don't know what she said.
Mike:	Billy wanted to do it for the whole school so his girlfriend Jackie could see him.
Billy:	Well, we wanted Jackie to be in it.
Amy:	Yeah, instead of me.
Billy:	Well, I had some trouble with the actors. I was trying to put this play together and here they are, jumping up and down, screaming, yelling, carrying on, and laughing! I said, "Stop, guys! We only have one day to get this together!" We were practicing on the last day.
Amy:	That's not what he said. He said, "You guys are going to keep doing this over until we do it perfect."
Mike:	He fired me and Amy. He fired me, like, seventeen times.
Billy:	We want to do another one.
Others:	Yeah!
Mike:	We'll use cue cards again.
Billy:	We're going to have 50 cue cards. It's going to take an hour.
Mike:	Two thousand! The whole day!

Hat Day. On another day, Whitemarsh Elementary's third annual hat day, the entire student body sat on the floor in the gym, the perimeter lined with parents. A phonograph rang out with player piano-style songs like "In the Good Ol' Summertime," as Erb, in a madras golf cap, stepped to the microphone to welcome everyone and to thank the PTO for the specially printed pencils to be given to all the children.

In riotous headgear, each class paraded around the gym twice and across the stage. Some hats were entirely home-made, like the baked bread dough one boy cooked over a bowl and wore. A few were purchased, like one boy's baseball cap sprouting stuffed antlers. Some were seasonal, one covered with shamrocks. Some were pretty, one a flowered grapevine wreath. One was taller than the wearers, a six-foot stovepipe hat whose brim reached it's wearer's shoulders, eyeholes cut into the hatband. Some looked uncomfortable, like the hat made of leggos. Many required careful balancing, like the table with complete place settings. Long balloons twisted around one child's head. A chef's cap was adorned with real food. A boy wore flashing Christmas lights. Hats were adorned with rockets, candy wrappers, cotton balls, Barbie and friends, mittens, popcorn fringe, a papier-mâché dinosaur.

Teachers reassured the few without millinery: "You'll make one next year."

"Yeah!"

Is that fine arts? Well, it was self-expression. It was seeing and using materials in a new, unique way. It was creative. Sometimes it was even aesthetic. It certainly was fun. It was also indicative of the nurturing of creativity and initiative that I thought an important part of the story of arts education here.

Conclusion

Summarizing, the four elements which, I concluded, most profoundly affected arts education at Whitemarsh and Colonial Elementary Schools were: (1) the stability and security of relationships with and among district personnel owing to their longevity; (2) the continuous development of local curriculum by those teaching it; (3) the subordinate value of the arts to the people here as evidenced by educational priorities, administrative support, scheduling, and the assignment of arts teachers; and (4) the strong, continuous leadership Pat Iannelli had provided in the early years of the fine arts coordinatorship. Other factors also contributed positively or negatively to children's school experience of the arts.

The highly structured, analytic approach to instruction favored by the district had also been taken in the arts. When I questioned Iannelli about the wisdom of this approach, using Bob Stake's metaphor: "Do we really want to make the arts one of the other seven dwarfs?" she answered:

> I guess it's a matter of being a dwarf or an orphan. We were an orphan, only providing prep time to classroom teachers. Maybe some people still see the arts as a step-child. Maybe we've only provided a foster home. But it is a home. We're part of the curricular family unit. It's better than no family at all but it is only a start.

A Whitemarsh Elementary School student hangs onto her hat topped with a papier-mâché dinosaur as she parades around the gym with her class on hat day.

Chapter 7:
Oakwood School
Townsend, New Hampshire

■ *Nancy Ellis*

The woes of arts education in our public schools have been amply catalogued (Getty Center, 1985; Eisner, 1986). Problems are seen to arise from teachers who follow their own preferences and inadvertently contribute to arts programs that are production oriented, haphazardly planned, unchallenging, and, at worst, miseducative. From another perspective, Howard Gardner (1990) recommended that we should take a closer look at models of art education invented by ordinary teachers. He suggested that we need not despise the pluralism of a broad repertoire of approaches in practice, for in the diverse and pluralistic wealth of wise teachers' practice we may discover unique ways of uniting curriculum theory with classroom application. He argued that we need a broad repertoire of approaches and we need to make significant changes, not just stop-gap measures, in order to improve art education.

In this case study I describe an ordinary elementary school in an old New Hampshire mill town, where some teachers struggle and others blossom. The questions I raise have to do with meaning: What do the arts mean to these teachers and how do teachers understand the arts within the context of school days when they also teach reading, writing, math, science, and social studies? What can we learn about arts education by comparing the teachers who struggle with those who blossom? In this ordinary school, are there wise teachers who can contribute to our knowledge of a broad repertoire of good practices in art education? What are the implications for teacher recruitment and preparation?

The Setting. Oakwood Elementary School is in Townsend, a small industrial city in New Hampshire. Townsend's population is composed mainly of white, working class families. Although the community is not wealthy, most of the funds for school programs are provided through local property taxes. State support for education is minimal because there are neither sales taxes nor personal income taxes in New Hampshire. In Townsend, local property taxes do not provide adequate funds for state-mandated requirements for schools. Development of adequate educational programs to meet state requirements appears to be impossible.

Townsend was first settled about 1630 by the British. It was first incorporated as a parish in the early part of the eighteenth century. Situated on a small river that cascades over rapids and a waterfall near the center of town, it was the site of a thriving woolen and cotton mill. Townsend's mill was well known as one of the largest broadcloth and carpet mills in the United States during the middle of the nineteenth century. However, the town did not continue to grow rapidly, and eventually, the mill gave way to other small manufacturing enterprises. In 1850 the population was 4,943, and in 1985 the population had increased to only 11,000. Mainly the descendants of early British and later French settlers, today's inhabitants of Townsend represent little ethnic or racial diversity. The income level of the majority of working-class residents is generally low but "adequate". The largest employer in Townsend is a General Electric plant that manufactures electric meters. I learned that meter technology here has not changed in the past 50 years. Other smaller industries in the town and a naval shipyard in a neighboring town provide additional employment. Most parents expect their children to graduate from high school and find jobs in the local industries.

A state university nearby enrolls more than 10,000 students, but few students or faculty are residents of Townsend. Townsend has three elementary schools, a middle school for grades 6 through 8, and a high school. The junior high and high schools have visual arts and music specialists. At the elementary level one music teacher serves all three elementary schools and there is no visual arts consultant.

Oakwood Elementary School is located in a well kept neighborhood several blocks away from the central downtown area. Built in 1980, the school architecture was planned by the district school superintendent and a principal, along with a community advisory committee of teachers and parents. Oakwood enrolls 400 students and employs 17 full time teachers and 8 teaching support staff members.

I interviewed the district superintendent, school principal, most of the teachers, and some students, parents, and volunteers. I observed and video-taped nine art lessons. Normally, my role at the school was that of a supervisor of interns, students from the university. During the academic year of 1988-1989 I visited the school regularly every week to observe progress of the interns. I made many casual observations of teachers, and talked informally with them many times. I video-taped art lessons and conducted most of the more formal, taped interviews for this case study during three weeks in December and January.

The Arts at Oakwood. Dance, drama, music, and visual arts took their places at the periphery of the "regular" curricula at Oakwood. There was no district arts curriculum framework or syllabus, and there were no state guidelines for the arts. Project Potential, a school-wide program funded mainly by Oakwood parents, occasionally brought visiting artists and other special programs to the school and made teachers with special talents available to all the students.

The principal, Dennis Harrington, avowed that he believed the arts are as critical as reading and math for helping people "find themselves" and for "unleashing talent," yet "from a political standpoint, in terms of getting monies [for the school], you still have to focus on that basic core of support for reading, writing, and computing."

The district superintendent's most recent staffing priority was a librarian position, not an elementary arts consultant. Mr. Harrington's provision for arts education was Project Potential, primarily designed as a program for gifted and talented children with the secondary purpose of reaching all students to some extent. Indeed, through Project Potential, all Oakwood children saw occasional demonstrations by visiting artists and teachers in a variety of disciplines. For every Project

Potential project, two children from each class were selected, on the basis of interest and teacher recommendation, to attend extended sessions led by the visiting expert. Topics depended mainly on the available talent and ranged from pysanki (traditional Ukrainian egg dying) and painting to astronomy.

Dance was the rarest of the arts at Oakwood. Three years previously, a volunteer ballet troupe had performed the *Nutcracker Suite*. The principal and several teachers described that particular performance for me and remembered that some children had appeared profoundly impressed by it. Apparently, even some "tough boys" had liked it. They said that, on rare occasions, teachers still planned field trips to dance performances. During the year of this study there were no dance performances performed at the school, and none were attended by any of the classes.

Drama was more common. Classes performed plays (from commercially distributed collections of children's plays) for other classes and for parents. There would be flurries of cardboard scenery painting, line memorization, and rehearsals. The culmination would be an evening performance when proud parents and grandparents would sit in folding chairs holding restless siblings or stand in aisles, armed with video cameras on tripods, to record brief and bashful attempts at formal acting and reciting. These performances were produced according to formulae prescribed by the scripts and school performance traditions. Focus was on performance, not on the meaning or elements of drama. Plays were chosen because scripts were conveniently available and related to a holiday theme.

Occasionally a class went on a field trip to view a professional theater production in a nearby town. The first grade saw a performance of Charles Dickens' *A Christmas Carol* the week before Christmas. After the performance I interviewed a first-grade teacher.

Ellis:	Why did you think it was important for your class to see *A Christmas Carol*?
First-grade teacher:	It's important for the children to be exposed to different arts. It's important to discriminate between one artist and another, between this version [of *A Christmas Carol*] and the Mickey Mouse version. They think the Mickey Mouse version is the first version and this one [Dickens' version] we saw yesterday is the takeoff. They need exposure.
Ellis:	Why is it important for children to have such exposure?
First-grade teacher:	I think it is important to expose children to as many different and varied experiences as possible. A lot of children in this town are disadvantaged. They don't have the opportunity for a lot of different experiences.

Her rationale appeared to be the extension and enrichment of experience, but she seemed unable to tell me *why* she thought exposure to a variety of the arts, or even discriminating between Mickey Mouse and Dickens, was important.

Althea Miles, a certificated music teacher came to Oakwood to teach music to each class once a week. The classes I observed were predominantly rehearsals of children's songs. Classes were fast-paced, enjoyable—mostly singing. It was difficult to ascertain why Ms. Miles thought music was important. Its place seemed taken for granted.

Ellis: What do you usually do in music classes?

Miles: At the beginning of class, we do a little extra credit thing on the composer of the month. We have time for this because we don't have concerts in this school. We've tried to listen to things that are appropriate for that month. For instance, like election day, it was a very patriotic time ... John Philip Sousa's *Stars and Stripes Forever* and all the marches ... we practiced the meter, practiced marching and all that stuff. Then I do two or three activities in my lesson plan for the class, some singing, a little appreciation time, maybe work with elements of music, some variety.

Ellis: Do you ever talk about what makes music important?

Miles: Boy, that's a hard question. Maybe what I do is try to make them aware of all the places that we will find music. Everywhere you go there is music ... social occasions, holidays. People have written music for every occasion thinkable. It is part of going shopping, part of television, movies, part of everything. And therefore it must be a very important part of our lives.

Children were "exposed" to the music of a variety of composers. They listened, sang, learned to read notes, and clapped to different rhythms. Educational or musical significance of the music teacher's lessons seemed not often discussed.

I interviewed a primary teacher who supplemented the music teacher's classes with music lessons in her own classroom. She said:

> I don't usually plan my music lessons. They just kind of happen. I take out the bag of instruments and let the children bang around. The kids enjoy listening to me play my flute. I don't teach them anything directly when I do that. I talk about the notes. We do a lot of rhythmic clapping with math, too.

Unlike her reading and math lessons, her music lessons lacked purpose. She seemed particularly unconcerned about what it was the students learned in music. "Banging around" was said to be legitimate in music. The same approach would not have been acceptable in reading or math. Why was it legitimate in music?

Most of the Oakwood teachers said they tried to teach an art lesson at least once each week. Nine teachers agreed to let me video-tape visual arts lessons. They engaged children in a variety of projects such as tempera paintings on cotton quilt squares, Christmas tree ornaments, "stained glass windows" made of black construction paper and colored tissue paper, Santa masks with coat hangers and cotton, greeting cards, weaving, landscape drawings, sponge paintings, and tissue paper wreaths.

Mary Palm's Sponge Printing Lesson. I observed Ms. Palm teach her fifth-grade class a lesson on sponge painting. While a teaching intern taught the rest of the class, Palm worked with children in groups of six or seven. On a table covered neatly with newspaper she laid out materials: sponges, scissors, several kinds of paper, and some green tempera paint in a flat pan in the center of the table. She introduced the lesson by showing children a final product, then demonstrated cutting a sponge the shape of a spruce tree and printing it with green paint on both absorbent paper and glazed paper. Finally, she showed children how to mount the print on a black piece of construction paper. Each child was to make two prints: one to hang in the hallway and one to take home. Children dutifully made their prints, matted them, and hung them in the hallway near the office. Most of the children made trees. A few made green candy canes. There was no critique of the final products. I asked children if they enjoyed art and one said, "It's funner than a lot of other stuff we do..."

Trying indirectly to learn about teachers' purposes for teaching art, I asked Palm some questions about her art lessons.

Ellis: How would you introduce an art lesson that would benefit students you consider gifted in visual art?

Palm: Well, let's say you're introducing something in front of the class and you say, "We are all going to try to draw mice. You can design any kind of mouse you want." I would say it has to be a certain size and it has to be neat. I would like some shading. Then I would draw a mouse on the board and I would say, "Try to get it as realistic as you can." I would draw some shading just as an example. I'd show them where I would shade it in different places. Then I would show them how to shade in different ways — like cross hatching. But I don't think you can teach a kid how to draw. They have to know somehow.

Ellis: What would you hope students would learn by the end of the year?

Palm: One example would be shading. How to use different media. Some geometric art as well as realistic art. I would want them to know that art is more than just *drawing* a picture.

Even after much probing on my part, Mary Palm did not mention aesthetic judgment, art criticism, or art history. There seemed to be production boundaries around her notions of what counted as art education. When I asked her what would be important in the elementary art curriculum, she focused on the types of things she would have students do, such as "practical things that go along with the different media." We talked about artists we both knew. She had favorites: "Andrew Wyeth's paintings are very good, but Picasso's are not so good. It's important for a work of art to get the point across." It was not clear to me what she thought "the point" was. Perhaps it was the recognizable image, the narrative, art as mimesis. She said class field trips to art museums would be nice, but she rarely led her classes to museums because she thought parents and the community, represented by the School Board, would not support that kind of activity. She asserted:

> This is a sports community ... always has been, always will be. That's the priority. When the state says, "You have to have an art teacher," [the School Board] will hire an art teacher to deal with all three elementary schools. You'll have someone who has to deal with not enough time, not enough materials, no one to talk to—the same thing I had to deal with my first year of teaching. It would be just like the music. The music specialist is limited on supplies she can buy. They cut one of the music people this year. They don't cut sports because that is the priority.

Curious about Palm's background, I asked her how she had prepared for a teaching career. I was surprised to find out that, twenty years previously, she had prepared to become an art teacher. She majored in graphic arts at a four-year teacher's college in New Hampshire. After that she taught art as the specialist in a public school for one year. I asked about her first job and she recalled:

> I taught eight classes a day for 20 minutes apiece. I taught in three different schools. In the elementary classrooms, basically what I did was prepare lesson plans and get materials together. I would introduce a lesson and teachers would follow up. Then I would teach at the high school one day a week. It was a choice group of students, like an elective. But I had to haul water up three flights of stairs. [There was no supply of water closer to the art room.] There was no one there to help, no one to talk to. I lasted one year. I was burned out by the end of that year.
>
> At the elementary level I basically went along with holidays so children would have something to do after they finished up their reading and other work. That was what the teachers wanted. At high school I introduced different kinds of media, but I didn't do much teaching.

After her first year of teaching art, Palm went back to the state college to take courses for certification in general elementary classrooms. She decided to teach elementary grades because, as an undergraduate, she had already taken a few elementary methods courses.

Like Mary Palm, most of the other Oakwood teachers focused on projects they dubbed "art." To better understand what aesthetic criteria Oakwood teachers valued, I asked them to describe how they might guide a student to make an especially "good" piece of art work. Some I asked to tell me how they judged the merit of students' completed work. Answers from Sarah Good, Evelyn Hargraves, and Rae Simpson were as follows:

Good: They [the pictures] look nice, when they have defined edges, they are centered on the paper so it doesn't hang off the edge, they are neat, they are pasted down well if they used paste. Maybe originality, something they can invent ... so that it gives you the idea, the impression of something, and it's interesting.

Hargraves: I suppose I'd end up looking at which was the neatest, most different, well presented. I wouldn't want the ones colored all over the whole paper. I'd want the ones that showed they spent time on it. I'd need to take an art course to know what kids can do.

Simpson: I talk a lot about not doing something like their neighbor. Everybody's creative. It's just a matter of helping them become confident. ...We don't usually talk about their pictures. We don't "interact" with the work, just talk sometimes about what's there.

The emphasis in production was on neatness, originality, detail, effort, and care. Creative expression was mentioned, but there was little talk about meanings of the expression, whether replicative or creative.

In contrast to the majority of teachers at Oakwood, two were different. Karolina Bodner, a teacher in grades 3 and 4, used what she called a "process approach" to infuse meaning into every part of her curriculum, including the arts. Joan Whittier, a second-grade teacher, seemed to have a way of planning lessons that reminded me of branching trees. Every branch off the main theme led to additional interesting, meaningful, connected ideas and information. Although one will not find the source of Joan Whittier's approach in current educational literature (Whittier had been planning her lessons the same way for many years), a recent book by Lilian Katz (1989) describes a similar technique she calls the "project approach."

Process and Conferencing. Karolina Bodner taught a third/fourth grade combined class. A slender, wiry woman in her late thirties, Bodner regularly wore sneakers and a full skirt. Sometimes a pair of wire-rimmed glasses was perched on her nose. She characterized her style of teaching as "process oriented." She illustrated her concept of "process" teaching by contrasting her approach to art education with other approaches:

> In most schools I've ever been in—where I've been a student or that I've experienced as an adult—art means the art teacher comes in with a cart or children go to the art room. The teacher demonstrates "the" project. The kids have about 20 minutes to "do it" and then the materials get collected and the project gets collected and the only conferencing that happens is accidentally when the kids go down the hall and see it displayed and talk about it informally amongst each other. They don't get the benefit of learning from what they've done, of learning what's worked and what hasn't. They don't go through that learning, researching, questioning that you have to do (for everything, whether it's science, social studies) for you to feel like you're in control of it. That might be one reason why so many people feel that they don't know anything about art: because they haven't learned the process enough to feel involved or immersed in it.

Bodner's classroom was a visual feast. Plants filled the windows. Weaving, posters, God's eyes, paintings, and drawings covered the walls. Shelves held rows and stacks of books, jars, nests, hives, baskets, boxes, and materials of all sorts. In one corner was an area for animals and insects. There were mice, adult and baby rabbits, tarantulas, grasshoppers, meal worms, and a big mayonnaise jar containing over twenty pet flies that had hatched from larvae found in the room. Fresh wood shavings for the cages, scales for weighing, and food for feeding the animals were stacked under a spare desk.

I observed Karolina Bodner organize an extended activity in which children made greeting cards. For the first hour, she elicited from individual children their intentions. She asked questions such as: For whom do you want to make a card? What message do you want the card to contain? How do you want the recipient to feel when they receive your card? How will you get the message across? Would you use any special techniques such as printing, stenciling, fancy cutouts, or pop-ups?

Some children were interested in learning special techniques from their peers. Bodner helped them organize groups so they could share the teaching with one another. For example, one child showed several others how to make a pop-up "talking mouth" that popped up when the card was opened. The children went to work in orderly fashion, some working alone and others working together. Bodner offered help when children requested it. When a boy wanted to make cutout letters, Bodner set up a board and showed him how to tape the paper to the board and cut out the letters with a sharp mat knife.

Searching for her ideas about art criticism and aesthetics, I asked Bodner how she would follow-up an art lesson. In reply, she described the conferencing process as she used it in art lessons:

Bodner: Usually with any drawing project (in science, social studies, whatever got it started) we "conference" at different stages. We might take the drawings all out in the common room and stick them all up on the wall and have the kids spend about 5 minutes just looking at them. Then we have a group conference. [They talk about] what they like about the different things; what's working about the different projects; suggestions; what they think. Then we give the person who did the work a chance ... they might say, "Well, I was planning on doing this and this" or "I'm not finished yet." Which is fine. We do that as adults. Then they can make a decision about whether they'll do this or that or not when they go back to work independently.

Ellis: Will you "conference" about the cards they made today?

Bodner: Oh, yes. Very definitely.

I observed a continuation of the card-making activity the next day. Bodner began by asking how they would describe a successful greeting card. With a magic marker on a large piece of newsprint she wrote criteria volunteered by students:

> It's done carefully, shows a lot of thought.
> The colors go together.
> It isn't messy.

The children's criteria reflected other teachers' descriptions of good art work.

Bodner took the class to an empty classroom. She spread the cards out on tables and allowed the children to mill around, looking at the cards for a few minutes. Then she called students together in a circle on the carpet and dumped all the cards in the center. She asked children, one by one, to choose any card they wanted to talk about. The children were asked to talk about the card—what message they thought their classmate, the "artist," was trying to convey and how well the card actually conveyed the intended message. Some cards were clearly unfinished. In many cases the "artist" was unknown by the class at this point. After the class' critique the "artist" was invited to speak, to explain, defend, or rebut. Bodner reminded the class several times that greeting cards are usually made in editions of many copies, that the cards the children made could be revised, recopied, and finished in alternate ways. Later, she told me:

> This situation [a self-contained classroom] gives someone in my position the chance to integrate a process approach to the arts totally into all curriculum areas, including math, on a daily basis. I personally feel this method is much more appropriate and effective than a spotty program of 40 minutes a week by a frustrated "art teacher" reduced to doing isolated, short, "manageable" projects and teaching spotty techniques. Most teachers don't have the same humanities or fine arts background [I've had] and perhaps don't have the same commitment to a process approach to learning. How and what should we be providing students consistently, on a yearly basis, to ensure their development as aesthetically rich, self-assured, creative, expressive people?

On making meaning, she commented:

> You're using that time to get to know the material, working with it, and playing around with it. Then the important thing is taking time to share the different results kids are getting and what it means. For instance, with crayons—if you just talk about it and then do it and collect all the things, it doesn't have the same effect as having a discussion, conferencing, part way through so the kids understand their results. That way kids are encouraged to think and experiment with a new technique.

Bodner had reservations about the adoption of a district-wide curriculum. She recognized possibilities for constraint within which she might find it difficult to teach her way. Were a prosaic district curriculum guide to set requirements and permissions for art education, her teaching methods might fall outside the boundaries.

Searching for a way to understand reasons why Bodner's approach to teaching differed from many of the other teachers' approaches I had seen at Oakwood, I asked her how and where she had learned to teach. She explained that she was trained "on the job" during the late 1960s. She recalled her first days in the public schools:

> I started teaching in 1968-69. I trained for a year in a classroom under EDFA [Educational Development Funding Act] where we trained in the classroom for a year under a Master Teacher and went to a lot of workshops and courses. But right from the beginning I was very process oriented. And we did journals. I've always done journals, even in that

period of time when people didn't talk about journals or writing very much. I read a book, *Teacher,* by Sylvia Ashton-Warner (1963) and that affected me. I was teaching first grade. I didn't use a basal reader. Most of the reading came from children's drawings and from their own words.

I studied drawing and painting at a small New Hampshire art gallery for two hours a week after school two years during high school. In college I took art courses and became "totally immersed in art courses" during my junior and senior years, but I was majoring in language. Studio courses were very competitive and they scared me. I earned money by making long, droopy earrings (they were in style then) and cutting mats for art students, printers, and clients working with public television.

After college I taught painting at the Army Education Center in West Berlin. It was wonderful. The students were army officers' wives. Most of them had never painted in their lives and thought they couldn't do it. But they were bored and wanted something fun to do. And so I would just take them outside and we'd paint or I'd set up a still life. We talked about them a whole lot. We did group conferencing. After the course was over, I went to homes to continue individual conferencing. I don't know why—I just did it. It wasn't because I'd read about it. I do very little reading about what you're supposed to do. Very little. I skim through books. Pick up things. But I've been told I should do more reading. It would help me be more articulate, help me become more of an advocate. I snuck in the back door. I guess I'm a big example of learning through experience.

Although Bodner admitted that she felt she should keep up with current trends in education by reading, she expanded her experience and knowledge by traveling. For example, during the year of this study she led a group of teachers on an exchange trip to Russia during spring vacation, hosted a group of Russian teachers on their visit to the United States, and spent six weeks during the summer in Pakistan with the extended family of one of her third-grade students.

Apparently Bodner's early interest and "immersion" in art classes during college, experience teaching painting in West Berlin, extensive travel, and attention to the folk art of the countries she visits have supplemented her understanding and fed her imagination for many possibilities in art education. Her capacity for making connections between children's expressive work in writing and the arts stems from a wealth of experience and a commitment to what she calls the "process approach."

The Project Approach. The hallway outside Joan Whittier's second-grade classroom was hung with images that changed from week to week. There were prints of serigraphs, mosaics, water colors, oil paintings, and cut paper. One week in December a collection of doves carrying olive branches appeared (doves on greeting cards, a dove on a United Nations poster, and all sorts of prints of doves). Whittier had asked the second graders to bring any pictures they could find as part of their thinking and learning about peace, peace on earth and peace in the classroom. Inside the classroom was a live dove caged for close observation, available for use as a model for student drawings and three dimensional paper doves. Soon the children's doves and peace messages filled the classroom.

A week or so later the doves gave way to other birds—crows, owls, etc. Many drawings and field sketches by Audubon and a variety of naturalists were displayed and available for desktop scrutiny. There were samples of feathers, diagrams of bird skeletons, and even parts of a road-killed ruffed grouse. The theme was extended to a study of birds' habits and bird biology. Flocks of wild crows came close to the classroom windows attracted by bits of raw meat left as bait by Whittier's students, and a stuffed crow from the university museum followed as a subject for the children's drawing. There was always an air of anticipation and orderly excitement. ...Where would the curriculum go next and how would the children and Whittier extend the topics at hand? Whatever it was, Ms. Whittier would impress the children with the fact that it was important and that she cared deeply about it.

Whittier had taught elementary school in Townsend for 22 years. I invited her to try to account for her enthusiasm for the arts and passion for teaching and learning. She told me of her university advisor:

> ...a person alive, unconventional, demanding, and eccentric, she had moved her students out of their narrow confines into the whole world of the arts. ... I was doing things I never dreamed would be requirements for my master's degree. At the time I wondered why I was doing all these things, but now I know. I was learning to see art in my everyday environment and to value ethnic diversity.

Professor Sigmund Abeles, a long-time friend and neighbor of Ms. Whittier and a sculptor and painter of some renown, was invited by Whittier to participate in a two-day art exhibit at the school in the all-purpose room. Out of the gallery exhibition grew a series of brief visits by Abeles to Whittier's classroom. Abeles had been stopping at Whittier's room for a few minutes once each week for several weeks. He would draw on the blackboard, perhaps explain what an art term meant, and examine the week's drawings in portfolios and displays. Although Abeles provided no formal teaching of "how to draw," the presence of an artist for a few minutes in the classroom was exciting and motivating for the students. These visits inspired a series of remarkable drawings by the second graders.

Whittier encouraged children to draw one object in the room for 15-25 minutes every day with pencils on white paper, the same object every day for a week. One week the children would draw their sneakers or shoes placed on the their desks, and another week they would draw their hats and gloves. Other subjects were the coat closet, toys, a papier-mâché Chinese dragon made by last year's second-grade class, and the stuffed crow from the university. In the early weeks some of the children's drawings were almost unrecognizable but as time went on the children's powers of observation and representation improved remarkably. Children saved their drawings throughout and at the end of each week put them in chronological order and selected their favorites for display. Portfolios of collected works were kept by children in their desks. Ms. Whittier reported, "The children loved seeing their own progress in the portfolios even though they weren't consciously *trying* to make progress."

Many of the drawings by these second graders became as detailed and as sensitive as some I had seen done by high school students and adults. Whittier told me that Abeles had made a similar observation. She was struck by the way this contradicted some of the literature on development of young children's observational and representational skills. She exclaimed, "The changes I saw in a given week were so amazing. It was not that a child would become such a better drawer, but that repetition of drawing the same thing, day after day, forced them to focus." Her pupils had looked at many artists' prints and drawings, they had drawn frequently, and now they saw themselves as artists.

Whittier borrowed a figure sculpted by Abeles more than twenty years ago. It was a life-size resin sculpture of a ten-year-old girl in party dress, standing with arms at repose and hands clasped in front. At times, glancing from the side, I mistook the sculpture for a live child standing by the bookshelves. The model had been Kaethe Zemach, daughter of the Abeles' 1960s next door neighbors, Harry and Margot Zemach, authors and illustrators of many children's books. The sculpture helped Whittier pique the children's curiosity about art, literature, and history, even what the world was like twenty years ago. Ms. Whittier asked the class, "What can Kaethe tell us?" The live child, Kaethe, was now a grown woman, Kaethe Zemach-Bersin, a recently published writer and illustrator of the children's book, *The Funny Dream* (1989). Ms. Whittier read Kaethe's book to her class and this began an exploration of all of the Zemach's books. Sculpture, drawing, literature, and illustration were interwoven in a tapestry of meaningful connection and perhaps unforgettable experience. History became part of the present and children saw their own drawings exhibited next to works of renowned artists.

A further extension of Kaethe's story was an introduction to the works of Kaethe's namesake, artist Kaethe Kollwitz. Kollwitz's drawings of the poor and the persecuted in Nazi Germany were displayed in the classroom, another vehicle for taking the study of history back a generation, to Europe and opportunity to study striking examples of fine pencil and charcoal drawing on plain white paper, simple media available to every child.

Questions arose from my encounters in Whittier's classroom. Would the absent district curriculum guide have been help or hindrance to the integrated plans that developed in unique directions with each year's second-grade class? Whittier answered:

> I teach out of my passions and the children's interests. If a guide were prescriptive or restrictive it would be a hindrance. I would most likely disregard it. However, I am always interested in learning and I often look to curriculum guides for new ideas and strategies, for keeping "current." And I like to check on myself to see that in the broadest sense I am meeting the basic objectives and goals of a given discipline or curriculum.

Joan Whittier did not place high priority on "exposing" children to varieties of media. Rather, she used common materials (pencils and white paper, crayons and construction paper) for production and display. Her priorities had to do with building observational skills, making art relevant to history, science, literature, math, and to the children themselves.

I asked Whittier for her advice; how can we fill the schools with teachers who are bursting with excitement about learning and teaching? She thought a moment. "Find those with a grounding in a liberal arts education and the ability to make connections—those who are eager and continuous learners, who are curious and questioning—those with lively minds, self-disciplined, with an ability to focus, who show enthusiasm, even passion—and turn them loose."

Recruitment and Preparation of Teachers. This New Hampshire case study raises three important sets of issues related to preparatory programs for new teachers, recruitment of teachers, and inservice programs for experienced teachers. Regarding recruitment, is it preferable to attract teachers to the field who, like Karolina Bodner and Joan Whittier, are enthusiastic, passionate, curious, eager, self-disciplined, and focused? Or is it better to expect programs in teacher education to produce such teachers, to light the fires of excitement? Is it feasible to expect that inservice programs can challenge and transform ordinary teachers, help them take risks to explore and try new teaching approaches, and expand the boundaries of their practice? What possibilities for change can we anticipate if teachers are content with the status quo of an arts curriculum that merely exposes children uncritically to activities like sponge painting and production of look-alike holiday projects in the guise of art education?

First, the recruitment of teachers who have exceptional qualities and potential requires a professional workplace that is attractive to such people. If teaching encourages teachers to solve problems, to think reflectively and critically, and to make autonomous decisions, then those who prefer to engage in those activities may choose educational careers. On the other hand, if the teaching profession encourages teachers to follow formulaic procedures, teach ready-made curricula, to depend on others to solve problems, and to obey orders and mandates uncritically, then those who fit that job description will apply.

Second, teacher preparation programs can help ensure that teachers entering the profession: 1) are educated people, 2) understand and accept their responsibility for stewardship of schools as institutions in a democratic society, 3) approach their work thoughtfully and reflectively, and 4) have the skills and attitudes necessary to contribute to ongoing school renewal efforts (Goodlad, 1990; Edmundson, 1990). Educated people have a broad background in the liberal arts; they are inspired, curious, and interested in learning. Maxine Greene (1988) argued that well informed people have learned to "see" in new ways. They may have experienced the arts as occasions for new visions, new modes of defamiliarization (making the ordinary world strange). The well-informed have seen aspects of experience ordinarily never seen and they have dealt earnestly with knotty philosophical, moral, and practical issues that envelop schools. Educational foundations courses in teacher preparation programs can provide new visions and perspectives to inform and educate beginning teachers. Well informed, educated teachers will have been interns and student teachers in classrooms where they have had opportunities to observe teachers reflect and solve problems and they will have formed their own habits of reflection and problem-solving. They will not be complacent with the status quo. They will be committed to finding solutions to current problems in the schools.

A third set of issues regarding teacher preparation is related to experienced teachers' inservice programs. Programs that build on teachers' knowledge and their already acquired wisdom of practice can open new visions of how education can be conducted. Inservice programs can challenge teachers by proposing new perspectives on their usual ways of doing the seemingly ordinary things in schools, by making the familiar strange. Such inservice programs can help teachers reflect on what they already know and what they think is important regarding purposes of schools, education in a democratic society, and idiosyncratic content areas.

The implementation of innovations is effectively encouraged when teachers have opportunities for choice and mutual adaptation of the innovation (Berman & McLaughlin, 1978). Inservice programs are useful to teachers when they provide opportunities for teachers to appraise critically and adapt new materials to their particular interests and requirements and to integrate old teaching strategies with new ones. Inservice programs are not so helpful, not so long lasting, and not so enthusiastically implemented when teachers are expected to adopt an outsider's ready-made innovation.

The issues of recruitment and preparation of teachers are large. What can be done by a single teacher educator to improve arts education for youngsters? Teacher educators' jobs may include teaching courses, supervising interns, conducting research, and providing consulting services to states, local districts, schools, and teachers. At every turn, they might suggest new visions of ordinary experience through various forms of the arts.

At Oakwood the research I was conducting stimulated conversation about arts education and planning of visual arts lessons among teachers and the principal. For Karolina Bodner and Joan Whittier the research process provided recognition for their integration of the "process" and "project" approaches for the arts within their ordinary classroom routines. For other teachers whose vision was narrower, my study did not automatically open new vistas. As an art educator, Mary Palm seemed disillusioned, resigned to classroom teaching. She said, "This is a sports community, always has been, always will be." Karolina Bodner and Joan Whittier viewed the same community in a different way. Joan Whittier frequently invited local writers and artists such as Sigmund Abeles to visit her classroom. It seemed that she could find artists and gifted members of the community at every turn. Karolina Bodner reveled in folk arts she uncovered locally as well as from Pakistan and Russia. Her class enjoyed the informal presence of a resident artist all year. Every week for two or three full days, George Lalarge, a local visual artist who had retired from another career, was a welcome volunteer. He sat with students, conversed with them, and sometimes sketched or painted images of them. He loaned many of his finished works to the school for regular display and for a yearly art show of children's works hung together with works of other local artists. The Dad's Club at Oakwood raised some of the money for visiting artists and the yearly art show. And yet, the superintendent told me that the community was not interested in the arts. I was quite puzzled by the many divergent views of the same community. There were spokespersons with diverse views, yet there was a lack of open debate. Perhaps a teacher educator would do well to stimulate informed debate among educators and community members at the local level, to help give voice to teachers, parents, and administrators who might support the arts more effectively if they were encouraged to speak and work together.

What else can a single teacher educator do? In teaching courses, the familiar status quo of the classroom can be expanded with new perspectives, new questions. Teacher educators can give teachers experiences in the arts by demonstrating presentations of new visions with poetry, stories, visual images, music, and even dance to teach and encourage teachers to question and explore. Teaching should be more than telling; showing how, and then giving students (teachers-as-students) opportunities to experience.

Curriculum Guides. Would elementary classroom teachers benefit from a district or state curriculum guide in the arts? Sequential, articulated K-12 curriculum guides for four disciplines in art (production, art history, art criticism, and aesthetics) are recommended by Getty Center for Education in the Arts (1985) for school districts. Adoption of curriculum guidelines alone is unlikely to change education in the arts in today's schools. However, an agreed-upon agenda for art education can provide some cohesion, purposeful direction, and benchmarks for teachers. Three of the teachers I interviewed at Oakwood School said they would appreciate having specific guidelines for art education. Karolina Bodner and Joan Whittier made ambivalent comments about the desirability of district or state guidelines. They applauded the advantages of a curriculum guide as an idea bank but recoiled from a mandated curriculum that might constrain their interests and wide-ranging ideas for integrating the arts into the various content areas they taught. Mutual adaptation of broad guidelines might help but mandated adoption of a specific, detailed program would be sure to cause problems.

Evolutionary Change. Over time, what evolutionary changes may serve to improve arts education? Rather than suggesting options such as offering teachers prepared, prepackaged arts programs, I propose five other possibilities. The first one is to de-isolate teachers and encourage them to work together to develop programs that are appropriate to their interests and the local communities' interests and resources. School leaders could identify and publicly recognize teachers who find ways to bring arts to their classrooms frequently, in enlightened ways. Ample opportunities might be provided for those exceptional teachers to serve as educative resources for their colleagues.

Teachers are notoriously isolated in their work (Lortie, 1975). Things were no different at Oakwood School. I asked Karolina Bodner whether she had given any workshops or demonstrations of her techniques for teachers at Oakwood. No, she answered, but she had been invited to give workshops at several other schools. What if there had been ample opportunities for Whittier and Bodner to share their excitement with other teachers at Oakwood? One can only guess. Both had worked at Oakwood more than twelve years. Without recognition of the necessity for formal opportunities to share ideas, teachers are not likely to learn from one another (Ellis, 1990).

The second suggestion is to expect changes resulting from inservice education to transform teaching slowly, with follow-up over sustained periods of time. Inservice education, conceived as series of opportunities structured over extended periods of time for teachers to receive follow-up supervision, have been found to result in change more consistently than short-term workshops and programs with no follow-up (Ellis, 1990). Teachers need to feel comfortable dropping old practices before they adopt new ones. Pedagogical change is a gradual process—it takes time (Fullan, 1982).

The third suggested possibility is for teacher leaders and administrators to respect what teachers already know about education and the arts. I advise: encourage them to build arts education programs on the basis of their own wisdom of practice. Don't be overly critical of individual teachers' approaches that may seem at first to be too project-oriented (as Joan Whittier's approach might seem to some critics) or too heavily weighted on process (as Karolina Bodner's strategies might seem to be).

The fourth suggestion is for administrators to provide non-mandatory curriculum guidelines that suggest an articulated K-12 arts program with components of aesthetics, criticism, production, and arts history. All of the teachers I interviewed at Oakwood expressed a desire for some form of arts guidelines. Joanne Batchelder, a second-/third-grade teacher whose background included an arts minor at a state teacher's college, read a letter to parents and teachers congregated to view the winter art show. She wrote:

> I have mixed emotions about the art gallery. No doubt each teacher at [Oakwood] is creative enough to come up with a thoughtful art project. Many of the works were clever and offered students a chance to participate in a worthwhile art experience—printing, drawing, water colors, etc. However, I strongly feel the public needs to know this is no substitute for a sequential art program. These experiences are sporadic and should only be a complement to a regular art program. To be a truly civilized society we need to be literate in all the arts—visual, musical, literature as well as the physical and social sciences. In developing an appreciation for the order and beauty in our world, we may be inspired to learn to work in harmony with it—to care and keep it for future generations.

Batchelder spent part of the summer following this study at an institute for elementary classroom teachers learning about the history of American art at the National Gallery of Art in Washington, D.C. Dependant on her own informational and financial resources, she embarked on a personal quest for new visions in the arts.

The fifth recommendation is for administrators at local and state levels to provide strong incentives for teachers to attend courses and conferences on the arts. Many teachers seem to enjoy challenges and opportunities for learning new content through personal contact and experience. For example, Karolina Bodner travels widely and collects many kinds of folk art. She enjoys staying in the homes of people in the countries she visits, and she is willing to change her life style in order to visit with friends in countries such as Pakistan and eastern Europe. In the local community of Townsend both Bodner and Whittier had a wealth of friends and acquaintances whom they lured into classrooms to share their interests and expertise with the students.

Conclusions

The teacher comes to school with theories about learning, notions about what is important in the curriculum and ways of planning. At the elementary level, the teacher's theories are played out in self-contained classrooms—in the reading curriculum, the math curriculum, the social studies curriculum, the science curriculum, and the arts curricula. The teacher applies her theories about knowledge and learning, along with her particular configuration of interests and expertise, to teaching across the various subjects and content areas. Joan Whittier knew how to link themes across disciplines, how to incorporate history and literature with visual arts. Karolina Bodner used a "process approach" for reading and writing and then applied that approach to other portions of the curriculum, including art. Both teachers used what they knew about pedagogy and planning and applied that knowledge to unique applications for teaching the arts. In their early education and as beginning teachers, both had experiences that opened their eyes to new possibilities and new visions of the world.

Chapter 8:
Luther Burbank Elementary School Las Lomas, California[1]

■ *Robert Stake*

I wanted to spend a few days in a classroom in which the teacher contributed to arts education—without even trying. Not so much to find that teaching to be artistic, embodying elegance, but where some subject matter was treated as elegant and precious, where ideas esteemed and savored by the teacher were very much a part of ordinary teaching, perhaps where a skill was reverently addressed. I didn't seek a master teacher epitomizing a master artist but a classroom where one could observe deep caring for what was taught, where a good but not extraordinary teacher was helping children move along (perhaps) toward what Harry Broudy (1972) has called, "enlightened cherishing."

During my Anacortes visit (see an earlier chapter) I observed a few teachers who not only were excellent instructors but who treated their subject matter with respect, even awe, who—whether the subject was math, language, or science—quietly invited learners to share in something of beauty. Of course they seldom characterized their own teaching that way. Nor is it how I would characterize most teaching, certainly not my own. But I felt that many teachers, at moments, convey just such esteem about what they are teaching or about what a youngster has put together. Esteem for scientific or social beholdings may help kids understand esteem for the arts.

Aesthetics and Cherishing. A few weeks earlier at a meeting of arts education researchers, Howard Gardner remarked that perhaps the best way to advance arts education in this country would be to draw teachers toward more aesthetic treatment of their regular subject matter. Not to use art to introduce or illustrate the subject matter, nor to draw connections between that subject matter and the subject matter of the arts, but to handle some of their nonarts subject matter with a greater attention to aesthetics. That is, to esteem, to illuminate quality, to savor, to cultivate the aesthetic experience.[2] I wanted to study opportunities for teaching about cherishing in a more or less ordinary elementary school classroom.

In our collection of case studies for the National Arts Education Research Center we had not yet looked at a California school. For further balance, we

---

[1]The names of community and people have been anonymized and certain happenings have been modified to facilitate the disguise.

[2]If you, the reader, are finding the purpose of this case study troublingly obscure, you may want to turn to the last section of this California study to read what Madeleine Grumet has said about aesthetics in the classroom.

needed another suburban school. I deliberately decided to stay away from Los Angeles because Getty activity there encourages discipline-based arts (DBAE). This Getty-DBAE interested us greatly but the arts education literature contains the Getty case studies (McLaughlin, Thomas & Peterson, 1984) to illustrate that orientation. As a second issue, I was curious about the consistency of views of arts education across several decades so I looked for a community with low mobility, an unlikelihood in a California suburb, talking about arts education with people who had gone to school there at least 10 years ago. After discussions with several California teachers and a Sacramento demographer, I chose a community I will call Las Lomas. Hearing my needs, Los Lomas School Superintendent Cynthia Cochran and Curriculum Coordinator Paula Demars suggested I observe the classroom of Gene Frielander at the Luther Burbank Elementary School. When I chatted with Gene I emphasized the second issue. I didn't mention looking for examples of cherishing embedded in classroom teaching.

As a community, Las Lomas has much to savor. Nestled in grassy hills and vineyards, it is nicely distanced from urban blight and urban splendor. More or less a part of the East Bay area, it is a remarkably stable settlement. The years have been kind to near-downtown's semi-circle of relatively inexpensive bungalows. Two miles out, beyond the expressway, along winding streets and culs-de-sac, are the forerunners of long distance commuter communities. An oil refinery and government offices are visible principal employers. The town has several elementary schools, one junior high and El Capitan Senior High. Luther Burbank Elementary has four fourth-grade classrooms. In that same neighborhood a century ago, Luther Burbank, naturalist, temporarily made his home.

Mr. Free's Class

On May 11, 1988, I arrive at the school at 7:30 a.m. to meet Gene Frielander in his fourth-grade classroom. We have talked previously on the phone, even last night, but this is our first meeting. His welcome again is warm and he hands over a packet of materials to acquaint me with school and community. He alerts me to his emphasis on geography and history and indicates that a music session, a trip to the library, an assembly, and a film will consume a good bit of the day. I am warned that the children may be restless. "Right after standardized testing generally is not good visitation time. Demeanor changes, theirs and mine. I have to be a little tougher on them, maybe a little narrow-minded."

As 9- and 10-year-olds drift in, greeting "Mr. Free", he cajoles them to remain outside until entry time. Most do. At the appointed hour, the group swells to almost 30, noisily, slowly working their way in. In comes Amy Harris, the vocal music teacher, carrying a CASIO portable keyboard. As Mr. Free leaves, Harris distributes duplicated song sheets and tries to quiet things down. In half a dozen minutes, she has the children singing the "Fifty States Song", an alphabetical listing of the states set to music: "When I was small I studied U.S. geography..."

In fine voice and with keyboard flourish, she stirs a tepid chorus, gaining momentum in the "Presidents Song," a companion listing of U.S. presidents from George Washington to George Bush. Harris gathers the blue-sheeted lyrics and hands out a white-sheeted quiz on the 41 presidents' names. "List as many as you can, in order, ...want to see how the song is working, ...not worried about spelling, ...no need for first names, ...etc." She falls short of quieting them; they persist in mild protest, uncertainty and distraction. "No, it is not to be a group effort." "I'd hate to put names on the board" (the "assertive discipline" move). "There's too much talking in here." Keith claims to know Nixon and Eisenhower but not their order. Finally, "Okay, who has the most?" Five more minutes of individual response to "Then who came next?" "Jefferson." "Van Buren." "John Quincy Adams." The sheets are left on the tables.

"Now, today is the last time we have to sing before the concert. Does everyone know the words? Let's try 'Kids.'" (From the green sheet, I learn "Kids" is from *Bye, Bye Birdie*.) Three verses, Mrs. Harris again the driving voice, jaunty, Broadwayish, pulling 27 sopranos. Then "Food, Glorious Food." "If you are interested in a lead or solo part, please let me know." The students are animated, few seem captivated but all more than tolerant of what is happening. Yesterday was the last of two weeks of California Achievement Program testing; maybe this is release. "Louder, please." Keith shouts the last "GLORIOUS FOOD!" and draws a mild reprimand. Then "There's No Business Like Show Business." It is going better. They speak four lines, then sing ten, twice around. "We're almost there. Work on 'Glorious Food.' Now let's end with a folk song that the first, second, and third graders sang in their concert. It's 'A May Day Carol,' on the second blue sheet. You can catch it right away."

The period is over. The session has been full, the conducting business-like. The students kept finding diversions here and there, yet gave the impression most would know the words at the concert. None seemed to dismiss Harris as irrelevant but few threw themselves into the performance. Annies (Little Orphan) they aren't. Nothing of cherishing this go.

Preparations. Mr. Free has had his prep period; now the students get theirs. Each day at this early hour: a few informal minutes for snacks, toilet, announcements and the like. Questions need answering. The number of kids wanting main entrées (hamburgers today) is needed by the cafeteria manager. Pledge of allegiance to the flag. The class sells itself Corn Nuts. Today, a long introduction to Bob Stake.

I am treated by the teacher as if I were a learned person, by the students as if I were an interesting person. Knowing of Mr. Free's emphasis on geography and history, I answer questions (Where do you live?) by pointing on the map to Illinois, (Where were you born?) to Nebraska, and (Have you ever lived in another country?) to Sweden. Knowing they have just read a biography of Benjamin Franklin, I brag that he and I are cousins, quickly sketching the family tree on the blackboard. Perhaps encouraged by the teacher, the questions continue one-on-one throughout the day. Various gifts of drawings and paper foldings are brought to me, including at times when no one is to leave their seat or to talk. Admonitions are given vigorously, sometimes with the threat of "name on the board," but Mr. Free's respect and (I believe I may say) love for the children are so apparent that the threats are half-empty. He greatly wants their attention. They just as greatly want his.

Luther Burbank Elementary School
Las Lomas, California

Library. Frances Kaskowski is the library media assistant. Hired part-time, she is a parent with a library science baccalaureate. Every second week, the fourth graders go en masse to the library for 30 minutes' instruction. Today Kaskowski has them in seats around three library tables to hear and watch her reading *Jumanje* by Chris Van Allsburg. She tells them the illustrations, much like those of his *Polar Express*, are powerful, a special use of perspective drawing. "Note how you are looking down from above in this scene." She reads to them, holding the book over head so all may see the illustrations. It is a story about two children playing a board game that brings wild animals suddenly alive in their home. At first, lots of wiggling, some whispering, but the reading is dramatic and attention waxes. Some are chuckling as a lion and later monkeys appear in the living room. After half a dozen species arrive, rolling a double six gets rid of them all. The story is over. There is no analysis or pause for reflection. Kaskowski says, "Discussion or analysis has never been a part of the library visit. For one thing, there is not enough time. The focus is to encourage good reading habits." She announces that all library books not previously turned in, should be. Now it is time for all to look for books containing illustrations and descriptions of the animals they have chosen for individual written reports. Kids work together, seeming to find what they need.

Four years ago, district administrators decided to add literature (although the elementary teachers had voted for science) to physical education and music as subjects to be taught by specialists during the teachers' daily 45-minute prep period. Just now, Jeanne Johnson, the literature specialist, is on maternity leave. Her substitute is Anna Kuster. Library visits are handled by Kaskowski. In her twice-a-month session, Kaskowski reads a story or works with kids on assigned projects. There is no mistaking the awe she has for her books. "It's essential that we build up the fairy tale collection. That's a must for this age." On another day, she reads of blood and tears being woven into a Chinese tapestry. She grimaces and sticks out her tongue. At the end, the kids applaud.

Spelling. Back in their own room, Mr. Free announces they will practice spelling their animal names in a version of the Password game. The class is divided into halves and a team representative for each sits at the front table. Spelling words, from ARMADILLO to GAZELLE, a word list drawn up by the students to reflect their wildlife project, are shuffled. Alternatively a team member knowing the answer verbalizes a one-word hint to other members who do not, prompting them to guess the name of the animal selected. When someone guesses the right animal, to get points, the team has to spell the animal correctly in unison. Then both teams together spell it. After initial confusion, it goes reasonably well. With WOLF, it goes like this:

Team A rep: Fierce.

Team A volunteer: Lion.

Team A rep: No.

Team B rep: Mammal.

Team B volunteer: Elephant.

Team B rep:	No.
Team A rep:	Wolverine.
Team A volunteer:	Wolf.
Team B rep:	Yes!
Mr. Free:	Team A, spell it.
Team A:	W-O-L-F.
Mr. Free:	Everybody, spell it.
Everybody:	W-O-L-F.

Students participate enthusiastically, vigorously waving hands to volunteer, wandering from their seats, interrupting, challenging the rules, etc. At any one moment, a few are standing, shouting, calling for arbitrary rulings. Mr. Free repeatedly calls for order, for quiet—but the oral group-spelling he himself orchestrates at higher decibels. When 27 animal names have been used, the score is totalled.

Then it's time to have a written quiz. With a sweet smile, Delle hands out paper. Mr. Free asks for volunteers, one by one, to choose an animal name from the same list. Finally, each of the pupils has spelled in writing the list of 27 animals. Together these two spelling exercises have taken more than an hour. There was more student engagement here than in the memorization and quizzing of presidents. And each of the students did get individual performance time, an accomplishment important to Mr. Free.

Friday, May 12

The kids are not at P.E., the scheduled opener for today, but are viewing a video tape of *Oliver* in conjunction with the upcoming concert June 1. Across the way Jim Bigley's fifth-grade class is getting a lecture on drugs from Bill Lee of the Las Lomas Police, the fourth and last in the series. Officer Lee is on full-time assignment to the district for this instruction and, although in uniform, is treated around the school as one of the teachers. He is giving the kids their final quiz with items such as:

T   F   *Drugs bought on the street are safe to use.*

Amy Harris comes to Mr. Free's room to arrange to have four kids miss class to participate in the Drama Club's play *Goin' Buggy* at Las Lomas Elementary School next week. The kids return from P.E. Kathryn leads the pledge of allegiance. Two girls go off to raise the school flag.

Reading. It is 9 a.m. Mr. Free has the pupils open reading books to page 36. "Who'll Feed My Cubs?" He reads aloud. "No food! No food!" Pause. "Keith, do that later." Keith struggles to prolong the interruption. "No, Keith, later." Keith responds soundlessly, dramatically, not disrespectfully, but as if injured, as if amazed his concerns are being treated shabbily. Mr. Free reads two paragraphs aloud, the class increasingly follows along. "Now read the rest to yourselves. We'll have a quiz as we usually do on Friday."

WINGS TO ADVENTURE
WHO'LL FEED MY CUBS
pp 366-376
Quiz #10

When finished study
extra copy of
Spelling Words #1-27
Test after recess

Using Science workbook
Sentences #1-27

On the board Mr. Free has written the book and assignments shown above, amid other notices to left and right:

(Left Board)	(Right Board)
Reminders	5/8/81
Track Meet — Th May 18, 3 pm	**Reading**
Happenings	Complete CTBS Tests
	Start level 24
	Wk Bk pp. 161-165
	Wings to Adventure pp. 342-352
Math/Science Fair	**Math**
May 11 7-9 pm	Complete CTBS Tests
El Capitan High School	Continue story problems, etc.
Assembly	**Language Arts**
Thurs Time?	Complete CTBS tests
	Identify animals/organize
	spelling sentences with each
	#1-27 for trial test Thurs
Softball game - Fri	**Science**
	start reports
Thurs	**Social Studies**
right after lunch	Complete CTBS tests
1:05–1:45	Start California stories/info/etc.
Dental Check	Indian Legends, etc.
Wed 9 am	Start US Maps
	Films: Luther Burbank, The Bear

At 9:16, Mr. Free writes "Pizza - Lunch Count" on the board and asks for a show of hands. Sixteen hands go up. Frank wants to take the order in; Mr. Free says, "OK, when you are finished." Reading continues amid a few whispers; children begin approaching him, asking questions quietly. It has been an on-task session. At

9:20, Mr. Free makes an announcement again about the quiz. Individual questions, mostly about procedures, get louder. "Sh—sh—sh—sh." At 9:25, it is still quiet. Carmen asks to go outdoors to cough. Keith gets up and examines something behind Mr. Free's desk. Carmen comes over to show me the spelling list. Soon Beth and Delle join us.

9:25. "Who is not finished?" Three hands go up. "No talking." "Sh—sh—sh." At Mr. Free's nod, Christopher comes to the front to dismiss the class for recess. He finds Row 2 quiet, in their seats, watching him. "Row 2." As they pass out the door, he excuses Row 3. "Walk quietly," says Mr. Free. "Row 4." "Row 5." Mr. Free comments, "This table needs to get their act together." "Row 1." Stuart has remained at his desk. Mr. Free wants him to leave too, but says, "Stuart, it looks like you've cleaned house today. It looks good. Yesterday, I thought it was a garage sale." To me Mr. Free comments, "Things are better today. There was so much wind yesterday—all classes were upset—off the wall."

After the children return, boys in one line, girls in another, Mr. Free wants to write on the board. He sends Alicia to the office to get two sticks of chalk. Matt is agitated by something. Mr. Free finds that Keith, Stuart, and Matt have squabbled at recess. And Frank has a bruised lip. Soon all are quiet at their seats; the chalk delivered. It is time for the quiz on "Who'll Feed My Cubs?" with items such as:

4. After the poisoned animals were gone, what did Mary predict was going to happen to the farm animals?

Beth approaches Mr. Free to clarify what "predict" means. Mr. Free stops the quiz to ask, "Who knows what 'predict' means?" They work out a definition and the quiz continues.

10:00. The quiz is over. "We'll go over the answers today. Be sure your names are on your paper." Pause. "Who is talking? Tricia?" He goes to the board and writes her name on the list. "Today we were looking for details of the story." (Perhaps, for me, he is alluding to the distinction between recall and comprehension.) "Do not talk to anyone." He designates how the papers should be collected. "All tests in?" The room is astir. "How many can count to three? If you can, raise your right hand." Then, "I want attention up here, complete attention up here." He presses on, quietly, barely a decibel above the general murmur, but insistent. "Thad, Thomas, everyone. Everybody, raise both hands. Elizabeth, Yvonne, Richard." Still lacking Keith's attention, he goes to the board and puts a check after his name. "Sh—sh—sh." There are five names on the board, one with a check. Now six. Finally and with requisite concentration, they identify correct answers to the quiz, some supplied by children but arbitrated by Mr. Free.

10:15. Budhiashi passes out 4 1/4" x 11" lined sheets. "When's snack time?" "I'll let you know." First comes oral spelling in unison, later spelling on the lined sheets the 27 animal names as they are called off.

As I said at the outset, I am watching for indication that certain knowledge or skill is really special, is cherished, by teacher or pupil. Nothing yet. And not surprisingly, no one questions the importance of spelling correctly, even WOLF and CHIMPANZEE.

A Week Later, Thursday Morning, May 18

The first thing today is an "assembly" put on by Wildlife Associates, a naturalist group. Everyone in the school is gathered in the cafeteria. Two women talk and display a turkey vulture, a raven, a peregrine falcon, a barn owl and a golden eagle, all tethered. They describe each bird's distinctive characteristics, behavior patterns, defense mechanisms and the circumstances by which it came into captivity. One strong theme is prevention of cruelty to animals.

The students sit on the floor. In the beginning, Mike O'Sullivan, the principal, gradually establishes quiet and reminds them of appropriate behavior at an assembly. The students wiggle and whisper, a few wander and are shooed back, but most pay attention, especially when the birds are on display. The presentation has a naturalist's orientation, with an occasional reference to beauty of plumage or flight. To close the program, a presenter asks the children to take a pledge. They repeat after her: "I will never hurt an animal—in my whole life.—I will always protect animals." Back in the classroom, after Delle leads the pledge of allegiance and after new snacking rules are announced, Mr. Frielander asks, "How many enjoyed assembly this morning?" There is a general affirmative, vocal and raising of hands.

Sharing Something Dear. After admonishing three who left designated play areas and subduing his returnees once again, Mr. Frielander reads a poem aloud, "Feather or Fur." The pupils somewhat reluctantly follow along in their reader. He makes and asks no comment on the poem. Next is the story of Wufu, a brown bat. Pausing before reading, he catches their attention. His face is solemn. His voice has a somber quality now.

> This morning at the assembly, you all took the pledge not to harm animals. That's very important. On the way to school this morning I was very disturbed. If anyone should know better—the head of a department in college should. This man works in a science department. A professor. He knows better. But he became very selfish. Wild animals not endangered should be left in their habitats. This professor decided to start his own special collection. He asked a student to join him hunting for a certain kind of animal. The student did not know he would be shooting and stuffing animals for the professor's own house. This was a professor from the great University of California where many have studied how to protect animals. The student reported it to the Wildlife Department. Watch tonight for the story in the papers or on TV.

Mr. Free relaxes a moment,[3] smiles, moves quickly to the reading lesson, pointing at the assignment written on the blackboard. "Now pages 160-170. I'll tell you when to stop." He starts reading aloud the story of Wufu. Then, "Read silently to yourself." This session runs half an hour or so. The blackboard indicates that those who finish first are to move into a review of spelling words. There are questions about this and that, some whispered, some blurted; there are reminders about snacking rules. Increasingly, children get up and move about. Finally Jeni's

---

[3]This incident is discussed further at the end of the chapter on curriculum.

name goes up on the infractions list. That quiets things a while but soon more disturbance and more names on the list.

Wildlife Reports. Attention is redirected to preparation of wildlife reports. From a large colorful Martin-Marietta ad taken from a magazine, each child has identified an animal to study. From old magazines they have cut pictures of their topical animals. Mr. Frielander has spirit-duplicated a four-page manual on producing a report. He quizzes them on rules about getting started: "What is first?" Stuart says, "Knowing where you are going." "Well, even before that you need to know something. What?" "Where you are." "Right. First you need to know where you are, then where you are going. What is #2?" Barry says, "You need tools." "Right. You've been watching Dr. Bob Stake doing his research here in this classroom. Pretty soon we will ask him to tell us how he works. But let's think for a moment about his tools. He has a pencil and paper and some other things in his briefcase and his brain. These are some of his tools. You need to think about what your tools are. (Pause.) And what is #3? (No answer.) Well, you also need to decide how you are going to limit your report. You can't tell everything. You have to decide what to say and what not to say."

It is time for second recess. Routines continue. Mr. Free and I go to the teachers' room for a snack. On the table we find a plate of fruit, crackers and cheese, attractively arranged. We overhear a casual discussion of how a particular textbook had been selected and the related staff development session coming up. Sally Wilks reads aloud a highly literate three-page student paper about California in general and waste disposal in particular.

And so it went. After the second recess, I did as asked and spoke to the class about my own report-making. I mentioned theme-development and need of other people to help me. I mentioned that only a small percent of my observations would be included in the report but that I never knew which until I was through writing. And I mentioned that although I worked from a plan not unlike Mr. Frielander's handout, composing my first drafts is spontaneous more than preplanned. I answered a number of questions such as "In what other states are you visiting classrooms?" and "Do they have skateboards in Illinois?"

I then indicated that I had questions to ask them and took the rest of the period before lunch learning whether or not they had parents who had gone to school in Las Lomas and how much the kids participated in music, art, drama and dance. Each of my questions was met with numerous pleas for better definition ("Do you mean Las Lomas or anywhere in the county?"). And they offered comments, particularly ones like "When my brother gets out of the army, he is going to be an artist." At the break, Mr. Free said, "There is lots of interest in the arts. The kids are so sophisticated, take for example, Sebastian's dancing. They see so much on television. We need to provide them with activities, plays and the like, give them opportunity to take part." Curriculum coordinator Paula Demars had told me there are more informal and out-of-school opportunities for arts learnings for ten-year-olds than there were 20 years ago.

Tangrams. The first lesson after lunch is math. Started yesterday and continuing through tomorrow, the topic is Tangrams (angular symmetric shaped pieces from which other figures can be assembled). A form of puzzle, a Tangram is used for accustoming kids to triangles and squares, with particular attention to areas. On the blackboard are displayed, mounted on black construction paper, three assembled Tangram figures: a yellow rabbit, a red coolie running and an orange sailboat. In fatherly manner, Mr. Free says, "Yesterday Tricia said she could not do it. At first it was frustrating but after trying awhile she found she could do it. Today I want you to take one of the figures and to work it out. Stick with it until you get it." Then with a note of severity he tries to bring order to Table 2. "Matt, see my head. (pointing) Your head. Brain? Use it." He works with individuals who are not getting the hang of this Tangram business, confirms the accomplishments of those who are. After further developing their skills in assembling prescribed figures, the kids are to make their own or mimic a favorite and paste together a two-color montage. "Tomorrow you'll be creative. You'll be able to do one of our art ones." In today's session the kids vigorously work in twos or threes, heeding admonition for quiet at first but gradually drifting into robust group work, and finally into an easy ambiance. The activity ends as Mr. Free prepares to show "that bear film" he had intended to show last week.

Visual Arts. Since I arrived in this room nine days ago, I have not seen a period of instruction in the visual arts. Gene Frielander tells me that most of their artwork is integrated with other studies, e.g., Tangrams, United States maps, the Westward Movement mural, poetry as part of a reading lesson but that occasionally they do art for art's sake. This artwork usually follows seasonal or holiday themes, often for room decorations: "munchkins" for St. Patrick's Day, Christmas trees for Christmas. For art criticism or analysis, Mr. Frielander says he has the students judge work other students are doing, perhaps to choose a "picture of the month." A recent class project was making representations of ships of early discoverers. The main purpose of this activity, Mr. Frielander says, is "to explore our own creativity, to extend the talents within us."

I am adding to my understanding of Paula Demars' comment that for the past few years the arts have had a smaller place in the elementary school formal curriculum here than they had a generation ago. We had talked about examples of integrating the arts into other instruction, noting that these examples could be seen as opportunities for craftwork and respite from ordinary basic skills routines. I asked if arts knowledge or skill is being learned in integration activities such as the Tangrams. She said, "Not necessarily. However, teaching songs of an era in history could and does teach knowledge and skill."

Gene Frielander

Gene Frielander drives a tenderly-kept 1954 Olds sedan a 50-mile round trip each schoolday from his home in Almond Grove. When he first moved to the coast in the early '60s, housing was much less expensive out in the valley, so he located in Almond Grove. He joined a development group and obtained a nice tract of land for home and orchard. Born and raised on a farm in the mountains, he took teacher training at one of the state colleges. He taught in a one-room school high in the mountains, later in a larger school. He worked toward an administrative and supervisory certificate. To up his income, he took a job teaching exceptional and mentally retarded children in Almond Grove, then took a position with the Las Lomas elementary schools for ten years at grade 6, then 5-6, and now in grade 4 at

Luther Burbank where he is also assistant principal. His wife teaches second grade in Almond Grove.

Gene Frielander is a thoroughly professional teacher. He thinks about what he is doing. He sees his fourth-grade youngsters moving ahead, soon on to junior high school, toward situations in which they will need to be more independent. Already, the kids want more independence than he wants to give them and they want to hang on to dependencies he wants them to give up. By chalking out weeklong and even monthlong assignments (visualized earlier), he hopes to nudge them toward a longer-range perspective of their schoolwork. He says:

> As a fourth-grade teacher, each year I get children whose previous school experience is one of lesson assignments finished right in class that day. There has to be a transition period, a development of independence. That independence and accountability has to start in the fourth grade. Some children are pretty self-sufficient when they come in but a great number are not. For both parent and child, this is frustrating. At the beginning of the year, I tell parents I may be calling sometime about a problem of work not getting done. Many think, "No, not my child." But when it happens they look inside a drawer in the boy or girl's bedroom and find the assignments not completed. I require the child be present at parent conferences so we can have three-way communication about getting assignments finished.

These assignments are "studies." The process of study is a strong orientation with Frielander. He didn't emphasize the word but "study" says it better than "learning" or "teaching." "Study" says it better than "knowledge" or "skill." The children are learning knowledge and skill, very important, but the task at hand is to pay attention, to put one's mind to it, to study.

A Study-Ethic. What I have been seeing in Gene Frielander's room reminds me that a study-ethic is consistent with the widespread emphasis on deportment and socialization. Most people agree that in order for children to learn lessons they need to ignore the interesting non-academic things of student life: folding paper airplanes, passing gas, putting pennies in the pizza party jar. The teacher tries to lower distraction levels. It is not just because parents and administrators think that quiet rooms are good rooms. Suppression of normal scanning behavior facilitates attention to instructional routine. It is not greatly overstated to say that fourth-grade children vary in degrees of hyperactivity. Of course a few are troublingly passive. But as a group they press for action. Mr. Frielander's pupils seemed to have little yearning for collective action but great yearning for interaction. Sometimes aggressive, usually not, they almost always appeared well within society's bounds on aggression. They resisted study.

I interpreted many off-lesson forays of the pupils as attention-seeking although it seemed just as reasonable to see it as conviviality. At least for the ten-year-old, it's a pattern of normal living—a norm from which uninterrupted concentration is a large deviation. We of the schools threaten and entice children into that kind of deviant behavior, that concentration, making great pretense that purposive and rule-fixed behavior is normal student behavior. Training, harnessing the energy and spirit of the ten-year-old is hard work, high on priority lists in most elementary schools and part of the self image of most teachers.

Mr. Frielander is a civilized trainer, more than that, a humane trainer. He treats the children with care. When Matt and Stuart push each other, he sends them to the bench on the patio outside his window, obligating them to talk it over until they understand how the other feels and then work it out. The five minutes he allows seem enough. When Vonda disregards his requirement that all sit at their own desks, he asks for an explanation. Often, after repeatedly asking for quiet, he says, "Raise your hand if you're talking."

When warnings and shushings fail, Mr. Frielander resorts to "assertive discipline," a districtwide formalized succession of warnings and tallies that ends in loss of privilege, such as a field trip, or punishment, such as to up to three hours of Saturday morning "staying in," (supervised by a special teacher hired by the district for that purpose). Assertive discipline starts with writing an offender's name on the board. Subsequent offenses draw a checkmark. In Jim Bigley's room at the far side of the patio, Alan has four checks by his name. One more and he misses next week's field trip to Marine World.

Mr. Frielander is a considerate trainer. He thinks about what he is accomplishing, how much it may be hurting. He expects different admonitions to work with different children. Finding girls more docile, he is more severe with boys. Within each group he differentiates. James bruises more quickly than Peter. One at a time, the children are assigned turns administering the pledge of allegiance and monitoring dismissal for recess. They are drawn into sharing the burden of administering law and order and restraining deviancy, unproductivity and inefficiency. The shepherding is continuous and concerted. I interpret it as not merely a reaction to waywardness but a deliberated plan of squelching immaturity, fostering responsibility and independence, and guiding study.

Gene Frielander does not seem offended by waywardness. He does not take it as personal assault. He does little to investigate the reason Vonda was not at her seat or the events that culminated in Matt hitting Stuart. Perhaps it would postpone study that much longer. The students work to increase personal exchange with their teacher and he works to decrease it. They like him. He likes them. And liking each other is not what it is all about. Study is.

Sharing That Held Dear. This elongated account of the discipline kept by Gene Frielander may seem out of place in a case study of the cherishings that occur in a classroom. It might be said that he cherished a class deep in study. But keeping order was close to the very definition of his job, his career. He did not appear to savor the at-work class even though he worked hard to attain it.

I asked, "Is there a particular aspect of your job you cherish?" Carefully he said, "I worry about how kids treat each other. I want to help them develop their nonindividual self, to see how others see them. I want to be fair and open, to treat others nicely, and I want them to also."

Asking about the content of education, I said, "Think back about your teaching the last few months. Can you recall an instance in which you brought the attention of the children to something very important to you, not necessarily in the lesson, some attention to an idea or object you valued very much?"

> Something personal I share with the children? (After long hesitation) You probably have noticed that our children put up the flag and take it down. No one had been doing it. In social studies, I said, "Why is that?" They didn't know. I said, "Well, why don't we find out?" So they went down and asked Vito (the janitor). He said we didn't have a flag. I told them I have one. And we volunteered to raise it each morning and lower it each afternoon.
>
> And I said, "Let's study this U.S. flag, our national symbol. I have something real personal I'd like to share with you. I had a brother killed in Okinawa in World War II." I was just a kid. I can identify with their feelings. These things happen to children.
>
> I have the flag from his coffin. I also have a flag flown over the capital in Washington—from our Congressman. That is very special. Fortunately, I had it in my room when the other school burned down so I still have it.
>
> I take the time to go through it all, why I have it in my room, why it is about five times bigger, why it has 48 stars. The Purple Heart I have not brought in but I may. These things tie social studies with giving life for country. It's a personal thing, very personal.

Ideologies Vying. In Gene Frielander's classroom, forthright sharing of beliefs-held-dear happened occasionally. Study orientation was a constant thing. Frielander's work orientation was admired by teachers, parents, and administrators. On one occasion he surprised me by referring to Luther Burbank School as a "party school." Parties were part of the self-image of school; parties, performances and games—fun things. But these were regularly and repeatedly identified as reward for and relief from hard work.

Hard work was not what characterized Gene Frielander's room. The pupils were as dedicated to relieving themselves from work as the teacher was to imposing it. Two ideologies stood face to face, a work ethic and a play ethic. Here, each and neither won. Quite a bit of learning was occurring and school "wasn't all that bad."

But vying also were two other ideologies, a basis skills ethic and an arts ethic. And the arts regularly lost. Mr. Frielander's incessant taskmaster role pretty much ruled out an aesthetician role. In any half hour about as far as he would go would be to say, "Delle, I really like the way you raised your hand before speaking," or to tell Miles, "The fact that your Minnesota and Wisconsin don't fit perfectly isn't as important as getting them to look good together." It appeared to me that establishing his priority as "study" greatly undercut opportunities for drawing them into awakenings of elegance, harmony and awe. He established a work pace. Respite came at recess, in daydreams, at the bench on the patio. The elegance of a bookbinding or of the nuances of Amy Harris' chording seemed obscured by higher priority for academic and social skills.

It would be a mistake to conclude that there are no aesthetic moments in any person's day and, certainly at times, the youngsters in Gene Frielander's class found something of beauty in their day. Were priorities to change, there easily could be more. Frielander had the ability to get students to examine the qualities of patriotism. As Howard Gardner suggested, cherishing might go beyond mere awe to become enlightened cherishing, that is, caring might be developed into aesthetic sophistication. Just as Frielander cherished the flag, he cherished certain parts of nature, his orchard and the animals of the wilderness. His respect for wildlife particularly caught my attention. To verify it, I asked him if the following were accurate:

> Last week, you assigned each child the making of a report on a wild animal. You asked the children not only to gather information but to see the need for special treatment of wild animals, for protection, for humane consideration. You were not just announcing an assignment, you were asking them to share your commitment.

He said, "Yes, I have such feelings, strong feelings. When I have an opportunity, I do that. It's part of me." I asked him if there was a connection between the wildlife he had them study and the trees and landscaping he treasured at home. Again he agreed.

He acknowledged the competition for minutes of the school day but not the conflict between thoughtful appreciation and prespecified performance. He noted that many aims vie for the pupil's mind and the teacher's as well, and many aims are simultaneously pursued. Parents vary in their expectations. A teacher plays different roles at different times. But here in this class, getting children on-task appeared preemptive of efforts to hold an idea dear. Many presume that after discipline wins, aesthetics can flourish. But discipline seldom wins for long; it seems constantly to need rewinning. If there is to be aesthetics in the fourth-grade classroom it probably requires a respite in the study ethic. Aesthetics requires study but study strictly imposed defies the aesthetic. Deportment ranks so high at Luther Burbank that any battle for aesthetic learning may be lost in advance regardless of how many minutes are won in the weekly curriculum.

The Arts in the Children's Lives

The fine arts are easily located in this cosmopolitan environment but the fine arts were found not to be prominent in the lives of these children. Gathered in Mr. Frielander's fourth grade classroom, the following table[4] indicates the children's statements of their own participation in popular and fine arts.

---

[4]These questions were asked broadly and restated. After general description of what was being asked and an explanation of the response categories, question #1 went something like, "Do you listen much to music? It could be any kind of music, rock, classical, choir, your mother playing the piano. It could be live music, on the radio, listening to your own albums. Do you often listen to music?" Dance included tap dance, ballet, break dance. Art included drawing, making posters, crafts. Drama included soap opera, cartoons (if they have a long story to tell), and play fantasy.

Of the 27 children in the room,

when I asked:	this many said "lots"	this many said "some"	this many said "none"
Do you often listen to music?	20	6	1
Do you often make music?	10	6	9
Have you taken music lessons?	4	4	16
Do you watch dancing?	6	8	13
Do you dance (any style)?	9	4	12
Have you taken dance lessons?	0	3	17
Do you often look at artwork?	6	14	7
Do you often make artwork?	16	7	3
Have you taken art lessons?	2	2	19
Do you often watch drama?	15	4	7
Do you participate in drama?	7	8	8
Have you had drama instruction?	3	0	18

The children seemed to enjoy answering the questions. Many asked about specific activities and discussed answers among themselves. Other evidence verified their attachment to popular music, for many the choice was "rap." From comments, I concluded that these activities were not often done with adults. Few saw themselves as having formal instruction in the arts.

In interviews[5] with parents of seven children, I found confirmation. And except from one parent, there was not strong support for arts in the classroom. They voiced the opinion that the school system has a responsibility to provide a few opportunities for the more interested students to be involved in performances and exhibits. The idea that arts should be important for all the children and the idea that arts experience contributes to an important refinement in children's thinking were not found to be common ideas among these parents. Using self portraits and self-descriptions Mr. Free shared with me, I prepared a short biography on the seven children. Here are excerpts:

Sebastian Klaus. Somehow it seems Sebastian is always first at bat, always hits the ball over the fielder's head, and keeps running no matter who has the ball. The walls of his room at home are covered with pennants and posters—Jose Conseco and Will Clark looming large. For music Sebastian likes rap. He likes to dance and the other kids know it. Sebastian had written this self-description (verbatim):

> I'm ten years old. I was born in January, 1979. I'm five feet tall. I have Brown hair. My eyes are brown. I have two dads one mom. Two brothers one sister and my mom is just about to have a baby. I have a lot of friends. My hobby is collecting baseball cards. I live in a brown house off of Venicia. I like to wacth "(Just the ten of us)." My favorite

---

[5] I selected the parents who had been in the community the longest. I met them at school, cafe, or home, wherever they preferred, chatted with them half an hour or so, sometimes with the child present. I had nine standard questions ranging across how schools were changing through the child's arts activities to their impressions of Mr. Free's teaching—but we talked also about anything on their minds regarding education.

> movie is "(Vica Virca)." My favorite song is "(M. C. Shad)." My favorite number is 8. I like baseball, football, soccer. My hobby is sports and baseball cards. My favorite actor is [erased]

Tracy Wainwright, Sebastian's mother, likes the way teachers today mix art with stories. She says, "Sebastian took flute lessons for a while but didn't like it. Now that he has his own stereo he spends a lot of time at home listening to music but it's a kind I don't like."

Elizabeth Porterfield. Beth is a live wire. One of the smallest in the class, she is also one of the most active and one of the least intimidated by mild disciplinary admonition.

> I am 9 years old. My Birthday is August, 1979. I am 48 inches tall. My hair is brown. I have blue-green eyes. My friend is Tricia Scriver. I have a dog. My favorite food is ice creem. My favorite color is red. I like swimming my hero is my dad.

Her mom Bonnie and her step-dad Ed live in a wooded cluster of tiny homes on Arroyo Street, not far from the center of town. Bonnie said she likes the way Gene Frielander tries to teach responsibility early. She likes his emphasis on science projects, e.g., solids and liquids (her example mentioned sand, salt, sugar, coffee and tea). "He gets involved but he lets them think for themselves."

Noting that art includes maps and lettering, Bonnie endorsed efforts to integrate the arts with other subject matters. She regretted that the district offered so few options, would like to see more attention in band given to music history and music theory. She suggested having some dance education in grades 1-4, perhaps folk and square dancing.

Emmanuel Aydelotte. Right now Emmanuel's biggest interest is in baseball cards. He trades with his cousins, keeps track of how many he collects and knows the value of individual cards. He wants to get the most valuable one. His aquarium has been a second special interest this spring. Earlier, a pet bird didn't work out. Music is a major interest, especially rap.

His mother, Estelle Winter, works. Often after school, alone, Emmanuel draws, works his Etch-a-Sketch, builds "amazing things" with Lego blocks and wood scraps. A stack of his drawings can be found on the shelf at home and sculptures assembled of found objects decorate his room. Though he has an art kit, he has not shown interest in drawing lessons.

Estelle told me she remembered art projects every holiday when she was in school, about the same she thought as today. Then she corrected herself, saying, "Well, they don't bring anything home on holidays—for example, Mother's Day." She didn't know why this was so. She understood that theatre and dance were available "on the side." Emmanuel brought the notices home but didn't choose to participate. "That's okay with me." Estelle has come to see Mr. Frielander several times. She asked that Emmanuel be dealt with firmly.

Andy Norman. When I first spoke to Andy he immediately wanted to show me the classroom computer. We waited until recess and he happily explained how it worked. He was disappointed that there was little software but was attentive to each option available. In class, Andy was one of the last to engage and one of the first to disengage. His description of himself was brief:

> I am nine years old. My favorite color is orange. My favorite sport is baseball. I have brown hair. My favorite number is 10 I have two cats and a dog and a catipillar

His father, Fred Norman, was a nurse at nearby Valley Hospital. He and Andy's mother monitored Andy's progress carefully. Fred told me:

> There's not nearly enough emphasis on the arts. They're needed for a rounded education. Doctors are an example. Some are prima donnas in academic terms but, due to a sole emphasis on academics, are lacking in life skills. The arts are needed for self-esteem, personal satisfaction. Andy is an example. He's not successful in other areas but the encouragement he gets in music offsets an otherwise negative situation.

Alicia Miller. Earlier in the year, Alicia tried to learn to play the recorder but found it not very interesting and dropped out. She likes drawing, is "always coloring pictures and stuff." She paints. She has a little art set with paints, chalks, paper. Her mother, Irja Miller, says, "She was given this when we were having some family trouble."

Alicia likes to watch ballet on the PBS channel and VCR movies which her dad rents. She is interested in science, likes science programs on TV. Her mother says, "I don't like TV myself and don't allow Alicia to watch much other than PBS." Alicia wrote about herself:

> Hi. I'm nine years old. I have brown hair and brown eyes. They're are six people in my family. I have three fish and a cat. My favorite colors are blue and pink. I like tennis and baseball.

Harris Witzny. When Harris sketched a home scene, he had himself watching TV. In his own handwriting he described himself:

> I am 10 years old. My birthday in March. I am 4 foot 7. My hair is brown. My eyes are blue. I live in a house. My favorite food is pizza. My favorite color is green. My favorite sport is football. My favorite subject is eating. My favorite t.v. show is Loony Tunes. My favorite movie is Police Academy. I am good at math. I like plaing football. I am smart. My hobby is collecting baseball cards. My family was very proud of me when I saved them $250. My family will never forget when I asked if frogs have teeth. When I grow up I want to program computers.

Harris' mother, Belinda Witzny, is "into crafts myself, mainly dough art. I do occasional demonstrations in school." She says it's not related to her career, buying for an apparel store. She tells me:

At Luther Burbank today we have an after-school drama class. It's elective. No one is turned away. Elective is better than required. You get the kids who are really interested. They put on a play, a cute production. The teachers did the staging, kids played the parts, furnished their own costumes. No, as far as I know, no improvisation; they always went by the script.

Harris enjoys drawing in the gifted and talented program once a week. Also he did some construction with straws. At home he constructs airplanes, satellite dishes and such things. Yes, sometimes he makes up stories to fit his constructions. I would say it is creativity more than aesthetics.

Richard Woefle. It's Richard, not Dick or Rich. Richard is a quiet kid, a full-time wearer of his A's baseball cap, second in a GBGBG sequence of siblings. With his brothers and sisters, he likes to "dress up," such as in his mom's witch costume and act something out. He likes to build things out of junk, recently a two-wheeled cart. He loves to play with plaster of paris. Sometimes he makes masks, paints them, uses yarn for hair. Richard wrote...

I am ten years old. I have brown eys and brown hair. There are 7 in my family. My favorite subject is science. My best friend is Arie Levin. I live in Las Lomas. My favorite ball team is the A's. I like wild life.

Richard's dad, a steamfitter, Malcolm Woefle, was just laid off. Malcolm thought that Richard could profit from more art and music, more opportunity to be creative and innovative. "It might build his self-esteem." He has participated in the after-school drama class which recently produced *Gone Buggy*. Richard's mother Ellen adds "We wouldn't want it to replace the ABC things. It's better if it is after school or on the weekend." They deny effort made to display or keep the art things he makes—then Ellen recalls, "Oh, yes, his ceramic penguin in my china closet."

Parent Views. The parents of these seven children all had long acquaintance with elementary schools in Las Lomas. From their generation to this, they saw little change in arts education, but they remembered little of their own elementary arts and were not watching the present version closely. It was not of high importance to them. What was being taught in the arts was of less importance than what was being taught in other areas—and that content was not of high importance either. The parents were far more interested in pedagogy than curriculum, more attentive to how teachers taught than what they taught. They wanted the students working. They wanted the teachers to make sure they worked. Those who had come to understand Gene Frielander's efforts to develop kids' responsibility for overseeing their own schoolwork, endorsed the idea.

It is not uncommon for people troubled by the quality of our schools to advocate a return to former practices, e.g., back to the basics, emphasis on phonics, strict rules on decorum. There were such expressions among these parents—but not about art. They saw the arts as not noticeably changed. They did not urge that specialist teachers be available for school art and music. Indirectly they declared that options in purpose or practice of school art were not important choices. Although the state of California has become more explicit about goals for school art, calling for a more academic approach to the arts, these parents were inclined to have schools and the community provide after-hours arts for the children with special interests rather than arts as general education.

I had asked Paula Demars, the curriculum coordinator, if the content of the elementary music program had changed, if oral and instrumental music teachers were pursuing the same purposes that music teachers had 20 years ago. She said:

> Content hasn't changed but has been stretched to become more integrated with core subjects (i.e., social studies, literature). Oral and instrumental teachers are pursuing the same purposes; however, I feel they are increasingly frustrated because of other demands on their curriculum (content integration) and scheduling conflicts.

The Teacher's Views. I asked Gene Frielander about changes in instruction of the arts over the years. He said that because more than three quarters of the children had been dropping out of fourth-grade instrumental music, the class was changed from instruction in particular instruments (e.g., saxophone, clarinet; to half a year instruction on the flute or recorder). The drop-out ratio stayed high but investment losses in time and instruments diminished. I asked him if he ever introduced music into his teaching of other subjects.

> Oh, yes. I enjoy listening to music and sometimes add a little to the social studies, some of the old favorites, *Home on the Range* and the patriotic songs, of course the *Star Spangled Banner*, to match the historical events of the country. I occasionally bring in some cultural records, Spanish on Cinco de Mayo. On St. Patrick's Day, we had a sing-along. We enjoy that.

As to the visual arts, Mr. Frielander noted that periodically an art docent (funded by the American Association of University Women) will "come and show Rembrandt prints and such. I don't infringe upon their area." As to his own use of art, he said it was not one of his strong areas. I mentioned the Tangrams and the Westward Movement mural.

> Yes, I will take a subject area and display it visually. I do that all the time. It's good experience for the kids and enhancing to the classroom environment. And from home I bring pictures or posters from the 60s, such as by Peter Max, noting how color is used. That is a "time gone by" for these kids. I try to fill it in.

> Many years ago, I would teach the kids a little round dancing. I brought in some of the Greek appreciation records and we would do some very simple dances with a nice beat. Later I became involved with square dancing and, when the district suspended music instruction, I offered some simple square dances. But now, as do most of the teachers, I feel that the music program is fulfilling that section of the curriculum. We are so pressed for time to get through the academics.

Luther Burbank Elementary School
Las Lomas, California

And drama? Yes, I frequently refer to programs on television or community theatre. Kids are aware. Many go to Bowman Pavilion, many know the stars performing there. They are in tune with it. If a particular program fits in, for example, with Luther Burbank and his life, we get into it. We do not have a big push as some districts do. Not a bad idea, but the funding to take a busload to Oakland... I can't remember when last we did that.

Clamor from parents to have art field trips or artists in the schools? No, not that I am aware of. Parents change. From the early '60s to early '70s our PTA had a fair participation of parents. Then a period when teachers would triply outnumber parents. Now, in the last 5-6 years we've had parents push to get involved in school activities. For ten years we had no assemblies. Now, 3-4 times a year, the PTA brings someone in—like the Wildlife Associates this week. It's been a real positive thing for our school.

The Principal's Views. In his office on my final day of visiting Las Lomas, I talked with Mike O'Sullivan, principal of both Luther Burbank and Las Lomas Elementary Schools. Mike had grown up in Las Lomas, had been a star athlete, was everyone's friend. Here are a few of his words about music education:

When the district set aside "prep time" for teachers, it was felt that teachers should be relieved of teaching music. Teachers don't have musical talent as they did in the old days. It used to be that an elementary teacher had to take piano to get a teaching credential, at least able to play chop-sticks. So now we have a professional just to teach music. Amy does a fantastic job. We have a music *program*. The kids get a uniform approach, one planned by the district where it wasn't before.

The parents feel the program's working. This is a blue collar community. If you were just east or just west of here you might get a different answer. I play poker with the high school band leader every Tuesday night. We talk about building up the feeder system. The junior high band director teaches instrumental music here at Luther Burbank too. He knows that if he cannot get excitement going in third and fourth grade, he is not going to have a pool to choose from. Like any other activity, like little league baseball, you have thousands of kids involved but you only have 15 on the high school varsity. Band is exactly the same way. You have to have the masses in order to have a quality program in the high school. You also have to have the numbers to justify the cost.

I have seen it happen two ways. The philosophy of a director when I first started teaching here was to bring along "a few good men." It didn't work. The band did have a few good ones who stayed in the program. But the high school band went from 135-150 down to 80-90. Pretty soon you don't have a marching band. And if you don't have a marching band you don't have an orchestra or jazz band. The jazz band has kept our musical program together because the band director is a hot-shot. He takes the jazz band to Reno. He takes them to Hawaii every other year.

> That's an incentive. Playing for the pleasure of playing isn't enough for kids... .

The Superintendent's Views. In her office at the Las Lomas Schools Building, I talked twice at length with Cynthia Cochran. Having come up through the ranks, buoyant with a new doctorate (University of Southern California) and strong support from staff and community, she was finishing her first year as district superintendent. The following are excerpts from the interviews:

> The Board view of the arts here appears the same as elsewhere. Everybody says they want to do everything. When you look at the curriculum, what are they doing? Lofty intentions...

> Historically, the district has had a strong, visible music program, one that got lots of kids involved. When kids get connected to school, parents are happy. Instrumental music has been popular. Prop 13 [1978 tax reduction referendum] forced us to drop both art and music from the elementary curriculum. It wasn't until 1983-84 that we were able to restore them.

> Both the Las Lomas Arts Association and the Las Lomas Educational Foundation provide supplemental grants, some for music education and drama. The drama program at the high school has been in decline for 12 years. We just passed a $25 million bond issue to build a new high school. A prominent feature will be a performing arts facility—a theater for 450 people, a place for dance, a place for instrumental and vocal music—for both school performances and community groups.

> We've raised a generation of people with video and television experience with little sense of what it's like to be part of a live audience. We want to make them part of a live audience. This year we were able to get the Contra Costa Ballet for a series of performances of the *Nutcracker* at Samuel Ingram School. Our vocal music teacher was instrumental in arranging it. That's the kind of outreach you get when you have specialists around. Those people not only deliver a curriculum but move that curriculum out into the community and find things in the community to reinforce arts in the schools.

> Arts education is not seen as a problem needing fixing. Nobody's come to me and said why aren't you doing this. People are happy with a modest elementary arts program based on performance and exhibition, offering opportunity for creativity and personal expression as well.

It was the curriculum coordinator, Paula Demars, who noted how much in tune were these student, parent and professional voices. People were not completely happy with the schools, but most agreed on what the schools were supposed to do and that fourth-grade education in Gene Frielander's classroom was pretty good. Arts education was not seen to be a shortcoming.

Aesthetics and the Fourth Grade

Before I left for California I had asked Madeleine Grumet what I should watch for if I wanted to observe aesthetics in the classroom. She suggested I look for processes that we associate with aesthetic knowledge. She said,

> If we work from Susanne Langer's (1953) thesis that aesthetic objects are forms that express the artist's knowledge about feeling, then one might also look for teachers and/or students who move to expressive forms other than discursive logic to express their understanding. The student who imitates, who gestures, who draws, sculpts or sings his understanding is caught in a moment of aesthetic process. Similarly, expression that is contingent on context and presentational persuasion rather than representational accuracy might be deemed aesthetic. Forms of expression that use the body, the classroom, that draw upon movement, touch, sound and color as expressive media are aesthetic. And any sense that teachers and students are working to find some new formulation in language or another code to express their mutual understanding is aesthetic, I think, as well.

> There is a collective process that verges on ritual that you might look for when a group of kids, a class, maybe, creates a space for itself marked with objects, a configuration of furniture, displays that mark their collective experience.

In my short visit, I looked for a good example of such aesthetic expression by pupils in Mr. Free's classroom but did not find it. I did find something on a field trip with another Luther Burbank fourth-grade class.

Collective Ritual. Nina Bortolio took her fourth graders on a field trip to Luther Burbank House. Not far from the orchard and vineyards cultivated by this great naturalist was an old adobe house built by one of the town's first settlers. The house stood just beyond the citrus trees at the base of the grand hill to the west, too low for a view of the river.

The sun was beaming warm as a group of five children undertook their task of making adobe bricks—as perhaps had the early settlers. They gathered at a six-foot-wide shallow pit under a weeping Deodor pine, dumped a barrow load of black dirt in the pit, added a few inches of water, took off their shoes, rolled up their jeans and began tramping round and round to mix adobe, round and round in a circle of productivity. Their space and purchase were nicely circumscribed.

Gret Neilsen, a park ranger, took off her shoes and socks and joined the circle. Partly because of her presence, the work began in sobriety but, as they warmed to the task, as the pit became slippery and as the ranger voiced no warning, the mud climbed higher on legs, and arms as well. Slowly childsplay insinuated. The slipping became more frequent, as did bumping and brushing. Round and round they went and down and up.

Ranger Neilsen withdrew. A blonde girl's hair suddenly had a tassel of mud. Giggling and haphazard swelled. The most animated boy became mud to his chest. A parent said "Enough!" They hand-scooped the slurry into the form and patted it flat, still moved by dual persuasions. Then, with little attention to the destiny of their bricks, they moved off to hose away the muck. Gret Neilsen smiled a shy smile and shook her head. The warm sun assured a reasonable completion of the task.

It is likely the moment will be remembered. Of course the five had been muddy before but, this time, it was at the intersection of historic story and possibly stern authority. They previously had mixed work and play but, this time, with something of the blessing of the Sierra Club. More than memorable, it was a special learning. The ritual of their play, the choreography of their experience, was not credited as arts learning—but perhaps it could have been. True, it was the clowning of artisans more than designing by artists. The episode was too unconscious to be aesthetic. It was not enlightened cherishing because the experience did not evoke real scrutiny from those novitiate eyes. They did not realize intellectually what others might find aesthetic in their circlings in the mud. They may cherish without enlightenment.

Wisdom is not prerequisite to cherishing. Each of these adobe makers was well experienced in cherishing: a Joe Conseco baseball card, playing older person to a new baby brother, gaining the attention of a visiting researcher. Enlightened cherishing—as Harry Broudy taught us—is the expansion of our valuings to a realization of the intricacies, the multiple meanings of the object or episode, and stretching beyond the connections between these meanings and the preciousness of things, not only to oneself, but as valued by friend or mother or society. The cherishing becomes enlightened when the child ponders the fact that having fun in the mud can be fun, elegant, and a bit naughty for a park ranger too.

Cherishings are a given. It is not necessary for a school system to invent them. The children come to school in the morning with cherishings. Beth cuddles three porcelain dolls. Matt whimpers as the teacher threatens to remove his Oakland A's baseball cap. The music teacher wants to add vocal timing to the collection of cherishings, the classroom teacher wants to add respect for the flag. School should have its lists of cherishings but the way to draw the child more fully into aesthetics may be by developing enlightenment of the child's own, rather than the teacher's. Do we analyze the elegance of a sticker collection, of embroidery on a bowling shirt, of a crayola self-portrait? In our better moments we pay attention, even fawn. In some of our best moments, we draw the child into analysis and self-enlightenment. Perhaps.

I asked Paula Demars if it made sense to her to have classroom teachers contribute to arts education by drawing the attention of children to what individually they and the teacher find worthy of cherishing, by considering what cherishing means, and ultimately by pointing out parallels to the cherishing of art and music. She said,

> Yes, it makes a great deal of sense. The responsibility may be seen as a burden by some teachers but if teachers saw showing their artistic side (appreciation and/or skills) as an opportunity to be more human, I feel it would help emphasize the art of teaching and be more relaxing and enjoyable for the teacher. We have to help teachers see teaching as a

whole, not as departments of information to be poured into youngsters. Perhaps helping teachers trust their own judgment to infuse the arts into the curriculum would help.

The Curriculum. In Las Lomas in the fourth grade, there is little obligation for the teaching of aesthetics. The system directly calls first for socialization and second for academics. Indirectly, there is a demand that the teachers be humane, although it is just as acceptable to be seen as strict as to be seen as kind. The system does not require being aesthetic or teaching aesthetics.

When, indirectly (for it appears not to arise directly), the question comes up as to the aesthetic quality of teaching, of a classroom or of an experience, emphasis is likely to be put on individual attention given to children or humane consideration given to personal experience. The aesthetic quality of schooling and the need for children learning about aesthetic quality are not a high priority in this school. The uniqueness of Mr. Frielander's room appears small, not enough to discourage belief that the same low priority would be found in fourth grades elsewhere in Las Lomas and across the country.

Teachers have limited options to construct an environment to fit their teaching styles. Room area, illumination, access to the outdoors, desk and chair equipment, chalkboards and exhibit space are pretty well fixed, constraining, imperfect in cleanliness and repair. But there are alternative ways to use those spaces. Not all arrangements, not all uses, are acceptable to principal, parents, and other teachers but the teacher can use the visual as well as the procedural environment to convey: teacher authority, the importance of basic skills, the dignity of the individual child or the cultural roots of what we consider to be an education. The budget for amenities is minuscule but the teacher can cast a mood with plants, posters, flags, slogans, photographs, exhibits. Some are brought by students, most by the teacher. It happens. Alas, it is not apparent that the system puts any demand on the teacher that the mood be, even in part, reverent of beauty, harmony, balance, elegance, the fine arts.

Teachers are largely free to interject nuance and interpretation into their subject matters. Gene Frielander puts naturalist, patriotic, historical, and geographic twists on reading assignments. He does not interject a fine arts twist. He did not draw attention to objects of art brought or created by the first settlers of California. He has been a folk dance enthusiast but he does not draw attention to the imagery of dance. He is a sophisticated gardener and may draw student attention to the structural or biological properties of leaves but not to the elegance of leaves. He does not choose to. He is not expected to. Parents, other teachers, the district curriculum coordinator, and the larger society do not urge him to be sure to attend to the aesthetic sophistication of his pupils.

Some teachers at Luther Burbank, of course, move further toward art education than others. And the principal may commend the effort. Teachers are not indifferent to what draws approval. But right now, the approval for maintaining an aesthetic environment and of including aesthetics within the curriculum is insufficient to draw more than the effort felt needed by the individual teacher.

Parent Views of Subject Matter. I asked parents how schools today were different from the elementary schools of their childhood. Almost without exception they directed my attention to discipline, maturation, and socialization but not to choices of knowledge taught. I asked parents if any changes should be made in the fourth-grade curriculum. They did not treat it as a question about which they had grounds for an opinion, but also did not acknowledge that it was an important question. Some endorsed the basics, the "A-B-C's", meaning, I believe, decoding of printed text, arithmetic operations, spelling, grammar, and a complex of place names such as the capitals of the states. These elementary school children were seen to be in the elementary and elemental stages of thinking. The parents did not indicate that such processes as logic, interpretation, exemplification, composition and dealing with probabilities were important learnings at this age even though much along each of these lines was being learned.

Were their children totally unsophisticated in these "higher mental processes," most parents would be aware that the child had problems. In the area of language acquisition and use, for example, parents expect their children to make sense, to tell about a happening with coherence, to make some rather fine discriminations. Certain kinds of complicated, sophisticated use of language are expected and found in ordinary, everyday human communication. People are unaware of the linguistic complications they require.

More important, they are not of the belief that sophistication is to be pursued in the fourth-grade classroom by engagement in sophisticated discourse. Rather they believe that the basic elements of language need to be mastered before more sophisticated relationships be taught. Many parents, as well as educators, probably have difficulty conceptualizing what it is that is being taught if the teacher teaches logic, interpretation, exemplification, probabilities and composition. Clearly, many believe that if you cannot specify (in ways that they can understand) what behaviors or test performances are to be achieved, then you should not claim you are teaching them. People, as represented by the parents in my small set of interviews, appeared to believe that the high proportion of fourth grade time should be spent mastering elementary reading and arithmetic operations.

Aesthetics extends the language arts even beyond the examples cited above, (i.e., beyond logic, interpretation, exemplification, probabilities, and composition). Aesthetics is among the most complex interpretations, drawing both upon recognition of intricacy and value. I could have included it above as one of the sophisticated learnings and (usually unconscious) teachings that defies specification and wins little popular support for inclusion within the fourth-grade curriculum. The patterning, the texture, the balance, the internal consistency of the object or performance or experience can be taught but are subject to different interpretation. Relevance to artistic tradition can be taught—but not with hope of success if only taught offhandedly in moments here and there. The popular view is that teachers should have developed and children should be developing ideas of what is elegant. Yet the value issues are problematic. And there is no opening in an already stuffed curriculum.

I asked the parents about art and music. As a group they knew of little happening for their fourth grader this year. They were aware that *music* was at least a weekly classroom experience, saw it accurately as performance-oriented, appreciated the opportunity for their child to explore learning to play an instrument (the recorder), were not much aware of its occasional integration into social studies and language arts, believed it needed no expansion over what they perceived and preferred anything additional as elective rather than required, and did not volunteer the opinion that it was important to have holiday or PTA performances.

As to *the visual arts*, the parents recognized that the children were not bringing home much in the way of artwork, did not see the absence of specialists or artists in the schools as problematic, and felt that out-of-school opportunities (most devised by the children themselves) for drawing and more advanced visual expression were adequate.

I asked them also about drama and dance. No one said that the school should be doing more. The after-school drama elective was acknowledged and, in the one instance availed, appreciated. No one said, "I wish *Mr. Free* would teach some of what he knows about folk dancing." No one suggested that an analysis of the dramatic within reading might raise the child's artistic sensitivities or could be useful in understanding the role of media in our society.

In these interviews there was essentially no parental voice suggesting that the arts are a part of or even a service to formal education for fourth graders. Not every parent was happy with this teacher or that but most showed a confidence in educators to decide what should be taught. They did not indicate that these decisions were very difficult, that they needed extended study, that inservice education was important to keep teachers abreast of new ideas about knowledge children need to know.

Rather, to the parents, certain truths were self-evident. One was that in the fourth grade you do two things. You obligate children to be students and you impart a competence in the elements of language, mathematics and nomenclature of the social system. Other curricular matters could become important, such as violations of social convention or inclusion of offensive reading material, but whether or not a teacher teaches a smattering of art history or organizes moments for creative expression are trivial choices. The parents of these children did not show an interest in questions of arts in the curriculum.

A Curriculum Too Full. The parents spoke of their priorities. With little attribution to these priorities as root to policy and practice, the educators in charge of education in this fourth-grade room, Superintendent Cochran, Curriculum Coordinator Paula Demars, Principal Mike O'Sullivan, and Teacher Gene Frielander reflected those priorities. They had a vastly more complex picture of the pedagogy and knowledge base involved but they stayed pretty close to community expectation.

There are many contentions as to what the curriculum should be. The philosophers of education, the state legislature, the staff of the state superintendent, special interests of all kinds, specialists in human development, curriculum researchers, textbook authors, and developers of achievement tests—across and within their groups, all have different ideas of what an education is and what should be done in the fourth grade to attain it. Educators in the Las Lomas schools were aware of most of these advocacies and had a few of their own. They found workable compromises.

Even though Luther Burbank Elementary School teachers were aware that a number of things get taught simultaneously, they were secure in the knowledge that everything cannot be taught simultaneously. And they saw the curriculum as overly full. They did not agree that four hours of DARE (drug education) should be squeezed into the semester but, largely because a specialist, Officer Bill Lee, would teach it, they acquiesced. They felt fourth-grade science was getting short shrift. Though the community and his classroom were both pretty homogeneous, Mr. Frielander felt need for more emphasis on minority culture studies. Already he included quite a bit without departing from his massive 27x40 (student by topic) instructional record. As never they can, neither lesson plans nor report card nor conversation in the teacher lounge told the diversification of topical coverage in the classroom. Regularly, there were deliberated and spontaneous responses to what the children needed. The curriculum was full, yet the new was constantly appearing.

It is not unlikely that because of my visit Gene Frielander modified his teaching a little. And if his is typical of other classrooms in which we make our inquiries, he later reflected upon our questions and responded with a change or two, at least for a short while. It is a human capacity and a human condition. But he did not modify his teaching much to allow for the fact that I was connected with the National Arts Education Research Center. I told him that I was interested in all his teaching, that mainly I wanted to see how teachers deal with new state mandates and other pressures, and how parents of his children see changes since they went to school. He could have faked an emphasis on art projects, beyond the poetry, the U.S. map coloring and paste-up project, the Tangrams; or alerted Amy Harris to emphasize the aesthetics of music. He did little of this. He is "professional." He had a job to do.

Similarly when he reads in his journals or hears in a staff development session that Elliot Eisner contends that the arts are a primary vehicle for teaching imagery, context and metaphor, Frielander may agree and next week modify his lesson a bit—but the curriculum is full, the parents have strong expectations, and he understands what he is good at.

Enlightened Cherishing. In my opening paragraphs, I indicated my desire to investigate Howard Gardner's claim that teachers might contribute more to arts education by expanding upon what they themselves cherish than by trying to teach the arts society cherishes. I looked carefully for what Gene Frielander cherished and pondered how he might exploit it pedagogically. If Gene Frielander were to become persuaded that he should teach more of the fine arts and if he were to follow Gardner's suggestion, he might expand upon what he cherishes or what his children cherish to an enlightenment about cherishing and on toward the art that society cherishes. Right now he is encouraged by arts educators first to identify what the society cherishes and then to studies of similarities and differences with what coached children produce. In his shrewd way, I think, he would point out that the two roads are unlikely to end up at the same destination.

In one way or another, his pupils indicated that they cherished things: an article of clothing, a pet, a kind of music, a particular baseball card. Could he draw them into seeing that special article in a different way, not only to expand on intricacies but to examine own-feelings and relate them to the generic feeling of cherishing, those of others as well? Would he expose his own cherishings, of flags and a particular almond tree, to their analysis? Would he work to improve the moments he teaches primarily for aesthetic purposes, redirecting his own cherishing to draw youngsters into the study of cherishing? These personal reverences would repel many arts educators.[6] It would not be an easy task.

But neither is it easy for Mr. Free to fulfill the state mandate to teach the fine arts. For music, he can rely on the specialist teacher but for the fourth grade in Las Lomas, there are no specialists in visual arts, drama, and dance. From what I have seen, Gene Frielander's inclination is to go for the video presentation more than to get the students working on their own, and certainly more than to sophisticate their own expressiveness. Having watched teachers much less competent than he, I am confident that with relatively little preparation he could have children analyzing works in many art forms. He could (already occasionally does) supervise sessions where creative expression is the aim. Incidental, not concerted. No prizes will bestow upon the dance, drama, and visual arts instruction of his fourth graders. Nor, I suspect, upon that of the fourth graders across the lanai or in most of California. The state cannot expect the schools to provide a high quality arts program without teachers qualified, persuaded, and properly supported and while the state is in effect telling them so much else is more important.

Today's teachers or tomorrow's will not be ready to teach the arts well. They will not have to because the curriculum does not have room for the arts. Mandates will be written but dollars will not be made available to employ teachers suitably qualified and time will not be reallocated. It is possible that standardization of learnings will diminish and some greater involvement of elementary school children in elective participation in the arts will emerge. Before he retires, Frielander might be caught up in such a turn and find himself teaching folk dance, possibly even its analysis, tasks at which he would excel. To have teachers teach the art they understand, to back away from standardization, would require a major shift of thinking about school reform. The arts education community is unlikely to cause destandardization or perhaps even to be supportive of it.

A smaller correction does seem possible. It could be some institutionalization of Howard Gardner's surmise. Not only would teachers be expected to integrate arts into other subject matters, as they are now, but they would advance children toward aesthetic education occasionally by studying existing cherishings, such as Gene Frielander's cherishing of America, animals of the wild, and those 27 children in his room and in addition, studying *their* cherishings. The moments, the objects, the experience are there. Many of the cherishings, such as the making of adobe bricks, resist prespecification, yet are subject to wonder and better acquaintance. It is not troubling to a child to look for the similarities between a trip to A's Stadium and the San Francisco Symphony, to examine elements common to a coin collection and a collection of Van Gogh's. It is less palatable to arts educators.

---

[6] Does the worry about bad art supercede inquiry into the nature of cherishing? Regarding concern about arousing passion in the young, Plato quoted Socrates: "...in all of them poetry feeds and waters the passions instead of drying them up; she lets them rule, although they ought to be controlled." Republic Book X, p. 606.

Chapter 9:
Webster County School District
San Sebastian, Texas

■ *Linda Mabry*

San Sebastian is a minor Texas port located on Sebastian Bay, an inlet of Matagorda Bay claimed for France by LaSalle in the seventeenth century and maintained as a retreat by his contemporary, the pirate Jean LaFitte. As settlers arrived, cattle moved through the port to the surrounding scrub brush ranches on the flat, coastal plains. In the middle of this century, aluminum, petroleum, and chemical industries clustered within a twenty-mile radius of San Sebastian to mine and process the bay area's natural resources. In the 1980s, many of these plants fell on hard times and, while some new industrial complexes located in the area, overall local economic decline mirrored a statewide downturn.

Ethnic Populations. Ethnically in 1988 when this study was started, 48% of Webster County Independent School District students were Caucasian, 45% Hispanic, 4% Asian, and 3% Afro-Americans. San Sebastian businessmen and public officials comprised an old guard joined by those industrial executives who became permanent residents. Ranchers, Czech family farmers, and most of the industrial plant workers made up the rest of the Caucasian population. Hispanics included Mexican-Americans (some illegal "alia"), South Americans, and Cubans. In recent years, small numbers of Asians had arrived. In nearby Bar Harbor, Taiwanese had come to work in a Taiwanese plastics factory, often in managerial positions, most intending to return to Taiwan. In Driftwood, also nearby, Vietnamese refugees had become permanent residents and, through sheer diligence, had taken over crabbing operations from the locals. In the 1970s, this economic usurpation sparked violence and ended in a murder, dramatically exaggerated in the movie "Alamo Bay."

Few, if any, residents enjoyed a socioeconomic level above mid-middle class, although the wealthier, nearly all Caucasian, were building new homes in a residential development overlooking the bay. The transient Taiwanese, probably the next most affluent group, arrived with education and economic position. There was considerable range in the financial status of Hispanics but many lived at or near poverty level. In political ascendancy at the time of this study, Hispanics were a majority on the Board of Education for the first time and an Hispanic was a mayoral candidate. The original Vietnamese settlers were "boat people" escaping with no money and no possessions in the aftermath of the American withdrawal from their homeland. Some arrived speaking English; some not. They feared newcoming countrymen might be North Vietnamese assassins. They maintained a communal existence, pooling wages, paying cash, slowly accepting and gaining acceptance from neighbors who admired their industry and predicted their eventual success. Afro-Americans were disproportionately the county's poorest residents.

Schools. The district maintained one high school (enrollment 1206), three middle schools (enrollment 877), and eight elementary schools (enrollment 2295). Most of the schools were located in San Sebastian, population about 20,000, but three outlying communities were also part of Webster County Independent School District. South of San Sebastian, on opposite sides of a peninsula, were fishing villages: Point Aden with Point Aden Elementary School, and Driftwood with Driftwood Elementary and Deaf Smith Middle Schools. Bar Harbor, a largely blue-collar company town toward the northeast across Sebastian Bay, had Bar Harbor Elementary School. A one-time junior college, later affiliated with a large university, was a half-hour commute inland.

Local Orientation to the Arts. Working people in a small, coastal community at least two hours from a sizable city; ethnically diverse people interacting with little friction but maintaining nearly tangible separations may seem unlikely enthusiasts or advocates for the arts or arts education. Newcomers from cities were disappointed in arts opportunities. Yet, the president of the local Art Guild called the community an "art colony," naming local painters who lived and worked in the area. Between these extremes, there was a wide range of opinions regarding community interest in the arts. Were the arts thriving in San Sebastian? The answer depended upon whom I asked.

Research Issues and Activities

The San Sebastian case study of arts and arts education was second in our series, undertaken after Bob Stake's in Anacortes, Washington. My research agenda in Texas began with these questions: What arts education does the school district offer the youngsters? What out-of-school arts opportunities are available? Do schools connect with out-of-school arts opportunities? What are potential resources for arts education? What are the messages from the culture to youngsters about knowledge and participation in the arts?

Personal experience in the community suggested to me that ethnicity might affect children's access to the arts. In 1955, the year after *Brown versus the Board of Education of Topeka, Kansas* forbade racial segregation in schools, my family moved to San Sebastian and I was enrolled in the third grade in WCISD. We were unaware that our last name was identical to that of a local, well-known Afro-American family. Perhaps school officials wrongly assumed I would be the first child to integrate county schools in assigning me to the teacher reputed to be the "meanest" in the school. For the first time, I attended school with Hispanic children and I will never forget the unfairness and cruelty with which I thought my darker-skinned classmates were treated. In returning to my home town, I wanted to learn whether there was differential access to the arts for minority children.

A graduate of Webster High School '66, I remembered community theatre productions, high school choir and band performances, and an annual art contest at the county fair. During the week of my fieldwork, I reviewed arts curricula, interviewed seven administrators, observed and interviewed eighteen school teachers and four private arts teachers, and talked with twelve parents, families, arts representatives, and residents. In this narrative of what I learned, names and places are given pseudonyms.

Immediate Influences on School Arts

The District's Prescribed Curriculum. Webster County Independent School District arts teachers were to follow a curriculum guide called *Essential Elements*. Subdividing the overall curriculum by subject areas and then by grade level, this document listed goals and broadly sketched classroom activities for pursuance of those goals. For fine arts K-6, instructional elements were categorized under "art," "music," and "theatre arts." An example:

Fine arts, grade 3 shall include the following essential elements:

Theatre Arts

(A) Expressive use of the body and voice. The student shall be provided opportunities to:

  (i) develop body awareness and spatial perception using rhythmic and imitative movement, sensory awareness, and pantomime;

  (ii) imitate sounds and dialogue; and

  (iii) recall sensory and emotional experiences.

(B) Creative drama. The student shall be provided opportunities to dramatize literary selections using shadow play, pantomime, and imitative dialogue.

(C) Aesthetic growth through appreciation of theatrical events. The student shall be provided opportunities to view theatrical events emphasizing player-audience relationships and audience etiquette.

Within the previous five years, Georgia Rose, visual arts teacher and head of the fine arts department at WHS, had headed a team which drafted the district's written visual arts curriculum document. However, $2500 in development funds ran out before the middle school section could be completed.

WCISD Superintendent Alton Waterford said teachers were aware of the *Essential Elements* but that:

> People are more important than curricula. It's concerned me occasionally when I've seen choral teachers who've just come in and opened a book and said, "What do y'all want to sing?" By the time those students are in seventh grade, they don't want to be in choir any more. I find that the talented teacher knows the craft and content and has a curriculum in mind.

Loss of K-1 Music and Art Specialists. In 1985, visual arts and music specialists were removed from grades K-1. Primary classroom teachers assumed the obligation to teach fine arts. Most of them remained uncomfortable with the responsibility. Preparation and enthusiasm as well as familiarity with the *Essential Elements* varied from teacher to teacher.

A kindergarten teacher spoke familiarly of the *Essential Elements* in music as including, at her grade level, making and playing rhythm instruments and using such media as movies and phonograph records. She used a Scott-Foresman textbook, which presented forms of music such as marches and waltzes, and the school's resource room, which contained classical tapes and instruments and audio-visual equipment. An accomplished pianist, she was considered well-trained in music, an exception on the faculty. Two first-grade teachers explained,

> Usually we just pick something we have a record for or use a songbook. You always hope there will be some in the class who sing well. Music teachers might feel like we don't know anything.

These two felt they devoted adequate time to the visual arts and they mentioned poetry recitals. But because of their lack of training, they gave little time to music.

A first-grade teacher said her class sang parodies, listened, and played games to phonograph records. In the visual arts, she said "color, cut, and paste" activities were integrated into other subject areas. She listed as theatre arts activities the adapting of stories and having students "describe a picture they've drawn." She recognized the limitations of her training: "I feel my students are cheated by having me."

I observed a kindergarten student's crayon drawing for the upcoming county fair. The teacher pointed to a blank area on the paper and said, "Christina, draw some more things on the picture." When I asked about the *Essential Elements*, this teacher said the activities were "OK" and searched unsuccessfully for her copy of the document.

Elementary Improvisations. With the district employing music and visual arts specialists in grades above K-1, teacher preparation in the arts improved with grade level. The *Essential Elements*' impact on teaching also increased at higher grade levels. A music specialist serving three elementary schools said:

> Somehow, some way, I have to incorporate *Essential Elements* into everything I do. There are areas of participation, singing, playing rhythm instruments. At the elementary level, mainly we sing all different kinds of music. Theory comes in recognizing notes going up and down, fast and slow, short and long—all of those. Lots of listening and understanding and performance. I think "doing" is emphasized. The district would also like other music cultures studied.

Elementary music specialist Juanita Callas acknowledged that she spent a lot of time teaching the *Essential Elements* but considered "enjoyment [to be] most important" in elementary grades. She wanted students to appreciate the work of famous composers and to see their influence on modern music. She said she used filmstrips, history, biography, listening, and interpretive movement (marching, standing at a musical cue, flag waving) to augment listening. Research on living composers was one class activity. She let kids bring records, almost invariably rock and roll or country and western, once each six weeks for the class to hear. She projected lyrics on a screen for them to sing along "if the words don't drive you to drugs." She said, "Kids do learn to appreciate. By the end of the year, when they have a free choice of what music to listen to, they choose a classical piece."

A visual arts teacher mentioned that the *Essential Elements* emphasized the importance of arts appreciation. Forty-five-minute classes were too short to include art history, so she "settled for" presenting reproductions of masterworks from library books. She wanted to give her students the opportunity to create with a variety of media but found supplies lacking. Of aesthetics, she conceded, "Most teachers are not trained in that area, so I'm glad I had some classes. But we do less aesthetics than anything else."

Observation of an Elementary Art Class. Beatrice Slattery taught visual arts to fourth and fifth graders and joined forces with Juanita Callas to introduce theatre arts into their elementary school. Trained to teach physical education and history, hired as an art teacher because she had maintained classroom discipline as a substitute teacher, Slattery was the only specialist I met without specific training in the arts. She demonstrated skill as a teacher of art history and facilitator of student art production.

In a small room with long tables, pupils are finding sandpainting materials with a remarkably business-like attitude. As they begin to work, Slattery says, "Stop a minute." She tells them how to keep sand colors from mixing together and how to spread glue. "Don't do what Thomas is doing. When you put on the glue, you have to use your good ol' fingers and spread it so you don't have a big, thick layer." Then she reviews "our color schemes," options for today's assignment: warm, complementary, analogous (adjacent on the color wheel), and monochromatic—"but we can't use that one for this project. After this, we're going to be talking about Van Gogh. Van Gogh said, 'I don't have to use a realistic color scheme.'" Van Gogh is the subject of one bulletin board in the room; four others are devoted to color.

Irrespective of race, students have chosen places around tables. There is some well-behaved movement and chatter as they concentrate on their work. Although the color schemes impose limitations, there seems to be no pre-assigned subject matter for the children's projects. Their emergent designs suggest familiarity with the artistic motifs of Native Americans of the Southwest.

Aside, Slattery explains to me that she likes to begin or end each project with information about a "master artist." She wants students to learn four to six things about the artist's life and media. She then gives a review sheet and a paper-pencil test. She mentions teaching about reliefs, busts, and "in-the-round" sculpture, student creations of newspaper and masking tape. She mentions the mobiles of Alexander Calder and sculptures by Henry Moore, saying she feels constrained to stick primarily to realistic work but would like to study abstract pieces, too. "I want to do Moore next time."

In describing her curriculum, Slattery says she tries to "do" the district's prescribed *Essential Elements*. Her copy is at hand, laminated. She thumbs through the pages, explaining Element Two which includes drawing, painting, sculpture, and photography. "But we don't have clay—there's no money for that or a kiln. Two schools share a kiln that we could borrow if we had clay but that kiln is clear across town. And I just can't figure out how to do photography with our set-up. I'd like to do some weaving. For printmaking, we usually do relief with cardboard or, for the fourth graders, styrofoam."

She shows me "Color Cards" she has made and organized in a box detailing lessons she has developed to articulate the *Essential Elements* and her own instructional priorities.

On paper, the *Essential Elements* unfolded sequentially through the grades. But whereas Slattery allowed for experimentation within broad project guidelines, taught about classical and contemporary artists and art, and limited her suggestions about student work to technique, her counterpart at a middle school perceived her task differently.

Observation of a Middle School Art Class. At a WCISD middle school, Edna Landry geared her visual arts lessons solely toward production, explaining,

> It's too dull to students to study artists' work. I don't want them to just learn who did what. But I did bring in some things from Picasso's blue period when we were talking about drawing.

She spoke of a distinction between arts and crafts, a distinction I didn't capture. Displayed student work included African-style masks, colored pencil drawings, Oriental-looking paintings—notable for their sameness in size, color, position of subject against background.

Today, students are quietly painting chlorine bleach onto black paper, which will turn gold after the bleach dries. Landry walks among tables, warmly suggesting changes or additions such as "Do a border" or "Add some feathers to the neck of the bird." She offers no aesthetic rationale for her suggestions and does not invite students' critical judgment. The kids accept her suggestions without question. One interchange:

Student: We did this in kindergarten.

Landry: Well, yeah, you might have done something like this in kindergarten but you have a lot more ability now. I bet we wouldn't want to hang the pictures you did in kindergarten out in the hall. [There is no student artwork in the hall.] Don't you think that's right?

Students: (murmuring around the room) Right. Right.

One student:
(after a pause) You *know* she's right.

I saw little or no divergent thinking, creative exploration, individual expression. Students accepted this friendly woman's judgment and conformed. I wondered about the concepts of art they were developing.

Curricular Interpretations at the High School. WHS fine arts department head Georgia Rose's visual arts teaching was renowned throughout the community for its high standards. A fine arts curriculum coordinator from El Paso, the most distant point in the state, attending the annual National Art Education Association convention the previous week, spoke approvingly of her.

Rose taught fundamentals of drawing, painting, and design until Texas's 1985 House Bill 72 mandated the inclusion of many studio arts not previously incorporated into her lessons. Knowledgeable about the Getty Center for Education in the Arts (1985) recommendations for discipline-based arts education, she commented on teaching the disciplines of art history, art criticism, art production, and aesthetics:

> It's hard to isolate art production from art history in teaching. I present information about different periods in art from a Western orientation. Also, individual and group evaluation of the students' artwork at the end of every project allows us to include art criticism and aesthetics.

When I arrived at the WHS theatre arts classroom, the WHS theatre teacher was giving an optional extra-credit quiz about the previous evening's televised Academy Awards. She turned on a videotape of the Oscars presentations and, in the hallway, discussed the *Essential Elements*. For theatre, the prescribed elements included movement, voice, acting, and enabling students to see a live performance. She felt free to supplement the curriculum at will, perceiving that "there's not a great deal of substance" in it. Of one element, she candidly conceded,

> I don't know how to "develop aesthetic growth." I'm more practical than aesthetic, although this is not a performance-oriented class. After school, I have a theatre production class which is approved by the Texas Education Agency for credit.

Each year, she selected a period of theatre history as a thematic focus. One year, she chose "the Greeks" and pupils studied Sophocles's *Oedipus*. "I'm doing American musical comedy again this year. That's a popular topic. I begin with the British underpinnings of Gilbert and Sullivan."

Dance first entered Webster County schools at high school level. A first-year WHS dance teacher instructed classes and sponsored the WHS drill team. The bodily movements I observed in her classes in the gym were reminiscent of aerobics or gymnastics. The teacher confided, "It really upsets me that we didn't get to ballet this year. I may do it first next year." She did not mention the *Essential Elements* when asked about her teaching plans and goals.

For the week of my fieldwork, choirs and bands were absorbed in rehearsals for upcoming annual University Interscholastic League contest, at which both had long histories of winning "sweepstakes," top marks in each of several performance events. I saw no theory or non-performance music learning opportunities.

For all instruction in fine arts, the *Essential Elements* were intended to ensure a prescribed sequence, PK-12. In fact, teachers implemented the curriculum so individually that the actual sequence from one grade to the next was unclear. Teachers at upper grades expected little background knowledge or skill from their incoming students. Teacher perceptions of the meaningfulness and prescriptiveness of the *Essential Elements* also varied by subject area. WCISD's only WHS dance instructor did not mention the *Essential Elements*; the high school theatre teacher thought the formal curriculum "lightweight;" visual arts specialists were hampered by supplies needed to implement prescribed activities; and music specialists were focused entirely on performance at the middle and high schools.

Holidays, Competitions, and Performances as Curricular Determinants

In most primary classrooms, holidays dominated the arts curriculum. Two first-grade teachers ruefully conceded that their social studies and fine arts lessons fixated on holidays, especially Christmas. Visual arts contests, such as the county fair and an annual Art Guild event, loomed large at every grade level. During the April week of my observations, students in school and in private visual art classes were preparing entries for the county fair art contest.

Music competitions for middle and high school band and chorus commandeered instruction, already performance-heavy, for months at a time. There were few signs that music instruction was systematic or developmental except for increasing performance skills. Elementary music teacher Juanita Callas, who chose not to emphasize performance, lamented that contests and programs left too little class time to teach music fundamentals: "You end up having to teach by rote, so you have kids who can play but can't read music."

At the high school, music instruction and performance were inseparable. The WHS assistant band director described

> four bands here now: the concert band, which prepares students for the symphonic band, which prepares students for the honors band—and the stage band, which takes seventeen performers from the other groups to perform jazz and rock.

The WHS high school choir director sponsored the "Golden Revue" partly because individual performance opportunities enticed some students to join the choir. Like the bands, the choir was preparing earnestly "for contest" or, as one student phrased it, "the big C." In band and choir, performances and contests demanded huge amounts of class time and after-school time from students and teachers.

The superintendent partly judged the quality of visual arts instruction in the primary grades partly on the basis of contest entries:

> I look at the art of kindergartners and first graders at the fair and other competitions and it appears to me that the students are continuing [in the absence of arts specialists] to do good work.

A visual arts teacher confirmed that her program gained parental and community respect when her students did well in contests. The following observations of two middle and high school groups illustrate the dominance of performance and contests.

Observation of Middle School Band Class. Bryant Middle School band director Bob Wolfe stands before concentric crescents of students taking their places, instruments in hand. "OK, concert F scale. Get a big ol' fat sound." They begin to warm up before rehearsing for the upcoming UIL regional contest. Next, he asks for "Eighth notes, short tone. Heads up." As the volume rises and falls to his moving hands, a girl passes out musical scores.

A few adjustments are made before the band begins to play from sheet music. "I want snare drum and bass drum right in the middle and y'all can set the rest of 'em wherever y'all think best," Wolfe directs the percussion section. He listens to each flautist in turn, advising "sharp" or "flat" and telling one player, "Pull that flute in whenever it starts to nosedive on you." French horns are directed to "Relax, open your throat. Relax more" until they achieve a round, faraway sound. When the oboe sounds reedy, Wolfe says, "Do it again. Can you blow more air through it?"

A new piece of music is to be sight-read for practice today; the two Spring contest events are concert performance and sight-reading. A hush falls even before Wolfe admonishes, "If anyone talks at contest, I'll have to ask you to leave the room and that would be pretty embarrassing in front of your friends and the judges." I reflect on the unlikelihood of such an occurrence—the kids will be too scared to misbehave at contest and he wouldn't easily give up a player at that moment.

Told to "finger through it at your own pace," student fingers silently depress valves and keys. Wolfe shares some information: "We do know that the sight-reading piece at contest will be on the E-flat concert scale." He begins to preview today's music, pointing out changes in tempo and key, fermatas, slurs, and repeat signs. "'Lento' is a slow tempo," he instructs them. "Please put your eyeballs on all these places that I ask you to."

The class is quiet, attentive, palpably tense. Wolfe's voice is calming, almost sleepy-sounding. Now, he counts each measure; the students tap their feet with him, silently fingering their instruments or tapping drumsticks in the air. This routine seems familiar to them. He points to sections to show them when they will enter and notes again key changes and fermatas. "Please study this," he says and all seem to be doing so.

A saxophone player opens an exterior door to let in the assistant band director from the high school. A few students glance that direction momentarily.

"In that concert room," Wolfe says softly, "I don't care if the bearded fat lady from the circus comes in, I want your eyes glued to that music. I don't care if the cymbals drop and make the loudest sound and you jump out of your seat, I want your eyes glued to the music." He is not threatening but emphasizing the importance of attentiveness.

They play the piece. The entrances are timely. The sound is round and warm. The cornets begin a solo and then hesitate as if they had not expected to suddenly find themselves playing alone. Through it all, Wolfe is silent, relying, as contest requires, on his hand and baton. The cornets falter again and a saxophone player grimaces. Feet tap in soft, careful unison. Eyes are indeed glued to the music, Wolfe's hands in peripheral view directing tempo changes and entrances.

"OK, pretty good job," Wolfe comments at the end. "Some of you did really well. Altos, you were great. You went softer when I wanted you to and, if everybody'd do that, we'd be in a lot better shape. Clarinets, I need more from you. And your solos," he turns to the cornets, "It's got to be louder. You've just gotta take a chance and go all out for it. Terry," he adds to a saxophone, "you didn't even know that was your entrance, did you? That stand's got to be a lot higher so you can see me." Terry smiles sheepishly and raises his music stand.

"OK, get your contest music in order." As they sift through folders, Wolfe reminds them, "We've worked on these for a long time but you'll have only one chance to play it there." He mentions the time students should arrive to load the bus for the trip to contest; apparently, they know the date. A girl asks the time of day when they will perform and he tells her.

The band plays four notes of the first concert piece before he stops them. "I'm sorry. I lied. When I set a tempo, I'm trying to think in my mind. I'll give you a very definite cue," he explains, then adds, "By the way, the judges say that foot-tapping hurts the music. They invariably comment on that, so tap softly if you need to."

He looks tense, his conducting emphatic but not dramatic. This piece is obviously well-rehearsed. The foot-tappers are unheard.

"Right at the end," he directs after the piece is finished, "write the word, 'freeze.' Don't take your horn down 'til I take my hand down." The students silently write on their music.

There is no need for Wolfe to announce the next piece, again well-rehearsed, or the third, which requires some percussion set-up. A trombonist helps the timpanist get his music in place just in time.

Afterward: "It's a shame that so many good-sounding parts are being messed up by a few things," Wolfe says, looking more disappointed than he sounds. "The number one thing is watching; that's number one. The number two thing is playing together. The number three thing is playing in tune." He becomes increasingly specific, "We're not entering together on the first piece. I don't think we'd get a 4 or a 5 [the top score is 1] or anything embarrassing like that but I do think we'd get a 3." County bands win Ones with a regularity unbroken in memory, so this prediction is devastating. "The note clarity, rhythmic clarity is just not there at all." To sections, "Tubas, you're bobbling notes. Cornets, it's 'da da de de breath.' About five of you are taking a whole beat to take a breath—'da da...' I know this has got to be boring the heck out of you 'cause we've said this a million times. Flutes, I guarantee you that the problem we're having here is going to cost us. So, what can we do about it? What you can do about it is roll out slightly and keep your head up and your airstream moving." The band looks tense as he concludes. "OK, pack up."

Wolfe tells me that it was his plan "to get them serious" by scaring them a bit.

"I disagree with him," the high school assistant director confides privately, his appearance part of the regular schedule. Usually he hears individuals play on a pull-out basis but practice for contest has preempted this routine. "I'm going to tell him to have them more relaxed. Right now, I think they need to know they're close. They think it's out of reach."

Observation of Drill Team After-School Rehearsal. The WHS auditorium, which seats nearly 2000 including balcony, is an enviable facility. For their dance program tomorrow night, the drill team has painted a backdrop with firecrackers and red shrapnel letters proclaiming, "DANCE EXPLOSION." Two or three people at a table before the raised stage operate huge Peavy amplifiers and sophisticated-looking recording equipment.

The curtain opens and five girls in pink, Cinderella-type dresses begin a graceful dance. Mid-number, they switch to something jazzier, something which stops as abruptly as the movements contrast with the costumes. The girls hold positions as if paralyzed while the curtain closes.

Two plump girls in short black and white diagonal skirts stand in an exaggerated posture waiting futilely for music. An electronic voice is heard: "Guess what! I messed up my song." During a brief flurry to find the song, one dancer is heard to say, "That freaked me," and the other replies, "*You* freaked!" Once begun, their energetic and jazzy dance ends suddenly with the two doing the splits.

A pair of girls in formfitting unitards complete another acrobatic, jazzy number despite a couple of flubs. The curtain closes, knocking over the flag; a woman and a young boy come up from the audience to raise it, Iwo Jima-style.

As five Hispanic girls in multicolored unitards perform next, I note that Hispanics are well-represented on the drill team. An Afro-American will appear later.

All of the dances combine modern dance movements and gymnastics. Rock music prevails. In an uninterrupted pattern, costumes and routines show more influence from MTV than from Martha Graham or Alvin Ailey. The following night, glitches are corrected as the girls perform before a small crowd of relatives and friends.

Attempts to Integrate the Arts and Academics

Camouflage in Primary Grades. "They teach the arts all day long," a PK-1 principal said proudly of his faculty's combined teaching of the arts with other subjects. He said that such integration was appropriate.

Two first-grade teachers offered a different explanation, that subject integration was the only way they could fill the state-required forty minutes of art per day. My observations suggested that subject integration also provided structure for lessons, enabling primary teachers untrained in the arts to cope with state and district arts requirements. Integration seemed less a way to teach the arts than to camouflage the feebleness with which they were taught in primary grades.

Integrating subjects was formidably difficult for those elementary arts specialists assigned to several schools. One described arriving early for classes and staying during her planning period to "keep in touch" with classroom teachers, a strategy that had not yet produced collaboration. Beatrice Slattery, teaching visual arts in a single school, felt that teachers of academic subjects were less willing to integrate subject matters than they had been in the past. A history teacher was interested in singing states' songs but, beyond that, Slattery found building linkages frustrating because colleagues "just don't see the intellectual carry-over."

"I see carry-overs, especially theatre into reading, but also there's counting in time signatures and note values," her music colleague, Juanita Callas added. "But I think most teachers don't see what we do as basic."

Departmentalization inevitably complicated efforts to integrate the arts and academics in upper grades. The WHS choir director said,

> I try to help teachers in academic subject areas to understand. I tell them I teach math, science, and foreign language—and concepts way above critical thinking. I teach music as another language. I teach my students to read the score.

But she found little support, no integrative opportunities.

Getty Center for Education in the Arts personnel have objected to integrating the arts and academics, claiming that this inevitably pushes the arts into a supportive role (Getty, 1985). And in trying to persuade classroom teachers that the arts deserve collaborative attention, specialists may inadvertently undermine the arts as merely instrumental to learning in academics (Eisner, 1990).

Teacher Training, Dedication, and Leadership

In 1985, redistribution of WCISD personnel took music and art specialists out of K-1 classes. A PK-1 principal acknowledged the continuing "apprehensiveness" of faculty to teach visual arts and music three years later. Still he claimed, "The primary teachers don't realize all the good things they're doing. I don't know that we lost that much, if anything." Another principal reckoned the loss as greater. Faculty said they felt unprepared to teach music and spent fewer minutes per week doing so than the district mandated.

Campaigning for Specialists in a Remote School. Point Aden Elementary School did not *lose* K-1 arts specialists in 1985—it had *never* had any. But Principal Carolyn Sommers recognized the need for trained faculty and succeeded in obtaining them even during a period of cutbacks in arts personnel.

> I fought to get our music specialist. I did it in a very systematic way, having worked under the assistant superintendent for four or five years. I just kept writing letters, saying, "I know that you're going to give me a music teacher soon."
>
> Two years ago, our third grade was in the top five percent in the state on the TEAMS [Texas Educational Assessment of Minimal Skills] test. Well, when that comes out in the paper and I go in and ask for an art teacher, it's more likely I'll get an art teacher. We used our intellectual achievement to impress the Board.
>
> I knew which teachers I wanted. I had total faith in our music teacher because I had seen what she did at another school. I told her, "I'll get you the materials you need." And our visual arts specialist is just superb. She can get those kids to do so much with their limited backgrounds.

Teacher Training and Quality of Instruction. Arts teaching after grade one in Webster County schools was done by specialists, most of whom were well-trained. The amount of specialized training these people had had—and the quality of instruction—tended to increase at higher grade levels, with some exceptions. A visual arts teacher with a master's degree and experience as a commercial artist said, "It would affect performance across the board" if all had earned masters' degrees.

Beatrice Slattery was of a different kind. Having earned no college credit in art "but always doing crafts," she was competent and dedicated.

Inservice Training in the Arts. Of inservices in the arts, Superintendent Waterford reported,

> Teachers as a total group have not responded as I would have hoped. Taking training and staff development and expanding their skills—they simply haven't done that except occasionally.

A kindergarten teacher confirmed that only four teachers had attended a recent visual arts inservice. But two first-grade teachers observed the arts were always represented among inservice choices and well-attended. They recalled a "neat one" in theatre arts about "what we were doing all along but we didn't call it that. We called it stories and poems and puppets." They remembered inservices in the visual arts, fewer in music. A high school teacher said there were no inservices in dance.

At all levels, teacher training in the arts usually presaged dedicated, respected arts instruction. Inservice training had not been a remedy for lack of training.

Examples of Leadership. To a secluded fishing village with few signs of artistic life, Principal Carolyn Sommers of Point Aden Elementary School had brought brightly hand-painted outfits, flowers and table silver, and the savvy and experience to obtain the school's first music and visual arts specialists. She made a virtue of the remoteness of the site, glorying in the opportunity to handle everyday matters with creative flair, partly because the school sometimes seemed "forgotten" by the district.

Georgia Rose, the visual arts teacher and fine arts department head at Webster High School, mixed the Getty-identified disciplines with state and local prescriptions in her lessons, adding a generous splash of respect for her students. Her expertise and dedication could not completely overcome obstacles involved with scheduling electives but did attract students to her classes and did win community respect and a budding statewide reputation.

Smiling Juanita Callas and stern Beatrice Slattery in elementary music and art were contrasts in many ways. Callas had long experience and training in music; Slattery had recently come to the visual arts with degrees in other subjects and dabblings in crafts. Callas strongly felt that enjoyment was more important than anything else she might convey to her students; Slattery strove to implement the *Essential Elements* and to impart familiarity with master artists and various media and modes of representation. As a team, they also offered students theatre opportunities. Working together, each brought a personal philosophy of arts education and a certainty about desirable educational outcomes.

Art Materials

Principals' Responsibility. Assistant Superintendent T. M. Peters explained, "To a large degree, the fine arts budget is determined by the principal. Each principal gets a per-pupil dollar amount and then allocates that according to campus-set priorities." Such an arrangement made the purchase of art supplies largely discretionary by principals.

Point Aden Elementary's Carolyn Sommers described her allocations:

> I have a per-pupil budget but it has to be approved and it has to cover certain things, like teacher training, my travel to state meetings, supplies, the library, things like that. This year I told teachers, "If you feel something has value, bring it to me and I will get it for you until the money's gone." I did set aside, last year, money for art and for music because I believe in that very deeply.

Teachers' Problem. An elementary visual arts teacher was concerned about supplies in the three schools she served. At one, there was "nothing" at the beginning of the year and obtaining even paper clips required requisitioning. She also taught computer literacy at the same school and, contrastingly, could get any supplies she wanted for that course. She said:

> We just got six new computers I wasn't even expecting but we have only one drying rack for 400 art students in two schools—we had *none* until I hounded them. Requisitions are granted more readily for any subject other than art. The principals would spend more for art but they're under pressure to spend to improve achievement test scores. Most of the principals support me as much as they can.

This teacher, who wanted children to see professional work, found the district's collection of prints and reproductions relatively inaccessible at the high school; she used library book illustrations. She was interested in teaching computer-generated art but lacked software and hardware; she was considering disguising her purpose, requisitioning these as if for her computer literacy class. Obtaining clay was difficult.

This art teacher's struggle was indicative of a general problem in teaching visual arts. Elementary specialists complained that they could not address all of the *Essential Elements* because they could not procure the necessary supplies for such activities as pottery, photography, and weaving. In primary grades, parents were to provide such supplies as crayons and waterpaints but not all did so.

With regard to supplies, music fared better in WCISD schools. A kindergarten teacher described as "adequate" her school's tapes of classical music, listening stations, videocassette recorder, autoharp, and melody bells. Band instruments were purchased by parents or loaned to students by the schools.

Administrative Policies and Priorities

The Texas legislature's 1985 House Bill 72 resulted, directly and indirectly, in state and district policy changes. The new law mandated, among other things, student and teacher evaluation and three high school diploma options. Implementing HB 72 cost local dollars, leading to Webster County Independent School District personnel cutbacks and reassignments and to new policy regarding teacher-pupil ratios. Changes affected assessment of student achievement, teacher appraisal, high school graduation requirements, and staffing.

Student Assessment: A Change Agent in Educational Priorities. Two batteries of achievement tests were being given annually in WCISD: the Texas Educational Assessment of Minimal Skills (TEAMS) and the California Achievement Test (CAT). Scores were published by school and grade level in the local newspaper. When I arrived in mid-April, most classes were just completing TEAMS testing. The effects of testing upon instruction, including arts instruction, were prominent in the minds of many administrators and teachers.

Superintendent Waterford shared some of his concerns about testing.

> No one can speak up against a student learning how to read and write and cipher. But the state has put so much emphasis on these skills that I think it has had a negative impact on other areas of the curriculum, including the arts. We're talking about a fifteen-year trend now where testing results have become everything.

On one occasion, results of tests translated into pro-arts clout, when Principal Carolyn Sommers's students at Point Aden Elementary "had more hundred percents" than any school in the district. As noted, she used these results as leverage for obtaining arts specialists.

But primary teachers held testing to be detrimental to their arts instruction. A first-grade teacher conceded,

> It's been ages since we had music. A lot of teachers are taking as much time as they can to get their kids ready for the tests. Their scores affect your salary. Some years you're lucky and the kids do well; some not.

Two other first-grade teachers said they had taught no art or music for four months in order to prepare students for testing.

Superintendent Waterford again:

> I think the emphasis on testing cannot help but undermine the importance of arts in the minds of faculty. There's no measure taken, in effect, saying, "It's not important enough to check." When I was teaching, I spent a lot of time making sure my students knew those concepts that would be on the tests. Tests lead instruction.

Teacher Appraisal System and the Arts, a Mismatch. House Bill 72's guidelines for teacher appraisal made no distinction between academic teachers and arts teachers. Arts teachers unanimously regarded the appraisal system as inappropriate for their teaching. Georgia Rose, fine arts department head at WHS, said the appraisal system

> probably works a lot better in academic classes. The appraisal instrument is hard to adjust for the fine arts. The risk is that it encourages arts teachers to ditch their plans [in order] to meet the personnel evaluation criteria.

An elementary visual arts teacher said she was advised by principals and "everybody" to have a "canned lesson" ready for unannounced evaluation observations. "Usually, in art, you're continuing something you've started in a previous lesson and you wouldn't have the required lesson introduction," for instance.

The assistant WHS band director, due to retire in seven years, balked at appraisal demands. "I won't put on a show; I'm not going to play games."

A first-grade teacher complained that a formal requirement to keep classrooms neat, partly enforced *via* spot checks, inhibited "doing fun things like art."

In contrast, Principal Jerri Bell in Driftwood felt that the concept of teacher appraisals was "good" and pointed out that the appraisal instrument was constructed by teachers. Her opinion:

> Teachers need to do the job. Before the appraisal system, some hadn't for twenty years. But it wigs out some teachers—even good ones. The district people and appraisers know that and announce visits two weeks or more in advance. Teachers are more conscious now of what's needed in lessons. Some of them returned to the university for classes.

Even so, she thought the appraisals took too much time, that it might be wise to reduce appraisals to one every three years.

Graduation Requirements: Calling For But Squeezing the Arts. House Bill 72 specified three different options for high school diplomas, each requiring two semesters of fine arts. A regular diploma allowed seven electives; advanced and advanced honors diplomas allowed only three, preventing college prep students from taking, for instance, chorus or band in each of the four years of high school.

WHS fine arts department head Georgia Rose observed the effects of HB 72. She said the numbers of students enrolled in entry level visual arts classes increased; the numbers of "top echelon" academic achievers enrolled in arts classes increased; but special services students were somehow driven out. "They feel inadequate," she says. But in the end, "all those who take Art II or III or IV are kids working toward regular diplomas."

The high school theatre arts teacher claimed that the bill

> changed the climate in my classroom. I now have advanced and advanced-honors students getting a fine arts credit even though they choose not to be in band and they can't paint.

The assistant WHS band director observed,

> There used to be too many elective slots, not too few. Now, we expect to lose the honors students from band. The ones who need band for social identification stay.

He also noted that, when computer literacy was added to middle school course requirements, fewer students joined middle school band.

> Students who don't take band in eighth grade rarely join in high school because there are no beginning programs, no personnel to teach beginners, and no empty slots in the school's daily schedule.

Declining membership was a more critical problem in chorus, said the high school chorus director. "It's better in band because kids can choose that as a P.E. option."

An Example of Embattled Dedication. A number of arts teachers exhibited impressive commitment. Prominent among them was the WHS choir director, who said,

> The choir leaves me physically and mentally exhausted—it's that demanding. I teach on roller skates. I keep lists of things I have to do and I wake up in the middle of the night to add things to the lists.

With graduation requirements and scheduling making choir the most endangered of arts electives at both middle and high school levels, her most draining effort was ensuring the choir's survival.

> The principal told me that the choir is going to die but I refuse to die. This year, I wanted to recruit 30 freshmen but I only got fifteen. Doesn't that make you want to cry?

The choir director sponsored an annual performance for soloists and ensembles partly as an incentive for students to join choir. She also helped student vocalists by teaching microphone technique and by preparing background tapes for them from a library of 800 songs.

> Preparing one song might take me four hours. I have to check the range and voice type beforehand. And I may have to bring in other instruments.

Personnel Cutbacks and Redistribution. Cutbacks often cost art teachers' jobs. Assistant Superintendent T. M. Peters sketched personnel decisions in the past three years.

> When House Bill 72 went into effect, the district budget escalated. That's a difficult situation to define and defend to the public. During this period, we changed superintendents. Whether there was a direct relationship there, I don't know. But I know the current superintendent has brought about a great many budgetary reform efforts.
>
> In the last three years, this district has had a flat budget [no increased expenditures] in spite of the fact that we have been losing state appropriations and in spite of the fact that we have managed to give teachers pay increases. Now, the only way that we were able to do that was to hold a tight line on staff because salaries are 80% of the budget. Last year, we cut about ten positions out of about 300 across the district. We'll probably cut another ten positions this year.
>
> We cut the position of coordinator of fine arts and a number of other coordinators' positions. A fine arts department head was added at the high school to give the arts people a voice in policy and scheduling. They elected Georgia Rose to the position.
>
> And some personnel have been reassigned because of district needs rather than individuals' desires. There's been negative feedback on that.

Superintendent Waterford amplified the district's economic context:

> In this school district, we have not had a financial crunch. We haven't raised taxes even up to what we thought was the effective tax rate the last two years. We had nearly $5 million on balance on a $72 million budget. Our tax rate is below the state average. Our teachers are still making $3,000 above the state base. We always have some complaints—you have that anywhere—but most of the complaints about taxes are relatively hollow.

A K-1 principal noted wryly that the state considered the district "wealthy." As such, according to legislative formula, the district had to contribute money—about $4 million in 1983-88—to the state for distribution to poorer districts. Although he thought San Sebastian's citizenry unconcerned, this principal anticipated a rise in local taxes and possible opposition by the community's tax league, composed largely of business and banking people.

Dr. Waterford described the fine arts personnel:

> We have about 25 people involved in the arts, five or eight percent of a $17 million budget. Most of that goes to salaries. Enrollment is decreasing, so we're losing about two teachers a year. If there's anything a school superintendent doesn't want to face, it's declining enrollment. It's depressing. At the elementary level, attrition will take care of [faculty cuts] but, at the high school and middle school, it's much more complicated. This year, we released two teachers who had three years' experience and we've never had to do that before. That's upsetting. Especially in the elementary school, the specialized teachers—art and music teachers—they're the most vulnerable. But you have to do what you have to do.
>
> In the past, a fine arts person might have taught music plus some math or something. Now, we're saying teachers need a full day of work and we want, for instance, music teachers teaching only music. In the primary grades, where HB 72 requires so many minutes of this and so many minutes of that, it became nearly impossible to send in a specialist.

Point Aden's Principal Carolyn Sommers described the changes as disorderly.

> It was fruit-basket turn-over. Principals were retiring and we at the central office were told we were in line for those positions. So, everyone applied for a school and no one went to the school applied for. Last year, three elementary principals were suddenly reshuffled. That just rocked everyone. We're all waiting to see what's next.

Three years of retrenchment and sudden personnel shifts had fostered anxiety among arts specialists. An elementary visual arts teacher said she felt lucky to have retained a job. An elementary music teacher said:

> I've had a different assignment every year and, next year, I'm not sure what's going to happen. I've been told I may stay at the elementary level or I may be pulled off of elementary altogether and go back to directing the middle school choirs plus assisting at the high school.

The New Teacher-Pupil Ratio. Assistant Superintendent Peters explained:

> We staffed at the elementary level according to HB 72, which is 22:1. At the high school and middle school, the district set a ratio of 19:1. Principals decide which positions fall under the axe. We eliminated one course in music theory that usually attracted two students. We like to have a minimum of ten in a class but we've allowed some with less than ten. Next year, we authorized an exemption so we can add one person in secondary music and we're letting the music faculty decide where that person will serve.

Despite this additional position, the assistant WHS band director felt the 19:1 ratio hurt band and choir. "We could use more personnel."

In sum, three years of sweeping state and district reforms may have sharpened academic instruction and may have stirred administrators to address some fiscal problems. But the reforms also removed arts specialists K-1, frightened those in grades 2-12, and reduced almost to invisibility elective options for academically high-achieving adolescents.

Evidence For and Against Administrative Support for the Arts. When asked, administrators carefully voiced curricular and fiscal support for arts education. Assistant Superintendent T. M. Peters cited specific actions favoring the arts, noting that budget-tightening efforts

> have not hit hardest in the fine arts; they've hit hardest in the vocational education area—marine vocational programs, automotive programs, home economics. Although fine arts enrollment has dramatically decreased as a consequence of HB 72, we have not cut any of our fine arts staff. On outlying campuses, we've increased staff. Recommendations for cutting programs come from principals but the district forbade cuts in high school fine arts faculty. I would say that's a strong commitment to fine arts.

> Also, fine arts budgets are largely determined by principals but, last year, the district bought new band uniforms and, this year, we bought dance costumes for the drill team. So, district supplemental budgets support the fine arts.

The most arts-enthusiastic principal I met was Carolyn Sommers at Point Aden Elementary School. Wearing hand-painted clothing, decorating her office with soft colors and fresh flowers, purchasing arts supplies, rewarding students by setting a lunch table with lace, silver, candles, and flowers—all bespoke her arts values and her effort to create an aesthetic environment in her remote school. She smiled,

> You know the poem, "If I have twopence, I'll spend one for a loaf of bread and one for hyacinths to feed my soul." I deeply believe, of all the little souls that need to be fed, these children do.

> On paper, the district has a commitment to the arts and they certainly did provide me with teachers. On the other hand, the quality we have at Point Aden, I believe, is a direct result of my commitment and of my teachers' commitment.

Another elementary principal differed.

> The superintendent is very much in favor of fine arts. If anything stops him from promoting it—and I don't see that happening—it's that he looks at the whole child.

A third principal, Jerri Bell of outlying Driftwood Elementary and Deaf Smith Middle Schools, related different curricular priorities. Piloting a mastery learning program which was decreasing failure and dropout rates and receiving national recognition, she saw the arts as secondary in importance for her students, 55% of whom were recipients of free lunches. Despite her bachelor's degree in theatre, she maintained, "You've got to teach them how to read and write; then it's time to improve the arts."

As for faculty, a first-grade teacher doubted the district's priority on the arts.

> The administration talks money, money, money but what do they do? Build a new administration building or a covered track. What we need is arts specialists in primary grades again.

An elementary arts specialist said the superintendent "toots his own horn" while threatening the arts with scheduling and budgetary constraints.

But the WHS theatre arts teacher described Superintendent Waterford as

> extremely supportive. His son Andy was in speech and drama and was one of the most beautiful kids I've ever taught in my life. He was in the one-act play contest and won the speech and drama award also.

She added archly, "It was not political." Regarding support from her principal, she said, "He lets me do my own thing. I didn't get the budget increase I requested but others didn't either."

Arts Education Goals and Benefits: A Sampler of Opinions

Superintendent Waterford voiced a widespread belief:

> Appreciation is more important than performance. A few students will major in music in college and it will develop into a vocational interest for them and that's important. But, I think for most of the students, the communication of it, the appreciation of it, is the ultimate benefit. I feel the same thing about art and theatre arts.

Point Aden Principal Carolyn Sommers amplified:

> I definitely believe that there is a connection between intellectual productivity and productivity in the arts. My two goals are that we equip students to earn a living but that we also equip them to celebrate life. The arts—I think that's celebration. I would like to see more appreciation in the curriculum.

As did many administrators, a PK-1 principal spoke first about the arts experiences of his own offspring, then offered general arts education goals:

> I think the arts develop the child more fully—intellectual ability, the ability to judge and reason and decide, appreciation for the finer things in life. In primary grades, I want to make sure every kindergartner and every first grader has a chance to perform on stage.

Elementary visual arts teacher Beatrice Slattery was specific:

> My goal is not that all students become artists but that they know and appreciate and experience art. I want them to recognize works of master artists in museums and not to fear the fine arts. I want to do more practical arts [not crafts] and to help kids appreciate abstract art in class.

Elementary music specialist Juanita Callas enumerated her goals without hesitation:

> My goals are: number one, that the students love music; number two, that they are able to read music; and number three, that they know basic theory. For most adults, music is important for enjoyment, which depends on exposure in childhood.

Said Georgia Rose of the high school visual arts program:

> I feel everybody needs the arts. We devote too much energy to developing the left brain hemisphere. The arts will make a person more successful, better able to understand life and to work with different kinds of people.

Questions. Teaching the arts as a means of expression, as a way of knowing, as a conveyor of cultural values or wisdom were rarely mentioned in discussions of arts education goals in San Sebastian. Rather, most school people focused on appreciation, viewing that as a sufficient justification of arts curricula. If asked, teachers, administrators, and parents defined appreciation simply as enjoyment or relaxation without seeming to imply the complex of cognitive and affective responses aestheticians take the term to mean (Beardsley, 1982).

But is it reasonable to expend precious educational time and energy developing and implementing arts curricula aimed at the simple-seeming goal of appreciation? Or is appreciation a complex rationale intuitively understood, an ultimate goal which subsumes a myriad of hard-to-state sub-goals?

Schools' Limited Use of Limited Community Arts Resources

From the Guadelupe Library thirty miles away, Point Aden's Principal Carolyn Sommers checked out a Millet reproduction, recordings of a Shakespearean play and a Broadway musical, and a book of poetry by Robert Browning. At a PTA presentation, she shared these items to encourage parents to bring home the arts. Rarely, if ever, did others in the schools mention use of relatively scarce outside arts resources.

One of two private dance teachers was disappointed that none of the 100+ WHS dance students took dance outside of school. "At the most, we've had three of four students come over here. They stop after five minutes of warm-up and never come back. They think they're dancers but all they know is to kick and to imitate." Even more disappointing were the students who came only to choreograph routines for drill team auditions.

A private piano teacher saw her work and that of other piano teachers as supporting the schools but unacknowledged by teachers and administrators:

> Every band and choir student that already knows music is a plus for the schools. Bands and choirs use accompanists but never realize that value. Piano students cannot get out of school for auditions. Extracurricular activities are scheduled right after school, conflicting with piano lessons. We can't do anything about it—we've tried and tried. We support what they're doing but they don't support us.

An artist and private art teacher said neither she nor any other local artist had ever been invited to classrooms or inservices.

The Webster Civic Theatre director related an effort to expose students to professional performances.

> About four years ago, the city Arts Council funded lodging for one of the Theatre of Texas traveling groups. After the performers arrived, I discovered the Thespians (WHS drama club) hadn't received the notices I had sent for student volunteers. The auditorium was locked. Students were coming from all over the county for the performance. It was embarrassing. We looked like a bunch of ninnies.

Community Attitudes Toward the Arts and Arts Education

Residents in and out of schools expressed a variety of opinions regarding local interest in the arts. The WHS assistant band director claimed:

> San Sebastian is musically backwards which is strange because Guadelupe is only 30 miles away and not that much bigger but it has a symphony and a band.

The Junior Service League sponsored a concert series which, according to one member, lasted only

> about ten years until we finally let it fold for lack of support. We sold about 400-500 tickets to some events, then had maybe 150 people show up—and that [high school] auditorium will seat 1900. We did things like asking the artist to come in the day before for student performances but nothing worked. People liked big choir groups but individual solo concerts were poorly attended. They wanted country and western. We did get one or two C&W groups but we felt that was defeating the purpose.

> There are segments of the community definitely interested in the arts. But people are just too busy to care sometimes. They were apathetic.

A painter and private art teacher said of local tastes:

> Some parents would take kids out of art class if their painting became too non-representational, so I give lots of opportunities to explore and learn "accidentally." I send a letter home trying to educate parents to appreciate children's art. I try to brainwash students into realizing art can be a lot of different things. A lot of them change their thinking but some do not.
>
> I struggle with that in my own paintings. I exaggerate color but, except for my own enjoyment, I would not paint non-representationally because it wouldn't sell. And I'm probably the loosest artist in the county.

The presence of local painters and attendance at two annual events sponsored by the Art Guild prompted the guild president to report, "A lot of people think that San Sebastian is rather outstanding in having such a large art colony." But local residents reportedly purchased crafts rather than art at the guild's annual festival. "There are a lot of good buys among the artworks but San Sebastian people don't know that."

The Webster Civic Theatre was experiencing a temporary "rest," according to its director. Since its beginning in the mid-1950s, the group had survived years-long hiatuses beginning in 1971, 1980, and 1986. "For some people, bowling is more important than rehearsal," she said. Others were tireless, including the director who often rehearsed after a day of driving a school bus and working as a secretary or dental assistant. She noted,

> Theatre takes so much time and working people are tired and busy. That affects our audiences too, although they're not too tired for beer and barn dancing.

Audiences in previous years had numbered only 75 to 200 per performance "but those that came loved it," she recalled. Patrons' annual contributions had helped defray the costs of "triumphs." The set for *Teahouse of the August Moon* had folded into the ceiling; props had included a live goat. The set for *Gaslight* had used $50,000 of borrowed antiques; costumes had included a 100-year-old petticoat. As for the future:

> We'll get back on again. There's a resurgence every five years or so. The tide comes in, the tide goes out; the baby gets big; the kids grow up and move out. I never say that theatre is dead in Webster County, just resting.

Among families, a newly arrived Afro-American foursome seemed eager to attend arts performances. Particularly fond of theatre and music, somewhat less interested in dance except Afro-American dance, they attended arts events fairly frequently, often driving to Houston or Guadelupe to expose the two young children to the arts. They said local events were few and poorly publicized.

The Caucasian wife of a plant executive said, "I wish my husband enjoyed music more because we could enjoy going to concerts but it doesn't interest him at all. We don't go." Her husband enlarged,

> It's more than not interesting to me. It's actually a negative experience. I don't know where that comes from but I don't have the appreciation for music. Maybe it's lack of exposure as a child.

Another Caucasian family liked plays, music, and ballet but said, "It's a hard job to find culture here." They traveled to San Antonio museums to spur a son's interest but "When he tells his friends about what he saw, they're not interested."

Appreciation for the fine arts is often an acquired but sublime taste. In a town of less than 20,000 residents, it is perhaps not surprising either that relatively few people hungered for the arts or that those who did sometimes expended considerable effort to import or to find the arts elsewhere.

Qualified Community Support for School Arts. Superintendent Waterford said:

> I think, in general, parents and the public are surprised at how well students are doing. We had a couple of students whose art was good enough to go up to the state capitol. It's my thought that the general public has a lot of support for the arts here. They view the arts as a way of avoiding being thought uncultured. Probably it's purely status-seeking but, nonetheless, that gives us an opportunity to put school programs into place.

No parents lobbied the school board for the arts, as they did for teacher issues and tax issues. Most school personnel described parents as valuing arts education but only after academics; some mentioned the back-to-basics movement. A kindergarten teacher thought college-educated parents more interested in the arts than other parents; other teachers thought the same group excessively academic in orientation.

To one college-educated Afro-American parent, school arts were as important as academics. An Austin resident before moving to San Sebastian, she had protested a back-to-basics policy and had become a spokesperson for a parents' arts advocacy group. She was satisfied with school arts here, specifically mentioning her daughter's kindergarten teacher as being "good and creative."

Teachers cited some evidence of community support. The WHS choir director said, "The administration support is mostly lip service but the community doesn't realize this. They really love the choir." A visual arts specialist credited parents with raising money for art supplies. The WHS assistant band director observed, "Once they purchase instruments in sixth grade, the parents have an investment in band. That's partly what keeps kids in band."

One parent remembered, "A couple of years ago, the community raised money to send the high school band to Nashville. The community support was phenomenal." He speculated that local economic decline had eroded support for the arts, saying,

> Seventeen hundred jobs were lost at one plant alone. A lot of them were management-level jobs. There's just not a big enough population of the type of people that are interested in the arts here.

Interest in Private Lessons. Private lessons were available in San Sebastian in the visual arts, music, and dance but not in theatre. Ethnicity, socioeconomic status, and parents' educational attainment and other influences affected enrollment in lessons.

> People who've been exposed to art want their kids exposed too. Mostly, these are people with some education beyond high school. Lots of them have moved here from somewhere else.

So said a painter and private art teacher, who also observed that the recent economic downturn had led to declining numbers in adult classes.

On the other hand, an experienced piano teacher reckoned, "Parents want the child to play the piano if they didn't have lessons when they were younger or if they want the child to have everything."

A Caucasian parent provided her son and daughter with piano lessons because of her own yearning to be able to play. She added,

> I don't know if you'd call it art but my daughter took twirling for five years. I think we started with that instead of tap dance because of a special they offered over the summer.

In private dance classes, jazz was popular but ballet unprofitable. Few could afford the three to four classes per week needed for good training. One teacher was phasing out tap dance because of declining student interest. She noted ruefully, "Sometimes we hear kids get mad and say, 'I don't care! I only take dance lessons because of the costumes!' Most of them stop at junior high."

A painter and private art teacher said her students want to win rosettes in local competitions.

> I try to tell them it's not important to win. I think it's good to see your painting in a different context. And for the most part, I think people feel good when their work is shown. I have this little speech: "It's OK to feel good if you win a rosette but next week you have to get back to work" and vice versa. But kids and parents think it's embarrassing to take classes and not win.

Taiwanese parents were anxious for their children to excel when they return to their homeland. Children of one Bar Harbor family took piano, art, and gymnastics lessons in addition to afterschool math instruction from their parents and Saturday Chinese lessons. A daughter's photograph had recently appeared in the local newspaper as winner of an art contest. Violin lessons were desired but the nearest teacher was about forty miles away in Guadelupe; some Taiwanese did commute to these lessons.

Gender-related expectations surfaced in the comments of an Hispanic father who had encouraged his daughters in the arts and his sons in the sciences. He said,

> Karen has talent. She paints and she took dance lessons and piano. Theresa has talent, too, but she couldn't care less. I can't honestly tell why. The boys wouldn't take piano but John took guitar.

"I honestly don't know if the remoteness of these communities prevents people from developing more interest," an elementary music teacher said of Bar Harbor, Driftwood, and Point Aden. She estimated that three Point Aden and five or six Driftwood students took piano lessons, that there was perhaps one piano teacher in Point Aden and one in Bar Harbor.

Popular arts were of interest to the community. From a hotel-motel tax amounting to about $10,000 per year, San Sebastian's Cultural Council granted funds for various arts activities. The Art Guild president told of good attendance for a sweatshirt and T-shirt painting class. The guild was awarded a grant for the fabric painting class but thereafter felt that applying was "too much work with no volunteers."

Encouraging Arts Careers. No one expected that more than a very few Webster County students would pursue arts careers. Yet teachers radiated pride when noting former pupils who had become artists or arts teachers. A couple of small local scholarships promoted further study and, sometimes perhaps, careers. Parents feared arts careers would mean economic hardship for their children.

The WHS assistant band director said that two or three band graduates per year pursued careers in music. He named home-grown musicians, the colleges they had attended, and where they were teaching. A piano teacher also tracked the music professions of WHS students, not necessarily students of hers. A private dance instructor beamed as she spoke of an Hispanic male who had attended her jazz, ballet, and tap classes for years, then accepted a scholarship and position from Martha Graham.

The Art Guild sponsored private lessons in the visual arts, an arts and crafts fair, a judged art show, and offered one or two $300 scholarships annually. The guild president explained that scholarship applicants must have been accepted to an arts or architecture post-secondary school and must have submitted a portfolio of work; scholastic ability was not an important criterion. She said

> It's not a lot of money but the scholarship becomes part of the student's resume. Some years, we have no qualified applicants. Winning at the art show also helps kids who are interested in art careers to establish a reputation.

"We used to give drama scholarships to high school students," the Webster Civic Theatre director recalled, "but the WHS theatre arts teacher didn't help so we stopped."

How much external encouragement is needed to develop vocational interest in the arts? How much encouragement is it reasonable to expect of communities, especially where the stereotype of the starving artist persists? A painter and art teacher recalled that she did not study art as a schoolchild partly because her family moved frequently. A couple of schools she attended offered "a little art and I loved it but I never thought I could paint or draw. I thought it was like magic." She took art classes as an adult and "thought everybody learned as easily as I did." She realized others' struggles and recognized her own talent five years later when she began to teach art.

Another painter and teacher thought her interest in art came entirely "from within. I didn't have any arts training when I went to school. I wanted some but now I think that a class might have stifled creativity." She would nevertheless like schools to provide more arts education and from an early age. "Learning techniques would save a lot of experimentation time but, frankly, I forgot all the art history I learned in college."

A WHS senior, unaware that he would soon be awarded the Art Guild scholarship, could not identify the origins of his interest in the visual arts: "I've been interested in art as long as I can remember." His interest was evidently strong for the arts competed for time with his many other interests. He was an outstanding football player, second in the state in weightlifting, and selected journalism and French as electives in addition to art.

His father regarded a career in the arts as "OK. If any of my four children want it, I'd help."

But his mother gasped and admitted, "I've tried to discourage that because it's hard to get a job."

"I would suggest they study something they could fall back on, like being an art teacher," his father amended.

A Taiwanese eighth grader described music classes at Bar Harbor Elementary School as "boring. You sing the same songs over and over and they're sorta stupid." Visual arts classes were

> OK, but there are too many students, so the teacher can't help you much. You can do waterpaint and crayon encaustic but that's about all. Private lessons are better. You learn more and your parents get after you, scold you, if you don't accomplish something. I don't want to be an artist. I'm not that interested.

Her mother said she would encourage a career in the arts but expected her daughters to marry, to be supported financially by their future husbands.

An Hispanic parent generalized,

> The Hispanic child is born with artistic talent. It's inbred. Hispanics at the upper [socioeconomic] level might push for art careers but most

would want their kids to get a regular kind of job. I always think of the arts as the pastime of those with leisure and money.

Surprisingly, an illegal alien speaking through a translator said he would happily support any decision by his children to follow a career in the arts. He felt that he could provide emotional support, opportunities for practice, and transportation. (He rode a bicycle.) Less surprising was the pride of his economically secure translator as she mentioned that her niece, WHS '77, was earning a master's degree in architecture, and would soon tour France and study in Rome and Greece.

An Afro-American mother of two, who persistently sought cultural opportunities for her children, said of an arts career for her dramatically inclined son, "I've thought about it but it's hard to get started. I think I'd also want something else for him, something secure. Theatre would be a good minor." She recalled her brother's fifteen-year struggle in gospel music before achieving economic security.

Principal Jerri Bell said of the Vietnamese in Driftwood,

> I don't think they would encourage their kids toward careers in the arts. I think they put a lot of pressure on their kids for engineering and technical fields for economic reasons. They are going to succeed; I promise you that.

A Caucasian plant executive said,

> If one of my children wanted to be an artist of some kind, my only reservation would be adequate financial compensation. That comes from being poor as I grew up.

The Art Guild president, a mother of six, seemed less concerned about artists' economic well-being. Of her youngest daughter, who won recognition as a pianist and then studied chemical engineering, she sometimes said, "I wish she had stayed with her music."

Ethnicity's Effects on Access to Arts Education

When the subject of ethnicity in school arts came up, the WHS assistant band director reached for lists of band members. He counted:

Honors Band	15 Hispanics	55 Caucasians	1 Asian	
Symphonic Band	24 Hispanics	"about 50% Caucasians"	2 Asians	
Concert Band	18 Hispanics	"just over 50% Caucasians"	1 Asian	1 Afro-American

He appeared dumfounded when asked for an explanation as to why the greatest concentration of Caucasians was in the honors band and somewhat pained when I suggested that someone might interpret his figures as evidence that Caucasians advanced more readily than other ethnic groups. "I just never thought about that before." He explained that students were placed based on teachers' knowledge of their playing ability, with a few changes based on ability demonstrated at band camp and a few to accommodate students' schedules. "At most, we get two Afro-Americans a year. Hispanics in the band get more family support than Caucasians in many cases."

An Hispanic elementary principal offered a possible explanation: "Probably there are not very many minority students in the top high school band and choir because, by then, some of them have dropped out of school."

WHS visual arts teacher Georgia Rose estimated that 75% of her students were males, many Hispanic. She hypothesized:

> Number one, I think art is more ingrained in Mexican-American culture, not isolated as it is in Western culture; and, number two, oftentimes, the boys mature at a later rate. Arts classes are more informal, less structured.

On the subject of ethnicity, the WHS theatre arts teacher commented only, "I have one Afro-American freshman girl in my class who is failing everything but theatre. And an Hispanic had the lead in the last play." But a parent said that Hispanic students avoided high school drama and speech classes, believing the teacher to be prejudiced.

As the WHS choir rehearsed for contest, I heard an Hispanic girl hit a very high solo note. The note was breathtakingly clear; I discovered I had goosebumps. A student sitting next to me, ineligible to participate in contest because of grades, confided, "She's the only one who can get that high."

"Why are there so few Hispanics in the choir?" I whispered.

The student shrugged, "I don't know. I never thought about it."

The choir director later said only that the ethnic composition of the choir fluctuated from year to year.

Participation in private arts lessons also varied by ethnicity. A piano teacher said,

> I started teaching piano in 1958. I have had maybe ten Spanish students in thirty years. The ones I get are excellent students but I would assume there's just not a lot of money for lessons [among Hispanics generally]. Over the years, I have had two Negro students. I have a little Negro student now that's just absolutely one of my favorites because she works so hard. She's very musical.

A private visual arts teacher reflected,

> The Hispanic children take lessons only if they're already good. I don't think it's a matter of money but that they need to show promise. The Caucasians come to learn to draw. I've never had a black child in class.

A private dance teacher estimated that 60% of her students were Hispanic. She felt that Hispanics were more family-oriented, distinguished by their love for their children. Resultingly, Hispanic kids were "wonderful students," often trying harder to learn and to please than did Caucasians. Of Afro-Americans she had had one, the same student, for the past four years. Of a total 180 students, she had had as many as twenty Taiwanese who, she noted, learned more quickly than any other group.

An Hispanic mother of four, thought Hispanics especially sensitive to art and music, recalling her father's and her children's constant radio-listening. It was her son who was to receive the Art Guild scholarship. A daughter had played Cinderella in a middle school play, won three medals for duet acting and poetry reading, took gymnastics lessons from a dance teacher, learned to play piano from an uncle, and was an officer in the drill team; she planned to enroll in vocational education to become a secretary. A freshman son didn't like choir in middle school but said, "There was nothing else to take." An eighth grade son chose to take art but declared himself, like his brother, more interested in athletics.

A wealthier Hispanic mother felt Hispanics had equal access to the arts in San Sebastian but "social problems" interfered—language difficulties with which teachers were impatient. None of her children felt discrimination in the local schools but she had taught them to speak only English so that they would not acquire an accent. "Spanish is such a musical language," she explained, "that it predisposes toward some sounds which affect the speaking of English."

An Afro-American mother said race affects children—"there's always some"—but a general openness and intelligence spared children injustice in San Sebastian.

> Being new, my son was nervous about try-outs for school plays this year but that helped him get established. He wanted to do it. He learns his lines on his own.

But she "pushed" piano lessons; there is daily practice. "I feel it will be good for him in the long run but I feel bad about having to force him to continue. There is also the investment." A daughter was interested in dance lessons but times conflicted with classes the mother was taking at Guadelupe College and "I was not comfortable with the carpool situation."

A poorer Afro-American parent said his children, two particularly, liked to draw "but not at school." His statement that there were no private visual arts classes indicated he was unaware of the Art Guild teacher-artists.

Of the "17% Vietnamese at Deaf Smith Middle School and 16% at Driftwood Elementary; just almost even for the Hispanics and Anglos," Principal Jerri Bell said:

> Most Vietnamese students at Deaf Smith were originally boat people that came with nothing. The Vietnamese in Driftwood have been fairly permanent and make a good living, most of them. They are not as educated as the Taiwanese and no Vietnamese will go back [to Vietnam because of the political situation]. I open the school to them to teach their kids Vietnamese in Saturday classes.
>
> In school, they're on a par with or better than other students if we get them as English speakers. If we have to teach them English, they're immediately behind. We get them into a federally-funded migrant program, although they're not really migrant.
>
> Some of the things they put out in art are just excellent. You can see they have talent. They are good at portraits and fine detail, very creative. Generally, the best artist in the school every year will be a Vietnamese. I have some Hispanics and some Anglos that are excellent, too.
>
> When I schedule them for high school, almost all the Vietnamese want to take art, although most of the other kids prefer to do something new. In the past couple of years, they've been signing up for band and choir, too. They seem interested in music. We think that, before, they were afraid they couldn't afford instruments or they didn't want to ask. Vietnamese are proud. They don't understand things like rent, lease. They pool their money and buy everything in cash. That kind of spilled over into the schools.
>
> Their parents are never really willing to let them go on our field trips or camping trips. Some of them get to go; the ones that have been in the States ten to fourteen years are more relaxed. We're going to San Antonio to the Art Institute on Wednesday, taking the whole seventh grade. I'll bet two or three Vietnamese won't go.

The most striking effect of ethnicity on access to instruction came in private piano lessons. A long-time resident and piano teacher, who referred to Taiwanese as Chinese and to Vietnamese as Taiwanese, related:

> An excellent music teacher here in town got rid of all her students except Chinese because, she says, "They really work and I'm not going to waste my time." She flat gave the rest their walking papers. There are enough students to keep classes full. I have found myself doing the same thing with a few students.
>
> The Taiwanese seem to be smart but they do not have the monetary advantages. The Chinese can afford to pay me $100 a month for three kids to take piano. The three kids will also be taking art lessons and other lessons.
>
> I had one Chinese student who, after five years, didn't like taking piano. I said, "Let him stop. He doesn't have to take piano." That was like

committing sacrilege. His parents wouldn't dream of such a thing but his heart really wasn't in music.

Socioeconomics and Minorities' Involvement in the Arts. As previously noted with some private arts teachers, school teachers expected both ethnicity and socioeconomic status to have a negative effect on access to the arts, minorities to be less affluent than Caucasians. Yet people consistently cited exceptions, often for reasons they associated with ethnic interest.

The WHS assistant band director did not think Hispanic families' financial situations prevented students from joining band because "most of the Latins are on sax and those cost over $1000—they're the most expensive of the student-provided instruments."

The WHS theatre arts teacher on school trips to plays:

> Students have to pay for themselves; I'm not going to go through fund-raising! Surprisingly, a good representation of Hispanics realize this is a cultural experience that they otherwise wouldn't provide.

Of seven students planning to take the next field trip, three were Hispanics and one was Afro-American.

An Illegal Alien's View. Manuel smiled and his eyes lit up when he related that his stepson Antonio loved music, loved to dance. A younger child, two-year-old Manny, danced and loved music even more, he said. He couldn't tell about the baby yet, only three months old and "very jolly."

Manuel played accordion but looked embarrassed when he shared this and claimed not to play well. Without acknowledging the expense of lessons, he said he himself wanted to train the three children on the accordion. He already had the boys listen and pay attention while he played. Their hands were too small to manipulate the keyboard but Manny liked to crawl beneath the accordion and push buttons while his father was playing.

The translator suspected Manuel's desire for the arts was greater than that of most illegal "alia." She found him atypical in other ways, too: a family man, an older man, married to a woman abandoned by her husband, his children born in the U.S. He wanted to stay in the U.S. and had his green card but had to wait for five years for final permission.

Manuel took Antonio to and from school on his bicycle. He was able to drive but afraid to test. The test was written in Spanish but he suspected that he would somehow be tricked. This suspicion pervaded thinking in other areas as well, perhaps including the arts. But opportunities to study the arts would be greater in San Sebastian than in Mexico where, the translator said, villages had little or no art besides an occasional "traveling tent" offering performances.

Ethnic and Non-Western Art. In visual arts, Georgia Rose at WHS seemed sensitive to Hispanic concerns and political progress. She encouraged Asian students to present and display cultural artifacts. And a Taiwanese student said her private art teacher had shown Chinese paintings in class. Other than that, I found little evidence of cultural diversity in arts offerings, other than radio stations playing music of Hispanic origin.

Conclusion

Clearly there were some places in Webster County Independent School District and in San Sebastian where the arts did thrive.

School district efforts to promote the arts were apparent, some said insufficient. Among teachers, specialist training and dedication nearly always increased with grade level; quality of instruction nearly always mirrored this rise. Private arts teachers and sponsors seemed ready to assist the schools but were uninvited. No arts advocates demanded more or better arts classes in the schools; most parents, even arts enthusiasts, declared themselves satisfied. Ethnic groups presented different interests in school arts.

The district lacked an explicated arts philosophy. Administrators often offered no more rationale for arts instruction than that exposure to culture is good. Frequent references to the district curriculum guide, *Essential Elements*, implied that mere statement of lessons and learning objectives was sufficient. Administrators' priorities strongly impacted teacher perceptions of the relative importance of the arts; most administrators at the school and district level thought other matters more important. An historically undervalued subject needs more support to gain a real footing in the curriculum.

Educational policies, even those designed to promote arts instruction, often had negative consequences. The same state mandates which required fine arts study for high school graduation also limited many of the brighter students to little more than a single course. The district teacher-pupil ratio encouraged personalized attention to students but the number of students required to hold a class usually precluded advanced offerings in high school arts. The teacher appraisal system may have raised the quality of instruction generally but it also failed to recognize differences thought significant between teaching the arts and teaching academics. Although WCISD in some ways had protected and augmented the numbers of arts teachers in the previous three years, it had also sacrificed specialists in the primary grades, stirring up resentment and anxiety.

Pitted against academics and athletics, the arts did not compete well for formal educational priority here. Parents were even more insistent upon traditional scholastic subjects than were school people. Many wanted good school arts programs, whether or not they could define "good," but only after reading and mathematics had been well learned. TEAMS and CAT testing intensified this insistence.

Most people in and out of schools said fine arts were a means of relaxation, something to enjoy lightly, rather than a means of seeing or understanding or communicating or developing creative skills and habits. With notable exceptions, nearly every adult expressed reservations about encouraging students to pursue arts careers. Students seemed to have absorbed these reservations.

Ethnicity—coupled with but not necessarily dominated by—socioeconomics gave some students a better chance at arts opportunities in and out of school. Caucasians often concentrated on academics in upper grades at the expense of the arts, sometimes compensating for underattention to school arts with private lessons. Taiwanese concentrated even more on academics but also were greatly over-represented in private music and visual arts classes. Hispanics sometimes overcame financial, language, and some discrimination difficulties to become involved in the school and community arts they loved. Afro-Americans and, to an even greater degree, Vietnamese were largely left out of private lessons, although Vietnamese did well in school arts. School personnel seemed unconcerned by patterns of ethnic enrollment and participation in arts electives.

Many arts instructors taught well, some very well. Some principals supported their efforts. WCISD showed some tangible signs of support, too. Many students brought supplies, entered competitions, took more than one arts elective. Many parents provided funds, transportation, and encouragement for out-of-school arts experiences. Within every group, some individuals made noteworthy efforts.

In the schools, leadership by individuals created pockets of commendable arts education. These people had strong personal commitment to the arts and to arts education. Despite differing goals and philosophies, each valued appreciating, enjoying, even cherishing art. Each was familiar with school and community expectations for arts education and eager to extend those expectations. For these reasons, people like Principal Carolyn Sommers, Fine Arts Department Head Georgia Rose, the team of visual arts specialist Beatrice Slattery and music specialist Juanita Callas, and others were assets to the community and schools of Webster County.

The range of interest in the arts and in arts education in San Sebastian was large, fed by ethnic diversity, socioeconomic differences within the community's relatively narrow band, education levels, experiences in other locations, and local opportunities. In the schools, the arts competed with other subjects for fiscal resources, time in the daily schedule and after school, and career preparation. All students had some exposure to the arts in elementary schools and beyond. Some students found ways to participate more, opportunities to learn more. Some parents and school people encouraged them; some worked very hard to do so.

A range of interest is to be expected, of course, even in a small town. Each town has its own particular sources of variation for its residents' perceptions of local arts. Some people in this town saw limitations stemming from San Sebastian's remoteness from cities, its economic woes, its ethnic composition. Some were overwhelmed by the struggle required to enhance arts opportunities. Others noted student awards, voluntary participation and enrollment, encouraging organizations and policies, and the presence of artists and enthusiasts. From disappointing backwater to art colony, many views of San Sebastian could be justified.

PART THREE: TRADITIONAL AND EMERGING ISSUES

Chapter 10: The Content of Elementary School Arts Education

In American elementary schools, teaching of the arts is largely teaching of custom. In teaching art and music and, occasionally, drama or dance, we teach the customs of the culture, honoring the stories of childhood, the first snowfall, the "Star-Spangled Banner." Children are coached in decorating and performing, joining in the traditions of holiday and celebration. The teacher of the arts is a preparer of shows. These exhibits and performances draw children's eyes and ears, also adults' eyes and ears, once again toward what we—primarily the middle class "we"—have come collectively and informally to recognize, our rituals and seasonal symbols.

Much of the coaching is rather formal. "Clean your brush before dipping into the yellow" and "When I raise my hand like this, sing very softly." Only occasional, much less formal, is the teaching of the arts' own content. Only incidental are references to such artistry as Whistler's mother, regal accoutrement, jazz chording, art deco lineage, Hamlet's soliloquy—incidental and rare.

Art and music classes, play practice, and synchronous movement certainly can be fun, a welcome change of pace from the regular classroom but each is a job for teachers to get done, a job needing sense of purpose and concerted effort, aiming toward exhibition. In many ways, the teaching of elementary school arts is teaching about work, not about drudgery but about craft pointed toward celebration, honors and fulfillment of duty. Work, production, conforming, obligation—they're important. Mixed now and again with pleasure and pride, in its way it is a *values clarification* exercise, not so much to crystalize the values of the individual child but to make crystalline those of a cultural majority.

Most classroom teachers do not find it easy to think of the arts as fundamental to education. Yes, all children need to follow directions, to make an effort regardless of talent or aptitude, to work quietly, to learn to limn and scissor straighter lines. But no, there is nothing critical about any particular learning in the arts or even the aesthetic experience (Beardsley, 1970). One doesn't learn these things. One participates. One prepares for the exhibition. To be a good student in the arts is to be acculturated, to join the custom.

Differentiation and Standardization of Aims. From room to room, from school to school, from year to year, there is little effort to voice the purposes of art education or to assure agreement as to those purposes. Articulated purpose is not essential to effective instruction (Polanyi, 1958) but in recent years greater and greater implication is to be found in official pronouncements that "essential" learning *will be specified*. School district syllabi are increasingly claiming the need for and more explicitly stating certain purposes of arts education (Chapman, 1982).

These goal statements are broad, elevated, and in tune with the aspirations of most specialists in arts education.

As mentioned earlier, in our 1985 case study for the Getty Center (Stake, McTaggart & Munski, 1984), working with elementary school teachers, we identified seven more or less latent purposes, namely to develop a youngster's (1) cultural knowledge base, (2) imaging and other critical thinking skills, (3) artistic expressiveness, (4) self-understanding, (5) membership in and support for the world of art, (6) opportunities for enjoyment and change of pace, and (7) appreciation and cherishing of the arts. As outcomes, the first six were seen to constitute a background for the seventh: appreciation, a cherishing of the arts, or better, an enlightened cherishing, an aesthetic beholding of the arts.[1]

With repeated questioning and patient listening, we discerned these aims again in '88 and '89. Diligence was needed—perhaps because articulating arts goals was not an ordinary task for teachers, one some felt uncomfortable with. After all, the next question is likely to be, "And how do you measure your success with that goal?" Priority was certainly not equal across the seven purposes. Two purposes were stated most frequently: cultural knowledge (informally known) and opportunities for enjoyment and change of pace. Artistic expressiveness or creativity was an aim often voiced but, as Liora Bresler will relate in the next chapter, not so frequently pursued, except as "creativity" is used to signify "productivity."

One goal seldom mentioned or pursued in the classrooms we visited was that of fostering cognitive skills. Well out of earshot were the exquisite arguments of Harry Broudy and Elliot Eisner[2] that study of the arts sophisticates the powers of imagery, illustration, allusion, and metaphor. Most educators in these schools were unaware of such claims. Nor did it appear unconsciously expected that participation in the arts or beholding of artistry would enhance mental and verbal imagery.

Unlike the high school arts teacher, most elementary classroom teachers and many itinerant specialists (serving two or three elementary schools) appeared seldom to identify with an art as discipline or life force. When specially trained, a high school drama teacher is likely to see himself/herself a member of the theatre arts community and to be as interested in preserving and enhancing that art form as in preserving and enhancing education. (This is common among science, math, and literature teachers and athletics coaches as well—they hold allegiance to their content fields.) But in the elementary grades, the arts are seldom seen as special preserve or knowledge-base, more often as a valued experience, background, a cultural enhancement. More will be said about the intellectual peripherality of arts teaching next when we discuss integration of arts instruction into teaching the other subject matters of the elementary curriculum. The point here is that in the elemen-

---

[1] We are impressed with the similarity of these purposes with those advocated by such spokespersons as Jerry Hausman (1963) and Arthur Efland (1979).

[2] The discipline-based advocacies of the J. Paul Getty Center for Education in the Arts have given new life to the writings of Harry Broudy (1977), Elliot Eisner (1982b) and others who called for seeing the arts as central to the process of education, central to the development of intellectual acuity.

tary school, the intellectual purposes are seldom voiced and seldom intentionally pursued. One or two teachers but not a small cadre of advocates can be found as agents for redirecting arts education toward the intellectual purposes of arts education.

According to Les McLean (1976), the standing of art education in the school is indicated by the ambiance of hallways and classrooms. Our Fifty States correspondent from New Mexico, Sculptor Harry Benjamin, wrote:

> In January I visited our local high school. I was surprised to find no hallway space allocated for display. The only visible posters were Fighting Colts posters in the gymnasium but not done by the Art classes. My experience was quite a shock. I found that I could not walk the hallways without permission from the principal who seemed reluctant to give it. The hallways I did get into were painted with bright orange enamel. There were very few windows.
>
> I have been aware for many years that the Art programs in our schools have been gradually fading away. It is happening even faster than I had imagined. When I was in high school we were bused to El Paso museums and to the University gallery on this campus to see exhibits. The same school systems are now complaining that their budgets prohibit such activities. It need not be. Last week at the Denver Museum of Art, I followed a teacher and her class. She was extremely good with the children. For a few minutes she had the class look at a very large painted construction, then had them turn and face the opposite direction. She asked questions like "What was the dominant color in the composition?" She was objective and direct, the students responded with enthusiasm.

At a nominal level, without providing appropriate funding, the states and districts have become increasingly explicit about the importance of the arts in K-12 learning. In practice, in allocating time to the arts, in requiring and rewarding special talents in teaching the arts, and in testing student achievement in the arts, the schools revealed to us a substantially lower priority. The teachers of the elementary schools we saw were able to read the signals pretty well. They understood they had neither the community nor the profession to fear if they failed to pursue the articulated aims of arts education.

Leading voices in education today call for standardized instruction, the same teaching and the same learning for all children (Adler, 1982). Under such thinking, the shortcomings of a majority of teachers draw public attention away from the many creative and proficient individualists among our teachers. Were the schools and the nation to capitalize on and encourage individual teachers to work from a syllabus *if they chose* and according to their own inclination if they did not, were we inspired to optimize differentiated (as well as standardized) growth of both teacher and children, the present circumstances would not appear so dismal and the opportunity for modest improvement would be enhanced.[3]

---

[3]This point is developed further in the chapter on Leadership which follows. The argument for empowering practitioners has been effectively made by Donald Schön (1982) and the argument for reducing the scale of education planning by Deborah Meier (1989).

Integration of the Arts into Other Instruction. Facing new and far-reaching state goal statements and finding no room in the schedule for additional arts instruction, school administrators speak of integration of the arts into reading, science and other classes. In the minds of most teachers we observed, integrated arts meant something like teaching the U.S. presidents' names in a song or making a mural of Westward-moving prairie schooners for a social studies unit. Arts components were seen by them as topical enhancements, motivators for learning basic skills objectives. As did the Getty case researchers (Day et al, 1984), we encountered few instances of integration where arts aims were as important as the other subject matter aims or even where the students were expected to learn something important in the disciplines of music, drama, dance or the visual arts. As pursued, inclusion of the arts through integration appeared to us to be of little value in meeting authentic arts goals.

Occasionally an integrated lesson drew our applause. In a classroom we noted 20 nine and ten-year-olds sprawled across a carpet floor, imaging the ocean depths, hearing the songs of humpback whales in the stillness of an early morning. Connie, their teacher, led them through visualization, then after several minutes of quiet listening and reflection, each child moved to a private spot to work out a haiku poem. Gordie wrote:

> *Deep in the ocean*
> *A whale floated sleeplessly*
> *Thinking about fish.*

The room was crowded with images of whale: books, posters, the children's own murals. For three weeks, classroom thoughts were drawn to the reality and wonder of whales. Habitats were researched; whale lengths became paper strips stretched down hallways; oatmeal was "krill" sieved from water with a "baleen" comb, ...

Most classrooms we visited were graphically alive but in contrast to Connie's room, failing to raise the question, "What is beauty?" We saw classrooms strong on caring, with many cared-for objects and activities from the popular arts: here a Michael Jackson album, there a Mexican blouse, next week a field trip to a drama festival. But formally and informally, there was little acknowledgement of discipline-based arts education. Few teachers felt ready to teach analysis or critical study. Fewer still felt *that* the way to use the few minutes available for the arts.

Discipline-Based Arts Education. In its bid to start a reform movement in visual arts education in America, the J. Paul Getty Center for Education in the Arts devised a strategy for de-emphasizing production in favor of emphasizing critical analysis of classical works, historical perspectives and an understanding of aesthetics (Getty Center, 1985). These emphases have long been integral to the ideology of arts educators, manifest in the writings of distinguished leaders such as Rudolph Arnheim (1954), Manuel Barkan (1955), and Ralph Smith (1989).

Unfortunately, most student teachers begin teacher training without training or experience in the arts. They take only a minor course or part of a course to learn what to do "during art." In that hasty preparatory sojourn, the dominant message to student-teachers has been to get their pupils into productive activities, developing techniques of making art and, occasionally, exploring ways of personal expression.

Most graduates headed for classroom teaching in grades K-6 have had no more than the opportunity to learn a few techniques and identify manuals of prospective projects—with little attention to the cognitive side of visual art and even less about the *disciplines* of music, drama, and dance.

Leilani Lattin Duke and her staff at the Getty Center have created in Los Angeles a DBAE model for full-scale restructuring of district programs. With summer institutes for teachers and administrators and subsequently with sponsored activities around the country, the Getty people have pushed for corporate or top-to-bottom commitment to discipline-based arts curricula.

Arts education program innovators have successfully demonstrated that, with relatively small staff development and small but real commitments from administrators, teachers with little training can participate effectively in discipline-based programs, at least at levels of sophistication well above what is happening in their schools now.[4] Before long, they can help students identify the elements of classical and popular works, recognize major periods and outstanding works, and experience a more cognitive approach to producing and appreciating the arts. It is far less than the needed restructuring and almost without attention to aesthetics—still, a major improvement.

But even this much DBAE takes more class time than is now available. And teachers already have too much to do (Cuban, 1984). Yet the real problem is that the knowledge of the arts is not seen by public, parents, and school leaders as a respectable part of education, certainly not instrumental in increasing wage-earning capacity (Kaagan, 1990). The collective opinion of the people is something like:

> Kids with interest and talent should have school opportunity to go further in the arts. The other kids? No. No required arts. The kids have enough to do. The teachers have enough to do. But all kids should get better at what they're good at. The arts *will be important for a few.*

Popular philosophy of school art is *laissez-faire*. Unlike with reading and writing, there is, with the arts, little public call for compensatory education. If a kid is ignorant of the arts, that's okay with most parents and teachers. *We* don't agree but we think that, given the teachers today in American elementary schools, a *laissez-faire* philosophy is actually more constructive than a standardizing, essential-skills philosophy. The arts have a special opportunity in being different.

Across the board, elementary school policy is based on the idea that there are certain knowledges and skills that everyone should work on until mastery. Schools, then, are devoted to drill, to fostering mental habits. In a short while, these are habits at which more than half the class is sufficiently good (for the time being) and at which a small percentage of students are floundering and will never do well. Contemporary pedagogy *can* be seen as finding out which learning makes children miserable and teaching it.

---

[4]We noted particularly the staff development work of Kent Anderson in Milwaukee, Stephanie Runyan in Virginia Beach, Virginia, and Nancy Roucher and Michele Olsen in Decatur, Illinois, all described in Day et al. (1984).

Core-curriculum advocates such as Gary Fenstermacher and John Goodlad (1983) and E. D. Hirsch, Jr. (1987) have helped legitimate the already popular notion that if kids are going to benefit from public funds, all of them should learn the rudiments of a common education. Combining "minimum competency" with a notion that it's not fair to teach what some children have little chance of learning, American elementary schools administer large doses of standardized simplistics.

Simplistics are also standard fare in music and art classes. Many lessons are enjoyable, tradition-sustaining, but contain little intellectual content. Still, opportunity is there for teachers to pursue different arts objectives for the group and for individuals. In those two ways, student interest and teacher potential for providing unique experience, we found arts education healthier today than most of the rest of the elementary school curriculum.

As Getty Center people advocated, disciplined-based arts education leans toward standardization but is far from simplistic. It pushes students to make fine distinctions, to study complex relationships. It gives little sway to personal interpretation, seems bent on making young people audiences first before they become performers. A passivity and discipline orientation is in tune with what many parents and educators told us they wanted for arts education—and education more broadly—but they also indicated that schools need to teach communication skills and math rigorously, to get those scores up, so to speak, before taking time to teach the arts.

Band and Vocal Music Customs. America did not need Meredith Wilson's *Music Man* to become aware of people's love for the high school band. The band director is a special person in the community. A successful band is as awe-inspiring as a successful football team. Neither happens overnight. An expectation of excellence takes years to mature. Most of the star performers would not be star performers had not playing the scales successfully competed with other things ten-year-olds do after school.

For those ten-year-olds, the high school band director worked to assure availability of instruments and both beginning and intermediate instruction for them as they moved into middle school. Private lessons outside school were seldom available. Except for piano and guitar lessons, introduction to instrumental music was a school responsibility.

In Las Lomas, California we found the junior high school band director coming once a week to Luther Burbank Elementary to work with the pre-band group. In previous years, students had started with an instrument of their choice but too many parents and kids had been disappointed—with loss out-of-pocket. Now requiring smaller investments, third graders first learned to play flute or recorder. Those who stuck it out were encouraged to advance to a band instrument. Of the 80 or so fourth graders at this school, about a dozen were working on clarinets, trumpets and such.

In San Sebastian, Texas, we found out-of-school music lessons more or less unavailable for Anglos, Afro-Americans, and Hispanics. Taiwanese parents had booked nearly all the available hours and their kids were considered the most rewarding to work with. In Anacortes and both Chicago schools, violin lessons for children and their parents had no connection to the school curriculum but were promoted by the schools. In some ways customs changed but tradition marched steadily along toward halftime and graduation. The schools acted as middle-man or host, if not always the deliverer of services.

Vocal music had its own place in community tradition. Choruses and choirs were church as well as school endeavors. The schools promoted the exhibitive and competitive vocal program. In the grade school the choral presentations were for parents, often at PTA meetings. A holiday theme was common. In these groups, all children participated, including a few who were told to pretend to sing. Performance was the aim, little about music literature or theory was included.

"Boom boxes" were not as common as they had been 10 and 20 years earlier. In the communities we visited, as in the movie, *Do the Right Thing*, the boom-boxer was often a marginal person. The schools took little note what children were hearing on rock stations or MTV or what they did with aural software, occasionally a moan or sneer. If at least partly a school function, concerts, choirs, and folk festivals got announced, otherwise usually were ignored.

Music literacy was seldom an issue in discussions of the curriculum. Once primary school singing was completed, the ethic called for availability of opportunity for those with talent and interest. The tradition of American music is a rich one. We seemed not to be worried that the schools are contributing little to its vigor.

Personal Cherishing. *How does a child come to understand artistries the society has come to cherish?* As indicated in the Luther Burbank School description, Bob Stake was intrigued at one meeting when Howard Gardner suggested that for vitalizing arts education, we think about helping children realize what they cherish, what their parents cherish, what their teacher cherishes.

Drawn from chapter 8 is this reflection on a special moment in an ordinary day for a teacher untrained in arts education and under little obligation to teach the arts. Stake wrote, "For several days I took note of what the teacher, Mr. Frielander, cherished. One parent told me Mr. Free cherished the kids and I could see he treated them with considerable respect. He liked geography but nothing geographically awesome appeared during my stay. During the wildlife project, however, with spelling, writing, and science integrated, my record went like this:

> Next they are to read the story of *Wufu*, a brown bat. Pausing before beginning the reading, Mr. Free catches their attention. His face is solemn. His voice has a somber quality now.
>
> This morning at the assembly you all took the pledge not to harm animals. That is very important. On the way to school this morning I was very disturbed. If anyone should know better—the head of a department in college should be. This man works in a science department. A professor—he knows better—but he became very selfish. Wild animals not endangered should be left in their habitats. This professor decided to start his own special collection. He asked a student to join him hunting for a certain kind of animal. The student didn't know he would be shooting and stuffing animals for the professor's own

house. You should always be alert. Watch tonight for the story in the papers or on TV.

He relaxes, smiles, then begins to read *Wufu* aloud.

The normally rambunctious ten-year-olds had been caught up in what he was saying, recognizing this was not so much an appeal for humane treatment as much as a reverence for nature. Perhaps they were alerted by the solemn tone or an appeal for passion. It seemed what we used to call, "a teachable moment."[5] Was there a chance then for brief teaching about aesthetics? Could they have pondered what is beautiful about animals in the wild? Could they have pondered beauty in the magazine photos they had clipped? Can a teacher untrained in the teaching of art, utter words that help youngsters refine their views of art? Mr. Free might have needed only five words more.

According to Harry Broudy (1972), enlightened cherishing is at the center of aesthetics education, not only reaching a state of reverence but intellectualizing the revering. Through aesthetics education we come not just to recognize but to understand what we ourselves cherish and what society cherishes. Discipline-based arts education includes the study of holding the fine arts dear. How is that accomplished? Through experience with the arts, through critical analysis, and with the help of teachers who themselves cherish the arts.

---

[5] Another such moment occurred on a Luther Burbank fourth-grade field trip. See the final pages of chapter 8.

Chapter 11:
The Pedagogy of Arts Education

A commonality[1] among the arts is their role in school, a role that contrasts with the academic subjects. The arts in the school mark a special realm, a realm in which school grades and measurements are far less rigid, in which "other intelligences," typically not sanctioned by the school, are invited to share in the school day, a realm colored by notions of "fun" rather than work, the festive rather than the mundane, a connection with honorific customs.

That the arts were part of the fun realm was clear not only in function and value orientations but in schedules too. The arts often served as transition from work to leisure: at the end of the school day, of the week, of the semester, before holidays. Occasionally, transition went the other way: some teachers started the day with a few minutes of dance or classical music. Holidays provided themes and arts activities: drawing and coloring pumpkins, turkeys, and Easter eggs; preparing skits, bunny hats, illustrated Christmas program notes, songs and dances (like the "Chinese New Year" dance or the "Jingle Bells" dance) for school programs. An aesthetic beholding was rare.

Although teachers, principals, and parents occasionally acknowledged and praised a certain arts project or program, the arts were regularly marginal, almost always secondary to academics. Said a teacher voicing the opinions of many others "I never hear parents ask me about art. If they come to the conference at all, it's always math and reading." Parents and administrators were preoccupied with urgent matters such as progress and achievements in the academics, children's misbehavior, academic and disciplinary functions of the school. Our conversations with parents in school performances indicated that they were proud of the artistic accomplishments of their offspring. But when school productions ceased, in Danville, few parents raised their voice in protest.

That values are personal and controversial created a problem for teaching the arts. A concern raised by some teachers was parents' sensitivity to values in regard to the arts. Teachers felt vulnerable and prone to parents' criticism when venturing beyond facts to the subjective territory of values. Jeff Cooper, a fourth-grade teacher, expresses here the concerns of many:

> [One of the things you confront in art are questions like]: What does this song really say? What does this picture really say? You begin to question society's conventions. The artists were trying to get into val-

---

[1] In this volume we often refer to the arts as one entity. Commonalities among the arts are apparent in philosophy and in the broader, more general, educational goals. Aestheticians examine the arts as one discipline and attempt to arrive at all-encompassing meanings (Cassirer, 1944; Kant, 1827/1969; Langer, 1956).

ues. But many people don't want to teach values clarification. Realistically speaking, we are a social institution giving students ideals and guidelines for living in our society. But my ideals or values, many times, are not the same [as the parents']. A conflict between home and school can be academically damaging to the student.

Teaching The Different Arts

Major differences in the pedagogy of the four arts are rooted in differences in the art forms as well as in their historical and political evolution into schools. Important, too, are the different symbol systems, materials, techniques, and teachers' ability to draw on availability of curricular organizers (e.g., textbooks, school productions). Another difference is the cultural associations for each of the arts and the larger traditions of our society. The impact of cultural associations and concepts (e.g., those of text as compared with body movements, sounds, colors and shapes) on arts education is subtle but powerful.

Not only do different arts employ different media, but different materials function differently within each of the arts. Thus, the function of sound in poetry is different from its function in music and is different still from its function in drama. Movement, colors and shapes are functionally different in dance, in drama and in opera. Different notations—symbolizing specific aspects of the respective art—shape the art forms. Let us examine some of these influences of notation in the larger society. The cultural products of literate societies are different from those of oral societies. (See, for example, Ong, 1982; Barry, 1928/1971). One important difference is in composition, in terms of redundancy versus analytic linearity. Music evolving in musically non-literate traditions (e.g., Blackfoot Indians, the middle-eastern Bedouins, or improvised jazz) is structurally different from the occidental classical forms of symphonies and concerts, the latter featuring more themes and a more complex analytic development. These differences are even greater in verbal art forms—the *Bible*, Homer's *Iliad* and *Odyssey* as compared with modern literature. Redundancy is natural to temporal activities, thought and speech, music and dance. As Ong pointed out, in a primary oral medium, conceptualized knowledge not repeated soon vanishes. Oral societies invest great energy in saying over and over again what has been learned.

These differences of notation carry over to the arts education scene. Schools are to a great extent visual and spatial, emphasizing ready-made codifications into well-defined meanings. Visual arts and drama (in as much as it centers around written text, which it typically does) can use familiar materials. Music and dance follow different rules, not lending themselves easily to denotation. Their symbol systems utilize abstract qualities (like rhythm, texture, or form) as primary materials inherently different from that of common language. Music and dance are accessible to relatively few. Not surprisingly, the manifestations of music and dance in the schools tend to be the simplest and highly repetitive (see for example, in Chicago's Armstrong School the kindergarten music lessons and the dance for the "Bunny Frolic"). Compared with abstract musical parameters, lyrics are easy to learn. In both music and drama, we find an emphasis on words but little on enunciation, emphasis on rhythm but little on articulation and dynamic. In all the school arts, and especially in elementary school, the emphasis is on the "what" rather than the "how," stronger emphasis on verbal elements, venturing little into those other intelligences (Gardner, 1985) that arts educators highlight in their plea for arts education in the school.

Teacher Expertise. Classroom teachers' beliefs reflected these differences. Most classroom teachers we observed did not feel comfortable teaching music. Asked to prioritize, they decidedly felt more comfortable about teaching the visual arts. The following quotation was typical of what many teachers said:

> If they told me to teach music, I'd do it with a record player. So would the majority of the teachers in this district. Kids could sing along with the record. I was in choir in high school and, if I studied real hard, I could read the music, maybe. But it would be very, very difficult. I would fare better in teaching art. I don't think it's as rigid as music can be, as exact. I can be more flexible in art.

It is possible that teacher role as authority figure in language literacy accentuates (in their own eyes) their lack of musical literacy. Unlike music, the visual arts seem not to require special education; anybody can recognize colors and shapes, anybody can cut and glue.

Partly as a result of teachers' beliefs about music and visual arts and their priorities in requesting specialists, partly due to district priorities and the history of teaching the arts at the elementary level in the U.S. (e.g., an established history of music education as compared with dance as a non-curricular activity), music, more than other subjects, is likely to be taught by specialists. Dance shares with music the level of specialization required but not the tradition in the U.S. curriculum. When dance is taught, it too is likely to be taught by specialists—most often artists-in-residence. Specialists, in turn, shape the use of materials and resources, determine schedules, contents and pedagogies.

Both music and dance are taught by people often involved in community activities (e.g., conducting local choirs). In contrast, the visual arts and drama are typically taught by classroom teachers who lack formal background in the arts. A few classroom teachers have taken an art class or two not perceived as relevant at the time and the content of which they had long forgotten. That lack of background shapes a paradigm of art which we shall examine in a later section. It also influences teacher ability to draw on curricular organizers such as textbooks, their ability to develop and to use curricular guides. Finally, our observations showed time and again that classroom teachers with little background in the arts had little interest in attending and learning from artists-in-residence or other resource people in the arts when they were available.

Availability of resources and teacher ability to use them impact each other, creating a positive or negative cycle. The few textbooks (such as Laura Chapman's *Discovery Art*) did not make it to the library or teachers' rooms. Popular among teachers were a potpourri of popular magazines, inservice materials, and projects-craft books. Whereas music textbooks usually offer a structure and a systematic approach, in art the burden of creating a pedagogically sound curriculum out of an arbitrary collection of sources was left to teachers who lacked the requisite background. The lack of sequence and development of knowledge and skills was not perceived as a problem. As a result of the lack of teachers' background in the arts and the lack of resources, teachers chose projects that were mainly easy to teach, easy to manage, and attractive to youngsters. The result was a series of short projects, little development of or building on previously learned skills.

Our observations indicated that non-specialists seldom ventured into history or appreciation of the arts. Consequently, of the four arts, music was the most likely to include some degree of appreciation and history. Visual arts (with an occasional exception in the gifted program or in the hands of an artist-in-residence) and the rarer instances of dance and drama revolved around production.

Most districts had specific curriculum-guides in music and art. Music guidelines had been developed by music specialists and reflected knowledge of the subject matter and expectations grounded in classroom experience. Sometimes, guidelines existed but nobody in the school knew about them. Supervision of arts instruction existed often no more than that the principal required teachers to hand in children's art projects once a month, to change bulletin boards, or to prepare songs for an upcoming school program. Curriculum guides for dance or drama were a rarity.

The specific curricula in each of the subject matters dictated a different pedagogical approach. Music classes manifested a group work, teacher-centered approach. Children tended to do things as a whole class, playing songs on recorders, singing together, dancing within a group, listening to the teacher as he/she didactically explained musical concepts, or listening to a recording of a musical piece. The same is true for the rarer instances of drama and dance. In the performing arts, the goal was usually a whole group performance to be presented to a larger public.

In contrast, the subject matter of the visual arts was characterized by individual work, each child doing his/her own project. The projects were often similar—Valentine hearts and Easter bunnies, sometimes different, as in the free project lessons. Whether a choice was given or not, in visual art, one person's choice did not affect the class as a whole. There were exceptions. Making murals, initiated by out-of-school specialists (e.g., in Anacortes and in Armstrong and Dumas schools in Chicago) were an important exception. Still, messages about teamwork and collaboration were important in the arts curriculum.

Resources. At the schools of our study that had music specialists, music classes were typically held in special music rooms. When crowdedness forced giving up these rooms, they were moved to gyms and lunch room corners. Music rooms, the kingdoms of the music teacher, were typically well equipped with piano, auto harps, recorders, rhythm instruments (e.g., Orff drums, triangle bells), as well as record player, music books, and "musical decorations" (e.g., pictures of instruments, of composers). In contrast, a room dedicated to art was not common; art was taught in the regular classroom.

Music budgets often recognized specific needs such as tuning and maintenance of instruments or the acquisition of new instruments. Music textbooks were provided by districts. Art resources varied from one school to the other. In some, such as Danville, materials were available to teachers who requested them. The result was that motivated teachers obtained them while others wanted and had nothing.

Construction paper and crayons were common supplies across almost all schools, the poorer schools having shorter supply. Alternatively, teachers were given a minimum budget (often, something of the order of $30 per year) to buy needed materials, which meant that motivated teachers spent their own money. The more affluent districts, like Plymouth Meeting, had beautifully equipped rooms with everything from kilns to sinks, irons (to iron colors), long tables which provided more space for clay and print making. Materials for drama—costumes, curtains, sets—were uncommon. Drama space was near the school auditorium and gym, fulfilling a variety of roles. Materials for dance (e.g., wooden floors, video-tapes) were typically non-existent.

Some of our schools did have visual arts specialists. Usually, these specialists were well-trained and dedicated to sharing their concepts of what is artistic, how art is expressive and communicative, how to use aesthetic and critical judgment in producing a piece. When they had classrooms of their own, student work was displayed with originals by local artists and reproductions of classical works. Often, non-Western cultures were given attention, especially in response to students' ethnic backgrounds. Students work under such tutelage was not so constrained by demands for conformity—no rows of nearly identical subjects. More media were available for exploration and development of technique, more clay, more watercolor, more watercolor, more sculpture, more charcoal, more pastels. Specialists pushed harder for materials and facilities whereas classroom teachers were more likely to be satisfied with crayons, and, perhaps, tempera paint or watercolors if time and demands for classroom tidiness permitted. Music specialists focused on singing and playing recorders. Use of Orff and other instruments was common. The parameters of rhythm, melody, harmony and form were attended to. History and appreciation were often included, mostly in preparation for an out-of-school performance.

In addition to those inner resources, there were outer resources from which teachers did sometimes draw. Local people, those interested and involved in the arts were one such resource. Many communities, even small towns such as San Sebastian, Texas; Danville, Illinois; and Oakwood, New Hampshire are homes to a painter or two, a civic theatre group, a local band, piano, guitar and violin teachers, a dance studio. Private teachers often grasp their connections to the schools, supplying piano accompanists, preparing performers in the glee club for coordinated movement routines. Many would do more if invited; some who had tried had been turned down. Support from community arts consumers was often not sought.

Underused were performances (live and recorded), museums and galleries, fairs and exhibits, libraries and television (especially public broadcasting)—which could have been video-taped for classroom replay. Even where field trips were constrained by daunting logistic difficulties, professionals and amateurs could have been invited into the school but were not.

In many places, artist residencies were available—some free (as with the Chicago A.R.T. program), some available as grants from states (as from the Washington State Department of Education), some on a fee basis (as with Chicago's Urban Gateway Program).

Resources were important to learning. Equally important were the contexts of learnings. There were differences in classroom teaching when taught by the regular teacher compared to an in-school specialist or artist-in-residence; differences between any classroom teaching and the visiting performances in the school; differences between performances in the school and those in city concert halls and civic centers. Settings facilitate a certain set of mind. One invoked by the pilgrimage to the Krannert Center of Champaign was different from ones invoked by the familiar setting of the classroom. Performance, whether in or out of school, promotes the magic of music, enhancing the stage charisma of a performer. In a school situation, performers address eras, styles, cultures. Classroom learning is typically sequential whereas the one-time performances tended not to be followed. Development of skills (e.g., practicing enunciations, playing recorders, acquiring music notation) requires continuity. The building of attitudes and appreciation also needs continuity. Less tangible, less measurable, the role of continuity in building attitudes remains unacknowledged. Occasional exposures are seen by principals and teachers to evoke these attitudes. Critical listening skills were not a priority, perhaps because listening is associated with the more passive skills. In a society that emphasizes the active, the *doing*—listening is not regarded as a priority.

Contrast Between Belief and Practice

As we scanned *what is* in terms of arts education programs, we were intrigued by the relationship of actual offerings and practices to teacher beliefs. In this section we examine classroom teacher beliefs (discussed in greater detail in the Danville case-study) as reflected in their own practice. Teacher beliefs often contrast with their own practice. The context of schooling, as well as its aims and goals, provide us with a useful framework to understand these discrepancies. Our case studies portray lessons where following directions is primary, singing, cutting/gluing/coloring were the basic skills. Artworks, better characterized as "cute" than "expressive," were strikingly similar from school to school. So was the singing of songs in terms of expression. Most art lessons could be summed up as a pleasant experience, few seemed to invite *aesthetic* experience.

Teachers provided little guidance toward aesthetic qualities, individual experimentation with materials and ideas, or tools to convey expressivity. When choices existed (pink or blue, six or eight whiskers) they typically remained technical, rather than broadening visions or promoting understanding. An on-going evaluation of students' work consisted mostly of checking to see that they performed the task at hand, that directions had been followed. Acknowledgements consisted of expressions of personal likes or dislikes ("How neat," "I like that!" "Our first bunny!") with few attempts to substantiate and rarely referring to a quality in the work.

This is what many do. It is different from what they claim to believe. Recall the conversations with classroom teachers in the Danville case study and others. Goals expressed by teachers had to do with art as experience ("I think that anything that you do, that makes you think and makes you react, is art."); with art as the reflection of the spirit ("For me, art is a reflection of the inner self, whether its yours or someone's else."); with the role of art as promoting self-esteem ("I think it helps them to feel better about themselves. I think it builds their self-esteem. It makes them feel positive, that they were able to do something on their own."); and legitimizing uniqueness and self expression ("I try to teach my kids through the arts that they are unique human beings. What they have to offer, no one else has to offer."). Thus, we find a harsh discrepancy between what teachers do and what they say, routinized activities and products against the belief in expression.

Grading and Evaluation. Both music and art had general categories—satisfactory, unsatisfactory, excellent—for grades. In both, "satisfactory" was almost universally awarded. In the absence of more specific criteria, student effort was primary. The grading system reflected general belief in the formation of attitudes rather than measuring achievements in the arts. There were additional reasons for not giving more evaluative grades. In music, these were mostly technical. The group structure (i.e., singing and playing recorders as a group) as well as the temporal nature of music, makes individual evaluation difficult. In the visual arts as we shall see again later on, the lack of evaluation was partly due to teacher feelings of inadequacy to critique children's works. In lack of other criteria, such as technical or formal aspects of the artwork, evaluation was viewed as an evaluation of the child's personality and inborn talent, rather than specific skills.

A lack of criteria for evaluating art reinforced the ambivalence of purpose. ("If it satisfies you, then its art." "We don't tell them that what they do is ugly, or no, that's not right. Because it's whatever they want to make of it.") As the unique aspects of art were emphasized, teachers maintained that there are no criteria for evaluation. In visual arts, the only criterion sometimes was *artist satisfaction*. If indeed art is the expression of the individual inner self, how can it be judged? The notions that art could not and should not be evaluated came up when teachers talked about grading in art ("Art to me should not be graded; It's a personal thing. Who am I to say—no one is going to tell me that my art work is lousy, it may be great for me. So I have this bad thing for grading art. I always give S's unless it is an exceptional, exceptional case"). In music, singing in pitch was a gift rather than something acquired. Teacher avoidance of critical evaluation was closely tied with the perceived role of art as promoting self-esteem and expressing uniqueness.

Such goals and concerns about grading were expressed by teachers across grade and ability levels. Implicit in teacher talk about art as a reflection of the inner self and about their reluctance and inability to judge that reflection is the assumption that the reflection is spontaneous, "natural." They failed to address the cognitive processes that mediate an artistic idea and its expression as a *work* of art. Few teachers referred to art as an activity that involves thought, analysis, mental engagement. Few mentioned the teaching and learning of skills and knowledge, the refinements of aesthetic sensitivities, the experimentations, trials and errors, and decision making necessary to produce artworks. Teacher views highlighted self-expression and individuality, not the cognitive, deliberate and cultural. Interviews with school administrators and parents revealed that many of them shared this popular view of art as unique, unevaluable self-expression. While it is true that art often articulates feelings, the translation of feelings into artworks as well as the meaningful consumption of artworks requires an intellectual drawing on artistic traditions and techniques.

The Nature of Art. Teacher avowals about art revealed four underlying, interrelated views about the nature of art: (a) art is the exclusive domain of emotions (in contrast to cognition); (b) works of art are seen as direct manifestations of artists' emotions; (c) artist and audience emotions are interchangeable; (d) art is subjective, personal and individual (in contrast to inter-subjective and cultural). The merit in art is in its uniqueness and the original vision. These avowals are challenged by the idealists and their followers (e.g., Eisner, Cassirer, Goodman, Gombrich, Langer) who have spoken of making art also as a cognitive activity—thinking and problem solving within a variety of media and through various modes of representation. Eisner (1982b) and Perkins (1977) pointed out that our culture at large often regards the cognitive and the affective as two distinct, independent states.

Many teachers talked about emotions in a generic form, referring interchangeably to artist's emotions, to the feelings communicated within an artwork, and to audience emotions in experiencing art. A lack of distinction between artists and audience fits the spontaneity attributed both to the act of creation and to art consumption. Susanne Langer (1957) distinguished between the feelings of the artist and those articulated in the work of art when she pointed out that an artist working on a tragedy need not be in personal despair or violent upheaval. "Nobody," says Langer, "could work in such a state of mind; his mind would be occupied with the causes of his emotional upset." The distinction between self and artistic expression is crucial to the artistic process. Self-expression does not require composition and lucidity. It does not require mastery of skills and knowledge of traditions. Langer's vivid example of a screaming baby who gives his feeling far more release than any musician makes her point that a work of art makes feeling *perceivable* through a *symbol*, not inferable from a symptom. What artists express, then, is not necessarily their own actual feelings and ideas, but what they *know* about human feelings.

Teachers' implicit distinction between emotion and cognition appeared closely related to a distinction between the subjective and objective. Teachers referred to the subjective aspects of art in highlighting the uniqueness of artwork, their inability to evaluate artworks. The concept of intersubjectivity was rarely alluded to.

A fourth implicit underlying distinction in teachers' views of art was the view that doing art is *spontaneous* rather than *deliberate*. The erroneous association of emotions with spontaneity may be traced to the confusion between *feeling* emotions and *reacting* on them. That confusion is apparent in that even though we are more likely to react on the basis of heated emotions, we also react on the basis of thoughts and concepts, a "cooler" mode. Teachers' neglect of the role of planning, experimenting, and making decisions on the one hand, implying that artistic process is immediate on the other, creates the illusion of spontaneity and ease in the act of creating. William Butler Yeats refers to the consequent lowly status of artists as a result of deceptive ease:

> A line will take us hours maybe;
> Yet if it does not seem a moment's thought,
> Our stitching and unstitching has been naught.
> Better go down upon your marrow-bones
> And scrub a kitchen pavement, or break stones
> Like an old pauper, in all kinds of weather;
> For to articulate sweet sounds together
> Is to work harder than all these, and yet

> Be thought an idle by the noisy set
> Of bankers, schoolmasters, and clergymen
> The martyrs call the world.

— "Adam's Curse," by W.B. Yeats (1954)

As Yeats' words convey, it requires much effort to achieve apparently effortless, natural effects, effort not recognized by ordinary people. While many non-artists are oblivious to the toils and skills involved in producing artworks, practitioners in the arts have always operated on these knowledges, from ancient apprenticeships through the medieval guilds to our present schools of art. The curricula and practice of schools of all the arts attest to the importance of knowledge in production and invention, the knowledge of a vocabulary of forms and styles, media and materials. Individuality and original vision are important but they operate within and build upon existing schemas and knowledge. That is true not only for performers, conductors, and directors, but also of composers, artists and writers. Bernard Shaw, Rembrandt and Raphael, Palestrina, Bach and Handel are among those who used idioms of their times to achieve great expressive power. But even those revolutionaries such as Beckett and Ionesco, Beethoven, Debussy, Schoenberg, Monet and Picasso explored new artistic languages only in the contexts of familiarity with the past.

The view of spontaneity in the arts may be nurtured by our need to create heros and enhance the magic of creation. Despite much evidence to the contrary (e.g., artists' numerous drafts and revisions of a painting, a play or a musical composition), artwork is often regarded as a spontaneous act.

The creation of art involves active mental and physical effort. Its consumption, however, can happen on many different levels from the most superficial exposure to a deeper meaningful experience. While few artists can live with the notion that art is spontaneous, audiences can and do, particularly the audience that associates art with entertainment. It is particularly those teachers whose contact with the arts is from the perspective of the "audience" who view art as a spontaneous act. But an even more powerful factor in that view is the contextual role of school as we see in the following section.

Consequences for Classroom Practice of Art. Teachers' visions of art idealize the expression of children's uniqueness and inner selves. Their classroom practice often focuses on routinized activities and uniform products. The espoused ideology mutates into mechanical instruction. The four beliefs of the nature of art (identified in the previous section) contribute, we believe, to the mechanization. The beliefs clash with two key roles of the school in society: (a) the *cognitive* function of school and (b) the *disciplinary* function of school.

The primary role of schooling is widely regarded as the development of students' cognitive faculties, the acquisition of knowledge and the development and training of skills. Cognitive subject matter forms the basis of course content, mainly the academic subjects. Teachers' views of art, however, minimize cognition and knowledge. Accordingly, arts curricula are often lacking in intellectual substance. Rather than deal with a body of critical knowledge and studio skills, arts curricula are largely decorative, entertaining, and associated with the less important aspects of school life. As cognition is marginalized in the definition of art, art is expected to share little in education's cherished values.

The second way in which art and school values clash is subtle. Schools, by definition and function, are heavily structured environments centering around discipline, evaluation, and following rules (cf. Dreeben, 1968; Henry, 1966; Jackson, 1968). Schools aim to produce a similitude of results. They inculcate rules rather than break them. They are advocates of clear and well-defined standards. But these are the very opposites of the values many teachers associate in the abstract with art. The open-endedness and lack of criteria by which arts are beheld is incompatible with the omnipresent school practice of evaluation and the production of accountable results. Equally unacceptable is the expression of unique feelings and emotions. The school aims to reshape and subdue these feelings of independence rather than nurture and promote them.

As a result of these discrepancies, teachers find themselves in a double-bind when called upon to integrate the arts into the curriculum. Two sets of values are a dissonance: the open-ended, criteria-free, individualistic, experiential and exploratory on the one hand; the pre-determined, rule-governed, authoritative, disciplinary and structured on the other. Not only does arts instruction require the integration of different *contents*, it also involves a whole set of *pedagogies* which teachers typically have little practice in. How does this discrepancy resolve itself in classroom practice? A few teachers opt for art as respite from school. But as we observed time and again, the unique, open-ended aspects of art are regularly given up for the disciplining aspects of school. Assignments are based on imitation, where criteria are clear and easy to judge (e.g., cutting according to patterns). The reconciliation of the need to evaluate (as a means to maintain authority) with teachers' disdain of negative feedback in the arts, is done by giving unchallenging assignments in which everybody (that is everybody who tries) can succeed.

In the process of adjusting their concepts of art to academic practice, teachers give up an important, perhaps their most cherished, perception of art—expressivity and experience. The same imbalance between holistic and fragmented style, between the experiential and the mechanical, prevalent in academic subjects, prevails here too. In the ever-lasting pendulum swing between basics and the holistic, the current emphasis is on isolated skills, clearly measurable achievements, and standardized test-scores. Experiential meanings are often neglected within the school. Teachers and principal alike sense the loss, lament the imbalance. The arts, symbolizing the essence of experience and intuition, are regarded by teachers as capturing these lost qualities. Introducing more of the arts into the school promises for many to restore some balance. But the discrepancy is too large. As we so often heard, the pressure towards academics and achievements is much too strong for art to be legitimized. Only those few classroom teachers who have artistic background and most specialists, those who have practiced art seriously, have an alternative, realistic set of schemas and paradigms for teaching the arts. They also have the specific knowledge of subject-matter contents and of skills to do it. Our observations disclosed that many of these teachers were able to provide a middle ground between rigid and open-ended extremes, creating a domain where feelings can be conceptualized in materials and different modes of presentations, addressing the core of arts discipline, drawing on conceptual organizers inherent to the arts, e.g., form, texture, loudness, articulation. For the rest, an easy way to resolve that conflict was to adhere to recipe-like activities that imitate what is done in other subjects.

Deep-rooted ideas shape our aspirations and behaviors. As long as stereotypical views of art prevail; as long as the arts are regarded as a domain that cannot be taught and should not be evaluated; as long as there are no criteria for progress and learning; and most importantly, as long as the eminence of art in human knowledge remains unrecognized, art lessons are likely to remain as they are. To change practices of art instruction requires "consciousness raising," acknowledging that much of what is expressed is rooted in our culture and learned symbol system: a vital part of general education.

Chapter 12:
The Arts and Educational Leadership

Educational leadership, particularly the instructional leadership of principals, draws increasing research interest (see, for example, Maehr and Fyans, 1990; Krug, 1990). Our studies incidentally reflect that the relationship between arts education and leadership may be crucial in at least two ways: (1) because the arts are generally not considered integral to basic education, extraordinary leadership is necessary to ensure a genuine place in the curriculum; and (2) the creative habits of mind fostered by the arts correlate remarkably with effective instructional and administrative leadership.

In our research design, leadership at first was not an organizing issue but it became one. We expected to find—and did find—charismatic people of influence at various levels of school district hierarchy. But our collective experience and knowledge of the field pointed us in other directions: toward community influences on school arts in Anacortes and Danville, toward socioeconomic status and proximity to professional artists in Plymouth Meeting and Armstrong Elementary School in Chicago, toward ethnic proclivities in San Sebastian, and toward cherishing in general and its potential for transfer to the arts in Las Lomas, California. The exception perhaps was Principal Sylvia Peters at Alexandre Dumas Elementary, an all Afro-American school, in Chicago. Two visits to Dumas convinced us to examine the vitality of the arts there attributable to the generative and enthusiastic influence of Peters.

No, leadership as an issue just grew, like Harriet Beecher Stowe's Topsy, increasingly prominent as a way of understanding whether and why the arts flourished in American classrooms. Where we found the arts thriving, we found instructional leadership at some level committed to arts education.

Notions of Leadership

Like former U.S. Supreme Court Justice Potter Stewart, who said on the subject of pornography, "I don't know how to define it but I know it when I see it," we were uncomfortably aware that we seemed to recognize leadership in school settings, to sense its effects on arts education, but that we could not see requisite leadership traits or essential personality characteristics across situations. Not unexpectedly, the healthier, livelier classrooms were inevitably tended by a conscientious teacher. Dedication was important but not enough to guarantee robust arts learnings, for some dedicated teachers' classroom walls were hung with monotonous rows of nearly identical student work, their definitions of art interchangeable with their definitions of merely decorative handicrafts. Further, although nearly every administrator said the arts were important in his or her school district, most administrators were not seen as highly supportive by arts educators.

Nor did training unfailingly lead to instructional leadership in the arts. Dedication appeared to be necessary if not sufficient for exciting arts classes but some untrained teachers could produce that excitement and some trained teachers failed to produce it. For example, Beatrice Slattery in San Sebastian was trained to teach social studies but had brought her students to an eagerness for arts concepts and skills and appreciation. Similarly, a retired minister hired to teach visual arts in the K-12 school at tiny Wartrace, Tennessee favorably impressed Fifty States correspondent Wanda Johnson (Mabry *et al*, 1989). Turned around, Teri Marinari in Pennsylvania could teach the formal elements of music amazingly efficiently and thoroughly but it looked as though she and her students hated every minute of it. Other well-trained arts specialists felt their opportunity to lead constrained by lack of time or itinerancy. Yet those who led were as log-jammed as the rest.

Although important, facilities and resources neither ensured nor precluded student engagement in the arts. For instance, Dumas Elementary lacked facilities and supplies but embraced the arts and connected with professional arts opportunities in Chicago. And Colonial Elementary had much the most luxurious facilities we saw and, in many ways, an enviable arts program but largely ignored the rich arts possibilities of nearby Philadelphia.

Dedication, training, facilities and resources, and community opportunities certainly can benefit arts education but, at each site we studied, arts education was unique, a product of its special contexts and peculiar influences. Generalizations were hard to come by. Still, we discovered that, where we admired arts education, we found arts leadership.

Like the arts education situations we saw, leaders were unique—yet some commonalities were apparent. Recent literature on the subject of educational leadership (especially the writings of John Gardner, 1988-89) assisted analysis on this point. The following examples from our data offer evidence for two claims: one, leaders are needed to cultivate arts education and, two, arts education cultivates leaders.

Pat Iannelli. In Plymouth Meeting, Pennsylvania, where Pat Iannelli worked as a district fine arts curriculum coordinator before becoming a principal, community interest in academics and sports overshadowed arts education. Several years ago, a demographic downturn cut faculty positions drastically, leaving many music and visual arts specialists with part-time assignments and bruised professional egos. Coordinator Iannelli encouraged the staff's sense of professionalism and promoted the cause of arts education at the district level with tenacity and political skill. Her requests were usually granted if arguments were well-reasoned; the superintendent consented to her pursuing requests with the Board of Education, and the board nearly always responded favorably. Under Iannelli, the fine arts reached administrative equality with academic and other subject areas, gaining a curriculum coordinator, a separate budget, and continuous formal curriculum development. Although some were to divide energies between two or three schools, arts specialists were assigned full-time to their areas of specialization.

Iannelli set goals in line with an overall mission and worked hard to establish an enhanced place for the arts in the schools of her district. She sought a place where arts teachers could work productively and could share ideas in developing local arts education. Although a minority voice in her district, Iannelli was well-respected for leadership in arts education.

Carolyn Sommers. In San Sebastian, Texas, Carolyn Sommers was also a district curriculum coordinator who became a principal by request. Her tiny school was located in a remote, weathered fishing village. The community had no library, no movie theater, no piano teacher. Sommers welcomed the remoteness: "The people in the district office forget about me 'way out here and I can do what I like."

What she liked was the arts. She wore funky, hand-painted clothes; fresh flowers adorned her office; each day, a few children were invited to a table in the cafeteria set with silver and candles and flowers to be recognized for some accomplishment or other. At PTA meetings she told how the arts could be brought into homes. Until 1988, her school had never had an arts specialist. Sommers wrote letter after letter, thanking the district for the art and music teachers she was confident they would send her. She also upgraded academic learning and, when her school out-performed on standardized tests the other elementary schools in the district, her request was not refused. She not only got both music and visual arts specialists, she hand-picked them herself.

Sommers pursued a vision. She defined a mission for her staff. Ubiquitous in her small school, she monitored progress. She established a pleasant and productive workplace. She focused her school and made a difference in the lives of her students and community. She exercised leadership.

Sylvia Peters. Sylvia Peters was an Afro-American principal of an all-Afro-American inner city Chicago school, Alexandre Dumas Elementary. When she arrived five years before this study, it was a dirty school inhabited by two warring camps: children victimized by poverty, neglect, and violence; and teachers whose primary goal was to maintain enough order to survive the day. There were no visual arts or music specialists in Chicago's public elementary schools. Peters fired some teachers and some almost got *her* fired. And she did a few other things: she focused on teaching children as an aspect of caring about them and their families; she instituted strong curricula, especially in reading and character education; she cleaned up the school building—covering it with student murals and art, setting plants and a park bench in the foyer, planting flowers outside. She brought in the arts partly as a way to connect students with mainstream American culture, to help them express their confusions and dreams, to enrich their lives. She quoted poetry as she visited classrooms, an almost daily visitor. If she didn't show up, students were likely to send work to her, so important was her recognition of their efforts.

Artists and performers were brought into the school; field trips occurred regularly, sometimes even on Saturday. Dumas instituted the first in-school Suzuki violin program in the city. Teachers were inspired and enthusiastic, integrating the arts into as much of the school day as the limitations of their training permitted. Peters encouraged them to get the paints out and let the classrooms get messy. Students contributed annually—or more often—to art exhibits at the Oak Woods Cemetery gallery across the street. The public address system announced school pride in the children's chorus, in a student contributing to a publisher's reading textbook, and in various other accomplishments. One theme in Peters's efforts was,

"This school may be in the ghetto but this is *not* a ghetto school!" The reverberations of that statement could be heard in every corner of Dumas Elementary.

Against punishing odds, Peters was a determined leader, nowhere more persistent than in giving her students knowledge and appreciation of the arts. Her strong sense of mission was contagious, attracted the attention of a nearby business, and inspired litter pick-up in the school neighborhood. The faculty uniformly said that the arts were important in their school because the arts were important to their principal. "She doesn't force you to get into the arts," one teacher told me, "but, when you see how much fun everyone is having, you don't want to be left out!" Peters worked consciously to share power and responsibility with faculty and parents, to encourage sharing ideas and support. She modeled leadership and she developed it in those around her.

Arline Hersh. Dr. Arline Hersh, principal of Armstrong Elementary School in Chicago, had discovered as a teacher that role-playing helped maintain student attention. In her first principalship in 1983 at an all Afro-American school, the arts were used to improve attendance from 86% to 93%. At Armstrong, Hersh actively sought out artists-in-residence and other programs. She assigned teachers to participate in holiday programs. Although she lacked a deep understanding of the arts, she expended energy and know-how in offering arts exposure to students.

Not only administrators, who are in hierarchical positions endowed with influence, but also teachers may exercise leadership. While it could be argued that teachers' instructional leadership is inherent in the job, we found teachers whose influence extended beyond their classrooms to their administrators, other teachers, and their communities. Judy Rudnicke in Danville and Beatrice Slattery in San Sebastian are examples. Less easily defined is the leadership of teachers like Wilma Spangler in Plymouth Meeting who work within the confines of their own classrooms and committees and whose influence beyond classrooms is less obvious, less direct. Some examples of teachers' leadership follow.

Phyllis Ennes. As librarian, chair of the Cultural Education Planning Committee, and teacher of speech and drama at Anacortes Middle School, Ennes raised expectations for quality in artistic work and experience. By example, and by arranging special experiences for students, she helped other teachers raise standards. She spotlighted arts education in and out of school saying, "Many people do not understand what we do. We keep attention on children's actual accomplishments. We can anticipate only partly where learning will take children—and us."

Unlike many charismatic organizers, her style was not of exuberance but of subtlety, even sometimes of austerity. Many of her efforts were informal enlistments and encouragements, frowns and strategic protests when expectations appeared to be softening. Her attentions to her own teaching were thorough but her leadership outside classroom and library was never-ending. She recognized educational talent and personally supported local artists, parents, and professional colleagues, drawing them into school programs in ways far beyond the specification of district or state requirements.

Judy Rudnicke. A drama major as an undergraduate student, Judy Rudnicke taught gifted third graders in Danville. She contributed to her school's theatrical productions, sometimes by writing original scripts. She was also enthusiastic about visual arts, talking vivaciously about her excursions to museums and sharing with colleagues her ideas and reproductions by her favorite artist, Renoir. Her influence extended beyond her own classroom to the school *via* theater and advice and suggestion to other teachers.

Beatrice Slattery. Beatrice Slattery in San Sebastian taught visual arts to fourth and fifth graders. Slattery was trained to teach social studies and originally had very little background in visual arts except as a hobbyist in crafts. Employed as a substitute, she was offered the arts position because of her skills at maintaining discipline. In a cramped classroom, insufficient equipment and few supplies prevented her from teaching pottery and photography, for instance, as required by her district's sketchy curriculum guide. Still, she committed the curriculum guide to file cards and organized her continually developing activities. These activities covered as many media as she found materials for, basic concepts like color and form, and some art history and appreciation. Aware of the absence of theater instruction at her school and with the help of a music teacher, she introduced weekly in-school classes on poetry recitation and puppetry.

Slattery taught visual arts to each student in her school twice a week for half an hour at a time. To make the most of these short periods, she trained them to find materials and immediately set to work on ongoing projects, such as sandpaintings of Southwest Indian motifs. Informal discussion punctuated an atmosphere in which all students, with the occasional exception of her own daughter, were observed working busily on their projects. Educating herself as well as her students, she presented the work of famous artists and encouraged beginning appreciation of abstract art—which students and the small community found nearly incomprehensible.

Slattery's situation is familiar to many in arts education: little valuing, little instructional time, little teacher preparation. In such situations, there is usually little student learning. But in this case, Slattery went well beyond her district's expectations in setting goals. She established a task-oriented arts workplace and geared for both formal instruction and informal discussion.

Wilma Spangler. Wilma Spangler at Colonial Elementary School in Plymouth Meeting had little in common with Beatrice Slattery besides teaching visual arts to fourth and fifth graders. Spangler was a well-trained specialist in the arts who continued her education through arts workshops and seminars. Her classroom, especially designed for visual arts classes, was large and airy and contained large, steady worktables and stools for students, a kiln, a sink, abundant cupboards and cabinets, a glass display case, and other helpful items. What she yearned for was more instructional time than one period per week, an allocation which limited the kinds of activities she could develop.

Spangler's lessons went beyond the specifications in her district curriculum guide, a guide which she helped develop and which was continually revised in a five-year cycle of review, revision, pilot-testing, and implementation. Her lessons included various media, Western and non-western cultural expression and appreciation, technical exploration and craftsmanship, critical judgment, and aesthetics. In a voice sometimes barely above a whisper, she would introduce a project, discuss its historical underpinnings, demonstrate for the group a project's basic techniques and suggest possible variations, then consult with students individually on problems of artistic production. Her students attended to what she had to say and show, readily offered questions and comments, oriented to tasks quickly and persisted to completion, shared their problems and products with each other, and took turns politely—in short, they behaved pretty much as Wilma Spangler did.

Although she had worked on the district's visual arts curriculum, it was primarily within her classroom that Spangler showed leadership—in setting instructional goals which adapted and expanded the district curriculum, in steering an implicit course toward artistic skills and understanding and enjoyment, in monitoring student progress and achievement, and in creating a climate in which children eagerly learned and shared.

Research on Educational Leadership. These examples illustrate educational leadership. Based on long experience, former U.S. Secretary of Health, Education, and Welfare, John Gardner has written insightfully about leadership. Leadership is not tidy. Decisions are made and then revised or reversed. Misunderstandings are frequent, inconsistency inevitable. Achieving a goal may simply make the next goal more urgent. Inside every solution are the seeds of new problems (Gardner, 1988a).

In social situations, including schools, reaching goals and solving problems requires the exercise of power, which Gardner defined as "the capacity to ensure desired outcomes and prevent undesired ones" (Gardner, 1988d, p. 77). Leadership should not be, but often is, confused with status or prestige. Power may derive from a person's position or from intrinsic qualities, such as persuasiveness or beauty. Leaders always have some power but not all power-holders have leadership.

While leadership can be a potent influence, many factors contribute to social activity, including a group's internal dynamics, environment, and history. Recognizing that no leader ever fully controls outcomes helps in understanding why even diligent arts education leaders enjoy only limited success. The stereotypic image of leaders as smiling cult heroes trailed by an adoring entourage rarely fits leaders in education and even less often in arts education (Murphy, 1988). Scrappy opportunists, they practice the art of the possible, often creating the very possibilities within which they extend their influence. They know they are the caboose on the long train of educational priorities but they are not content to bump along silently. They are leaders in dissent, a minority in a context so indifferent or hostile that simple preservation of arts education is no small accomplishment.

Leadership develops within and in response to specific social realities; no traits guarantee effective leadership in all situations (Gardner, 1989a). Still, researchers have attempted to identify distinguishing characteristics of leaders (see, for example, Fuhr, 1989 and Gardner, 1989b). Gardner's list includes:

- They think longer-term than most people.

- They grasp the relationship of their unit and its task to the larger organization and to external contexts.

- They influence people beyond their organizational boundaries.

- They emphasize intangibles like vision, values, motivation.

- They possess the political skill to cope with the conflicting requirements of multiple constituencies.

- They renew and revise (rather than merely accept) structure and processes to fit an ever-changing reality (Gardner, 1988a).

In addition, he found,

> ...the leader has little choice but to be optimistic. The analyst, the critic, the journalist can afford not to be. But taking a positive view is not something that effective leaders have to work at: it is in their temperament, and no doubt had much to do with their attainment of a leadership role... Leaders must help people believe that they can be effective... (Gardner, 1989)

In schools, the principalship

> ... is the place for people who can recognize that great opportunities are often brilliantly disguised as insoluble problems... The scene may look discouraging—it is a big, noisy society—but principals have the power to make their case. (Koerner, 1988)

Our data offer instances of teachers and administrators recognizing opportunities for arts education within their different spheres of influence.

Leaders direct their attitudes and skills toward such general tasks as envisioning goals, affirming values, motivating others, managing organizations, achieving workable unity among conflicting groups, explaining, representing the group, serving as a symbol, and renewing and preserving values (Gardner, 1988b). Within these generalities, leaders must address particular tasks specific to the situation. Myriad influences within each context create tensions and reciprocal pressures. For example, leaders are never completely in charge nor are their followers completely submissive. Rather, a leader typically acts on personal judgment informed by constituency feedback. Communication skills are practiced at many levels, including the nonverbal and the symbolic. Leadership styles develop within the context of constituent needs and dynamic interaction with the culture partly defining what constitutes good leadership (Gardner, 1989a).

In our culture, some prevalent myths about leadership hamper its exercise. We are inclined to believe that, for every problem, a perfect—preferably simple—solution exists; that good leaders are free of bias; that real power is visible. Leaders themselves may have early faith that the reasonableness of their views will be apparent, that people will understand, that there is sufficient time for reflective and rational decision-making (Tyree, 1988).

We tend to discount intuitive processes in decision-making, intuition defined as an unconscious balancing of evidence and a compelling sense of "rightness" about the decision without certainty about how the conclusion was reached (Raudsepp, 1981). There exists the argument that intuition is needed and utilized for focusing on the whole where details are overwhelming, where time is short, and where complexity is great (Norris & Achilles, 1988)—often the case in schools. But, superintendents and principals in a recent study described themselves as more logical than intuitive, increasingly so at higher rungs on the hierarchical ladder (Norris, 1988).

Let us distinguish between leadership and power. Effective leaders do more than direct. Like Pericles, they refrain from making themselves indispensable. Gardner noted,

> Some individuals who have dazzling powers of personal leadership not only fail to build institutional strength but create dependency in those below them. They leave behind a weakened organization staffed by weakened people. In contrast, leaders who strengthen their people and have a gift for institution-building may create a legacy that will last for a very long time (Gardner, 1988d).

The people we observed and intuitively felt to be leaders, like everyone, wielded power toward desired outcomes. Often theirs was not a simple path from *status quo* to Utopia but a tortuous zig-zag over and around obstacles to quasi-Utopia. Sylvia Peters is a good example. Denied a principalship by the Chicago Board of Education until her potential was noticed by someone with political clout, her sense of Dumas School's mission met early determined resistance from the majority of the faculty and from some parents. Enormous efforts were required to build wide support from an initial cadre, to clean the building, to revamp the curriculum, to forge community connections, to change attitudes. Adjustments were made along the way. Peters maintained her vision through exhaustion and tears, encouraging her growing following and being encouraged by them. She distinguished between disagreements to be countered firmly, those to be handled gently and generously, and those to be ignored. She motivated students and teachers and parents partly by voicing her belief in their possibilities, empowering as well as inspiring them.

Peters' charismatic leadership was of obvious value; the improvements at Dumas were revolutionary and of a kind many would like to implement in our troubled schools. But how do school systems find and empower the people they seem to need? Graduate programs are better at recognizing potential leadership than at producing it. The prerequisite commitment to values can be found and nurtured in existing staff and it can be sought in candidates. We do not know *whether* it is possible to create charismatic leaders, much less *how*.

Current emphasis on compliance to standards and measurable accountability severely restricts divergent thinking and the exploration of personal influence. If schools are to nurture the varying potentials for leadership to be found in their personnel, then schools must learn to appreciate challenge and conflict, must free teachers and principals from conformity requirements. But schools are besieged by problems and criticism from within and without. In such situations, institutions are unlikely to tolerate or grant the very political freedoms which might rejuvenate them.

In arts education, then, the situation is nearly a Catch-22. Undervalued in every sense and manifestation, arts education is desperate for leaders that can create and preserve for it a toe-hold in the schools. But schools' narrowness in curriculum and organization isolates and disempowers arts education leaders and obstructs the development of others.

Persuasive Advocacy: An Arts Need

Two chapters back, we said that arts education across the United States is rarely substantive, often simplistic, and generally oriented toward performance rather than toward the development of creativity or analytic skills. The arts in schools, held in low priority when taught as separate subjects, also take a back seat to academics when subject matters are integrated. Because arts curricula are rarely well-articulated, arts teachers are freer to modify and adapt pedagogy, we said, suggesting this may be a blessing.

How might arts education—or any curricular subject matter—be expected to develop in an atmosphere of low public priority and high pedagogical freedom? Unsurprising are the innumerable variations in arts education to be found in the classrooms of the nation's over 15,000 school districts—a veritable crazy quilt. In his 1988 research for the National Endowment for the Arts, Brent Wilson found:

> There is inconsistency in the arts education that students receive in various parts of the country, in different school districts within states, in different schools within a single school district, and even within a single school.

And

> In practice, most of the curricular decisions regarding visual arts curricula are made by the 50,700 special art teachers and the approximately 576,378 classroom teachers whose responsibility it is to teach art in the schools of the U.S. (Wilson, 1988)

On both national and local scenes, we find social, economic, and other demands jockeying for position on the educational priority list. Always nationally and nearly always locally, we find arts education drained by budgetary shortage and swamped by competition for career training. Americans treat the scientist with reverence, invest dollars and faith in computer and other high-tech industries, and glance askance at that relatively rare curiosity, the artist. Employees gather at factories and laboratories but not at studios; stores run short of Nintendo games but not of paint sets. Suspicion about the practical utility of the arts pervades the national consciousness and limits the value placed on arts education for our offspring. Our kids *need* to learn how to survive in an economically and technologically competitive world. Do they *need* the arts? Most Americans think not. Some parents are satisfied if children enjoy music, pleased if they play an instrument, but see little point in their learning music theory or history or criticism or aesthetics.

Parent and Community Initiative. If parents were clamoring—and supporting tax referenda—for more arts in the school the leadership needs would still exist but would certainly be different. Parents see schools, in large part and increasingly in upper grades, as institutions to prepare their children for gainful employment as adults. Aware of the stereotype of the starving artist, few American parents encourage their sons and daughters to pursue careers in the arts or support childhood activities leading that direction. A typical comment was that of a Texas industrial executive who said, "My family was poor as I was growing up. I'd like my children to find jobs that would support them comfortably. Wouldn't you?"

Our San Sebastian case study showed that parental interest in and support for in- and out-of-school arts education sometimes varies according to ethnic roots. But sometimes ethnic interests overrode economic hindrances. Such data defied easy generalization about ethnic-related trends regarding parent interest in arts education.

Parent interest can be stimulated by student enthusiasm, as at Chicago's Dumas Elementary School. There, the arts were seen partly as a basis for rooting individual self-esteem and school-wide unity in ethnic pride, partly as a door to mainstream culture. Parents willingly and energetically supported the arts opportunities their neighborhood school was beginning to offer. They assisted with field trips, coordinated a Suzuki strings program, attended performances and exhibits, and enlarged the scope of family activities to include the arts.

Clearly, it would be a mistake to think a child's interest in the arts determined by family or ethnicity or socioeconomic status. As ever, children can and do surprise families and friends with vocational and avocational choices. But it is also apparent that these factors play a role in student participation in school arts, especially with middle and high school electives. Community and school attitudes and programs feed or starve student appetites.

Communities reflect and particularize national contexts. Each city and town and rural collective offers its own tradition of arts support and non-support, access and barriers to privilege. Some communities buck the national trend, celebrating the arts in ways that spill over into classrooms—but not many. In Anacortes, Washington, for instance, *community* arts were so strong that many citizens perceived little need for *school* arts. Within communities, pockets of arts interest and involvement are often found—civic theater, church or community choirs, a local artist or two—but their effects on classrooms is usually negligible even when those people *try* to have an effect. We found this to be the case in San Sebastian, Texas and in Danville, Illinois. One might think that cities' art museums, orchestras, live theater, and dance companies would inevitably find their way into schoolrooms. Sometimes they do but often logistics, transportation, funding, and a cascade of other community institutions competing for youth attention make high quality arts experiences inaccessible to all but the most determined. This was the case in Plymouth Meeting, Pennsylvania and Armstrong Elementary School, Chicago.

Facilities, materials, and hirings vary with local conditions. In Chicago Public Schools, many facilities were shockingly poor, materials nearly nonexistent, arts specialists absent. Contrastingly, in Plymouth Meeting, facilities or materials were in good supply and specialists were retained even during a sharp decline in student population.

From district to district, adherence to arts education syllabi also varies. The existence of formal arts curricula is not universal. Where we found arts curricula locally developed by coordinators and teachers and systematically reviewed and revised, as in Plymouth Meeting, curricular documents tended to be familiar to teachers. Guidelines structured course content. Where we found curricular guides prescribed without teacher input, teacher familiarity with and adherence to district objectives were haphazard.

Teachers undoubtedly have the strongest effect on students' arts experiences. Sometimes working in atmospheres of district support, sometimes in indifference. Some arts teachers are knowledgeable, devoted, creative, and inspiring; many who could be so described are specialists. Itinerant specialists, those assigned to two or more schools concurrently, lose time and energy transporting themselves and their materials, lack a familiar home base, and have difficulty perceiving themselves as *bona fide* members of faculties. Where financial belt-tightening occurs, arts specialists often worry that they will be considered expendable. This kind of worry affects teachers' willingness to try innovative approaches to teaching.

Specialists are more likely to take advantage of community arts resources than are classroom teachers required to teach the arts in the absence of specialists. Our Danville study shows that classroom teachers who teach the arts may have personal ties to the arts without sharing their appreciations with students. While classroom teachers of the arts have greater opportunity to integrate the arts into academic subject matter, they may or may not choose to do so. Classroom teachers sometimes respond to standardized student assessment by replacing instruction in the arts for instruction that might lead to higher test scores. Two first-grade teachers in San Sebastian, for instance, said that they hadn't taught art or music for three months, using that time to prepare their six- and seven-year-olds for Texas's statewide student testing.

Much is still unknown but study of contexts helps us understand the variety in arts education, the limited opportunities for lively arts classes, and the need for persuasive and persistent arts advocacy. We generally think American pluralism, our many competing values and activities, healthy. But we sometimes focus on fads that blind us to lasting values. On the other hand, familiarity and custom spotlight certain school aims and relegate the less familiar to increasing darkness. So it is with the arts. The pressure for accountability, the higher relative value accorded academics and technology by communities and schools, budget constraints, and the back-to-basics movement squeeze the arts. Against this national backdrop, it is not surprising that the arts are alive and well—really well—in relatively few classrooms and that the few real leaders must rewin old battles, must persistently and persuasively advocate for the arts against long odds.

Creative Habits of Mind: A Leadership Need

For the National Arts Education Research Center (NAERC), our task was partly to observe and ponder the problems of arts teaching in ordinary elementary schools. We were to describe contexts embedded within contexts, the classroom actors situated within these contexts. Descriptions of teachers, principals, coordinators, and superintendents naturally led to reflection about their effectiveness in these roles: Is Ms. Smith effective? What constitutes effectiveness in Ms. Smith's milieu? What is it about Ms. Smith or the environment that obstructs or enhances effectiveness?

We began to realize that, of the most able elementary principals we encountered during the current studies, most had a background in the arts. Prime examples included Sylvia Peters at Dumas Elementary in Chicago, Carolyn Sommers at Point Aden Elementary in Texas, former fine arts coordinator Pat Iannelli at Conshohocken Elementary in Pennsylvania. The skills that these principals exhibited were similar to the skills required of artists: the creation of novel ideas, adapting available materials and resources, imagining and accessing novel resources, persistence to completion.

There were exceptions. One effective principal with no apparent arts interest was Al Erb at Whitemarsh Elementary in Plymouth Meeting. Remarkably in tune with his various constituencies and alert to their conflicting needs and potential problems, Erb was a popular guiding force about whom only one muted criticism was heard: reluctance to try new ideas.

Jerri Bell in Driftwood, Texas seemed an exception, too—a dynamic principal gaining district and state recognition for significantly raising her students' academic achievement and lowering their drop-out rates when they went on to high school. Clearly Bell was an example of educational leadership, but the arts were not high on her agenda; basic skills and keeping kids in school were, even though Bell had received a drama scholarship in high school and had earned a bachelor's degree in theater.

Emerging from the data was the idea that the arts foster creative habits of mind that are also elements of leadership. Even the two potential exceptions, Erb and Bell, seemed to support this notion. But were we predisposed to find arts-interested administrators? Actually, having assumed that administrators were under-prioritizing arts education, we were surprised to find a few contradictions. We met more principals with little interest in the arts than with strong interest.

Curiosity about the apparent relationship between the arts and effective administrators led to a review of theories of creativity in aesthetics, recent literature on educational leadership (previously discussed), and cognitive psychology studies related to the development of creative insight.

Aesthetic Theories of Creativity. In the aesthetics literature, some theories of creativity focus on how artists generate ideas with seeming ease and fluidity and how they capitalize on those ideas to create something new. Two theories seemed particularly well-developed and reflective of the literature. In one, Monroe Beardsley termed the initial idea for an artwork its "incept" and the stretch of mental and physical activity between the incept and the finished artwork the "creative process." He posited an "inventive" stage in which a new idea is formed in the preconscious mind and enters consciousness as an incept, which itself suggests artistic possibilities. In the ensuing "selective" stage, the artist exercises critical judgment in recognizing and addressing deficiencies and potentialities, continuing until the artwork is completed (Beardsley, 1982).

Second, Larry Briskman argued that there can be no theory of creativity, then paradoxically offered his "Darwinian model" as a theoretical answer to the question, "How is creativity possible?" Based on Darwin's notions of random variation and selective retention, Briskman listed five steps in the process of creating an artwork, a scientific theory, or any other human invention. First, the creator interacts with the familiar relevant background (including such things as content, theory, current thinking and status, and history within the field of endeavor). Second, he "blindly" (but, because of his familiarity with background, not "randomly") generates possible solutions to a problem or possible expressions of an idea or feeling. Third, he evaluates the options he has generated and retains successful partial results. Fourth, merging these partial results with his background knowledge, he generates more options. Finally, he repeats the third and fourth steps as often as needed until he has completed the product (Briskman, 1981).

The two theories are similar in noting the generation of possibilities, with constant evaluation of those options, exercising of critical judgment as to whether the developing product may be wholly or partially satisfactory for its intended purpose, and persistence to completion. These two theories are also similar to descriptions of tasks discharged by leaders. Characteristic leadership tasks:

> envisioning goals;
> focusing energies;
> exercising judgment, making decisions, responding to change in a way that preserves basic values and enhances vitality;
> achieving a workable unity among internal and external conflicts

sound like steps listed in the creative process:

> imagining a goal or incept;
> generating possible solutions or expressions;
> exercising of critical judgment in selecting and retaining partial results;
> recognizing that a piece satisfactorily expresses an idea or emotion.

The tasks of a leader and the tasks of an artist are strikingly alike.

Schema Theory. Schema theory from cognitive psychology emphasizes the role of background, a component of creativity considered vital by Briskman. Schema theory explains why expertise correlates with creative insight. Rumelhart and Norman have said that people develop concepts—representing them as mental schema—in three ways: by adding new information to pre-existing schema ("accretion"), by modifying schema so that the new information can fit in ("tuning"), and by creating new schemata to represent new concepts ("restructuring") (Rumelhart and Norman, 1981). Expertise comes from knowledge (constructing many richly detailed concepts or schemata) and experience (making connections between concepts or schemata through practical application). From this background of knowledge and experience, experts comprehend patterns of relatedness and application options, which are potential springboards for creativity.

Background is also an emphasis in Gardner's list of distinguishing characteristics of leaders. He described leaders as people who grasp the relationship of their unit and its task to the larger organization and to external contexts and who understand intuitively the unconscious elements of their interactions with constituents. The point is that background knowledge helps to explain both how creativity is possible and how leaders use background knowledge creatively to deal with shifting constituent demands.

Creativity and Leadership. Much of an artist's work is imagining expressive possibilities and bringing them to fruition. At each step in that process, he or she critically evaluates the developing creation and imagines what else might be done with it. His or her generating ideas, evaluating and acting upon them, persisting until completion is like that of the leader who envisions goals and works to implement policies and practices that will achieve them. What we noticed about effective leaders in classrooms, schools, and district offices was their ability to come up with ideas for lessons and programs and organizational structures, to adapt these ideas to fit local needs and resources, to persist in imagining and exploiting options until the reality was achieved.

The point is not that artists and leaders are the same. One could argue that cooking and medicine and circus performance also fit the template. The point is that leadership requires creativity and persistence. The leaders we discovered who had arts training *could* exercise creativity and persistence, often outperforming those *without* training in the arts. Many leaders we met could think and act creatively and persistently partly *because* of the habits of mind they had learned *via* the arts.

PART FOUR: THE SEVERAL ARTS

Chapter 13:
The Several Arts

Music Education

Of all the arts, music—and with it, music education—has the strongest tradition in American society. Its recognition in community life dates to colonial days. Music education as a university discipline was established before the beginning of the century. As an educational subject in the schools, music is far more prevalent than theatre, dance, and film education. That there are music textbooks reflects the status of music education as a field; the variety of high-quality textbooks in music is unparalleled in the other arts. Though remaining isolated from much in the arts world, it is the closest the arts share in general education. It enjoys a greater place in general education than the other arts (Broudy, 1990).

We have discussed complex issues in the teaching of music. In schools without music specialists, classroom teachers longed for them more than for any other assistance. We found that trained music teachers based their work on musical concepts and incorporated development of skills within a thoughtful pedagogy. A few taught music theory and music history. In their traditional role as teachers of singing, music specialists developed technical skills such as reading music and playing recorders and introduced such musical parameters as rhythm, pitch, form and orchestration.

When specialists were not available, there was little music in the schools. In each school we found perhaps two or three non-specialist teachers with some performance background, typically in playing piano. By choice or obligation, some conducted music activities with their children; a few helped with other children. Music lessons without specialists featured simple songs, often centering on holidays and seasons. Where we observed, rhythm and pitch were accurate but the more sophisticated musical features, e.g., phrases, articulation, dynamics, harmony, were neglected. Goals, when articulated, were extramusical. In these schools without specialists, rarely was there attention to the development of musical skills. Ours is a society that does not cultivate nuances of sound, nuances of expression. With musical thinking not part of American education and culture, many good teachers, many good administrators, have essentially no knowledge of music education.

In most of our case study schools, teaching music was delegated only to those with specialized training. Listening to music was sometimes initiated by non-specialists, occasionally for the school as a whole. Many teachers were consumers of music. With radios and tape players everywhere, listening is an easy activity to provide. But rarely was time allotted for full-attention listening. Most teachers thought of music as background for eating, reading, working. It supported recreation at recess time and relaxation at the end of the day.

In a culture that places great emphasis on action, listening seems like nothing much to do. As a class activity, listening is a difficult assignment, seeming to need an elusive level of control. As was apparent in our downstate Illinois case study, music specialists and particularly classroom teachers had difficulty developing good listening environments. It may be that children are conditioned not to listen to music. Across the formative years, background radio, television, and Musak appear to be successfully ignored. A kindergartner may already be an expert at ignoring music. Much of the listening teachers request in the classroom also encourages children to be quiet more than to hear. Mobilizing student attention to subtle stimulation is a skill few teachers seem to have. Even more discouraging is the general lack of awareness that it could be different.

Dance Education

Dance has a marginal presence in the schools. Dance education programs are rarities even in college. Most people number many more musicians than dancers among their acquaintances. Radios and tapes allow easy access to music. Access to dance—either for observing or participation—requires technical spaces and equipment. Dance is a less common experience in and out of school.

On those few occasions in which we encountered dance in the elementary schools, it was closely tied to music. Even as synchronous movement—a sometimes part of physical education—music was a common accompaniment. We saw a Danville teacher start her classroom day with movement to the Muppets. In Anacortes a dancer-in-residence used drums and tambourine to set and keep the tempo. The joy of coordinated movement and the energy of the group emerge in marching bands and even in chorus but physical power is most apparent in dance.

As holiday fare, the most common dance activities featured folk and ethnic dancing. Many children got no further than a labored stepping. Except in Anacortes, Washington, and Whitemarsh, Pennsylvania, where dance was led by specialists, kinesthetic awareness was not a goal. Nor was the perception of conceptual organizers such as rhythm, line, texture, and form.

Theatre Education

At our schools, as elsewhere, performance arts have revolved around holidays and school gatherings. Parents and teachers remembered these special occasions, markers of the culture. Principals sometimes helped organize them. Drama and music were important components. Typically the themes were light, the sketches short: a variety show. The repertoire—literary, musical, kinesthetic—was seldom beyond the simplest. It often was festive, occasionally serious and honorific.

Madeleine Grumet (1980) has articulated the connection between school life and theatre:

> Schooling comprehends three forms of theatre. Theatre as ritual is associated with the formal school culture. Theatre as confrontation is associated with the counter-school culture. These first two forms

emerge in the daily interactions of school life, the former providing the ground for the latter. The third form, theatre as a deliberate aesthetic enterprise, most often collapses into the ritual of the school play that legitimizes the formal school culture. Creative dramatics programs celebrate feeling and fantasy but avoid the school situation, severing action from the situation from which it is derived. (p. 93)

The Spring Frolic and Christmas programs—important aesthetic enterprises within our schools—embodied and reflected explicit and implicit school values. Components always were short pieces with quick changes of scene and character, repetition dominating. There was little of depth, subtlety, nuance. The contents, whether messages about the nature of teaching and learning or holiday rituals, were one-dimensional, stereotypical, fully fitting within the discourse of the school.

As Grumet observed, theatre differs from ritual in providing an audience, a group in attendance not participating, sitting apart, watching, listening, judging, providing a challenge to the ritual scheme. Theatre reinforces the daily rituals: the schedules and grades, the straight lines of children and desks. The organization of its elements—the characters, the groupings on stage, the colors, the gestures, the rhythm and melodic lines—conspire to legitimize a particular point of view. School theatre becomes a ritual within a ritual, imitating the canonized categories of reality, filling the spaces of traditional formulas. There is little invitation to the children to experience a detachment, to reflect upon those daily routines. To invite reflection would threaten an already-threatened institution. Reflection violates a primary purpose of school, that of inculcating in children these elements of culture.

Theatre in school is art in the sense that it is a deliberate, formal set of symbols organized to project some images of the world it represents and to obscure others. Within its aesthetic form, some features of school life are highlighted and celebrated. Other features are muted. It is the ritual of "the school as a formal institution" which theatre arts maintain in a process that emphasizes authority, schematics, and sentimentality.

In Chicago Armstrong, Laura stumbles during tumbling, the other children groan, and she runs out in tears. John momentary forgets the text he is supposed to read. Dale daydreams in line as everybody moves to leave the stage. In this friendly atmosphere, the Caroline Lutgens of the world whisper the missing lines, hug the heartshaken. The principal applauds and comments humorously on the acoustics. Performance is secondary to positive feelings, to caring, to the well-being of the people gathered together.

What makes the play different from life is the script—the explicit, conscious plan directing gestures and sounds. Similar scripts are to be found in popular magazines and in our own rituals, calling for the simplest gestures—saluting, blowing out candles, waving goodbye. The gesture prevails over the content. For the classroom play, the skills are so general that any primary teacher in the country would find them accessible and comprehensible. That common denominator may well be the reason of the play's popularity among teachers.

A higher quality script is often presented on movie screens and television, more often on public television. In our observations, these were rarely introduced into the classroom. Only occasionally would a teacher refer to a television show—more likely if it were the Winter Olympics or Masterworks. Teachers said that they did not refer to programs because they did not want to exclude students: some parents would have conflicting viewing rules or preferences and not every child would have a chance to participate. Arts video or film presentations in school were rare, sometimes discouraged by principals; some regarded them as too passive.

Drama is a communal art and, as such, together with simplified forms of music and dance, lends itself easily to school as a model for interaction and work. Paradoxically, it was not the masterpieces but the lowest of television that appeared to influence school drama. Television commercials seemed to provide the strongest prototype for musicals and variety shows—in content as well as form. The simple, often naive messages, sometimes propaganda, fit nicely within these frameworks.

Visual Arts Education

Art instruction was a regular guest in most schools, once a month, once a week, some places more and some places less—in the lower grades happening more often. The average lesson or activity was 25 to 45 minutes, not allowing much time for "conferencing" (see the Chicago Armstrong case) finished pieces. For studio sessions, teachers drew ideas from a potpourri of popular magazines, inservice materials, and craft books. In other studies, textbooks offer pedagogical structure and an articulated approach, not in art. Meager stockrooms in many schools limited teacher choice as to activities.

In the classrooms we studied in Washington and Pennsylvania, the children were being taught the visual arts by specialist teachers. In the classrooms elsewhere the visual arts were taught by a classroom teacher, sometimes briefly augmented by a visiting artist.

With little arts preparation and little resource teacher assistance, many classroom teachers chose projects easy to teach, easy to control, product oriented, tied to cultural events, and attractive to youngsters. The result was a jumble of short, little-articulated projects. If the teacher perceived growing creative skills, it seemed to be acknowledged in terms of the children's ages more than in terms of previous artwork. When asked what they would do with more time, more resources, or improved conditions, most of these untrained teachers said they would do more of the same. Thus, neither time nor lack of materials seemed to them a major obstacle to comprehensive arts education.

In a great number of classrooms, painted turkeys, Christmas trees, Valentine hearts, spring bunnies went on display again and again year after year. Studio skills consisted of cutting, gluing, and aligning. Artwork, better characterized as "cute" than "expressive," was the style up and down many a hallway, not apparently less in metropolitan California than rural New Hampshire. All too many art lessons could be summed up as a pleasant experience, providing relief from the academic routines, without aesthetic compass.

Most classroom teachers provided little guidance, verbally or by example, as to aesthetic quality. Many did not urge experimentation with materials or arrangements. Many did not suggest that tools can be used expressively. When choices existed (pink or blue, six or eight whiskers), they typically remained technical, not drawn to broadening vision or promoting understanding. An on-going evaluation of fourth-grade work at our California school consisted mostly of checking to see the students had performed the task at hand, that directions had been followed. Acknowledgements consisted of expressions of personal likes or dislikes with few attempts to substantiate and rarely referring to a quality in the work.

Still, on some days a teacher would honor the expressive and sometimes whole schools would take up the arts with zest. In our Pennsylvania and Texas sites and in a longer report of teaching at Decatur, Illinois (Bresler, 1989), we describe teachers who have backgrounds as artists, who experienced art first-hand, and who skillfully taught in a variety of ways, emphasizing observation, planning, translation of sights into colors and shapes, and artistic expression of mood. In Anacortes and Chicago, artists-in-residence guided exploration into imagination, skill, cultural heritage and knowledge. At our Pennsylvania site we found schools where every child could expect such encounters almost every week but, in the schools at most of our sites, these experiences were not the expectation, not an integral part of school life, not part of teacher or administrator vision of what an education ought to be.

Final Summary

The four of us looked across the country at ordinary teaching in elementary schools to see how teachers are coping with their obligations to teach the arts. We found ourselves welcomed into classrooms and confidences in schools in eight communities and further informed by volunteer correspondents in our Fifty States Project.

Marginality of Arts in the Schools. We noted quickly the difference between the arts taught casually and occasionally by a classroom teacher and the brief perhaps weekly arts production activities led by a specialist teacher. We found extramural arts in a reasonable state of health, dominated by instrumental music, engaging but a small minority of children.

In the primary schools we visited it would be common for us to find a child having 30 minutes weekly of music, 45 minutes weekly of visual arts, and 3 hours altogether in a semester preparing a dramatic presentation for parents and another class. The music usually was taught by a specialist, the latter two directed by a teacher having essentially no training in the arts. Thanks to a teacher or volunteer willing more-or-less to donate time after school, violin, synchronous movement, photography or some such was availed by a small number for whom transportation home could be arranged.

We thought about trying to characterize the typical child but concluded there is no typical child, no typical school, no typical arts education in America. One child spends a weekly half-hour singing nearly-archaic folk songs, halfway across the country another has a half-hour of singing hymns. One small group has violin instruction, another saxophone instruction in a pre-band setting. One child is denied art for four months as his teacher responds to pressure to raise student reading scores; another in the same district creates a Navajo-inspired sandpainting under the watchful gaze of Van Gogh's self-portraits. One child recites poetry from memory at the front of a weekly theatre class, then takes part in a puppet play; another child will get to be in a play if Ms. Arnold decides after lunch that dramatic re-creation of Evangeline is an appropriate enrichment. Ms. Anderson is teaching her children to clog.

In our schools, popular arts and crafts predominated; the fine arts were seldom in evidence. Discipline-based arts education was relatively unknown, not a recognized need. The schools took too little advantage of out-of-school arts activities, occasionally arranging a field trip but ignoring what the children were learning independently out of school, failing to capitalize on community resources willing and ready to share. Teachers and curriculum specialists did not see the aesthetic education of their children as a high priority responsibility.

The teacher in the classroom was our focus but we began with and kept our belief that what happens in the classroom is greatly influenced by the nearby community and the society extending beyond. Very few teachers carefully drew youngsters toward a personal beholding of artistic works. Those teachers who did got little direction or commendation from administrators or parents. The message from the community to the school was "Keep art and music a part of the curriculum; keep it modest and conventional; continue the traditional performances and exhibits."

In perhaps half of our elementary schools the primary role of the visual arts was to support higher priority subject matter such as language arts, math, and social studies. In the other schools, too, that role was strong but it accompanied efforts to teach arts knowledge and skills. Teaching the arts for their cultural substance and their centrality to human expression was to be found schoolwide in perhaps a third of our schools, in only one or two classrooms in a second third of our schools, and essentially not at all in the remaining third.

Around the country we saw no *perestroika* for arts education in the American elementary schools, no public enthusiasm for greater emphasis on the arts or for increasing the quality of understandings of the arts. Campus-based and museum-based people remind us of the long crusade of leaders in arts education to wrest a greater share of the elementary school curriculum. School-based people tell us those efforts were and continue to be in vain.

There is public support for custom, for linking the arts with holidays and seasons. Some critics deride the practice, more for the opportunity-costs than for the triviality. Schools have a place in cultural tradition, as well as providing performances, exhibits, and relief from cognitive grind. But the communities fail to lament a recognized infrequence of creativity and individualistic expression. Not even noticed are the absence of encounters with art history and aesthetic beholding.

Instructional Reform. We do not believe generally that case studies alone are a good basis for setting educational policy. Case studies such as these can provoke reconsideration and resolve but seldom should indicate specific action to be taken. We do not provide a set of recommendations here partly because we did not study forthcoming decisions, the implications of choice, and the generality of problems.

Furthermore, we believe that the action needing to be taken is different for each school administrator, legislator, teacher, and parent, depending on their circumstances, depending on their experience and indignation. But, of course, we have notions as to which strategies are not working and which are. At the end of our New Hampshire case study, Nancy Ellis offered five recommendations that deserve rereading. Here we will comment on several arts-related instructional improvement strategies.

First is the curriculum improvement strategy, reforming what it is that the teachers teach, changing the notion of what schools can best contribute to education of children. Our summary of observations in Chapter 10 are pertinent. A better curriculum was the aim of many admirable projects at CEMREL and SWERL. The Getty Center has taken up the advocacy. Two of the recommendations of Stephen Kaagan (1990) are rally points, to increase instructional emphasis on reasoning and problem-solving and to develop exemplary DBAE materials. Unfortunately, in our schools we found little interest in changing what arts education is all about. Among the arts education spokespersons there, we found general agreement about the need—with disagreement as to priorities on content specifics, plenty to argue with Getty prescriptions. Even with limited prospects, the curriculum grand strategy seems essential; American education greatly needs to help students see the arts as historical, amenable to intellectualization, critical analysis and cherishing.

But as to specific facts, skills and attitudes, it is not apparent that different teachers should all be teaching the same things. Teacher responsibility for what they teach is important. Accountability can be achieved by encouraging the individual teacher to work from a syllabus if that brings out their best teaching but, if it does not, to advance alternative conceptualizations and activities. Often at the expense of standardization, it should be important to teachers to foster uniqueness in personal perception, their own as well as their students'.

One curricular substrategy, only weakly in evidence, featured the integrated lesson, what Nancy Ellis referred to in her New Hampshire case study as the "project method." Integrating the arts with social studies and other subjects *is* a common objective, a source of pride, often an extensive project handsomely left to the teacher to devise. Almost exclusively (Ellis' description of Ms. Whittier portrays an exception), integrated arts teaching right now, unfortunately, uses the graphic arts and music largely as a motivator and illustrator of something important outside the arts. To intellectualize the aesthetics in life we need to integrate the arts with personal cherishing. Could the grade school teacher perhaps be persuaded to commit annually to a small number of supplementary arts learnings, especially if grounded in matter the teacher holds dear? Moving from the teacher's personal cherishing to the essences of the arts is no small task, as Stake suggested here in his California case study, but the strategy seems worth further consideration.

Another curriculum substrategy is to get classrooms attending more to ambient education in home and community. In our Pennsylvania case study, we found a school arts program masterfully put together but isolated from the artistry of the neighborhood and metropolitan area around it. American children are enormously educated by Walkmen and television commercials, by sports figures and travel— alas, poorly educated in large part—with very little corrective from the schools. A few weeks after we finished our fieldwork, the sales of rap cassettes were embattled in court and newspapers but, to our recollection, only one teacher in our schools had said a word about rap. Most of the arts of the home, shopping mall, park, concert hall, church, and stadium are educating (Willis, 1977), some commendably, but almost entirely without educated critique. As is all education, arts education is vitalized by signs that people care. Field trips to the performing arts center are not the only way for schools to be a part of the best of community artistry. Paying attention to community arts is not a matter of budget, it a matter of paying attention. Here, too, improvement might start with leaders persuading authorities to commend the good things already happening.

And last we mention the educator-training grand strategy, the one to change how teachers and administrators are readied to create effective educational programs. Our summary of observations in Chapter 11 drew attention back to site observations where we met music and arts specialists who apparently arrived ready to teach a more discipline-based curriculum but found little colleague support, time-slot, or district authentication to do so. The problems we saw appeared to lie not with the training of specialists in arts education but with specialists in school management who saw the arts more as a promotional device for the schools than (perhaps because it has so little vocational promise) an educational domain of its own. Classroom teachers too might have benefitted by having better-educated administrators but many of them had arrived without proper college preparation for providing arts education. Most of those doing a good job had somehow gained experience or training beyond college of education requirements. Staff development programs in the schools were not making up the difference, keeping arts education in its marginal role and heeding little the inservice performances of such organizations as Project Heart (See Stake, McTaggart & Munski, 1977). As observed at the Washington site, Artists-in-Schools sometimes contributed to curriculum guides but though expected to do so, did little to improve readiness of classroom teachers to be arts teachers themselves. Professional continuing education strategies are essential but seem impotent without a substantial restructuring of schools and school systems.

As to the matter of restructuring the schools, we three researchers are entirely over our heads. We did make observations in a school, Chicago Dumas, that had undertaken so major a change, but we looked mostly at the ways teachers behave in their classrooms. In all our sites we noted many constraints on change but saw, too, some reason to hope.

One final strategy to mention is to improve the ambiance within the school. The easy half step is to improve decor. Our New Mexico correspondent found the schools he visited aesthetically offensive. With tasteful murals, banners, and stained glass panels in hallways, photographs of students and staff in offices, glass-shelved collections of cultural artifacts in a classroom window, fresh flowers and candles on a special student's table in the cafeteria, our case study schools in Anacortes, Washington, Point Aden, Texas, and the Chicago southside were pleasant places to be. The decor of many schools appears intended to hype the students more than to create living spaces. Garish school colors, an athletic motif, and student prizes egg on vanity and competition. Travel posters and holiday cut-outs reflect a people on the go. Raucous public address systems remind that the central office expects to be in charge. Most schools have small budgets for decor but at each of them some money and effort is spent.

But school ambiance is more than attractive visual stimuli. The visuals may be mere symbol of the openness of aesthetics and appreciation of the arts, the openness and appreciation itself still absent. That openness, that appreciation—an attitude of cherishing what is beautiful and meaningful in human life, a view that delights in unique perspective and self-expression—is missing from so many of our schools. Our children need to be encouraged to explore, to see and hear with other eyes and ears, to sense the power of understanding that can be gained from another's point of view, to translate their own thoughts and feelings into a socially communicable and engaging form. The school needs to provide an atmosphere not only to inform and educate but also to synthesize and share what is learned with what is known. The school needs to be a space to learn but also a place that tolerates and celebrates its growing learners and their artistic self-expression.

The Authorities. Almost never did we encounter connections—literal or spiritual—between the teachers we observed and the people who speak publicly for music and art education. Local curriculum coordinators and teachers appeared unconcerned about the advocacies and critiques of those who write in learned journals. Specialist teachers were knowledgeable about what their college-campus mentors and a few others believed but did not appear to participate in reform efforts such as discipline-based arts education. Differences in the teachers' and spokespersons' positions were notable in several ways.

Advocates for high quality arts education speak in one way or another about the place of the arts in general education (Eisner, 1982; Broudy, 1990). They emphasize the need for cultural understanding and linguistic sophistication, for creative expression and recognition of individualistic thinking. The teachers and school authorities we saw occasionally spoke of these aims but gave them low priority during art and music instruction. Perhaps more troublesome was the fact that most teachers and school officials seemed comfortable with arrangements that assigned much of the best arts instruction to instrumental music and special activities, often extracurriculars—catering to students with talent and interest, diminishing the effort to teach the arts as general education. Furthermore, in places with few specialist teachers, most educators voiced no protest at having the majority of children instructed by teachers who have essentially no qualification to teach the arts.

To us, it appeared that the authorities were out of touch with the practitioners. There was no alliance between them for improvement of school offerings in the arts. One problem was that the leaders were calling for revolutionary change whereas the teachers held little hope even for evolutionary change and considered protectionist strategies more appropriate than expansionist. In matters of school curricula, some incremental change occurs but revolutionary change does not. The visionaries, including a few school-based educators, were aware of that. But they cared so deeply that they could not tolerate having the arts taught rarely, crudely, and without intellectual force. They wanted the arts elevated to full standing in the curriculum. They were calling for respectable portions of the school week for arts instruction, for standardized objectives and examinations, and for recognition of the arts as intellectual disciplines. Given present-day public attitudes and financing, these advocacies are unrealistic.

In their ideology, arts education leaders are, in fact, part of the problem. They fail to contribute to modest change, change that would leave programs still weak and disjointed but change that would raise the quality of artistic experience of many youngsters.[1] Such modest changes would include assistance to untrained teachers needing rudimentary instruction in music theory, empathic critiques of art including critical discussion of Christmas programs and PTA presentations, recognition of arts activities in the community and programs on television, and encouragement of popular arts which individual teachers themselves have come to cherish. Like experts, connoisseurs and visionaries across the curriculum, national leaders in arts education sometimes give substance to the words of Voltaire, "The best is the enemy of the good."

Larger Impressions. In the 1960s, Newton Minew called television a vast wasteland. In the 1980s Terrell Bell called the schools a sea of mediocrity. And in writing up these case studies, our recollections have frequently been drawn to places where arts education was mediocrity and wasteland, to schools where aesthetic spirit was smothered. Like most people, we are quick to generalize. Such summary judgments are, at best, half-truths. Indignation is the fuel of reform. Some of the vignettes of this book might add to the fire but the truth is that things are bad *and* good in the best and worst of places.

In some abstract, population sense, the criticisms may be accurate but in a personal, real-school sense, they are not. An overview does not nicely describe the situation for real people. For years, the Gallup Poll on Education has shown that most people rate their neighborhood school higher than the nation's schools as a whole. It could be local pride or unwillingness to admit that local educators are not providing good schools but we think the reason is that people are more familiar with the local situation. National news reports of illiterate graduates, substance abuse, teacher strikes, and violence on school grounds are frightening. An occasional mishap close to home can be frightening too but usually is balanced by counter-evidence: the kids are getting satisfactory marks, teachers personally-known are hard at work, extramurals are winning the occasional award. It is easier to defuse simplistic complaints about the local curriculum than complaints about the nation's schools. The nation's schools are of much lower quality than they could be but no one ideal school system would delight many people. A local school faces a narrower set of demands.

In a typical middle school, only two teachers may be worthy of the name "arts educator." Still, each affects many children, some but for an aesthetic moment, some in ways that last a lifetime. Much more happens out of school. Even in the cruelty of the ghetto and the quiet of the village, through every child's spaces pass the signs of all artistries. Teachers and other adults help kids catch sight of a few. The children catch some by themselves.

---

[1] It would be tragic were there no idealists, no unrealistic zealots, among leaders in arts education. Not all of them need accommodate the constraints of today's schools. But as a community, the national spokespersons appeared to us so devoted to what teaching ought to be that they provided little assistance to improving what it is.

Learnings as Nebulae. Most signs are missed but the curious child still encounters a great range of objects and ideas worthy of cherishing, worthy of pondering. What is available to be learned is infinite, what is actually learned is nearly infinite. The total learning may be best symbolized as a vast nebula. The total is poorly represented by a list of information, an array of skills, or several test scores. What has been brought into experience, into meaning of one kind or another is beyond our count. Each nebula of learnings is personal, streaked with emotion, unique.

It makes some sense for educators to talk about cultural literacy (Hirsch, 1987) and a need for common aesthetic experience among interacting people but it makes sense also to talk about the cultivation of each individual's unique knowledge, sensitivity and experience (Pring, 1984).

Ours is a heterogeneous society, priding itself in individualistic interpretation of the good life (Bellah et al, 1985). The people watch what they please, pressure schools for programs and policies they prefer—with little regard to what the experts say. Instance by instance, they judge the acceptability of the school arts program by PTA recitals, opportunities for kids to learn to play an instrument, and refrigerator postings.

The public wants arts opportunities for all but it wants serious arts teaching only for those who are going to "work their butts off" practicing for the performance. Can it be in the public interest to evaluate a school arts program on the basis of what students collectively know and appreciate when the public doesn't believe that everybody *should* know and appreciate? State goals for the arts tell what the arts educators want, not what the public wants. Local teaching tells more about what the public wants, less about what the experts want.

Robust Diversities. Current state-legislature-mandated school reform is based on the idea that common teachings and minimum competencies are the first order of business of the schools. Much more emphasis should be on what the child is individually ready for and keen to learn and what individual schools can do for their communities. Chicago is not Plymouth Meeting is not Las Lomas. The careful reader probably has been reassured that what Sandra Henderson was doing for arts education in Dumas School, what John Fino was doing at Whitemarsh, and what Gene Frielander was doing at Luther Burbank, though unlikely to win arts education awards, was far more nicely tailored to the needs of parents and children than are most arts education syllabi produced by districts, states or regional laboratories. Guides and tests have their place but even poorly trained teachers can pay too diligent heed.

The tempo of school reform is set by repetitious student achievement testing. Administrators have committed the schools to attaining higher test scores and teachers increasingly are teaching to the tests (Shepard, 1991). What few people realize is that, although the tests consistently differentiate among fast and slow learners, tests do a poor job of identifying what is being learned among the vast learnings not directly covered (Stake, in press). The tests have not been validated for covering the content of an education.

Teachers always have taught far more broadly than the prescribed curriculum, introducing thousands of complexities covered by but not intentionally implied by statements of goal and objective, most not mentioned in the tests. Of course some teacher choices of both meta-thinking and minutiae are better than other choices but, by custom, experience, and intent, all teachers teach meanings and procedures far beyond their own awareness, farther still beyond design. Teachings and learnings are not adequately represented by goal statements and test scores which focus and summarize. An education is a nebula, itself having many constellations, each with multiple meanings, with much knowledge only loosely connected, maybe merely stored away.

Arts education has not greatly suffered the misperception and faulty focus of goal-setting and testing because it has not been regularly a part of standardized student assessment schemes—though plans exist to make that happen. Diffuse and diverse in purpose, fine arts education lacks widespread support. But the teaching of the arts is enriched by that ambivalence. The arts are curricula which allow for teacher choice, teacher creativity, teacher cherishing. The central administration, as in Anacortes and Plymouth Meeting, may boast of its district guide but it is a guide to be built upon, demanding little obedience. Though few teachers do, the arts are an area for teaching important concepts not fitting into more subject-dedicated courses. Such technical and wide-ranging topics as recursion and standards and willpower can be nicely developed in an arts project with little chance of drawing the question of "Who cares?" or "Will that be on the test?" or "Are the other fourth-grade teachers teaching that?" The support for the arts teacher is small but the freedom to educate is large.

A Need for Staying Power. In each school we found at least one teacher caring about the arts, willing to go well beyond custom and requirement to teach something of the arts. Often a classroom teacher was the leading voice for the arts. A few had substantial personal involvement in the fine arts. Most of the other teachers admired a classic or two. But more important to the potential for arts education, almost everyone cherished and invested something in the popular arts, e.g., the design of clothing, Fred Astaire movies, singing in the church choir. These customs and cherishings are modest resources for an arts curriculum but are underused, too seldom commended. In several schools the arts were thriving, in others they were occasional and peripheral. The call to do better was easy to read in official brochures but the will to do better was hard to find. The question for arts educators perhaps is not "How can we do it right?" but "How can we keep from losing the few-but-many good things we've got?"

Finale: Appendix

Appendix:
References and Related Works

Clem Adelman, Stephen Kemmis & David Jenkins. Rethinking case study: Notes from the Second Cambridge Conference. In Helen Simons (ed.), *Towards a Science of the Singular: Essays about Case Study in Educational Research and Evaluation*, 1980.

Mortimer Adler. *Paideia Proposal: An Educational Manifesto*. Macmillan, 1982.

Alliance for Arts Education. State of the arts: An interchange update. *Interchange*. John F. Kennedy Center for the Performing Arts, Summer, 1987.

Frances Anderson. *Art for All the Children*. Springfield, IL: Charles Thomas, 1978.

Rudolph Arnheim. *Art and Visual Perception*. Berkeley: University of California Press, 1954.

Rudolph Arnheim. *Art and Visual Perception: A Psychology of the Creative Eye*. Berkeley: University of California Press, 1965.

Sylvia Ashton-Warner. *Teacher*. Simon & Schuster, 1963.

Manuel Barkan. *A Foundation for Art Education*. New York: Ronald Press, 1955.

Manuel Barkan & Laura Chapman. *Guidelines for Art Instruction Through Television for the Elementary Schools*. Bloomington, IN: National Center for School and College Television, 1967.

Monroe Beardsley. *Aesthetics: Problems in the Philosophy of Criticism*. New York: Harcourt, Brace & World, 1958.

Monroe Beardsley. Aesthetic theory and educational theory. In Ralph Smith (ed.), *Aesthetic Concepts and Education*, 1970.

Monroe Beardsley. The creation of art. In Michael Wreen & Donald Callen (eds.), *The Aesthetic Point of View: Selected Essays*. Ithaca, NY: Cornell University Press, 1982.

Howard Becker, Blanche Geer, Everett Hughes & Anselm Strauss. *Boys in White: Student Culture in Medical School*. New Brunswick, NJ: Transaction Books, 1961.

Robert Bellah, Richard Madsen, William Sullivan, Ann Swindler, & Stephen Tipton. *Habits of the Heart.* Harper & Row, 1985.

Carl Bereiter. *Must We Educate?* Prentice Hall, 1974.

Paul Berman & Milbrey McLaughlin. *Federal Programs Supporting Educational Change, Vol. VIII, Implementing and Sustaining Innovations.* Rand, 1978.

Benjamin Bloom, Tom Hastings & George Madaus. *Handbook of Formative and Summative Evaluation of Student Learning.* McGraw-Hill, 1971.

Kathryn Bloom & Jane Remer. A rationale for the arts in education. New York: John D. Rockefeller III Fund, 1975.

Robert Bogdan & Sari Bicklen. *Qualitative Research for Education.* Allyn & Bacon, 1982.

Ernest Boyer. *High School: A Report on Secondary Education in America.* Carnegie Foundation for the Advancement of Teaching, 1st edition. Harper & Row, 1983.

Liora Bresler. The role of the computer in a music theory classroom: Integration, barriers and learning. Stanford University doctoral dissertation, 1987.

Larry Briskman. Creative product and creative process in science and art. In Denis Dutton & Michael Krausz (eds.), *The Concept of Creativity in Science and Art*, Boston: Kluwer-Nijhoff, 1981.

Urie Bronfenbrenner. The experimental ecology of education. *Educational Researcher,* 5(9), pp. 5-15, October, 1976.

Harry Broudy. *Enlightened Cherishing: An Essay in Aesthetic Education.* University of Illinois Press, 1972.

Harry Broudy. *The Whys and Hows of Aesthetic Education.* St. Louis: CEMREL, 1977.

Harry Broudy. The role of music in general education. *Bulletin of the Council for Research in Music Education,* 105, 23-43, 1990.

Frank Brouillet. Visual and performing arts curriculum guidelines for Washington schools. Olympia: State Department of Public Instruction, 1987.

California State Department of Education. *Visual and Performing Arts Framework for California Public Schools: Kindergarten through Grade Twelve.* Sacramento: State Department of Education, 1982.

Pat Carini. *Observation and Description: An Alternative Methodology for the Investigation of Human Phenomena.* North Dakota Study Group on Evaluation Monograph Series, Grand Forks: University of North Dakota, 1975.

Ernst Cassirer. *An Essay on Man.* Yale Universty Press, 1944.

Laura Chapman. *Instant Art, Instant Culture.* Teachers College Press, 1982.

Laura Chapman. *Discover Art.* Worcester, MA: Davis Publications, 1985.

Lois Choksy. *The Kodály Method.* Prentice Hall, 1974.

Michael Connelly & Jean Clandinin. *Personal Practical Knowledges and the Modes of Knowing: Relevance for Teaching and Learning. NSSE Yearbook* 2, 1985.

Eleanor Dale Costello. Kaleidoscope patterns: Art education in an elementary classroom. Vancouver: University of British Columbia masters thesis, 1988.

Larry Cuban. *How Teachers Taught: Consistency and Change in American Classrooms, 1890-1980.* Longman, 1984.

Michael Day. Diversity and innovation: Art education in the Milwaukee Public Schools. In Michael Day et al., *Art History, Art Criticism, and Art Production. Volume II: Case Studies of Seven Selected Sites*, 1984.

Michael Day, Elliot Eisner, Robert Stake, Brent Wilson & Marjorie Wilson. *Art History, Art Criticism, and Art Production. Volume II: Case Studies of Seven Selected Sites.* Rand Corporation, 1984.

Terry Denny. In defense of story telling as a first step in educational research. Paper presented at the International Reading Association, Houston, 1978.

Norman Denzin. *The Research Act.* Aldine, 1970.

John Dewey. *Art as Experience.* Minton, Balch, 1934.

Robert Dreeben. *On What is Learned in School.* Reading, MA: Addison-Wesley, 1968.

Elizabeth Drew. *Poetry, A Modern Guide to Its Understanding and Enjoyment.* New York: W. W. Norton, 1959.

David Ecker. *Improving the Teaching of Art Appreciation.* The Ohio State University, 1966.

Junius Eddy. Beyond "Enrichment:" Developing a comprehensive community-school arts curriculum. In Jerome Hausman, (ed.), *Arts and the Schools*, McGraw-Hill, 1980a.

Phyllis Edmundson. A normative look at the curriculum in teacher education. *Phi Delta Kappan,* 71(9), pp. 717-722, 1990.

Arthur Efland. School art style: A functional analysis. *Studies in Art Education,* 17(2), 1976.

Arthur Efland. *Planning Art Education in the Middle/Secondary Schools of Ohio.* Columbus: State Department of Education, 1977.

Arthur Efland. Conceptions of teaching in art education. *Art Education,* pp. 1-9, April, 1979.

Elliot Eisner. *The Educational Imagination.* Macmillan, 1979.

Elliot Eisner. *Educating Artistic Vision.* Macmillan, 1982(a).

Elliot Eisner. *Cognition and Curriculum.* New York: Longman, 1982(b).

Elliot Eisner. *The Role of Discipline-Based Art Education in America's Schools.* Monograph. Getty Center for Education in the Arts, 1986.

Freema Elbaz. *Teacher Thinking: A Study of Practical Knowledge.* The Netherlands: Croom-Helm, 1983.

Nancy Ellis. Collaborative interaction for the improvement of teaching. *Teaching and Teacher Education.* August, 1990.

Fred Erickson. Timing and context in everyday discourse. In Patrick Dickson (ed.), *Children Oral Communication Skills.* New York: Academic Press, 1981.

Fred Erickson. Qualitative methods in research on teaching. In Merlin Wittrock (ed.), *Handbook of Research on Teaching.* Macmillan, 1986.

Eleanor Farrar & Ernest House. The evaluation of PUSH/Excel: A case study. In Ernest House (ed.), *New Directions in Educational Evaluation.* Falmer, 1986.

Edmund Feldman. *Becoming Human Through Art.* Prentice Hall, 1970

Gary Fenstermacher & John Goodlad. *Individual Differences and the Common Curriculum.* National Society for the Study of Education, 82nd Yearbook, part 1, 1983.

Don Fuhr. Elements of good administrative leadership. *NASSP Bulletin,* March 1989.

Michael Fullan. *The Meaning of Educational Change.* New York: Teachers College Press, 1982.

Alec Gallup & Stanley Elam. The 20th annual Gallup Poll of the public's attitudes toward the public schools. *Phi Delta Kappan*, September, 1988.

Howard Gardner. *The Arts and Human Development*. New York: John Wiley, 1973.

Howard Gardner. *Frames of Mind: The Theory of Multiple Intelligences*. New York: Basic Books, 1983.

Howard Gardner. Remarks made as discussant at the annual conference of the National Art Education Association in Kansas City, MO, 1990.

John Gardner. Leaders and managers. *NASSP Bulletin*, September 1988a.

John Gardner. The tasks of leadership. *NASSP Bulletin*, October 1988b.

John Gardner. The heart of the matter—leader-constituent interaction. *NASSP Bulletin*, November 1988c.

John Gardner. Leadership and power. *NASSP Bulletin*, December 1988d.

John Gardner. The moral aspects of leadership. *NASSP Bulletin*, January 1989a.

John Gardner. Leadership: Attributes and context. *NASSP Bulletin*, February 1989b.

John Gardner. Leadership and the task of motivating. *NASSP Bulletin*, April 1989c.

Getty Center for Education in the Arts. *Beyond Creating: The Place for Art in America's Schools*. Los Angeles: Getty Center, 1985.

Barney Glaser & Ansel Strauss. *The Discovery of Grounded Theory: Strategies for Qualitative Research*. Aldine, 1967.

Anne Green Gilbert. *Teaching the Three R's Through Movement Experiences*. Minneapolis: Burgess, 1977.

Judith Goetz & Margaret LeCompte. *Ethnography and Qualitative Design in Educational Research*. San Francisco: Academic Press, 1984.

Ernst Gombrich. *Art and Illusion*. Princeton University Press, 1960.

John Goodlad. *A Place Called School, Prospects for the Future*. McGraw-Hill, 1984.

John Goodlad. Studying the education of educators: From conception to findings. *Phi Delta Kappan,* 71(9), 698-701, 1990.

John Goodlad & Jack Morrison. The arts and education. In Jerome Hausman (ed.), *Arts and the Schools*, McGraw-Hill, 1980a.

Ivor Goodson. *The Making of Curriculum: Collected Essays*. Falmer, 1988.

Edwin Gordon. *Learning Sequences in Music: Skill, Content, and Patterns*. Chicago: G. I. A. Publications, 1980.

Donald Graves. *Writing: Teachers and Children at Work*. Portsmouth, NH: Heinemann, 1983.

David Greene & Jane David. A research design for generalizing from multiple case studies. *Evaluation and Program Planning*, 7, pp. 73-85, 1984.

Maxine Greene. Teaching for aesthetic experience. In Music Educators National Conference, *Toward an Aesthetic Education*, 1971.

Madeleine Grumet. In search of theatre: Ritual, confrontation and the suspense of form. *Journal of Education, 162(1)*, 93-116.

Madeleine Grumet. The line is drawn. *Educational Leadership*, January, 1983.

Egon Guba. Toward a methodology of naturalistic inquiry in educational evaluation. *CSE Monograph Series in Evaluation*. Los Angeles: UCLA, 1978.

Egon Guba & Yvonna Lincoln. *Fourth Generation Evaluation*. Sage, 1989.

Gulbenkian Foundation. *The Arts in Schools*. The Foundation, 1982.

David Hamilton. Some contrasting assumptions about case study research and survey analysis. In Helen Simons (ed.), *Towards a Science of the Singular: Essays about Case Study in Educational Research and Evaluation*. East Anglia: Centre for Applied Research in Education, 1980.

David Hamilton. *Towards a Theory of Schooling*. Falmer, 1989.

David Hamilton, David Jenkins, Christine King, Barry MacDonald & Malcolm Parlett (eds.). *Beyond the Numbers Game: A Reader in Educational Evaluation*. Macmillan, 1977.

Jane Hansen. *When Writers Read*. Portsmouth, NH: Heinemann, 1987.

B. Harrison. *An Arts-Based Approach to English*. Hodder & Stoughton, 1982.

Jerome Hausman. Research on teaching the visual arts. In Nate Gage (ed.), *Handbook of Research on Teaching*. Rand McNally, 1963.

Jerome Hausman. A contemporary aesthetics curriculum. In *National Music Educators Conference, 1971*.

Jerome Hausman (ed.). *Arts and the Schools*. McGraw-Hill, 1980a.

Jerome Hausman. The domain of the arts. In Jerome Hausman (ed.), *Arts and the Schools*. McGraw-Hill, 1980b.

Robert Havighurst. *The public schools of Chicago: A survey for the Board of Education of the City of Chicago*. 1964.

Jules Henry. *On Education*. Random House, 1966.

E. D. Hirsch, Jr. *Cultural Literacy What Every Amerian Needs to Know*. Houghton Mifflan, 1987.

Burnett Hobgood. *Master Teachers of Theatre*. Carbondale, IL: SIU Press, 1988.

Phil Jackson. *Life in Classrooms*. Holt, Reinhart & Winston, 1968.

Richard Jaeger (ed.). *Complementary Methods for Research in Education*. AERA, 1988.

David Jenkins, Helen Simons & Rob Walker. 'Thou art my goddess': Naturalistic inquiry and educational evaluation. *Cambridge Journal of Education, II*(3), pp. 169-189, 1981.

Joint statement issued by the American Association of School Administrators and the Music Educators National Conference, Joint Committee AASA/MENC, MENC, 1201 16th Street, Washington, DC, 1965.

Stephen Kaagan. *Aesthetic Persuasion: Pressing the Cause of Arts Education in American Schools,* (p. 7). Los Angeles: Getty Center, 1990

Immanuel Kant. *Kritik der Urteilskraft*. (Hebrew translation by Hugo Bergman & Nathan Rothenstrich.) Jerusalem: Bialik Institute, 1827/1969.

Lilian Katz & Sylvia Chard. *Engaging Children's Minds: The Project Approach*. Norwood, NJ: Ablex, 1989.

Stephen Kemmis. The imagination of the case and the invention of the study. In Helen Simons (ed.), *Towards a Science of the Singular: Essays about Case Study in Educational Research and Evaluation*, 1980.

Tom Koerner. Principals and leadership—An interview with John Gardner. *NAASP Bulletin*, September 1988.

Samuel Krug. Leadership and learning: A measurement-based approach for analyzing school effectiveness and developing effective school leaders. Project report for the National Center for School Leadership, University of Illinois at Urbana-Champaign, 1990.

Saville Kushner. *Working dreams: Innovation in a conservatoire.* East Anglia: Centre for Applied Research in Education, 1985.

David Labaree. *The Making of an American High School.* Yale University Press, 1988.

Susanne Langer. *Feeling and Form.* Charles Scribner's Sons, 1953.

Susanne Langer. *Problems of Art.* Charles Scribner's Sons, 1957.

Charles Leonhard. Human potential and aesthetic experience. *Music Educators Journal,* 54, April, 1967.

Charles Leonhard. *The Status of Arts Education in American Public Schools: Report on a Survey Conducted by The National Arts Education Research Center at the University of Illinois.* Urbana-Champaign, IL: Council for Research in Music Education (University of Illinois), 1991.

Yvonna Lincoln & Egon Guba. *Naturalistic Inquiry.* Sage, 1985.

Yvonna Lincoln & Egon Guba. Criteria for Assessing Naturalistic Inquiries as Reports. Paper presented at the Annual Meeting of the American Education Research Association, New Orleans, 1988.

Dan Lortie. *Schoolteacher.* University of Chicago Press, 1975.

Viktor Lowenfeld. *Creative and Mental Growth.* Macmillan, 1947.

Ulf Lundgren & Sten Pettersson (eds.). *Code, Context and Curriculum Processes: Seven papers Presented at the Annual Meeting of the American Educational Research Association 1979.* Stockholm Institute of Education, Department of Educational Research, 1979.

Linda Mabry. Drama in a junior high school in Danville. Unpublished paper. CIRCE, University of Illinois, 1988.

Linda Mabry, Robert Stake, Liora Bresler, & Jonathan Block. *Notebook of the Fifty States Project.* Unpublished compiled notes from correspondents, Center for Instructional Research and Curriculum Evaluation, University of Illinois at Urbana-Champaign (for the National Arts Education Research Center), 1989.

Barry MacDonald, Clem Adelman, Saville Kushner & Rob Walker. *Bread and Dreams: A Case Study of Bilingual Schooling in the U.S.A.* CARE Occasional Publication No. 12. Norwich: F. Crowe & Sons, 1982.

James Macdonald. The domain of curriculum. *Journal of Curriculum and Supervision,* 1(3), Spring 1986, pp. 205-214.

Stanley Madeja. *Through the Arts to the Aesthetic.* St. Louis: CEMREL, 1977.

Stanley Madeja & Harry Kelly. The process of curriculum development for aesthetic education. In National Music Educators Conference, *Toward an Aesthetic Education*, 1971.

Martin Maehr & Jack Fyans. School culture, motivation, and achievement. Project report for the National Center for School Leadership, University of Illinois at Urbana-Champaign, 1990.

Gina May. The State of Arts Education in Washington Schools—K-12: A Preliminary Report. Olympia: Office of the Superintendent of Public Instruction, no date.

Milbrey McLaughlin & Margaret Thomas. *Art History, Art Criticism, and Art Production, Volume I: Comparing the Process of Change Across Districts*. Rand Corporation, 1984.

Milbrey McLaughlin, Margaret Thomas & Joyce Peterson. Art history, art criticism, and art production: An examination of art education in selected school districts. Volume III, Executive Summary. Santa Monica: Rand Corporation, 1984.

Leslie McLean. Judging the quality of a school as a place where the arts might thrive. In Robert Stake (ed.), *Evaluating the Arts in Education: A Responsive Approach*. Merrill, 1975.

Leonard Meyer. *Emotion and Meaning in Music*. University of Chicago Press, 1956.

Matthew Miles & Michael Huberman. *Qualitative Data Analysis: A Sourcebook of New Methods*. SAGE, 1984.

Jerome Murphy. The unheroic side of leadership: Notes from the swamp. *Phi Delta Kappan*, May 1988, pp. 654-9.

Ruth Murray. *Dance in Elementary Education: A Program for Boys and Girls*, third edition. Harper & Row, 1975.

Music Educators National Conference. *Toward an Aesthetic Education*. Reston, VA: Music Educators National Conference, 1971.

Music Educators National Conference. Dan Steinel (ed.). *Arts in Schools State by State*. (2nd ed.) Reston, VA: Music Educators National Conference, 1988.

Dan Nadaner. Responding to the image world: A proposal for art curricula. *Art Education*, 38(1), pp. 9-12, January 1985.

National Assessment of Educational Progress. *Results from the Second National Art Assessment*. Report 10-A-01. Denver: Educational Commission of the States, December, 1981.

National Endowment for the Arts. *Toward Civilization*. National Endowment for the Arts, May, 1988.

Cynthia Norris. A discussion of brain hemisphere characteristics and creative leadership among selected educational administrators in Tennessee. University of Tennessee, doctoral dissertation, 1984.

Cynthia Norris & Charles Achilles. Intuitive leadership: A new dimension for education leadership. *Planning and Changing*, Summer 1988.

Allan Odden & David Marsh. How state education reforms can improve secondary schools. Policy paper #PC 87-12-13 SDE Sacramento: California State Department of Education, 1987.

Walter Ong. *Orality and Literacy*. New York: Methuen. 1982.

DeWitt Parker. *The Analysis of Art*. Yale University Press, 1926.

Michael Parsons. *How We Understand Art*. New York: Cambridge University Press, 1987.

David Perkins. Invisible art. *Art Education, 36*(1), 1983.

Alan Peshkin, *Growing Up American: Schooling and the Survival of Community*. University of Chicago Press, 1979.

William Pinar & Madeleine Grumet. *Toward a Poor Curriculum*. Dubuque, IA: Kendall/Hunt Publishing Co., 1976.

Plato. *Republic*, Book X.

Michael Polanyi. *Personal Knowledge*. University of Chicago Press, 1958.

Richard Pring. *Personal and Social Education in the Curriculum*. London: Hodder and Stoughton, 1984.

Eugene Raudsepp. Can you trust your hunches? *Administrative Management*, October 1981.

Herman Regner (ed.). *Music for Children*. Orff-Schulwerk, volume 2. New York: Schott, 1977.

Bennett Reimer. *A Philosophy of Music Education*. Prentice-Hall, 1970.

Bennett Reimer. A comprehensive arts curriculum model. In *Design for Arts in Education*. July/August 1989, *90*(6), 2-16.

Ireene Robbins. Elementary teacher's arts and crafts ideas for every month of the year. The author, 1971.

David Rumelhart & Donald Norman. Analogical processes in learning. In John Anderson (ed.), *Cognitive Skills and their Acquisition*. Hillsdale, NJ: Lawrence Erlbaum, 1981.

Galen Saylor. *Who Planned the Curriculum?* West Lafayette: Kappa Delta Pi Press, 1982.

Henry Schaeffer-Simmern. *The Unfolding of Artistic Activity*. Berkeley: University of California Press, 1948.

Pat Scheyer & Robert Stake. A program's self-evaluation portfolio. CIRCE, University of Illinois, 1976.

Lelia Schoenberg. *The artist as resource in six Illinois school Districts*. Report on the Illinois Artist as Resource Pilot Study. Illinois Alliance for Arts Education, 1989.

Donald Schön. *The Reflective Practitioner*. Basic Books, 1983.

Shepard, Lorrie. (in press). Will national tests improve student learning? *Phi Delta Kappan.* (scheduled for November, 1991 publication).

Geraldine Siks. *Drama with Children*, second edition. Harper & Row, 1983.

Rawley Silver. Developing cognitive skills through art. In Lilian Katz (ed.), *Current Topics in Early Childhood Education.* Norwood, NJ: Ablex, 1982.

Helen Simons (ed.), *Towards a Science of the Singular: Essays about Case Study in Educational Research and Evaluation*. East Anglia: Centre for Applied Research in Education, 1980.

Helen Simons & John Elliott (eds.). *Rethinking Appraisal and Assessment*. Milton Keynes: Open University Press, 1989.

Louis Smith. The micro-ethnography of the classroom. *Psychology in the Schools*, 4, 1967, 216-221.

Louis Smith. An evolving logic of participant observation, educational ethnography and other case studies. In Lee Shulman (ed.), *Reviews of Research in Education,* Volume 6. Chicago: Peacock Press, 1978.

Louis Smith. Some not so random thoughts on doing fieldwork: The interplay of values. In Helen Simons (ed.), *Towards a Science of the Singular: Essays about Case Study in Educational Research and Evaluation.*, 1980.

Nancy Smith. Designing effective arts programs. In Jerome Hausman (ed), 1980.

Ralph Smith (ed.). *Aesthetic Concepts and Education*. University of Illinois Press, 1970.

Ralph Smith (ed.). *Aesthetics and Problems of Education*. University of Illinois Press, 1971(a).

Ralph Smith. The philosophical literature of aesthetic education. In Music Educators National Conference, *Toward an Aesthetic Education*, 1971(b).

Ralph Smith. *Excellence in Art Education: Ideas and Initiatives*. Reston, VA: National Art Education Association, 1986.

Ralph Smith. *The Sense of Art: A Study in Aesthetic Education*. Routledge, 1989.

Susan Sontag. *On Photography*. New York: Farrar, Straus & Giroux, 1977.

Lauren Sosniak. The tortoise, the hare, and the development of talent. In Michael Howe (ed.) *Encouraging the Development of Exceptional Abilities and Talents*. Leichester, UK: British Psychological Society, (in press).

Bernard Spodek. The past as prologue. Paper presented at the annual meeting of the American Education Research Association, New Orleans, 1984.

SRI International. Assessment of initiatives available to the National Science Foundation in science education. Volume 1, Problems and opportunities. Menlo Park, CA: SRI International, 1988.

Robert Stake (ed.). *Evaluating the Arts in Education: A Responsive Approach*. Columbus, OH: Merrill, 1975. Now available only through University Microfilms, Ann Arbor.

Robert Stake. The case study method in social inquiry. *Educational Researcher, (2)*, 5-8, 1978.

Robert Stake. Case study. In John Nisbet (ed.) *World Yearbook of Education, 1984/85*.

Robert Stake. An evolutionary view of educational improvement. In Ernest House (ed.), *New Directions in Educational Evaluation*. Falmer, 1986.

Robert Stake. (in press). *Validity and Invalidity of Standardized Testing of Mathematics Achievement*. National Center for Research in Mathematical Sciences Education.

Robert Stake & Jack Easley (eds.). *Case Studies in Science Education*. CIRCE, University of Illinois, 1977.

Robert Stake & Gordon Hoke. Evaluating an arts program: Movement and dance in a downstate district. *National Elementary Principal*, 55(3), February, 1976

Robert Stake, Robin McTaggart, & Marilyn Munski. An Illinois pair: A case study of school art in Champaign and Decatur. In Michael Day et al., *Art History, Art*

Criticism, and Art Production. Volume II: Case Studies of Seven Selected Sites, 1984.

Robert Stake & Deborah Trumbull. Naturalistic generalizations. *Review Journal of Philosophy & Social Science*, VII, 3-12, 1982.

Robert Stake and others. Evaluation study of the Indiana Department of Education Gifted and Talented Program. CIRCE, University of Illinois, 1986.

George Steiner. *Language and Silence*. New York: Antheneum, 1967.

Larry Tyree. Myths of leadership. *Community, Technological and Junior College Journal*, October-November 1988.

Paul Valéry. Degas danse dessin. In *Degas Manet Morisot* (David Paul, trans.). New York: Pantheon Books. 1960.

Georg Henrik von Wright. *Explanation and Understanding*. Cornell University Press, 1971.

Rob Walker. Case studies in science education: Pine City. In Robert Stake & Jack Easley (eds.), *Case Studies in Science Education*. CIRCE, University of Illinois, 1977.

Rob Walker. Making sense and losing meaning. In Helen Simons (ed.), *Towards a Science of the Singular: Essays about Case Study in Educational Research and Evaluation*, 1980.

Joel Weiss & Barbara Soren. *The Museum as Object: Schools and Community-Cultural Institutions*. Toronto: Ontario Institute for Studies in Education. Unpublished manuscript, 1988.

Alfred North Whitehead. *The Aims of Education*. New York: Mentor, 1949.

Elliot Wigginton (ed.). *The Foxfire Book*. Garden City: Anchor, 1972.

Paul Willis. *Learning to Labour: How Working Class Kids Get Working Class Jobs*. Westmead, Farnborough, Hauts, England: Saxon House, 1977.

Brent Wilson. Evaluation of learning in art education. In Bloom, Hastings, & Madaus, *Handbook of Formative and Summative Evaluation of Student Learning*. McGraw-Hill, 1971.

Brent Wilson. Tight structure, discipline, and quality: Art education in Virginia Beach. In Michael Day, et al., *Art History, Art Criticism, and Art Production. Volume II: Case Studies of Seven Selected Sites*, 1984.

Brent Wilson. *Toward Civilization: Overview from a Report on Arts Education*. National Endowment for the Arts, 1988.

Harry Wolcott. *The Man in the Principal's Office*. Holt, Rinehart & Winston, 1973.

W. B. Yeats. *The Collected Poems of W. B. Yeats*. New York: Macmillan, 1954.

Robert Yin. The case study as a serious research strategy. *Knowledge: Creations, Diffusion, Utilization, 3*, 1981.